The long road to recovery

Note to the reader from the UNU

This book is an outcome of a research project on "Community Responses to Industrial Hazards" carried out under the Environment Programme of the United Nations University. The project was initiated with a conference of the same title held in Minamata, Japan, in November 1992. The main objectives of the project were to study cases where societal disruption has been caused by serious environmental pollution, and to exchange information and lessons concerning the community recovery process following such disasters. The explicit concern was to learn from these experiences so as to avoid similar unfortunate episodes in the future and, where they cannot be avoided, to facilitate community rehabilitation.

The seven case-studies selected cover a variety of geographical locations in both industrialized and developing countries. The hazards analysed fall into the category of disaster "surprises," and range from industrial accidents to those caused by war. The book focuses on the relatively neglected issue of long-term recovery from industrial disasters. It calls for a new system for conceptualizing and managing industrial hazards and disasters.

The long road
to recovery:
Community
responses to
industrial disaster

Edited by James K. Mitchell

United Nations
University Press

TOKYO · NEW YORK · PARIS

United Nations University Press
The United Nations University, 53-70, Jingumae 5-chome, Shibuya-ku, Tokyo 150, Japan
Tel: (03) 3499-2811   Fax: (03) 3406-7345
Telex: J25442   Cable: UNATUNIV TOKYO

UNU Office in North America
2 United Nations Plaza, Room DC2-1462-70, New York, NY 10017, USA
Tel: (212) 963-6387   Fax: (212) 371-9454   Telex: 422311 UN UI

United Nations University Press is the publishing division of the United Nations University.

Typeset by Asco Trade Typesetting Limited, Hong Kong
Printed by Permanent Typesetting and Printing Co., Ltd., Hong Kong
Cover design by J.-M. Antenen, Geneva

UNUP-926
ISBN 92-808-0926-1
03000 P

Contents

Introduction   1
James K. Mitchell

1   Improving community responses to industrial disasters   10
James K. Mitchell

2   Responses to Minamata disease   41
Sadami Maruyama

3   Environmental contamination, community transformation, and the Centralia mine fire   60
Stephen R. Couch

4   Seveso: A paradoxical classic disaster   86
B. De Marchi, S. Funtowicz, and J. Ravetz

5   Long-term recovery from the Bhopal crisis   121
Paul Shrivastava

6   Iranian recovery from industrial devastation during war with Iraq   148
Hooshang Amirahmadi

Contents

7   The Chernobyl disaster: Its effect on Belarus and
     Ukraine   183
     David R. Marples

8   The *Exxon Valdez* oil spill, Alaska   231
     Nancy Y. Davis

9   Signposts on the road to recovery   273
     James K. Mitchell

     Contributors   292

     Index   293

Introduction

James K. Mitchell

In a gaunt building just outside the gates of Prague's Hradcany Castle, a recent exhibition of photographs chronicled the dismal fate of one of the world's most abused landscapes.[1] The portraits of environmental and social destruction in the north-east Czech Republic are graphic reminders of the visible consequences of chronic industrial disaster.[2] Here, nearly half a century of rapacious open pit coalmining has stripped away topsoil, gashed the topography, filled hollows with acid drainage, littered the ravaged countryside with discarded excavation machinery, killed off all but the hardiest vegetation, and covered the entire region in a semi-permanent pall of noxious smoke laden with sulphur, heavy metals, and radioactive elements. Close to one hundred villages and towns have been swallowed up and their inhabitants displaced. The health of half a million residents is seriously compromised and the region faces a staggering array of associated problems. The land has been poisoned. Most of the educated youth emigrate; crime rates are soaring; and the incidence of vandalism, alcoholism, and drug addiction has reached epidemic proportions.

The Prague exhibition documented a continuing problem that is largely overlooked by the throngs of tourists who have come to sample the vast sociopolitical, economic, and cultural changes now taking place in the Czech Republic and other parts of Eastern Europe. Most

1

of the vistors streamed past the exhibition without going in, intent on gazing at the architectural wonders of St. Vitus's Cathedral, the castle guards arrayed in new unintimidating sky-blue uniforms, and the sumptuous panorama of medieval Prague spread out below. For the small minority who entered to view them, the photographs seemed to be a kind of memorial to past environmental horrors that are assumed to have become museum pieces along with the former system of government. Sadly, that is a mistaken judgement: the legacy of these industrial disasters is very much a part of contemporary life. The problems remain unresolved (World Resources Institute 1993). In many respects, the plight of the Ore Mountains is a metaphor of modern industrial disasters. *Despite considerable successes in avoiding or mitigating some of these disasters, the consequences of others seem capable of outliving the human institutions that created them, condone them, or seek to manage them.*

Perversely, long-term recovery from industrial disasters is a subject that has received little attention from scholars and researchers. Most academic and professional writing focuses on cataloguing immediate disaster impacts and losses, identifying causes, and developing appropriate plans for intervention. There are relatively few accounts of short-term recovery in the weeks and months after industrial disasters while those that examine recovery over periods of 5, 10, 20, or 40 years are extremely scarce.

The 10 authors in this book have set out to rectify these omissions. *The Long Road to Recovery: Community Responses to Industrial Disaster* is based on papers delivered at an international conference held in Minamata, Japan, during November 1992. This was the second in a series of meetings organized by the United Nations University, Kumamoto prefectural government and the city of Minamata. At the first conference in 1991, worldwide industrial releases of toxic metals and their impacts were reviewed and a follow-up programme of research was suggested – including a scholarly assessment of recovery and rehabilitation (Carpenter 1992).

Contemporary thinking about industrial hazards is strongly influenced by the work of risk analysts. They are mainly concerned with establishing rational procedures for identifying potential failures in specific technologies, analysing the consequences of those events, and designing appropriate countermeasures in light of the variability of human judgments and preferences. Risk analysis draws on expertise from physical and chemical science, engineering, the biological sciences, and the health professions as well as inputs from social scien-

tists who are interested in issues of risk perception and risk judgement (e.g. Cothern, Mehlman, and Marcus 1988; National Research
Council 1993). Within the field there are differences between what
one observer has described as the "two cultures of risk analysis."
According to Jasanoff (1993), " 'hard' (quantitative) analysis represents risks as they 'really are,' whereas 'softer' (qualitative) work in
politics or sociology mostly explains why people refuse to accept the
pictures of reality that technical experts produce for them." Contributors to the present book mainly employ the "softer" social science
perspective. In different ways they underline the contextual character
of knowledge about industrial hazards and disasters and the importance of framing public policies in light of local experience and lay
knowledge as well as with respect to scientific findings that transcend
particular places. Effective public policy must take account of such
matters and blend the contributions of both "cultures." Unfortunately, to date there have been relatively few attempts to integrate
the two approaches.

This book also adopts a broad view of industrial disasters. Industry
is not simply the facilities and firms that turn raw materials and
energy resources into usable products; nor are industrial disasters just
the fires, explosions, leaks, spills, and other events that occur in those
places as a result of faulty design, improper operating procedures,
and other in-plant flaws (e.g. Seveso, Chernobyl, Bhopal). Some of
the most challenging industrial disasters of recent years have involved
external hazards such as extremes of nature and human conflict. For
example, the oil and gas industry has been afflicted by many such
problems. Among others, they include the fracture of Arctic oil pipelines during earthquakes in Russia, the ignition of petroleum products leaking from pipelines undermined by floods in Texas, seafloor
pipelines left exposed to collisions with passing ships after storms
redeployed covering sediments, and the deliberate destruction of oil
facilities during the 1992 Gulf War (National Research Council 1994;
El-Baz and Makharita 1994). Clearly, industrial facilities are often
susceptible to disaster-causing events that occur beyond their boundaries, and the effects of disasters do not necessarily stop at the plant
gates. Nor do disasters disappear with the decline or cessation of
industrial operations: major legacies of hazard may be left behind in
the form of dangerous wastes, ravaged environments, and moribund
communities (e.g. Minamata, Centralia, the Black Triangle). A comprehensive approach to public policy-making for industrial disasters
must take account of all these aspects of the problem.

The present study contains seven case-studies of events and consequences that can be broadly described as "industrial disaster surprises." All are connected with the process of industrial production and all are, in some sense, unprecedented. Nothing quite like them had ever occurred before in the same or similar contexts. The case-studies are arranged in chronological order and include one example of chronic chemical contamination (Minamata, Japan), a continuing underground fire (Centralia, USA), two sudden airborne releases of toxic chemicals (Seveso, Italy; Bhopal, India), a nuclear reactor explosion and fire (Chernobyl, USSR, and successor states), a seven-year-long military conflict that produced widespread destruction of industrial facilities (Iran–Iraq war), and a massive oil spill (*Exxon Valdez*, USA). The first of these disasters was initially detected almost fifty years ago (c. 1949); the most recent occurred in 1989.

Case-study authors are drawn from seven different countries and half a dozen separate disciplines. This provides a variety of interests and perspectives, but most contributions follow a similar format that is intended to allow for ease of comparison across the various sites. After this Introduction, the book opens with a call for a new system for conceptualizing and managing industrial hazards and disasters. James K. Mitchell, a geographer born in Northern Ireland and working in the United States, assesses the changing global burden of industrial disasters and suggests that surprises should be distinguished from routine disasters because they pose increasingly serious problems for industrial managers, hazards professionals, and the general public. He develops a classification of surprises to serve as a point of departure for identifying robust and flexible coping strategies. Learning from – and transferring – the lessons of places that have experienced industrial disaster surprises lies at the heart of his proposed research strategy. This chapter serves as a springboard for the case-studies that follow.

Chapter 2 is a broad-based, victim-centred analysis of the notorious Minamata "disease," prepared by a professor in the Department of Literature at nearby Kumamoto University. Sadami Maruyama chronicles the toll that has been exacted by the long uphill struggle of different groups of victims to gain recognition and restitution. The community has become deeply and rancorously divided. Traditions of mutual assistance have been fractured, and a long-established myth of common interests between industry and citizens has been overturned. Nearly half a century after it appeared, Minamata's disaster is still a defining event in the lives of most residents. Although much has been

4

done to shape a new post-disaster future, many problems remain unresolved or unattended to. The author characterizes Minamata's experience as both a failure of government to protect the health and welfare of citizens who possessed little power to act in their own behalf and the outcome of a flawed public ethic that promoted unfettered economic development at the expense of citizens' rights to a safe environment.

Chapter 3 examines a small American town that is menaced by an expanding underground fire. Here, the term "recovery" takes on a special meaning because most of Centralia's population has moved away and the remainder are likely to follow. The town will soon cease to exist! Drawing on evidence from social surveys and detailed observations, Stephen Couch, an American sociologist, paints a picture of a former "company town" that lacked a political tradition of acting in defence of its resident's interests and was ill prepared for conflicts that developed in the wake of the fire. The Centralia case raises serious questions about the validity of existing "stage" models of post-disaster recovery in communities affected by "contamination" disasters. These posit a gradual return to "normal" after disaster that does not fit the Centralia case. Couch offers an alternative model that suggests that contamination disasters generate multiple interpretations of causation and risk, leading to intensive community conflict, alienation, and coping difficulties. Activities of recovery and emergency response occur simultaneously in repeated cycles, eventually culminating in one of two outcomes – relocation of the affected community or apparently successful technological fixes that permit it to continue in place.

Compared with Centralia, the long-term outcome of Seveso's dioxin contamination disaster has been different. Although in the period after the event there was a major controversy marked by physical attacks on people and property, as well as a general political crisis, not only did the affected community survive intact but the recovery period was marked by fewer of the rancorous tensions between industry, government, and the local population than occurred elsewhere. Far from retaining its initial well-justified association with a frightening disaster, the name Seveso has now come to be associated with successful high-technology management of chemical hazards! This curious development occurred not because the disaster itself was well managed in the affected community but rather because of the dramatic changes in European-wide public policy that it spurred. The Seveso experience is analysed in chapter 4 by a team of sociologists and philosophers of science from Italy and the United Kingdom. They focus on the formulation of new European Community regulations for chemical risk management that were developed after the accident. The so-called "Seveso Directive" is a precedent-breaking measure that seeks to reduce industrial accident risks by publicizing information about hazardous facilities and communicating it to groups that are responsible for public safety on a "need to know" basis. Although the Seveso Directive is something of a showpiece for rational top-down planning approaches to industrial safety, Bruna De Marchi and her colleagues suggest that its apparent success is perversely paradoxical for both scientists and public policy makers. They caution against drawing simplistic lessons from Seveso's deeply contradictory experience.

Paul Shrivastava's analysis of Bhopal (ch. 5) emphasizes the dizzying complexity of modern industrial disasters and their impacts on corporate management as well as surrounding populations. Because most involve mixes of technological and human causes that are both antecedent and proximate, it is difficult to attribute blame to any one culpable party. Nor is it always clear which is the appropriate judicial jurisdiction for resolving compensatory or punitive lawsuits. The continuing spread of multinational corporations into third world countries increases their exposure to legal actions abroad as well as at home. The author, a professor of management who was born and raised in Bhopal and now works in the United States, reminds us that industrial disasters rarely produce many – if any – "winners." In this case, not only were several thousand people killed or injured in India with only limited compensation, but the Union Carbide Corporation came close to collapse. It is clear that disaster impacts are not confined to the obvious victims. Corporate restructuring in the wake of industrial disaster carries with it the possibility of additional losses of jobs, income, and other benefits among employees, investors, and host communities associated with the offending firms.

The Bhopal chemical disaster mostly affected people in India and the United States, but the effects of Chernobyl's nuclear power station disaster involved large populations throughout much of Europe and Asia, as well as the world's entire nuclear power industry. The Canadian historian David Marples focuses on institutional effects of the Chernobyl disaster (ch. 6) during a recovery period that overlapped with dramatic changes in the geopolitical arrangements of Russia and Eastern Europe. Unlike Seveso, where the institutional

6

response has been toward greater centralized planning and management of industrial risks, the opposite process is at work in the Ukraine, Belarus, and – to a lesser extent – Russia. The difficult lessons of grass-roots institution building in a region of fragmenting states may be disquieting for those who hope to encourage greater decentralizing of risk-management decisions.

The Iran–Iraq war was not an industrial disaster in the conventional sense, but its effects were similar because military conflict inflicted heavy damage on industries, especially Persian Gulf oil facilities, and these in turn released hazardous materials into surrounding communities and ecosystems. Hooshang Amirahmadi adopts a planner's perspective on the post-war recovery process in Iran and shows very clearly how disasters and development are closely intertwined (ch. 7). He emphasizes the lack of detailed information about the environmental effects of wartime industrial disasters, the overwhelming priority given to economic issues, and the dominant role of centrally directed planning and management of recovery efforts (except in the housing sector). Despite the fact that such a strategy is poorly designed for responding to disasters with highly localized patterns of loss, the author suggests that most third world countries will probably favour centralized responses because national government institutions are significantly stronger than those at the local level. The influence of World Bank development policy is detectable in Iran's emphasis on giving priority to restoring selected industry, infrastructure, and services on key sites rather than an across-the-board programme of post-war recovery. Amirahmadi also argues that the all-too-common urge to blame external enemies for wartime losses is counter-productive to recovery efforts because it prolongs the state of tension between former combatants and diverts much-needed resources into defence budgets.

The *Exxon Valdez* experience clearly demonstrates that much more effort is devoted to assessing the impacts of disasters than the effectiveness of recovery (ch. 8). It also shows that there are important barriers to analysing recovery. For example, it has been difficult to gain a coherent and comprehensive picture of the recovery process in Prince William Sound because research has been commissioned and carried out by many different agencies and organizations, with only limited synthesis or coordination among the various groups. Also, one of the most remarkable side-effects of the disaster has been the gagging of social science research by legal constraints. Information that might be relevant to ongoing lawsuits is rarely permitted to be published until the legal proceedings end. It is effectively lost to the disaster-management system until too late to be of use in recovery efforts. Data on responses by fishing communities and native populations are particularly scarce. None the less, Nancy Davis, an American cultural anthropologist, is not persuaded that the small – and seemingly vulnerable – communities of southern Alaska have been stricken by this disaster beyond their capacity to make a substantial recovery.

In the book's final chapter, Mitchell draws together principal findings from the case-studies, examines their implications, and makes suggestions for future research on industrial disaster surprises. He highlights the record of slow, delayed, uneven, and incomplete recovery, as well as identifying a plethora of attempted institutional changes and their often paradoxical outcomes. He judges this as evidence that existing public policies are systematically undermatched and mismatched with the problems of industrial disaster surprises. The chapter ends with suggestions for repositioning industrial disaster public policy to take account of a much wider range of issues than those that are currently addressed.

Notes

1. "The Black Triangle: The Foothills of the Ore Mountains," an exhibition of photographs taken between 1990 and 1994 by Joseph Koudelka and displayed in the Salmovsky Palace from 29 June to 4 September 1994. The area of 300 square kilometres that is featured in this exhibition lies between the Ohre and Bilina rivers, tributaries of the Elbe. It is the southernmost extension of the notorious "Black Triangle" that includes larger sections of Poland and the former German Democratic Republic. Coal has been extracted from this part of the Ore Mountains since at least 1403, but production accelerated dramatically during the second half of the nineteenth century. By 1910 it reached 17 million tonnes per year (mostly from underground mines) and fluctuated thereafter until after World War II. Then, with the advent of open pit mining, production rose to around 40 million tonnes in 1960 and 53 million tonnes in 1992. Most of the coal is burned in local electricity-generating stations that are not equipped to remove its toxic constituents.
2. Research on industrial disasters is part of an evolving multidisciplinary enterprise that has yet to standardize terminology. While there is a significant level of agreement about the conceptual definition of disaster (i.e. the situation that occurs when human coping systems are overwhelmed by realized risks), operational definitions of disaster are notoriously variable because different individuals and different institutions have widely different coping capabilities and sensitivities to loss. Similarly, hazard is variously defined as a phenomenon, or a process, or a probability (Alexander 1993). Many languages have no word for hazard and it has not proved to be popular among international agencies. (It was for this reason that the name of the International Decade for Natural Hazard Reduction was changed to the International Decade for Natural Disaster Reduction when the original US-inspired proposal was taken up by the United Nations.) Similar problems attend the definition of terms such as

risk, vulnerability, and mitigation. No attempt has been made to standardize terminology in this book, although most authors generally subscribe to the view that industrial hazards are interactive systems of people, technologies, and environments that can be characterized in terms of risk (potential threat), exposure (populations and property at risk), vulnerability (potential for loss), and response (purposive adjustments).

References

Alexander, David. 1993. *Natural Disasters*. London: Chapman and Hall, pp. 4–9.

Carpenter, Richard A. 1992. *Industry, the Environment and Human Health: In Search of a Harmonious Relationship*. Report of a conference held at Minamata, Japan, 14–15 November 1991. Tokyo: The United Nations University.

Cothern, C. Richard, Myron A. Mehlman, and William L. Marcus. 1988. *Advances in Modern Environmental Toxicology, Vol. XV: Risk Assessment and Risk Management of Industrial and Environmental Chemicals*. Princeton: Princeton Scientific Publishing Co., Inc.

El-Baz, Farouk, and R.M. Makharita. 1994. *The Gulf War and the Environment*. New York: Gordon and Breach Science Publishers.

Jasanoff, Sheila. 1993. "Bridging the two cultures of risk analysis." *Risk Analysis* 13(2): 123–129.

National Research Council. 1993. *Issues in Risk Assessment*. Committee on risk assessment methodology, Board on Environmental Studies and Toxicology, Commission on Life Sciences. Washington, DC: National Academy Press.

———. 1994. *Improving the Safety of Marine Pipelines*. Committee on the Safety of Marine Pipelines, Marine Board, Commission on Engineering and Technical Systems. Washington, DC: National Academy Press.

World Resources Institute. 1993. "Central Europe." In: *World Resources 1992–93*. New York: Oxford University Press, pp. 57–74.

1

Improving community responses to industrial disasters

James K. Mitchell

Introduction

During the last several decades there has been a growing awareness of the expanding risks and consequences of major industrial disasters. This is reflected in official statistics, mass media reports, and the appearance of new public institutions that address the problem. The growth of industrial accident prevention companies and the blossoming of literature on industrial risk assessment are other expressions of the same trend (Bowonder and Linstone 1987; Covello and Merkhofer 1993; Cutter 1993; International Atomic Energy Agency 1992; Lewis 1990; Lave and Upton 1987; Lepkowski 1987; Mitchell 1990; National Research Council 1993; Rafter 1987; *Risk Analysis* 1994; Smith, Carpenter, and Faulstich 1988; United Nations Environment Programme 1993; United Nations 1994; Warner 1992).[1]

Industrial disasters are not simply safety problems that need to be resolved: they also have wider significance because they offer important opportunities to learn about the "goodness of fit" between society, technology, and environment and about how that fit can be strengthened or weakened by unexpected events (Roush 1993). This is the kind of information that will be invaluable to humanity during an era of deep and far-reaching societal and environmental change. However, if we are to make optimal use of such opportunities it may be necessary to modify the way we think about industrial disasters.

It is customary to view industrial disasters as "extreme events" that are different mainly in degree from more mundane disruptions to which industries and society have become adjusted. This chapter asserts that it is time to make a clear distinction between two types of industrial disasters – "routine" disasters and "surprises". As defined here, routine disasters are well understood by experts and susceptible to management using long-established principles and practices. They constitute the great majority of threats to human populations. Successful management of routine disasters mainly requires that society put into practice the ample stocks of knowledge and experience about them that already exist. Surprises, which confound both expert and lay expectations, are quite different and much less understood. They include disasters like Bhopal and Chernobyl and Minamata – events or their consequences or both – that lie outside the realm of previous experience.

It is advantageous to think of surprises as a coherent *class* of events that cuts across all types of hazards, rather than as extreme events that lie at the tails of different sets of statistical distributions.[2] Since surprises appear to be increasing, it is important to develop better ways of responding to them. Because surprises are unprecedented events, it is difficult to design specific anticipatory measures of the kind that have proved successful in reducing routine hazards. Improving reactive responses to surprises may offer better opportunities for coping with surprises, at least in the short run. Communities that have been affected by surprises should learn from each other's experience and disseminate that knowledge widely. By so doing, it may be possible to identify responses that are robust and flexible across a range of different surprises and therefore worthy of encouragement and emulation in communities elsewhere.

The nature of industrial disaster

Industrial *hazards* are threats to people and life-support systems that arise from the mass production of goods and services.[3] When these threats exceed human coping capabilities or the absorptive capacities of environmental systems they give rise to industrial *disasters*. Industrial hazards can occur at any stage in the production process, including extraction, processing, manufacture, transportation, storage, use, and disposal. Losses generally involve the release of damaging substances (e.g. chemicals, radioactivity, genetic materials) or damaging levels of energy from industrial facilities or equipment into surrounding environments. This usually occurs in the form of explosions, fires, spills, leaks, or wastes. Releases may occur because of factors that are internal to the industrial system (e.g. engineering flaws) or they may occur because of external factors (e.g. extremes of nature). Releases may be sudden and intensive, as in a power-plant explosion, or gradual and extensive, as in the build-up of ozone-destroying chemicals in the stratosphere or the progressive leakage of improperly disposed toxic wastes.

In a narrow sense the causes of industrial hazards and disasters are malfunctions, failures, or unanticipated side-effects of technological systems. But this is a misleading oversimplification. Many other factors are involved. The calculus of industrial hazard is a blend of industrial systems, people, and environments (fig. 1.1). These combine in different ways to create a specific hazard. For example, faulty equipment, operator error, and a south-westerly air flow all helped to

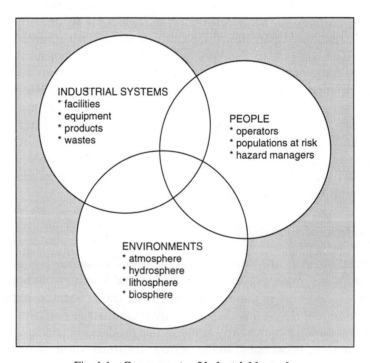

Fig. 1.1 **Components of industrial hazards**

shape the events that occurred at Three Mile Island nuclear power station (Sills, Wolf, and Shelanski 1982; Houts, Cleary, and Hu 1988). The *Challenger* space shuttle disaster involved, among others, a vulnerable fluid seal, cold weather, and an impatient launch team – although the official inquiry blamed only the seal.

Large-scale industrial disasters are one of the legacies of the Industrial Revolution; before 1800 they were few and far between. Historically, the effects of industrial disasters were typically confined to workplaces or to the transportation systems that shipped raw materials and finished goods. Accordingly, most public policies for disaster reduction emphasized safer industrial technologies and upgraded working conditions – at the mine face, on the foundry floor, in the machine shop and the power station, or on the ships and railroads that transported a majority of industrial products (Sax 1975; Chelius 1977; Rosner and Markowitz 1987; National Safety Council 1988; Whiteside 1990). Occasional extraordinary disasters affected larger populations that were not directly associated with the industrial production system. For example, in 1917 the explosion of a munitions ship in the harbour of Halifax, Nova Scotia, destroyed much of the surrounding city (Prince 1920). But it was not until comparatively recently that these latter kinds of industrial disasters became common. Since the 1970s there has been an increasing number of devastating events that produced significant "off-site" effects on the health and well-being of humans and other life-forms as well as on the non-living environment. The partial meltdown of a nuclear reactor core at Three Mile Island, Pennsylvania, in 1979 is a good example. It is estimated that over 140,000 people evacuated an area within 15 miles of the TMI power station (Houts, Cleary, and Hu 1988). As a result of the upsurge in off-site events, the context of the industrial disaster management problem has expanded considerably. Explanations of industrial hazards and disasters have also changed.

Increasingly, broad or quasi-universal explanations of industrial hazards are now emerging. Some of these focus on specific technical developments in the evolution of modern technology. Perrow highlights the growing importance of tightly coupled systems that leave little room for error and virtuaily guarantee failure. Accidents thus become "normal" (Perrow 1984). Lovins has made similar arguments about the inherent vulnerability of large centralized systems such as electricity transmission grids (Lovins 1981). Lagadec suggests that we increasingly live in "metastable" contexts where potential instabilities in technological systems and human systems are camouflaged or otherwise hidden from view. As a result, when perturbations occur they grow and spread quickly, undermining apparently well-designed safeguards against disaster (Lagadec 1990).

Other analysts locate the problem of hazard predominantly in the human components of technology. For example, Headrick believes that industrial hazards are an inevitable consequence of dominant cultural conceptions of technology (Headrick 1990). He argues that technological innovation is typically viewed as a "linear" process that connects the achievement of a particular intended result with the use of a specific device. Little thought is given to the larger contexts that promote unintended side-effects, including hazards. Slovic and others suggest that limited human abilities to assess risks in complex systems are a crucial component in the creation of hazard (Slovic 1987). Johnson and Covello (1987) remind us that risk is a socially constructed concept. Douglas and Wildavsky contend that all societies pay attention to risks selectively and that decisions about which risks we choose to confront are highly social and value-laden (Douglas and Wildavsky 1982; Douglas, 1992). Moreover, some hazards are subject to a process of social amplification that raises their salience, often out of proportion to the objective risks (Kasperson et al. 1988; Renn et al. 1993). There is also a growing awareness that the impacts of industrial hazards often fall disproportionately on disadvantaged and relatively powerless groups. It is suggested that once such groups are empowered to defend their interests, hazards will be less likely to develop or to continue (Dembo et al. 1988).

Finally, Beck contends that the citizens of economically advanced states have become part of a "risk society." This is "an epoch in which the dark sides of progress increasingly come to dominate social debate," when all of us must confront " ... the possibility of artificially produced self-annihilation" (Beck 1995, 2). This period is marked by the emergence of a distinction between "risks" and "threats." Beck reserves the term risks for the hazardous phenomena of early industrial societies. These, he believes, were limited, knowable, and capable of being compensated or insured against. By contrast, contemporary threats – whether nuclear, chemical, biological, or ecological – are: "(1) not limitable, either socially or temporally; (2) not accountable according to the prevailing rules of causality, guilt and liability; and (3) neither compensable nor insurable" (Beck 1995, 2).

From many of these perspectives, meaningful advances in risk reduction require social change as well as the development of technical solutions. In light of the range and variety of explanations that have been advanced, it is clear that industrial hazards and disasters are highly complex phenomena subject to a multitude of contextual influences (Burton and Kates 1986). As the next section shows, they also impose heavy burdens on society.

Industrial disaster burdens

Recent studies by the American think-tank Resources for the Future and the Swiss Reinsurance Company suggest that at least 10,000 people are killed each year in major industrial accidents and that insured losses are in the vicinity of US$5 billion annually.[4,5] The losses are increasing. In 1970, comparable figures were around 1,000 deaths with insured losses of US$1 billion (Marbacher 1990; Glickman, Golding, and Silverman 1992). However, these figures merely hint at the magnitude of the problem. The complete burden of industrial hazard and disaster is undoubtedly much larger. No comprehensive data on global losses have been compiled, and available figures mainly pertain to acute and intensive events. They do not report uninsured losses, or delayed losses associated with acute events, or losses due to chronic industrial pollution such as that which has affected places like Minamata, Japan.

Minamata's experience with industrial disaster has been long and painful (Ellis 1989; Minamata City and Kumamoto Prefecture 1988). It is now 60 years since methyl mercury compounds were first released from an industrial plant in the city and more than 40 years since Minamata Bay became a disposal location. A few years later, the symptoms of Minamata disease were first publicly reported and it has been almost 30 years since scientists identified its causes and aetiology. The community is still living through – and coping with – the aftermath of those events. Thousands of people have been identified as victims and thousands more seek official designation. Lives have been burdened by physical disfigurements and impaired functioning or cut short by premature death. Ecosystems have been contaminated, and local food supplies have been quarantined. The community's economic base and the livelihoods of its people have been eroded. There have been deep disagreements about the allocation of blame and about appropriate restitution and countermeasures. Anxiety and mistrust have taken root in private lives and public discourse. Decision-making has been marked by protests, riots, and protracted legal disputes as well as by attempts at mediation and reconciliation. Citizen action groups have

15

emerged to press disparate agendas, and new public institutions have been established to provide a permanent capacity for studying, managing, and memorializing the disaster. In the process, Minamata's identity has become inextricably bound up with the disease, both in the minds of its own residents and in the eyes of the outside world. Recovery continues but many uncertainties remain: the end of this disaster is not yet in sight!

Unfortunately, Minamata is only one entry in a growing list of places that have been grievously affected by industrial disasters. Others include Bhopal, Chernobyl, Seveso, and Times Beach.[6] Moreover, it is not just specific communities that are affected: whole regions – the coalfields of Silesia, the oil-stained shores of Prince William Sound, and the acid precipitation-damaged forests of south Germany – have been stigmatized by chronic releases of industrial effluents or by sudden catastrophic accidents involving industrial products (World Resources Institute 1992). In some cases, impacts more extreme than Minamata's have been recorded. The Kyshtym district of Russia provides a particularly chilling example that involved nuclear wastes – albeit most probably from military sources rather than civilian industries. Here, an area of about 1,500 square kilometres in the southern Ural Mountains is devoid of human occupation and most signs of life. Until 1957 it was home to about 200,000 people but most of the old settlements are now empty and large signs posted along nearby roads urge travellers not to stop in the vicinity. More than 30 years after soils, lakes, streams, vegetation, and animal life were contaminated by a catastrophic release of improperly stored nuclear wastes, much of the district remains abandoned (Medvedhev 1979). What became officially known in 1989 as "The East Ural Radioactive Trace" is an example of the worst kind of industrial or environmental disaster – one that results in the annihilation of affected communities and the demise or permanent relocation of their residents (Feshbach and Friendly 1992). Fortunately, such cases are still comparatively rare, and, with the reduction in East–West tensions, those that involve military–industrial facilities may be on the decline. The potential for catastrophic disasters associated with high-level civilian nuclear wastes is a continuing problem (*New York Times*, 5 March 1995). None the less, though deaths, injuries, economic loss, and disruption are attributes of industrial disaster, the bulk of experience suggests that most impacted communities survive and attempt to recover their former vitality.

The evolution of responses

The fact that most communities survive industrial disasters testifies to the resilience of people and the effectiveness of their responses to catastrophe. Indeed, over the long term, humans have demonstrated impressive abilities to cope with most industrial disasters, first by ameliorating their effects and then by finding effective ways to avoid, prevent, or control them by precautionary actions. Boiler explosions provide a good illustration. At one time in the early industrialization of Great Britain and the United States, boiler explosions were per-haps the most common industrial disaster (Hamilton 1973). They often led to catastrophic fires on board ships and trains as well as in factories, apartment buildings, and other places.[7] Now the problem of boiler explosions is much reduced as a consequence of improvements in industrial design, construction standards, worker safety, occupa-tional health, and other factors. Similar improvements have reduced the hazard of fires caused by faulty electrical equipment and the num-ber of collapses of high-rise buildings. Another more recent example has come to light in the wake of hurricane Andrew, the most disastrous storm ever to have affected the United States. Despite Andrew's size, intensity, and general destructiveness on land, it destroyed or dam-aged very few offshore oil and gas platforms. This positive outcome continues a long-term trend of improvement in platform survivability that has come about because of advances in knowledge about marine environments, design standards, building materials and construction practices, platform siting and installation procedures, and improved operation and maintenance actions (*New York Times*, 21 October 1992).

As these examples show, though they may be long lived (Iijima 1979; Glacken 1973), industrial hazards are neither permanent nor unchanging. The mix of hazard is always in flux. New hazards arise as a consequence of technological innovations, while existing hazards are reduced or eliminated by effective human responses. Through time, whole classes of hazard may be added to or dropped from the public agenda. Kirk Smith, a researcher at the East–West Center in Hawaii, argues that this process of change might be labelled "risk transition" and that it is comparable in importance to the so-called "demographic transition" that accompanied rapid economic devel-opment in many countries during the past century (Smith 1988).

The process of developing effective responses may require many decades or longer to reach completion. The recent history of hazardous industry regulation in Britain makes this point (Petts 1988; Myers and Read 1992). After World War II, demand for the products of refineries and chemical plants increased sharply throughout the world. This led to major changes in those industries, including new production processes (e.g. bulk liquefaction of gases), larger plants, bigger inventories, and expanded throughput of products. These changes were accompanied by an upsurge in explosions and fires, particularly during the 1950s and 1960s. But it was not until the early 1970s that public policy makers in the United Kingdom began to take action in response. And it took two more decades before comprehensive programmes of hazard management were put in place. In other words, in the United Kingdom the entire sequence, from the industrial innovations that triggered the hazards to the development of effective responses, stretched across four decades.

The history of coalmine disasters in the United States offers an even more salutary lesson. Numbers of mine disasters and disaster deaths rose throughout the nineteenth century to peak in the first decade of the twentieth. Thereafter they did not undergo a major decline until the 1930s. However, even as late as the 1960s, coalmine death rates were much higher in the United States than in coalmining countries of Europe (Curran 1993). Death rates were affected by changes in a wide range of factors including, among others, coal supplies and demand, mine size, levels of mechanization, coalfield labour demographics, unionization, worker education and training, laws and regulations, and mine safety programmes. Some of these changes worked toward reducing mine disasters and deaths, while others worked against that outcome.

Of course, the response process might be induced to unfold faster. For example, in developing countries it is theoretically possible to adopt production systems and related hazard controls at the same time by taking advantage of experience already acquired in developed countries. But, more typically, transfers of technology to developing countries often fail to modify the borrowed systems to take account of sociocultural circumstances in the receiving country. As a result, the potential for further disasters grows.

What has just been described might be labelled a *social learning model* of industrial hazard management. It assumes that few hazards are insurmountable in the long run. What is required is a period of time to gain experience of the hazard, scientific expertise to investigate it, and a public commitment to put the findings into practice.

Often, the process begins with reactive strategies that are intended to reduce the impacts of disasters and works toward creating anticipatory strategies that are intended to avoid the build-up of hazard. Gradually, a new hazard becomes familiar – by dint of repeated experience – and hazards managers are able to acquire a fund of knowledge about the utility of alternative coping mechanisms. In time, the match between hazard and response becomes closer and losses begin to decline. At this stage, what had once been a challenging new hazard would no longer constitute much of a threat.

Certainly, social learning of the type just noted plausibly explains the changing salience of boiler disasters, offshore platform failures and many other phenomena (Sheehan and Wedeen 1993). But such learning requires that hazards and disasters occur with sufficient frequency to provide a base of experience and opportunities for testing alternative responses. How, then, can we learn to cope with unprecedented events, sometimes of vast proportions? And what if these events signal that society is already pressing against the limits of the global environment's capacity to absorb them? The next section takes up this theme.

Routine disasters

So-called "man-made catastrophes" occur with considerable frequency throughout the world every year (fig. 1.2). In 1990 the Swiss Reinsurance Company recorded 191. These included 126 transportation accidents, 35 large explosions and fires, 8 mine disasters, 6 building collapses and 16 miscellaneous others (Marbacher 1991). About 25 of these disasters took place in exclusively industrial facilities, mainly chemical plants and power stations. The three most costly were petrochemicals explosions in Thailand (54 deaths), India (30 deaths; $28 million damage) and the United States (17 deaths; $220 million damage).

What is striking about the Swiss data is the unexceptional and repetitive nature of the events that they record. Dozens of the entries refer to aircraft and ships that went down during bad weather. Scores more are about buses, cars, and trains that collided or ran out of control. There are multiple cases of gas explosions in mines and factory fires. Although there might be only one such event in any country in a given year, these are hardly unprecedented disasters: they occur relatively often somewhere throughout the globe; their causes and characteristics are well known to engineers and safety managers;

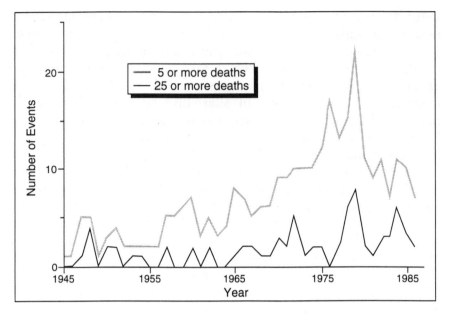

Fig. 1.2   **Global trends in industrial accidents**

and they can be reduced by applying more or less reliable counter-measures. In short, they are *"routine disasters"*. And because they dominate the global catalogue of losses, most of the global effort to reduce industrial hazards is, understandably, directed at them.[8] Moreover, that effort may be paying off. According to Resources for the Future, the global total of industrial accidents, which peaked in the late 1970s, is now decreasing[9] (fig. 1.2). Additional data for the United States indicate that this downward trend has taken place while levels of production have been rising (fig. 1.3). In other words, despite a growing potential for technological disasters (including industrial accidents), fewer of them seem to be occurring.

Surprises

But sprinkled here and there throughout the record is another kind of event, one that brings to light new and troubling dimensions of disaster. These can be labelled *"surprises"* (Kates 1985). Surprises are events that confound our expectations (Holling 1986). In the context of this subject they are also events that announce unprecedented hazards. In the lists of major disasters there may be only a few surprises each year but they are among the most important events.

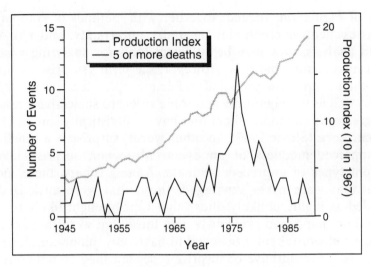

Fig. 1.3 **US trends in industrial accidents**

Progress in understanding – let alone managing – surprises is slow and limited.

Surprises arise from two interacting sources: (1) the events that we experience; and (2) the metaphors and concepts that we use to understand those events. In other words, surprises not only have unexpected practical consequences but also challenge us to devise new interpretive paradigms. Thus, surprises raise fundamental issues about the nature and roles of uncertainty and indeterminacy in human thought (Wynne 1992; O'Riordan and Rayner 1991; Ravetz and Funtowicz 1990; Funtowicz and Ravetz 1990, 1995). It is important to realize that the underlying thrust of this chapter is not about simply reclassifying events as surprises and routine hazards: it is about asking us to change the way we think about hazardous events and eventually to change the ways we seek to manage them.

For readers who are familiar with frequency/severity graphs of hazardous industrial phenomena, such as those that occur in quantitative risk analyses (e.g. Lowrance 1976; Lave 1982), a word of explanation is in order. Such graphs typically show a large number of high-probability/low-consequence events and a small number of low-probability/high-consequence events. Society is usually well adjusted to coping with the high-probability (common) events but less well equipped to deal with the low-probability (rare) ones. These graphs are useful devices for illustrating risk distributions and for suggesting alternative levels of risk that might be designated for purposes of regulation. Indeed, together with methods of comparative risk assessment, decision-making under uncertainty, and risk–cost–benefit analysis, they may be sufficient tools for analysing what are here called routine hazards. However, the term "surprise" connotes more than simply low probability. For example, rare events differ in kind as well as in magnitude, and some risks are subjectively assessed with greater dread than others that have a statistically similar chance of occurrence (Slovic 1987). In other words, surprise is a function of the unprecedentedness of an event. Moreover, surprise involves different types of unprecedentedness. Among others, these include events that were never envisaged, those that were envisaged but regarded as highly unlikely, those that were thought likely to occur but had not happened previously, and those that were thought likely to occur but (mistakenly) believed to have only minor consequences. These are representative of surprise types but they do not constitute an exhaustive list.

Many of the most spectacular industrial disasters of the post-World War II era can be described as surprises: these include Minamata, Three Mile Island, Love Canal, Seveso, Bhopal, Chernobyl, the Mississauga train derailment in Ontario, *Challenger*, so-called "forest death" in Europe,[10] *Exxon Valdez*, the Kuwait oil fires, stratospheric ozone depletion, acid precipitation, and greenhouse gas build-up in the atmosphere. This is a heterogeneous group. It contains some events that affected fixed facilities (e.g. Three Mile Island) and others that involved moving vehicles (e.g. Mississauga). Extensive processes (e.g. acid precipitation) are included as well as intensive events (e.g. Seveso). There are examples of mechanical systems, chemicals, and radiation. Acute events and chronic ones are both represented. Indeed, about the only characteristics that the group seem to share are hazardousness and surprise.

Surprises can be classified in terms of the *degree to which they connect with or depart from expectations*. For example, it is possible to divide them into three general groups: (1) unique events; (2) precursor events; and (3) superlative events. Some surprises are unprecedented because they are *one of a kind*. For example, Kyshtym appears to be the only significant example of a nuclear waste storage disaster; perhaps there will never be another like it. Other surprises are unprecedented because they are the *first of a kind*, each the precursor of what later turns out to be a sequence of related events. The destruction in flight of the world's first commercial jet airliner – the British Comet – is an example: a series of apparently mysterious

Comet crashes occurred at intervals until a lengthy investigation disclosed that metal fatigue was an unexpectedly serious problem in these aircraft. The sinking of the *Torrey Canyon* off the United Kingdom in the early 1970s was the first in a series of supertanker oil spills that brought increasingly greater damage to maritime ecosystems (Cowan 1968). Within a few years, much larger cargoes of oil were fetching up on vulnerable shores. A third type of surprise gains notoriety from being a *worst of a kind* event. Chernobyl stands as the worst in a series of nuclear power station accidents that includes earlier events like the Windscale incident (1957) and the accident at Three Mile Island (1979). Although it is currently the worst event of its kind, there is potential for others. A recent US General Accounting Office report indicates that 40 old Soviet-designed nuclear reactors without basic safety features are still operating in Russia and Eastern Europe (United States General Accounting Office 1991); 10 of these are of special concern (*New York Times*, 23 July 1995).

It is also possible to classify surprises in terms of the *degree to which they are susceptible to prediction and control*. Here, three groups of hazards stand out: (1) unsuspected hazards; (2) improperly managed hazards; and (3) instrumental hazards. *Unsuspected hazards* involve substances or activities that were regarded as harmless or benign until scientific evidence or human experience showed otherwise. DDT, asbestos, and chemical chlorofluorocarbons are representative examples. *Improperly managed hazards* involve failures of various kinds of hazard control systems. Most major industrial accidents are of this type. Well-known management failures have taken place at nuclear facilities (e.g. Windscale, Three Mile Island, Chernobyl), chemical plants (e.g. Seveso, Basle, Bhopal), and transportation systems (e.g. *Challenger, Exxon Valdez*), as well as in storage and disposal sites for toxic materials (e.g. Kyshtym, Times Beach, Love Canal, Minamata). *Instrumental hazards* are intended to cause harm and are consciously employed towards that end. They include sabotage, arson, and warfare (Matousek 1991). Military industrial technologies belong to this group (e.g. nuclear, biological, and chemical weapons such as defoliants and nerve agents; deliberate oil spills and oilfield conflagrations). The mismanaged wastes of military industrial technology are also an important form of improperly managed hazards.

Although instrumental hazards lie entirely within the domain of human control they have never been easy to prevent, control, or reduce. Certain military industrial technologies have been subject to controls (e.g. nuclear test ban treaty, SALT treaty) but many others are not controlled. There are strong pressures to continue to develop, test, and maintain most innovative weapons systems. Improperly managed hazards are outcomes of failed controls. They pose problems that might be ultimately solvable, but we have yet to find and adopt appropriate solutions. Unsuspected hazards are effectively unknown, at least until disaster strikes or is imminent. They lie at the outer limits of our awareness but, once identified, may be susceptible to control.

Some of the more complex surprises are blends of industrial hazard and natural hazard (Showalter and Myers 1994). For example, river floods provided the means by which a hazardous chemical – dioxin – was spread through the community of Times Beach, Missouri, leading to its eventual abandonment. Experts worry that rising sea levels may soon allow sea water to leach nuclear wastes that are buried on Pacific atolls, thereby bringing about serious – perhaps unprecedented – results (Walters 1992).

A further characteristic of recent industrial surprises deserves comment. Unlike previous industrial hazards, whose effects were mostly confined to people in close contact with the industries, many of the new surprises have demonstrated the potential to inflict delayed catastrophic losses on people and life-support systems often far removed from the industries themselves. Some of them can reach across space and time to affect vast numbers. The spread of radiation associated with the Chernobyl nuclear power station fire (1986) is an appropriate example. Although communities in the (then) USSR and Eastern Europe received most of the contamination, smaller levels of fallout circulated as far afield as the Alps, the British Isles, and Scandinavia (Smith and Clark 1989). Today an area of at least 13,000 square kilometres is officially classified as being heavily affected by radiation, but some of the worst contamination is known to lie outside this designated zone. Apart from those who died at the time of the accident, a minimum of one million people – mainly in Belarus and the Ukraine – live with the possibility of impaired health and truncated lives. They include an unknown number of former employees of the Chernobyl power station; an additional 600,000 people who took part in extinguishing the fire, building the concrete "sarcophagus" that entombs the stricken reactor, and decontaminating the vicinity; 135,000 evacuees from the so-called "exclusion zone" that was established after the fire; and 272,000 inhabitants of the surrounding "zone of strict control." The lives of others who live further afield have also been affected, by such measures as restrictions on food supplies that were exposed to fallout and changes in national energy policies that de-emphasized the use of nuclear power (Bojcun 1991; Brenton 1994). The effects may be felt for generations (Park 1989; Marples 1988).

Finally, some surprises raise the worrisome possibility that industrial hazards have evolved to the point where they are now capable of fundamentally altering global biogeochemical systems. Concern about human-induced climate change is a leading example (Mintzer 1992). Atmospheric build-up of chlorofluorocarbons is directly attributable to industrial processes. Increases in atmospheric carbon dioxide are also a function of industrial activities (especially power generation and vehicle use) as well as a function of the intensification of non-industrial activities (e.g. forest clearance for agriculture). It is widely believed that global warming might well affect the frequency and magnitude of conventional natural hazards, such as tropical cyclones and drought (Mitchell and Ericksen 1992). This example illustrates an important characteristic of evolving surprises – they are beginning to dissolve long-standing conceptual boundaries between what were thought of as natural hazards and what were considered industrial or human-made hazards. In the realm of global change surprises that are driven by industrial hazards, both the outcomes and the relative contributions of people and nature are in doubt. But there is unanimity that the issues are vitally important to the entire planet.

Coping with surprise

Surprises pose conceptual difficulties for hazard researchers and hazard managers. On the one hand, surprises can be viewed as extreme events or anomalies – outliers in the distribution of events to which they are most closely related. Thus, a toxic surprise like the dioxin cloud at Seveso is seen as a special case among all airborne toxic releases. Or the Chernobyl explosion and fire is seen as a more extreme kind of nuclear power station accident – an extension of events like Three Mile Island or Windscale. From this perspective, improved responses are likely to be found among measures that have proved to be effective against the most closely related class of events. On the other hand surprises are – to a greater or lesser degree – *unlike* other events. They are often indicators of abrupt or discontinuous change and may be forerunners of new sets of events (Brooks 1986). Existing responses are almost certainly mismatched with these new hazards and may be entirely inadequate. It is often necessary to learn about surprises and respond to them simultaneously. The process can stretch over many decades, with many frustrations and continuing losses along the way. Promising management approaches turn out to be blind alleys because they are based on flawed expectations about causes, behaviours, or actions that grew out of experience with other types of hazards.

The contradictions are illustrated by a recent example. After the Chernobyl explosion, British and Nordic scientists confidently expected that upland pastures that received moderate doses of fallout would not pose serious threats to livestock. They were forced to revise this judgement and institute restrictions on sheep farming when high levels of radioactivity showed up in animals that grazed these areas. Eventually, months after the event, it became clear that prevailing knowledge about the uptake and conversion of radioactivity in soils had been based on experience with alkaline soils; upland soils in Britain, Scandinavia, and elsewhere are highly acidic and respond quite differently (Wynne 1992).

As this example shows, there are dangers to managing surprises using principles that are applicable to routine hazards. Indeed, the very nature of surprises – many types but few cases of each, unusual amalgams of phenomena that we are accustomed to treat separately, increasingly potent and far-reaching in space and time, confounding of accepted wisdom – tends to frustrate conventional management. How can an appropriate alternative management system for surprises be fashioned?

It is too early to give an answer to that question for we are only now beginning to think systematically about surprise as a special kind of management problem. However, a first step towards the answer is to treat surprises as a heterogeneous but coherent class of events that shares the common characteristic of challenging our expectations. That is not to say that all surprises are the same; quite evidently they are not. Table 1.1 is one attempt to characterize some of the salient differences and similarities among surprises. It arranges a sample of surprises in a matrix whose axes roughly correspond to variables of control and experience. As portrayed here, prospects for control increase as we move from left to right and levels of experience increase as we move from top to bottom. This table provides a kind of conceptual "map" of surprise. Ideally, the boxes in the matrix might be filled with many more examples – say, all surprises that inflict more than some minimum amount of loss. This would permit identification

Table 1.1   **A matrix of surprises**[a]

Experience	Control		
	Unsuspected hazards	Improperly managed hazards	Instrumental hazards
One of a kind	Ozone depletion: chlorofluorocarbons	Kyshtym: nuclear wastes	Hiroshima, Nagasaki: atomic bombs
First of a kind	DDT: pesticide	Metal fatigue: Comet aircraft	World War I: poison gas
Worst of a kind	Minamata: methyl mercury bio-magnification	Chernobyl: nuclear power station	Kuwait: oil well fires

a. Control increases from left to right; experience increases from top to bottom.

of subcategories of surprise that currently impose the heaviest burdens on society. A time series of such assessments would provide useful information about the shifting nature of surprise and the rate at which some surprises undergo the transition to routine hazards.

The purpose of classifying surprises in this – or a similar – manner is to help structure investigations of responses and thereby to lay the basis for a surprise-management system. For example, warning systems, emergency-management schemes and recovery programmes are three of the many responses to hazard. It would be valuable to examine the record of success in employing these responses across the full range of surprises. It may be that certain actions are particularly flexible as well as effective and that others are restricted to one niche in the matrix. At this stage it is not possible to do more than indicate these general directions that investigations might take.

It should be realized that a system for managing surprise would supplement, not replace, existing systems of hazard management. Existing systems would continue to be applied to routine hazards, which constitute the bulk of all hazards that confront society. Indeed, a successful system for managing surprises would be one that facilitates the transition of surprises to routine hazards.

Reducing the impact of industrial disaster surprises: The range of choice

While we await the development of tools to manage surprises, it is both possible and necessary to improve the existing means of responding to them. Four broad sets of choices are available at present: (1) do nothing; (2) undertake research; (3) engage in mitigation; and (4) encourage adaptation. Which choice (or choices) offer(s) the best prospects for improvement?

Doing nothing is ruled out because of the stakes that are involved. If the scale of human intervention in natural systems is growing, and industrial hazards are an active ingredient of this process, it would be risky to ignore new types of industrial hazard – even if immediate losses are not heavy (e.g. Seveso). This is certainly one lesson of recent experience with ozone depletion, forest death, and greenhouse gases. However, doing nothing has often been a preferred alternative for governments that are accustomed to short-term decision-making.

Scientific and technical research to develop a better basis for action is clearly a second possible alternative. Given the novelty of industrial surprises, it is important to find out more about them so that adequate responses can be formulated. But the lack of similar cases poses difficulties in generalizing from a single experience or a small number of related experiences. Research findings are likely to emerge slowly and haltingly. This calls to mind an example from Japan. Most of what is known about the medical effects of atomic weapons explosions comes from the tragic experience of Hiroshima and Nagasaki (Harwell and Hutchinson 1985). But we are still debating the interpretation of these data almost 50 years after the events. A recent dispute concerns discrepancies between calculations of radiation emitted from the bombs and radiation doses received at ground level (Marshall 1992). Previous findings may have overstated or understated the hazard, though this has not prevented the data from playing a role as evidence in debates about nuclear policy. I am not saying here that it is impossible to make policy decisions about hazards without copious and reliable data on their observed effects. Obviously, one can conclude that nuclear weapons pose unacceptable risks or hazards, on the basis of other information. For example, scenario-building and simulation are alternative approaches. The point is that scientific research on surprises is usually slow and difficult and it does not necessarily produce results that can be replicated in the future.

Mitigation refers to actions that are designed to prevent, avoid, or reduce a hazard. Clearly, it is in the long-term interests of society to develop mitigation measures because they offer the best hope of permanent solutions to hazards of all kinds. For example, two types of mitigation have been proposed to combat the anticipated hazard of global warming, which is connected with the rapid industrialization of the Earth. The first focuses on reducing the emission of greenhouse gases that are believed to be the driving forces of warming. This would probably entail major restrictions on the burning of fossil fuels. The second type of mitigation turns the issue around and focuses not on reducing greenhouse gas emissions but on increasing the capacity of environments to absorb these gases. This involves reducing defor-estation and encouraging reforestation as well as somewhat visionary technological fixes such as seeding the oceans with carbon-absorbing chemicals. Both types of mitigation are controversial, in part because there is no consensus that human-induced global warming is indeed taking place. Although growing concentrations of carbon in the at-mosphere have been confirmed and constitute a clear case of sur-prise, there are still major gaps in knowledge that might confirm that actual warming is under way. So the policy arrangements are being developed on the basis of what are admittedly incomplete scientific data. It is expected to be many years, perhaps decades, before the scientific basis of global warming can be confirmed. By then, it may be too late to do anything but live with the consequences. What this example suggests is that it is very difficult to mitigate surprises – in part because it is difficult to analyse the surprises and in part because it may be necessary to adopt presumed countermeasures that have high costs and uncertain efficacy.

This brings us to the final major strategy – adaptation. Here the intent is not so much to prevent a surprise occurring but to make sure that society is able to cope with the resulting impacts. Attention is mainly focused on improving management of the emergency and subsequent recovery. Of the four possible sets of alternative adjust-ments to surprise, adaptation is perhaps the most promising. I will focus on one aspect of adaptation – improving the process of *recov-ery*. It should be possible to improve recovery from events such as Bhopal and *Exxon Valdez*, because many of the problems and issues of recovery are not specific to a particular hazard, they are generic across most or all hazards. For example, victims must be tended to and provided with assistance that will allow them to continue their lives, whether the distress is caused by toxic waste, or nuclear radia-tion, or any other hazard. Damaged or destroyed buildings must be rebuilt or replaced, whether the agent of destruction is a flood or a bomb. Degraded natural resources must be restored, whether con-taminated by an oil spill or leached by acid precipitation. It is not

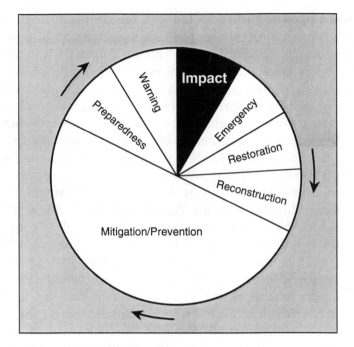

Fig. 1.4 **The disaster cycle**

necessary to wait for detailed scientific analysis of surprises before beginning recovery.

Recovering from surprise

What is known about disaster recovery comes mainly from studies of natural disasters (Anderson and Woodrow 1989; Bolin 1982; Bolin and Bolton 1986; Drabek 1986; Friesma et al. 1979; Geipel 1991; Hall and Landreth 1975; LaPlante 1988; May 1985, 1988; Perry and Mushkatel 1984; Rubin et al. 1985). These suggest that disasters are discrete phenomena with more or less well-marked beginnings and ends. They are also sequential phenomena, with each one helping to shape the one that follows (Haas, Kates, and Bowden 1977). In the wake of a disaster, communities are believed to pass through successively longer overlapping stages that are characterized by different problems, issues, and responses. These are commonly given labels like "emergency," "rehabilitation," "reconstruction," "revival," and "symbolic recovery" (fig. 1.4). As recovery progresses, attention turns from efforts to recoup past losses to planning for the future, including preparing for the next disaster. The characteristics of each period have been summarized by LaPlante:

The first period, the emergency phase, is typically a period of high consensus in the community, with much altruistic behavior aimed at preventing or reducing human suffering. Next, activities that will return the community to normal functioning are undertaken and initiate the second period, called the restoration phase. When a semblance of normal functioning is achieved, activities aimed at permanence begin the reconstruction phase: families return to home, work or school and community rebuilding gets under way. Family and individual needs may come into conflict with community goals at this stage of recovery ... a final stage ... reflects activity at essentially the community level, called the commemorative, betterment, and development reconstruction phase. During this time of second-stage community reconstruction, plans and actions decided upon during the earlier reconstruction are implemented. (LaPlante 1988, 220)

The entire cycle may take many years to reach completion, depending on such factors as the magnitude of the initial disaster, the amount of resources that are available to provide assistance, and whether the affected community is urban or rural. Though the speed and timing of recovery vary in different settings, the process is held to be essentially similar everywhere.

This stage model of disaster is widely employed by researchers. However, it is not universally accepted. For example, students of rural third world disasters have suggested that the pace of recovery is often strongly distorted by the demand for agricultural labour. In farming villages, recovery may occur in spurts during times when the community is not occupied with planting crops or harvesting them. Thus, recovery may take place in several cycles of activity of varying intensity separated by periods when little recovery occurs (Cuny 1983). Other analysts have criticized the stage model for focusing too much on aggregate conditions and economic factors and overlooking the more varied suite of problems that affects individuals and families. Recovery at the family level is believed to be a fourfold process that involves – in addition to economic recovery – emotional recovery, housing recovery, and quality of life recovery (Bolin 1982). A community might appear to be recovering from disaster but it could contain many families that are not recovering and may never do so. Thus, it is argued that the general stage model glosses over the multidimensionality of recovery and its internal contradictions.

Relatively little is known about the process of recovery from industrial disasters, particularly surprises, but the available information is

31

not comforting. As pointed out earlier, some communities that are affected by industrial disasters simply cease to exist. That is what happened at Times Beach and it may also be the fate of communities near Chernobyl. Such a dire outcome is almost unheard of among communities stricken by natural disasters. The post-World War II increase in global interconnectedness has made it possible for people everywhere to be aware of storm- and earthquake-ravaged communities and to facilitate the transfer of sustaining aid to them. Whereas Drabek could well say that (natural) disasters caused "... relatively minor ripples in the long term developmental cycle" (Drabek 1986, 251), industrial disasters can bring fundamental changes to impacted communities.

Industrial surprises are often protracted; some are, perhaps, interminable. It is questionable that one can speak of recovery from disaster when the process is not complete within the life-span of victims. In Minamata, recovery has taken at least four decades and is still incomplete. Awareness of toxic chemical wastes is a relatively recent phenomenon in most countries, but already there are communities that can look back on more than twenty years of experience, concern, and action. The entire planet may face the prospect of significant climate changes, whose effects will stretch from now well into the twenty-first century – and perhaps beyond. How long will recovery take for populations affected by such changes?

Recovery from industrial disasters is usually conflict laden. Probably the most enduring conflict revolves around the attribution of responsibility and blame. Although human agency can play a role in natural disasters, people are not generally held accountable for the occurrence of extreme natural events. It is easier for communities that are affected by natural disasters to unite around themes of common loss, common interests, and common action in support of community-wide goals for recovery. This does not necessarily mean that post-disaster conflicts are thereby avoided, but they are less likely to occur than in the accusatory atmosphere that surrounds many industrial disasters. Conflicts also tend to create winners and losers, with the potential for acrimony, recrimination, and resentment. Groups that seek to help can become embroiled in unrewarding actions. Speaking of one experience, Brown and Mikkelsen note:

It is important to remember that community efforts ... are difficult, painful, and lengthy. We have looked at efforts taking five or ten years or even longer, sapping energy, bringing loss and the pain of publicity, creating tensions in families and communities, and standing a good chance of failure. (Brown and Mikkelsen 1990, 198–199)

Not only are industrial surprises like Chernobyl likely to have very long-lived effects that effectively postpone and extend recovery into succeeding generations but also there is considerable doubt that recovery will take the form of a return to a stable pre-disaster state. Based on a review of several case-studies, Edelstein concluded that "... recovery to a 'post-disaster equilibrium' is difficult if not impossible" (Edelstein 1988, 9). Others have come to similar conclusions. In other words, it may be impossible to return to "normal" after a surprise. This suggests that the range of recovery strategies may include other choices. For example, instead of attempting to resurrect the *status quo ante*, "surprised" communities might either chose to (1) make recovery a process for realizing an entirely new and different future *in situ*, or (2) accept that recovery in any form is not possible at the existing site and make plans for relocation elsewhere.

Conclusions

What is known about recovery from industrial disaster surprises suggests that the process is disjointed, conflict ridden, long lasting and highly uncertain. Such characteristics are difficult to reconcile with the image of disaster recovery that is projected by existing research models and the professional literature. These sources tend to assume that recovery involves continuity of effort, a minimum level of agreement about community goals, and the attainment of identifiable short-term objectives on the way to a definite end-point when recovery is completed – usually within the lifetimes of victims. The gap between the hopeful expectations of this model and reality is wide. Too often, the length of time that is required to engage in and to complete recovery from industrial disasters has been underestimated. Too often, these disasters have been viewed as temporary perturbations, whose effects will cease sooner or later, thereby permitting affected communities to return to "normal". Too often, the predominant response has been to address disasters as separate and discrete events, and to ignore the broader contexts that facilitate disaster by promoting far-reaching changes in technology, environments, and society. In short, responses to industrial disasters are often flawed by inaccurate perceptions of the recovery process.

Society needs industrial technology; we will not be well served by rejecting it in fruitless pursuit of Arcadian or Utopian myths about a riskless society. However, if recovery from industrial disaster surprises is to be improved, it will be necessary to acquire a more sophisticated understanding of how the process actually takes place in specific communities. By chronicling the process of recovery in a wide range of disasters, the chapters in this volume aid in achieving that objective. As a fund of experience is accumulated from a large number of communities, we will be in a better position to identify the responses that have proved to be most effective and to replicate them. Improving recovery from events like Minamata and Bhopal is an essential and feasible step in building the global capacity to manage surprises. Beyond lies the considerably more difficult task of mitigating surprises.

Notes

1. For up-to-date information on industrial risk issues, the following periodicals provide useful starting points: *Industrial and Environmental Crisis Quarterly, Industry and Environment, Risk Analysis*, and *Risk: Health, Safety and Environment*. There is also a vast journal literature on the more general subject of industrial safety.
2. Many problems of statistical inference about uncertainty and extreme events seriously hamper risk analysis. See, for example, Hacking (1986) and Haimes, Barry, and Lambert (1994).
3. The term "hazard" is preferred over "risk" because it connotes an interactive system of risks and responses that affects industrial systems – not just single types of incident risks. This system includes various feedback relationships among different types and levels of risks, exposed populations, vulnerable groups, and deliberate or inadvertent responses, the whole being set within different sociotemporal and spatial contexts.
4. Throughout this volume, prices expressed in dollars are US dollars, and the term "billion" means a thousand million (10^9).
5. The interpretation of workplace fatalities is complicated by different definitions of "major industrial disasters." For example, in 1992 approximately 15,000 workers were killed in job-related industrial accidents in China – an increase of 3% over 1991 (*International Labor Review* 1993). Most of these deaths probably occurred singly and in small facilities, therefore failing to merit the label "major disasters." Such a pattern clearly exists in the United States. A recent analysis of 500,000 federal and state safety-inspection records, carried out by the Occupational Health and Safety Administration, lists 4,464 on-the-job deaths in US companies between 1988 and 1992 (*Wall Street Journal*, 3 February 1994). The vast majority of these deaths (4,337) occurred in workplaces with fewer than 20 employees.
6. It should be noted that problems resulting from two of these events (Seveso and Times Beach) were downgraded in revised assessments made by scientists several years after public concern was first raised. This in no way minimizes the extent to which each event constituted a disaster for the human populations that were affected when the events first came to light.
7. The first person to be killed in a railroad accident in the United States was the fireman on the country's first passenger locomotive, the boiler of which exploded in 1831. In 1865 a

boiler explosion and fire on board the *Sultana*, a Mississippi sternwheeler, killed more than 1,500 people – the largest loss of life in any American marine disaster.

8. Most natural hazards can be classified as routine. The International Decade for Natural Disaster Reduction (1990–2000), a UN-sponsored programme of collaborative actions among participating nations, assumes that a thoroughgoing commitment to applying existing unused knowledge about natural disasters would be sufficient to bring about major reductions in losses.

9. As defined by Resources for the Future, industrial accidents included explosions, fires, and toxic vapours associated with industrial materials or facilities but excluded mining accidents and passenger transportation accidents; see Glickman, Golding, and Silverman (1992).

10. Forest death (Waldsterben) is the name given to a collection of symptoms of die-back and die-off among trees in Germany that are believed to be linked to increased air pollution among other factors; see "Multiple pollutants and forest decline," in *World Resources 1986* (World Resources Institute 1986).

References

Anderson, Mary B., and Peter J. Woodrow. 1989. *Rising from the Ashes: Development Strategies in Times of Disaster*. Boulder, Colo.: Westview Press and Paris: UNESCO.

Beck, Ulrich. 1995. *Ecological Enlightenment: Essays on the Politics of the Risk Society*. Atlantic Highlands, New Jersey: Humanities Press.

Bocjun, Marko. 1991. "The legacy of Chernobyl." *New Scientist* (1765): 30–35 (20 April 1991).

Bolin, Robert C. 1982. *Long-term Family Recovery from Disaster*. Program on Environment and Behavior Monograph 36. Boulder, Colo.: Institute of Behavioral Science, University of Colorado.

———, and Patricia Bolton. 1986. *Race, Religion and Ethnicity in Disaster Recovery*. Program on Environment and Behavior Monograph 42. Boulder, Colo.: Institute of Behavioral Science, University of Colorado.

Bowonder, B., and H.A. Linstone. 1987. "Notes on the Bhopal accident: risk analysis and multiple perspectives." *Technological Forecasting and Social Change* 32(2): 183–202.

Brenton, Tony. 1994. *The Greening of Machiavelli: The Evolution of International Environmental Politics*. London: Royal Institute of International Affairs, pp. 130–131.

Brooks, H. 1986. "The typology of surprises in technology, institutions and development." In: W.C. Clark and R.E. Munn, eds. *Sustainable Development of the Biosphere*. Cambridge: Cambridge University Press, pp. 325–347.

Brown, Phil, and Edwin J. Mikkelsen. 1990. *No Safe Place: Toxic Waste, Leukemia, and Community Action*. Berkeley: University of California Press.

Burton, Ian, and Robert W. Kates. 1986. "The Great Climacteric, 1798–2048: The transition to a just and sustainable human environment." In: Robert W. Kates and Ian Burton, eds. *Themes from the Work of Gilbert F. White. Vol II: Geography, Resources, and Environment*. Chicago: University of Chicago Press, pp. 339–360.

Chelius, James Robert. 1977. *Workplace Safety and Health: The Role of Workers' Compensation*. Washington, DC: American Enterprise Institute for Public Policy Research.

Covello, Vincent T., and Miley W. Merkhofer. 1993. *Risk Assessment Methods: Approaches for Assessing Health and Environmental Risks*. New York: Plenum Press.

Cowan, Edward. 1968. *Oil and Water: The* Torrey Canyon *Disaster*. Philadelphia: J. B. Lippincott.

Cuny, Frederick. 1983. *Disasters and Development*. New York: Oxford University Press, pp. 40–44.

Curran, Daniel J. 1993. *Dead Laws for Dead Men: The Politics of Federal Coal Mine Health and Safety Legislation*. Pittsburgh: University of Pittsburgh Press.

Cutter, Susan L. 1993. *Living with Risk: The Geography of Technological Hazards*. London: Edward Arnold.

Dembo, David, Clarence J. Dias, Ayesha Kadwani, and Ward Morehouse (eds.). 1988. *Nothing to Lose but Our Lives: Empowerment to Oppose Industrial Hazards in a Transnational World*. New York: New Horizons Press.

Douglas, Mary. 1992. *Risk and Blame: Essays in Cultural Theory*. London: Routledge.

———, and Aaron Wildavsky. 1982. *Risk and Culture: An Essay on the Selection of Technological and Environmental Dangers*. Berkeley: University of California Press.

Drabek, Thomas E. 1986. *Human System Responses to Disaster: An Inventory of Sociological Findings*. New York: Springer-Verlag.

Edelstein, Michael R. 1988. *Contaminated Communities: The Social and Psychological Impacts of Residential Toxic Exposure*. Boulder, Colo.: Westview Press.

Ellis, Derek. 1989. *Environments at Risk: Case Histories of Impact Assessment*. Berlin: Springer-Verlag, pp. 38–69.

Feshbach, Murray, and Alfred Friendly, Jr. 1992. *Ecocide in the USSR: Health and Nature Under Siege*. New York: Basic Books.

Friesma, H. Paul, James Caporaso, Gerald Goldstein, Robert Lineberry, and Richard McCleary. 1979. *Aftermath: Communities After Natural Disasters*. Beverly Hills: Sage Publications.

Funtowicz, S.O. and J.R. Ravetz. 1990. *Uncertainty and Quality in Science for Policy*. Dordrecht: Kluwer Academic Press.

———, and ———. 1996. "Global risk, uncertainty and ignorance." In: J.X. Kasperson and R.E. Kasperson, eds. *Global Environmental Risk*. Tokyo: United Nations University Press (forthcoming.)

Geipel, Robert. 1991. *Long-term Consequences of Disasters: The Reconstruction of Fruili, Italy, in Its International Context 1976–1988*. New York: Springer-Verlag.

Glacken, Clarence J. 1973. *Traces on the Rhodian Shore: Nature and Culture in Western Thought from Ancient Times to the End of the Eighteenth Century*. Berkeley: University of California Press.

Glickman, Theodore S., Dominic Golding, and Emily D. Silverman. 1992. *Acts of God and Acts of Man: Recent Trends in Natural Disasters and Major Industrial Accidents*. Discussion Paper CRM 92-02. Washington, DC: Resources for the Future.

Haas, J. Eugene, Robert W. Kates and Martyn J. Bowden (eds.). 1977. *Reconstruction Following Disaster*. Cambridge: MIT Press.

Hacking, Ian. 1986. "Culpable ignorance of interference effects." In: Douglas MacLean, ed. *Values at Risk*. Totowa: Rowman and Allanheld, pp. 136–154.

Haimes, Yacov, Timothy Barry, and James H. Lambert. 1994. "Workshop Proceedings: When and how can you specify a probability distribution when you don't know much?" *Risk Analysis* 14: 661.

Hall, Philip S., and Patrick W. Landreth. 1975. "Assessing some long term consequences of a natural disaster." *Mass Emergencies* 1: 55–61.

Hamilton, David. 1973. *Technology, Man and the Environment*. London: Faber and Faber, p. 296.

Harwell, Mark A., and Thomas C. Hutchinson (eds.). 1985. *Environmental Consequences of Nuclear War, Vol 2*. Chichester: John Wiley and Sons.

Headrick, Daniel R. 1990. "Technological change." In: B.L. Turner, II, William C. Clark, Robert W. Kates, John F. Richards, Jessica T. Mathews, and William B. Meyer, eds. *The Earth as Transformed by Human Action: Global and Regional Changes in the Biosphere over the Past 300 Years*. Cambridge: Cambridge University Press and Clark University, pp. 55–68.

Holling, C.S. 1986. "The resilience of terrestrial ecosystems: local surprise and global change." In: W.C. Clark and R.E. Munn, eds. *Sustainable Development of the Biosphere*. Cambridge: Cambridge University Press, pp. 292–316.

Houts, Peter S., Paul D. Cleary, and Teh-Wei Hu. 1988. *The Three Mile Island Crisis: Psychological, Social, and Economic Impacts on the Surrounding Population*. University Park: Pennsylvania State University Press.

Iijima, Nobuko (ed). 1979. *Pollution Japan: Historical Chronology*. Elmsford: Pergamon Press.

International Atomic Energy Agency. 1992. *The Role of Probabilistic Safety Assessment and Probabilistic Safety Criteria in Nuclear Power Plant Safety*. Safety Series No. 106. Vienna: IAEA.

International Labor Review. 1993. Vol. 132, No. 2, pp. 128–129.

Johnson, Brandon B., and Vincent T. Covello (eds.). 1987. *The Social and Cultural Construction of Risk: Essays on Risk Selection and Perception*. Dordrecht/Boston: D. Reidel/Norwell,

Kasperson, R.E., O. Renn, P. Slovic, H. Brown, J. Emel, R. Gogle, J.X. Kasperson, and S. Ratick. 1988. "The social amplification of risk: A conceptual framework." *Risk Analysis* 8(2): 177–187.

Kates, Robert W. 1985. "Success, strain and surprise: An introduction." *Issues in Science and Technology* 2(1): 46–58.

Lagadec, Patrick. 1990. *States of Emergency: Technological Failures and Social Destabilization*. London: Butterworth-Heinemann.

LaPlante, Josephine M. 1988. "Recovery following disaster: Policy issues and recommendations." In: Louise K. Comfort, ed. *Managing Disaster: Strategies and Policy Perspectives*. Durham: Duke University Press, pp. 217–235.

Lave, Lester B. (ed.). 1982. *Quantitative Risk Assessment in Regulation*. Washington, DC: The Brookings Institution.

———, and Arthur C. Upton (eds.). 1987. *Toxic Chemicals, Health, and the Environment*. Baltimore: Johns Hopkins University Press.

Lepkowski, Will. 1987. "The disaster at Bhopal – Chemical safety in the Third World." In: Charles S. Pearson, ed. *Multinational Corporations, Environment, and the Third World: Business Matters*. Durham: Duke University Press, pp. 240–254.

Lewis, H.W. 1990. *Technological Risk*. New York: W.W. Norton.

Lovins, Amony B. 1981. *Energy Policies for Resilience and National Security*. San Francisco: Friends of the Earth.

Lowrance, W.W. 1976. *Of Acceptable Risk: Science and Determination of Safety*. Los Altos: William Kaufmann.

Marbacher, J. (ed.). 1990. "Natural catastrophes and major losses 1970–1989: Increasing catastrophe losses from forces of nature in the 1980s." *Sigma Economic Studies* 6/90. Zurich: Swiss Reinsurance Company.

Marples, David R. 1988. *The Social Impact of the Chernobyl Disaster*. New York: St. Martin's Press.

Marshall, Eliot. 1992. "Study casts doubt on Hiroshima data." *Science* 238: 394.

Matousek, Jiri. 1991. "The release in war of dangerous forces from chemical facilities." In: Arthur H. Westing, ed. *Environmental Hazards of War: Releasing Dangerous Forces in an Industrialized World*. London: Sage Publications, pp. 30–37.

May, Peter J. 1985. *Recovering from Catastrophes: Federal Disaster Relief Policy and Practices*. Westport: Greenwood Press.

———. 1988. "Disaster recovery and reconstruction," In: Louise K. Comfort, ed. *Managing Disaster: Strategies and Policy Perspectives*. Durham: Duke University Press, pp. 236–254.

Medvedev, Zhores A. 1979. *Nuclear Disaster in the Urals*. New York: Vintage Books.

Minamata City and Kumamoto Prefecture. 1988. *A Summary of the Minamata Disease*. Minamata, Japan: City of Minamata.

Mintzer, Irving M. (ed.). 1992. *Confronting Climate Change: Risks, Implications and Responses*. Cambridge: Cambridge University Press.

Mitchell, James K. 1990. "Human dimensions of environmental hazards: Complexity, disparity and the search for guidance." In: Andrew Kirby, ed. *Nothing to Fear: Risks and Hazards in American Society*. Tucson: University of Arizona Press, pp. 131–178.

———, and Neil J. Ericksen. 1992. "Effects of climate change on weather-related disasters." In: Irving M. Mintzer, ed. *Confronting Climate Change: Risks, Implications and Responses*. Cambridge: Cambridge University Press, pp. 141–152.

Myers, Bill, and Paul Read. 1992. "Emergency planning and pollution." In: Malcolm Newson, ed. *Managing the Human Impact on the Natural Environment: Patterns and Processes*. London: Belhaven Press, pp. 196–210.

National Research Council. 1993. *Issues in Risk Assessment*. Committee on risk assessment methodology, Board on Environmental Studies and Toxicology, Commission on Life Sciences. Washington, DC: National Academy Press.

National Safety Council. 1988. *Accident Prevention Manual for Industrial Operations: Administration and Programs*. Chicago: National Safety Council.

O'Riordan, T., and S. Rayner. 1991. "Risk management for global environmental change." *Global Environmental Change* 1(2): 91–108.

Park, Chris C. 1989. *Chernobyl: The Long Shadow*. London: Routledge.

Perrow, Charles. 1984. *Normal Accidents: Living with High-risk Technologies*. New York: Basic Books.

Perry, Ronald W., and Alvin H. Mushkatel. 1984. *Disaster Management: Warning Response and Community Relocation*. Westport: Quorum Books.

Petts, Judith. 1988. "Planning and hazardous installation control." *Progress in Planning*, 29: 1–75.

Prince, D.H. 1920. *Catastrophe and Social Change*. New York: Columbia University Press.

Rafter, Susan. 1987. *Risk Analysis and Risk Management: A Selected Bibliography*. Monticello, Ill.: Vance Bibliographies.

Ravetz, J.R., and S. Funtowicz. 1990. *Global Environmental Issues and the Emergence of Second-order Science*. London: Council for Science and Society.

Roush, Wade. 1993. "Learning from technological disasters." *Technology Review* 96(6): 50–57.

Renn, O., W. Burns, J.X. Kasperson, R.E. Kasperson, and P. Slovic. 1993. "The social amplification of risk: Theoretical foundations and empirical applications." *Journal of Social Issues* 48: 137–160.

Risk Analysis. 1994. *The Risk Assessment Paradigm after Ten Years: Policy and Practice Then, Now, and in the Future. Risk Analysis* 14(3). (Special issue.)

Rosner, David, and Gerald Markowitz (eds.). 1987. *Dying for Work: Workers' Safety and Health in Twentieth-century America*. Bloomington: Indiana University Press.

Rubin, Claire B., Martin D. Saperstein, and Daniel R. Barbee. 1985. *Community Recovery from a Major Natural Disaster*. Program on Environment and Behavior Monograph 41. Boulder, Colorado: Institute of Behavioral Science, University of Colorado.

Sax, N. Irving. 1975. *Dangerous Properties of Industrial Materials*. New York: Van Nostrand Reinhold.

Sheehan, Helen E., and Richard P. Wedeen (eds.). 1993. *Toxic Circles: Environmental Hazards from the Workplace into the Community*. New Brunswick: Rutgers University Press.

Showalter, Pamela S., and Mary F. Myers. 1994. "Natural disasters in the United States as release agents of oil, chemicals, or radiological materials between 1980–1989: Analysis and recommendations." *Risk Analysis* 14(2): 169–182.

Sills, David L., C.P. Wolf, and Vivien B. Shelanski. 1982. *Accident at Three Mile Island: The Human Dimensions*. Boulder: Westview Press.

Slovic, Paul. 1987. "Perception of risk." *Science* 236(4799): 280–285.

Smith, F.B., and M.J. Clark. 1989. *Airborne Debris from the Chernobyl Incident*. Meteorological Science Paper No. 2. London: Her Majesty's Stationery Office.

Smith, Kirk. 1988. *The Risk Transition*. Working Paper No. 10. Honolulu: East–West Center, Environment and Policy Institute.

———, Richard A. Carpenter, and M. Susanne Faulstich. 1988. *Risk Assessment of Hazardous Chemical Systems in Developing Countries*. Occasional papers of the East–West Environment and Policy Institute No. 5. Honolulu: East–West Center.

United Nations. 1994. *Industrial Accident Manual: Activities of Other United Nations Bodies and Programmes, International Organizations and Institutions*. Geneva: International Programme on Chemical Safety.

United Nations Environment Programme. 1993. *Intergovernmental Forum on Chemical Risk Assessment and Management*. Report of the governing council of United Nations Environment Programme, 17th session. New York. 11 June.

United States General Accounting Office. 1991. *Nuclear Power Safety: Chernobyl Accident Prompted Worldwide Actions but Further Efforts Needed*. GAO/NSIAD-92-28. November 1991. Washington, DC: USGAO.

Wall Street Journal. 1994. 3 February, Sec A, p. 1.

Walters, Robert. 1992. "Poison in the Pacific." *The Progressive* 56(7): 32–35.

Warner, Sir Frederick. 1992. *Risk: Analysis, Perception and Management.* Report of a Royal Society study group. London: Royal Society.

Whiteside, James. 1990. *Regulating Danger: The Struggle for Mine Safety in the Rocky Mountain Coal Industry.* Lincoln: University of Nebraska Press.

World Resources Institute. 1986. *World Resources 1986.* New York: Basic Books, pp. 203–226.

———. 1992. *World Resources 1992–93.* New York: Basic Books.

Wynne, Brian. 1992. "Uncertainty and environmental learning: Reconceiving science and policy in the preventive paradigm." *Global Environmental Change* 2(2): 111–127.

2

Responses to Minamata disease

Sadami Maruyama

Introduction

Minamata is a Japanese city of 34,000 people on the north-west coast of Kumamoto Prefecture in the island of Kyushu. It lies astride a small river that empties into Minamata Bay, an arm of the semi-enclosed Shiranui (Yatsushiro) Sea. This sea is about 50 miles long and 10 miles wide and is separated from the open ocean by a chain of small mountainous islands (fig. 2.1).

Minamata disease is the name given to mercury toxicosis (poisoning) that developed in people who ate contaminated seafood taken from Minamata Bay and adjacent coastal waters in the period after World War II. During this time, methyl mercury was dumped into the sea as an unwanted by-product of acetaldehyde processing at the Chisso Company Limited industrial plant in Minamata.[1]

Almost forty years have passed since Minamata disease was officially recognized in May 1956 but, despite an urgent need for relief of victims and restoration of fishing grounds, these and many other issues still remain to be resolved. Although resolution is complicated by the dispersion and diversity of victims, the slow and incomplete response is mainly due to the actions of individuals and organizations that confused and dragged out the entire recovery process.

This chapter emphasizes the victims' perspective and focuses on

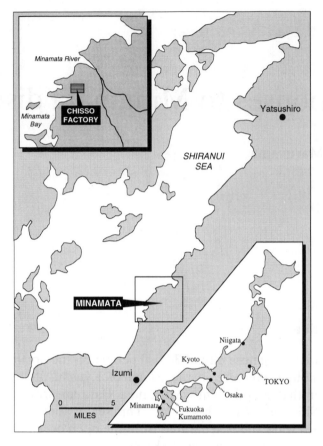

Fig. 2.1 **The Minamata region**

how governmental and corporate evasion of responsibility for the disaster frustrated attempts at providing needed relief and restitution.[2] It provides clues about what can be done to speed the recovery of any local community that has been hollowed out by lingering environmental disaster and offers guidance to prevent a recurrence of similar situations elsewhere.

Who are the victims of Minamata disease?

It is necessary to have a thorough understanding of the victims of Minamata disease before proceeding to an analysis of the disaster response. Victims can be divided into two groups – primary and secondary. The primary victims suffered physical disabilities and impairment, whereas the secondary victims experienced a variety of other losses (e.g. economic, social, psychological).

As of 31 March 1993, the official government tally of confirmed victims was 2,255 (both living and dead) with 2,376 others who are still seeking to be classified as victims.[3] The number of persons refused certification has climbed to 12,503. The actual total of victims is undoubtedly larger than the official figures because an unknown number of people died from the disease without certification or chose not to apply for certification. Some physicians estimate that at least half of the 200,000 people who lived along the coast of the Shiranui Sea in the late 1950s were affected by some form of mercury poisoning.

Patients who died when the disease entered an acute stage suffered incomparable misery. Others who survived carry severe physical and psychological scars. Those with minor symptoms such as ataxia and inertia often also exhibit signs of neurological disorder together with intellectual impairment. These afflictions hinder every aspect of their daily lives, including work and social relations. A large number of children acquired the disease before birth via transfer across the placenta from the mother.

Sadly, there is no effective means of medication for Minamata disease. Above all, there is no possibility of recovery for nerve cells that are destroyed by methyl mercury. Practically no research on probable means of treatment is under way. The primary victims of Minamata disease could not seek work and were forced to bear heavy medical and nursing costs. Usually, these costs were transferred to the victims' families because mutual aid among family members is traditional in this community. As a result, many poor families have had to scrape the bottom of the barrel just to make ends meet. By the end of 1959, only 43 per cent of households with Minamata disease patients were receiving any sort of public assistance. Entire households were faced with collapse. To make matters worse, the dismal symptoms of Minamata disease were unprecedented and therefore particularly threatening. This so-called "strange disease" was feared by residents of the fishing hamlets, who turned against the afflicted because they were thought to be carriers of contagion. The government's practice of disinfecting and isolating patients in hospitals provided grounds for these fears. Thus, patients lost the support of a normally friendly and cooperative community. They were deprived of mutual aid and their families were ostracized by neighbours.

When the cause of Minamata disease was finally identified, people who lived near, or fished in, the contaminated area came under even greater pressure from outsiders. The fact that fish were the medium by which the disease was spread, crippled the fisheries. Not only did regional catches decline because of pollution but sales of locally caught fish were entirely prohibited. As a result, fishermen became obsessed by the possibility that the disease might spread and did what they could to shut the disease out of their lives. Fishing cooperatives methodically plotted to conceal new cases of poisoning. Families with disease-afflicted persons became more and more alienated and isolated.

One fact was clear to all: the natural environment was being degraded. Evidence of marine pollution was clear before humans went down with Minamata disease. Fisheries were already in trouble. Some local fishermen tried to combat declining catches by turning to new fishing techniques and new locations, but they met with no success because pollution was widespread. As a result, many sold their boats and sought employment on shore. A great number of others moved away from the area. The widespread migration of victims accounts for the fact that many lawsuits were brought against Chisso, the prefecture of Kumamoto, and the national government by persons who lived in Osaka, Tokyo, Kyoto, Fukuoka, and elsewhere.

Minamata disease is typical of modern industrial pollution in so far as it manifests a wide geographic spread of impacts and casualties. Furthermore, like other industrial pollution disasters, most of the effects are concentrated in lower socio-economic groups such as labourers from primary industries – in this case fishermen and their families. But the natural environment also suffers heavily, and with it a variety of other groups who have recreation and tourism interests. Public beaches are particularly impaired, especially those that provide tidewater fishing, crabbing, and opportunities for leisure strolls. In other words, Minamata disease affects virtually every element of the local community. Most of these issues remain to be resolved before the problems of recovery can be said to have been properly addressed.

Official recognition of Minamata disease and the initial response

The first signs that something was amiss in the seas near Minamata appeared around 1949. Dead fish floated on top of the bay and shellfish emitted a noxious odour when opened. Soon, catches began to decline. By 1953, local residents reported that cats "danced" in circles before collapsing into the bay; seabirds and crows were also observed spiralling unexpectedly into the sea. Shortly thereafter, the first cases of human sickness were noted.

The immediate response of the local government and residents was vigorous and uncontroversial. A research committee was organized by the city of Minamata. Public health officials and the local medical association moved quickly to discover the cause of the disease and to search for preventive measures as well as appropriate treatments for the victims. Within two or three months it was clear that the worst-affected areas were fishing hamlets along the shores of the bay. The symptoms of an apparently contagious disease were also identified. Emergency actions were quickly mounted. Patients were admitted to a hospital isolation ward. Some experts suggested that they might be suffering from encephalitis japonica – sleeping sickness. Others thought that a possibly contagious disease was involved, so the government repeatedly disinfected places associated with large numbers of cases.

A change in the speed and effectiveness of responses came about after heavy metal poisoning of fish began to be suspected as the chief culprit. When industrial effluents from Chisso came under suspicion, there was a marked slackening of efforts to identify the disease and prevent its worsening. The entire matter was put into the hands of prefectural and national governments rather than local groups. In the process, local citizens lost the ability to bring about directly a speedy resolution of the problem. Some of the blame for this unproductive turn of events must be shared by the residents of Minamata, but it is clear that the main contributors to disaster were a combination of business practices that gave priority to production and ignored environmental pollution, and the principle of governmental promotion of industries at any cost – including dangerous pollution.

Chisso's grip on the local community

The making of Minamata

The city of Minamata grew along with the expansion of Chisso. Indeed, the city served as a model company town. The penetration of Chisso's influence and that of affiliated companies is shown by several statistics. Between 1956 and the early 1970s the industrial complex occupied 68 per cent of the city's land area and consumed 93 per cent of its water supply. Chisso-related businesses accounted for 30 per cent of retail sales, employed 19 per cent of the workforce and commissioned 66 per cent of all the shipping activity.

By the early 1960s, as Chisso started to invest in petrochemicals operations elsewhere, it began to reduce its stake in Minamata. But the company was still a pre-eminent force in the community (Nakamura 1975). For example, in 1960, despite privileged exemptions, Chisso accounted for 49 per cent of the city's total tax revenues (Funaba 1973). Chisso was Minamata's cashbox (Chisso 1955). Yet the extent of Chisso's influence on municipal policy was viewed as insufficient by company leaders, for employees were directed to involve themselves in municipal affairs and ensure that public policy was in accordance with Chisso's business operations.

The extent of Chisso's involvement in local government began during the period of rapid expansion after World War I. In 1925, the company entered its own candidates in local elections for the city council. The Plant Manager was among seven people elected to the council and a former Plant Director was elected Mayor. During the 20 years from 1950 to 1969, except for one brief period, the mayoral seat was continuously held by the Chisso Plant Manager.

Government penetration was not the only way that the Chisso company seized control of the local community. By identifying themselves as "Chisso of Minamata," corporate leaders also encouraged the belief that the firm and the community shared a "mutual destiny." These and other manoeuvres explain Chisso's success in taking control of the municipality but they do not account for their irresponsibility as managers of the local environment and the health of residents. From the outset, the company had a history of inflicting damage on the environment.

Environmental destruction before Minamata disease

In 1925, fishermen from Minamata demanded restitution from Chisso for damage caused by water pollution. They were fobbed off with a *mimaikin* – a consolation payment – and were required to drop all further complaints. But the pollution did not cease and further complaints were lodged in 1943 and 1954. In each case, Chisso used its power to limit compensation to small sums.

Local residents were also aware of other environmental problems that were traceable to actions taken by Chisso. These included dumping of effluent in the city's harbour that caused it to silt up and hampered shipping. Smoke, dust, noise, and vibrations were also widespread. Hazardous gases inflicted losses on crops and trees.

Complaints about pollution were always handled directly by the company without the intervention of the Minamata city government. As a result, there was no tradition of assistance to citizens by the local government. What might otherwise have surfaced as a social problem that would have necessitated the formulation of public policy was diverted into a series of private arrangements between the corporation and affected individuals. This means of responding to industrial pollution laid the groundwork for the later poor handling of Minamata disease.

Neglect in preventing the spread of disease

Manoeuvres to avoid a ban on fishing

Measures to prevent further outbreaks of Minamata disease should have been taken once the cause was identified, but no such action occurred. When it became clear that contaminated fish and shellfish were the principal carriers of toxins, a comprehensive ban on fishing should have been adopted immediately. Instead, the Kumamoto prefectural government argued that it was unlawful to impose a ban because not all the seafood in the bay was poisoned. Hence, the government requested fishermen to refrain voluntarily from fishing in the bay or selling catches from it. But fishermen who contravened the ban were not penalized, nor were they supervised. In time, the area of polluted waters expanded and the disease spread along the entire coastal region of the Shiranui Sea. Though there was public pressure to change existing laws and institute a compulsory ban, nothing was done to amend the legislation.

Here was a failure of government. Fishermen were asked to accept unilateral self-restraint, whereas Chisso's dumping operations were given implicit approval. In the process, no thorough warning of the dangers of consuming contaminated seafood was provided for local citizens. Daily catches continued to be distributed and the number of infected people rose. Had a proper ban been imposed at the outset, it is probable that the disease would have been checked in its early stages. Even today, no such action has ever been taken, though court battles to apportion responsibility for the failure are in progress. So far, three verdicts have been handed down in the lower courts, two of which hold government administrators negligent.

Obstacles to identifying the cause of Minamata disease

Early investigations of Minamata disease were conducted by the School of Medicine at Kumamoto University. These soon disclosed that toxins in seafood from the bay were responsible, but the precise causes were not readily identifiable. Chisso and government officials took the position that, without conclusive proof of a particular cause or causes, no effective public action could be taken. Thus, researchers were forced to undertake a laborious series of trial-and-error tests of every possible toxin. During this period, the Mayor of Minamata formally notified the Ministry of Health and Welfare that agrochemicals used in farming might be implicated. This action was without scientific foundation and is representative of many attempts to redirect attention away from Chisso's effluents.

Late in 1959, the medical research group concluded that a particular type of organic mercury was the toxin that gave rise to Minamata disease. Fishermen and local residents readily embraced this conclusion and generated sufficient pressure to compel Chisso to stop dumping wastes into the sea. But the corporation contested the validity of the research and insisted that the mechanisms that caused the formation of methyl mercury be elucidated. Their spokespeople offered various counter-arguments. Though these were often voiced by university professors who served as paid consultants to the company, the arguments were based on fraudulent information and lacked a sound scientific footing. None the less, they delayed official identification of methyl mercury as the offending substance, thereby frustrating causal linkage of Chisso and the disease. Paradoxically, Chisso's own research had come to the conclusion that mercury pollutants were responsible for Minamata disease, but the results of this work were withheld from the public. All these manoeuvres slowed effective responses to the disease.

Public attention was also diverted by the settlement of actions against Chisso brought by the fishing industry and disease victims. At this time (December 1959) there was a general sense that the disease was abating and no longer much of a social problem, so attention again shifted to other matters.

In 1963, the medical research group at Kumamoto University finally released an official report announcing that the causative substance of Minamata disease was methyl mercury found in industrial wastes discharged by the Chisso plant. Both the company and the government appeared unconcerned. Their stance was that Minamata disease had been resolved as a social problem.

Coincidentally, a new outbreak of organic mercury poisoning occurred soon thereafter in the Agano river basin of Niigata Prefecture (1965). Again the pollutants were dumped by industry and again the offending corporation – the Showa Denko K.K. – refused to admit that it was the perpetrator. But this time public concern for environmental pollution had grown and the national government was compelled to investigate the disease fully. These events led to publication of an official statement about the cause of the original Minamata disease. This was described as "methyl mercury compounds produced in the acetaldehyde acetic facilities of Chisso at Minamata."

Little by little, the cause of Minamata disease had come to be recognized officially, but the entire process took 12 years after human symptoms initially appeared. During this period, government agencies and leaders delayed official recognition and afflicted persons went uncompensated. Governmental controls and regulations on industrial wastes were sidestepped without any serious effort to come to grips with the problem.

Efforts to halt the dumping of contaminated wastes

In early 1957, the Minamata Fishermen's Cooperative called on Chisso to cease dumping mercury-contaminated wastes into the bay. The request contained two parts: (a) that "the release of polluted water into the sea be stopped" and (b) that "adequate waste water treatment facilities be installed and that evidence identifying the harmless nature of waste water after treatment be submitted." Had these proposals been accepted, the source of pollution would have been eliminated and further spread of the disease retarded. But Chisso flatly rejected the Cooperative's request and failed to accelerate the installation of improved waste water treatment facilities. By now, local residents were choosing to avoid seafood from the bay and the number of new cases of poisoning was declining. The corporation was thus able to argue that matters were under control and the fishermen's pleas could safely be ignored.

A new round of anxiety about the disease began in 1958 when additional cases were verified in villages at the southern end of Minamata. Chisso responded by re-routing the discharge of effluents from the bay to the lower reaches of the Minamata River. Soon thereafter, more new cases of the disease developed in the estuary. At this point, most observers would have concluded that the disease agents were closely connected with the effluents, but Chisso did not. From start to finish they offered stopgap measures and failed to take any definitive steps against pollution by the industrial wastes.

The following year (1959), new cases of disease sprang up in coastal regions all along the Shiranui Sea. Fishermen staged a large-scale protest against Chisso and demanded that the corporation "discontinue the release of effluents until facilities for treatment and purification are completed." Sentiment in the prefectural Assembly began shifting to the side of the fishermen and the Governor called for a special Assembly session to resolve the matter. However, the Japanese Ministry of International Trade and Industry (MITI) stepped in to declare that "the problem of industrial waste had been resolved." Chisso was to be allowed to continue operations if it ceased dumping wastes into the Minamata River and quickly completed water treatment facilities.

To the untutored eye, Chisso might have appeared to have taken some kind of countermeasures against pollution. By the end of 1959 they had completed two waste treatment facilities, neither of which was effective in removing organic mercury compounds dissolved in water. Aware of these shortcomings, the corporation never channelled any waste water from the acetaldehyde process into them. Yet, at the formal opening ceremonies, the President of Chisso made the gesture of drinking a cup of water that had supposedly undergone treatment! It had not, but the prefectural Governor and the other guests believed the ruse. In fact, the fishermen, the residents of Minamata, and onlookers everywhere were brainwashed by an effective but misleading public relations campaign.

Chisso thereafter dumped waste water from the acetaldehyde process into a collection pool and recirculated it for reuse, without taking all the steps necessary to stop the flow of methyl mercury. This did not occur until 1968, when the acetaldehyde process was changed. Gradually, methyl mercury was eliminated as a by-product. But a vast amount of mercury-tainted sediment had already been discharged into the sea, where it continued to contaminate fish and shellfish.[4]

Problems associated with relief and reparations

Relief

After the prompt admission of patients to hospitals at the initial stages of the Minamata disaster, there were few new developments in the arena of relief. Medical costs were privately borne at first, until patients began to be admitted to the Minamata Municipal Hospital in 1958. State relief for bedridden victims did not arrive for a period of five years. A special wing of the Municipal Hospital was opened in July 1959 to provide treatment for Minamata disease victims, but there were insufficient beds and at least 19 verified cases were cared for at home. Infants with the congenital form of Minamata disease endured lengthy delays before they were verified as official cases, because the medical diagnosis of these cases was slow. Many affected infants received no assistance.

Changes in methods of investigating Minamata disease and standards for treatment also had repercussions for victims. In the beginning, widespread epidemiological testing was carried out to identify causes of the disease. But once it was understood that heavy metal contamination of food supplies was involved, broad screening procedures halted and individual cases were turned over to local physicians. By this means, acute cases who manifested chronic symptoms became the standard for diagnosis and many persons with less advanced forms of the disease were left unattended.

Over the years since 1956, the government has gradually implemented more comprehensive measures for addressing Minamata disease. For example, medical treatment costs and a monthly allowance for nursing are provided to patients who manifest disease symptoms but have yet to be verified officially as victims. There is also a new medical examination and management programme that is aimed at improving health and sanitation among populations at risk. It remains to be seen whether the programme will be effective in addressing the needs of Minamata disease victims. Already, it is clear that there is bureaucratic pressure to reduce the number of persons who apply for certification as victims, so the programme may serve to deter people who should be receiving treatment.

Reparations

Efforts by victims to secure reparations from Chisso and the government continued throughout the four decades after 1956 but little was achieved. The *mimaikin* contract has already been noted as an example of the corporation's efforts to appear magnanimous without either admitting responsibility or incurring substantial costs.[5] Because of being ostracized by the community, victims found themselves in a weak position to contest such attempted resolutions of their plight. Had it not been for the timely occurrence of the "second Minamata disease" in Niigata, the policy of "stonewalling" might have worked for Chisso. But it was not until 1973 that a workable system of reparations by the company was agreed to – 17 years after the disease was officially recognized.

Reparations are tied directly to the disease certification process, because only persons who have been officially certified can qualify for assistance. This leaves many sufferers outside the aid system. They include victims who are refused certification, those still being processed, and those who have yet to apply. Standards for certification are very strict and are closely tied to the appearance of Hunter and Russell's syndrome.[6] By 1970, no more than 121 persons had been certified as victims. Since then, victims who were refused certification have made appeals against the screening methods. However, despite an apparent brief easing of standards, the new examination system – which was established in 1977 – has resulted in a near-total refusal of certification to applicants.

Frustrated first by Chisso and then by official procedures for determining who may be counted as a victim, aggrieved citizens redoubled their efforts to claim reparations from both the company and the government. The number of plaintiffs in all regional courts eventually exceeded 2,000 persons. Soon, the courts desired to pass their own judgement on Minamata disease, and a new category of victims came into being – those that were certified by court order rather than medical evidence.

Part of the reason that Chisso and the government dragged their feet in paying reparations was that the financial burdens of the disease were mounting up to impressive proportions. The combined total of reparations to victims and the sludge-removal project in Minamata Bay ate into corporate funds and made it difficult for Chisso to continue operating. The prospect of industrial closings and the advent of widespread public support for pollution prevention in Japan spurred the government to come to the company's aid. Bonds were issued by the Kumamoto prefectural government, and the capital thereby raised was lent to Chisso to subsidize reparations. It was further agreed that Chisso would have to repay the prefecture ¥150 billion by the end of 1992, with further sums to follow as additional reparations were settled.

Measures to aid the fisheries

The fishermen's place of work was directly contaminated by mercury, but at first – apart from increasing the number of artificial reefs and expanding areas open to fishing – nothing was done to help them. These measures proved ineffective and the local fishing industry faced imminent ruin. Kumamoto Prefecture then decided to encourage fishermen to convert their operations from taking local inshore finfish to deep-sea fishing for squid and cuttlefish. But the labour force was unfamiliar with the larger vessels, as well as the equipment necessary, and most fishermen did not want to spend a long time on the open sea. As a result, this effort foundered. Several other ideas for rescuing the fishing industry were tried without success, but the level of activity was sufficient to convince the national government and the Japanese parliament (Diet) that the issue was being attended to. Most of the draft ideas were, in fact, abandoned without being implemented.

The subsequent history of the fishermen's attempts to gain reparations is similar to that of the Minamata disease victims. Initially, Chisso refused to respond to their appeals (1958). After mercury pollution was identified as the disease's cause, a new round of appeals for aid was submitted by the fishermen (July 1959). In the end, the mayor's office negotiated a token payment from Chisso that was not to be considered reparation for problems related to Minamata disease. As more and more cases of disease appeared, relations between the fishermen and the corporation deteriorated to the point where the fishermen stormed Chisso's Minamata plant, thereby propelling the dispute into a major political problem. But once again the outcome was payment of limited reparations by the company, this time brokered by the Governor of Kumamoto Prefecture.

How the local community suppressed the victims

The vitality of the local community in Minamata was slowly sapped by repeated failures to arrive at a solution to the problems of Minamata disease. However, it was also the local citizens who helped to drag out the process of settlement. Chisso held the reins of political power in Minamata but, in disputes with people affected by Minamata disease, they could count on local residents to come to their aid. Workers from Chisso and affiliated companies turned their backs on the victims because they believed that their own livelihoods were threatened by any assault on the corporation. With a majority of the citizens behind them, Chisso commanded public officials and other local influentials. As a long-established local institution, the company took advantage of their ties – geographical, economic, and familial – to the area and were able to suppress victims' appeals. Though their claims for reparations were relatively modest, protesters were effectively penned into an isolated group. For example, when fishermen protested to Chisso in 1959, the Mayor and Chairman of Minamata City Council headed a delegation of 28 groups that lobbied the Governor against stopping industrial discharges from Chisso because that action "signed certain death for the local community." They followed this up with a request for the prefecture to provide "ample defense against acts of violence" and implored the Ministry of Health and Welfare to ignore arguments that might implicate Chisso as a cause of the disaster.

Although victims' protests grew throughout the 1960s into a fully fledged social movement – complete with support from external interest groups – Chisso's appeal to the existence of a "shared destiny" between the citizens and the company was a formidable obstacle. Even as late as 1968, when official recognition of the causes of Minamata disease had been secured, Chisso was able to bring together more than 2,500 persons representing 53 local groups in support of a concerted effort to rebuild the Chisso Minamata plant. At this time, the President of Chisso attempted to dampen the exultation of victims about the progress they were making in seeking commitments from the corporation by making a statement that "plant reconstruction depended on whether cooperation could be won from labor unions and the local community."

Again, in 1971, when local groups were battling in direct negotiations for reparation, the Mayor of Minamata pronounced that he "would defend Chisso even in the eyes of national consensus." (He later explained that he was forced to make this statement "for the sake of creating and maintaining jobs for the people.") Yet again, in 1975, Minamata City Council officially requested both the state and the prefecture to mitigate Chisso's burden of work for the removal of contaminated sludge from Minamata Bay. And once more, in 1977, an organization created and funded by the City Council campaigned to collect signatures in support of reconstruction of the Chisso plant.

In short, the carefully cultivated myth of "shared destiny" between city and company had taken deep root in the community. Opponents of "mutuality" were discriminated against and suppressed. The victims – not the disease – were now seen as the threat. They also became scapegoats for the community's problems. In this curious and troubling inversion of reality, Minamata disease itself became a taboo subject.

If something truly effective is to be done about the lingering impact of Minamata disease, a start must be made on fashioning a new concept of the community. The conception of "shared destiny" that served the interests of Chisso and many of its workers in earlier decades must be dismantled. It will be necessary to free the residents of Minamata from dependence on a single corporation and to diversify the economic foundations of the community. So far, existing approaches have not produced a solution to the ills that still blight the lives and landscape in Minamata. This alternative remains to be tried.

Conclusions

The victims of Minamata disease offer the following lessons to the world:
1. Industrial pollution causes disease, destroys ecosystems, and produces other types of irreparable damage. This means that complete recovery from industrial pollution is impossible. Accordingly, waste material that is produced as a result of industrial operations must not be dumped into any environmental sink until it is harmless.
2. The world's chemical industry is currently dumping newly created substances whose effects are not fully understood. Because it takes considerable time before the presence and effects of toxic substances can be identified, it is necessary to prevent the spread of pollution at the source.
3. Industrial degradation of the environment produces effects that can spread rapidly. It is, therefore, necessary to monitor the effect of pollutants and measure the damage, otherwise relief of victims and restoration of the environment will be delayed.
4. When a local community has no control over business operations that affect its environment, the possibility exists that the environment will be destroyed.
5. Any business that destroys the environment must bear the responsibility of making reparations to the victims and making good the environmental destruction.

55

Editor's postscript

Students of natural disasters have observed that communities typically move through characteristic stages of recovery after a major catastrophe. The last of these is a period marked by symbolic construction projects and other initiatives that memorialize the event and attest to the onset of a "new beginning." On a recent trip to Minamata (November 1992), participants in the Second Minamata International Conference (itself intended to be a therapeutic response to the community's problems) were taken on a tour of several such facilities. These included a waterfront park on reclaimed land that covered the site of Chisso's sludge-dumping operations; an ornamental bamboo garden and display centre that is intended both to demonstrate the aesthetic possibilities of landfills and to showcase a valuable but neglected bamboo handicrafts industry; and the newly opened Minamata Disease Data Hall, which contains officially selected photographs and other displays of information about the disease and its consequences.

To some extent, the existence of these projects reflects growing community willingness to reject Minamata's pariah status among Japanese cities and to fashion a new collective self-image and a new economic base in the manner suggested by Maruyama. However, it will probably be a long time before Minamata completes the intended transition from troubled industrial city to showplace centre of disaster tourism, traditional handicrafts, and ecodevelopment. The psychological and political gap that separates victims and non-victims is wide. Many victims are deeply suspicious of the motives of government and industry leaders who are promoting the community's new image. The existence of a privately supported "Disease Victims Museum," which contests official versions of local history, is only one indicator of the differences. Other signs of disunity emerged in a flurry of critical comments about the recovery process that were delivered by local citizens in the international conference audience. Such public displays of discord are unusual at conferences in Japan. Though invited by the conference organizers, representatives of the Chisso Corporation were notably absent.

It is probably too early to tell whether these recent developments signal the beginning of the end of Minamata's long struggle with the consequences of its namesake disease. What seems amply clear is that the recovery process has entered a new stage. At the very least, denial and foot-dragging have been replaced by recognition and willingness to make a start on the process of community regeneration. The need to face up to the realities of industrial hazard as soon as possible and to begin a broad search for appropriate solutions is one of the indispensable lessons of Minamata.

Chronology

1908

Chisso builds plant in Minamata.

1926

Chisso pays first retributions for damage incurred by local fisheries because of industrial pollution.

1932

Operations initiated at Chisso's acetaldehyde-processing plant where mercury is used as a catalyst.

1956

Minamata disease publicly recognized. Cause of disease identified as heavy metal poisoning via the ingestion of fish and shellfish. Chisso's industrial effluents suspected as source of contamination.

1957

Minamata Fishermen's Cooperative calls for end to dumping of industrial wastes in local waters and treatment of wastes before discharge.

1958

Chisso re-routes waste water produced in the acetaldehyde plant from Minamata Bay to a point near the Minamata River estuary. Pollution spreads across a large part of the Shiranui Sea.

1959

Organic mercury is identified as the substance that causes the disease. Fisherman adopt violent tactics in effort to stop dumping of industrial waste and to support demands for reparations. Symptoms of Minamata disease develop in a laboratory cat that was directly administered effluent from Chisso's plant in tests conducted at Chisso's research laboratory, but no official announcement is made. *Mimaikin* contract (simple expression of sympathy with little financial reimbursement) is concluded between Chisso and families of victims. (Contract later annulled in the First Lawsuit against Chisso, 1969–1973.)

1965

Cases of organic mercury poisoning in humans living in Niigata Prefecture are officially recognized in the so-called second Minamata disease.

1968

Operations at Chisso's acetaldehyde-processing plant cease. The government releases an official judgement that "Chisso (is) the cause."

1969

Victims and families bring civil action against Chisso seeking compensation. This becomes known as the First Lawsuit against Chisso.

1973

First Lawsuit against Chisso is decided in favour of the plaintiffs. An agreement on reparations is concluded between the victims and Chisso, constituting what was to become the retribution system that has continued to operate ever since.

1977

Removal of sludge from Minamata Bay begins. Project completed in 1990.

1980

Victims and families bring civil action against Chisso, the national government, and the Kumamoto prefectural government. This becomes known as the Third Lawsuit.

1987

The Third Lawsuit is decided in favour of the plaintiffs. It cites the national government and Kumamoto prefectural government as negligent about their responsibilities for protecting the public. The defendants (Chisso, Kumamoto prefectural government, national government) appeal against the decision.

1987

The former President of Chisso and the Plant Manager are found guilty of professional negligence leading to involuntary manslaughter.

1992

The Environmental Agency of Japan initiates a comprehensive programme for the relief of Minamata disease.

Notes

1. In 1965 a similar, but less well known, example of methyl mercury poisoning was recognized near a Showa Denko K.K. industrial plant in the Agano River basin of Niigata Prefecture.
2. Although the facts reported here are not contested by most analysts, other writers have

emphasized different aspects of the Minamata disease disaster. Apart from general overviews, the English-language literature on Minamata is relatively sparse; see Ui (1992) and
Ellis (1989).

3. Rulings are made on individual cases by a medical board of inquiry that examines the results
   of examinations conducted by prefectural authorities.

4. The sludge accumulated in Minamata Bay contained a high concentration of mercury. In
   1987, sludge was dredged and used to fill in the distal part of the bay with the intention of
   covering over 209 m^2 of sea bottom that contains mercury in concentrations of 25 ppm or
   more. Residents were alarmed that further contamination might be triggered by this action.
   They opposed the plan but it went ahead anyway and was completed in 1990, 14 years after
   initiation, at a cost of ¥48.5 billion. Nevertheless, fish and shellfish in the bay continue to
   exceed the provisional pollution control level stipulated by the national government (i.e.
   total mercury <0.44 ppm; methyl mercury <0.3 ppm). There is no sign that the ban on fishing in the bay will soon be raised.

5. The *mimaikin* contract was later annulled in legal proceedings that found Chisso guilty of
   violating public order and morale by "deliberately neglecting their responsibility to respond
   to the victims' proper and just claims for reparations, for further taking advantage of the
   ignorance and oppressed financial state of the victims' families and for tendering retribution
   in an extremely low sum." (Verdict from the First Lawsuit against Chisso, 1973.)

6. The syndrome is named after two investigators of methyl mercury poisoning at an agro-
   chemical factory in England. Their work provided important clues about the cause of Minamata disease.

References

Chisso. 1955. *Minamata Plant Newsletter*, September.

Ellis, Derek. 1989. *Environments at Risk: Case Histories of Impact Assessment*.
Berlin: Springer-Verlag, pp. 38–69.

Funaba, Masatomi. 1973. "Chisso and the community and municipality." *Research
into Industrial Pollution* 2(4).

Nakamura, Masafumi. 1975. "Structure and features of Chisso's local dominance in
Minamata." In: Kenji Kono, ed. *Transfiguration of the Local Community and
Resident Sentiment*.

Ui, Jun. 1992. "Minamata disease." In: Jun Ui, ed. *Industrial Pollution in Japan*.
Tokyo: United Nations University Press, pp. 103–132.

3

Environmental contamination, community transformation, and the Centralia mine fire

Stephen R. Couch

Introduction

An underground coalmine fire has been burning since 1962 in the small Pennsylvania community of Centralia. Between 1981 and 1992, severe social conflict about the fire disrupted the town and most of its one thousand inhabitants left, taking advantage of a voluntary relocation programme supported by the US Government. Today, only a relative handful (58) remain and soon they, too, are likely to depart as the result of a state government order. The final disposition of their homes will probably be decided by litigation.

At first glance, Centralia does not appear to fit the image of a typical toxic contamination disaster such as the one that affected Minamata, Japan. No one has died; claims of direct health damage have not been proven; there is no corporation to hold responsible. But, like Minamata and Love Canal, Times Beach, Three Mile Island, Bhopal, and other places, Centralia has partaken of what Kai Erikson calls a "new species of trouble" (Erikson 1991). Intense intracommunity conflict has taken place, conflict which ripped apart the bonds of communality and civility and tore at the very basis of the social fabric that binds people together. Unlike the "therapeutic community," which often aids recovery from natural disasters (Raphael 1986: 297–298), the "conflictual community" that developed in Centralia hinders the re-

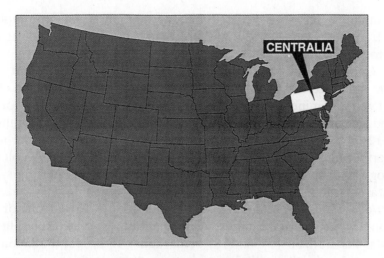

Fig. 3.1 **Location of Centralia**

solution of environmental contamination problems and stalls recovery. Moreover, the experience of this kind of destructive conflict changes for ever the ways in which people view their communities and their world.

Centralia: A dependent town

Centralia is located in the north-eastern United States, among the northern ranges of the Appalachian Mountains (fig. 3.1). A coalmining town from the beginning, it was settled in the late 1850s and 1860s by immigrants from Ireland, and later by people from Eastern and Southern Europe. By the latter part of the nineteenth century it had become a company town, with the Lehigh Valley Coal Company as its dominant institution. Agents of this New York-based firm made most decisions of importance.

Economically and socially, Centralia went through "boom" and "bust" periods during the late nineteenth and early twentieth centuries. The borough's population rose and fell in step with the demand for coal. In 1870, 1,342 residents lived there; two decades later, the population had risen to 2,761, only to fall to 2,048 by 1900 (Geschwindt 1984). The instability and upheaval brought about by these population shifts hampered the development of strong community institutions. As in other towns of Pennsylvania's anthracite region,

"Community ties were weak.... The population ... was too mobile, too transient, too quickly gathered and easily scattered again" (Bertoff 1965: 263).

In Centralia, the coal companies made their political and economic influence felt at all levels. Since locally elected officials often sided with the miners against the corporations, the companies worked to reduce local government power (Aurand 1971: 23–24). Communities resembled medieval fiefs (Auand 1971: 21), with even the most powerful police forces being company run (Couch 1984). A colonial analogy is even more apt: the anthracite region was peripheral to core areas along the eastern seaboard (cf. Nyden 1979; Gonzales-Casanova 1965; Hechter 1975). Coal and profits flowed out of the region to build distant cities, civic institutions, and urban upper classes. As Baltzell (1958: 118) remarked: "If Proper Philadelphia can be said to be the capital of an empire, then its chief colony is the anthracite ... region of northeastern Pennsylvania." Conversely, an upper class was missing throughout the anthracite region, and agents of the coal companies were the most influential members of the weak local middle class. Therefore, coalmining communities like Centralia lacked a tradition of collective decision-making in their own interests, a fact that continues to inhibit their responses to crises.

Residents were not entirely pawns of the coal companies. They took collective action in the form of strikes and trade union activity but the companies successfully resisted union organizing throughout the nineteenth century. A boatman's strike occurred on the Schuylkill Canal as early as 1835 (Schalek and Henning 1907: 158). Anthracite miners struck for the first time in 1842, dispersing only when the militia was called in (*History of Schuylkill County* 1881). The first organized miners' union appeared in Schuylkill County in 1848 (Eavenson 1942). Violent mine and railroad strikes occurred in 1869, 1871, 1877, 1897, 1900, and 1902 (Aurand 1971: 72, 80–81, 91–92, 106, 110–114, 129–130, 138–142). Centralia workers participated in many of these strikes, as well as some local strikes of their own.

While helping to solidify a class culture of distrust toward the coal companies, the strikes and union activities failed to create a strong internal political structure in Centralia (Homrighaus, Couch, and Kroll-Smith 1985). When the coal companies finally recognized the United Mine Workers' Union as a legitimate bargaining agent (1902), relative labour peace settled over the area. The Union might have become a seed-bed of stronger, more durable, community institutions had it not been for the decline of "King Coal." Beginning in the

1920s, and especially in the 1950s when alternative fuels became popular, anthracite coal production declined precipitously. By 1960, very little active mining was taking place in the area, and Centralia's population had declined to around 1,435 (Geschwindt 1984). At that time, the borough was home to a largely working-class population that included a high percentage of elderly persons. Though small, the population was at least stable. Many people had lived in Centralia all their lives and displayed a strong, sentimental (even nostalgic) attachment to the town. Most residents thought of it as a pleasant, tranquil place.

But Centralia was economically and politically weak; it lacked a firm economic base because new businesses were not keen to locate in a declining one-industry economy. Gradually it became a back-water, out of step with the economic needs of the time, peripheral to the larger society beyond the mountains. Some of its population developed the kind of fatalism Henry Caudill found in other areas of Appalachia (Caudill 1963) – a fatalism born of a long history of being first exploited and then ignored by outsiders. Many developed a sus-picious attitude toward the activities of large corporations and often viewed the institutions of government in a similar light.

The Centralia mine fire

The story of the Centralia mine fire began in 1962, when fire was discovered just outside the borough in an abandoned strip mine used as an illegal garbage dump (fig. 3.2). After initial fire-fighting efforts failed, the blaze ignited an outcropping of coal and spread under the town by way of abandoned mine shafts and tunnels. Slowly but inex-orably, about one-third of Centralia was directly affected by fires, an area locally known as the "impact zone."

Despite the prominence of coal companies in the town's past, the fire was not due to corporate malfeasance, because there was no active mining where the fire started. Moreover, while coal companies generally kept ownership of subsurface mineral rights throughout the anthracite region, Centralia was an exception – the borough had acquired these rights early in the twentieth century. Therefore, the responsibility for extinguishing or containing the fire fell to various branches of government.

Between 1962 and 1980, a number of engineering projects were undertaken in an attempt to deal with the fire, but all attempts failed. Thereafter, some people began to express concern about the fire's

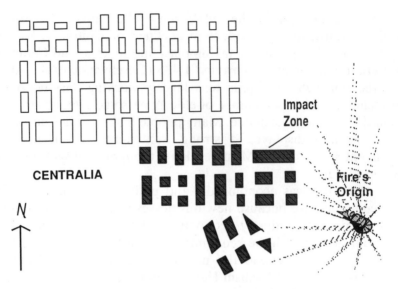

Fig. 3.2 **Origin of the Centralia mine fire**

potential health and safety effects. In 1969, three families were evacuated from their homes owing to the presence of poisonous gases. In 1976, supralethal concentrations of carbon monoxide were found pouring from a borehole within 27 feet of another Centralia home. Three years later, a service station was ordered to close because of rising gasoline temperatures in its underground storage tanks. Then, in 1970, the federal government purchased seven properties considered to be unsafe; others followed. More and more residents complained of physical illnesses that they attributed to the fire. Some, however, regarded such complaints as overreaction.

Indeed, the community was divided over the seriousness of the fire. Some residents, mostly in the "impact zone," viewed it as a dangerous and imminent threat that necessitated strong and swift action to protect residents. These people were also more likely to have children living at home and less likely to have lived in Centralia all their lives. Others, while feeling threatened, saw the fire as a distant hazard. Still others believed there was "no problem," that people were becoming concerned without good reason. According to such a view, coal-related hazards and disasters add an important element to local culture (Wallace 1981). The "disaster subculture" of the region integrated the mine fire into a normative response: people might not like it, but they would have to bear it! Moreover, many of those who had lived in Centralia for all or most of their lives felt a very strong attachment to their homes and land, making them reluctant even to consider the possibility of relocation due to hazard.

These different interpretations nourished a conflict that was just barely contained within the normal political system. The way was prepared for emergence of insurgent grass-roots groups on different sides of the issue. All that was needed was a dramatic event to illustrate that existing political institutions were unable to prevent a real calamity. That event took place on 12 February 1981, when a 12-year-old boy noticed a hole opening in the ground. As he approached it, the void widened and he fell in. Fortunately, the boy was able to hold onto a tree root until pulled to safety by a cousin. Confidence in the local political system had been dealt a grievous blow; it eroded away completely a few weeks later when an elderly man narrowly avoided death after being overcome by carbon monoxide in his home.

These two near-death incidents spurred a portion of the community to organize Concerned Citizens Against the Centralia Mine Fire. The Concerned Citizens were convinced that the fire posed a real and imminent danger to people who lived in the impact zone. By means of letter-writing campaigns, trips to the state and national capitols, and various marches and demonstrations, the Concerned Citizens urged government leaders to do whatever was necessary to protect residents from the fire, even if that meant relocation.

Concerned Citizens immediately sought and received the assistance of national environmental interest groups, including Rural American Women. From such organizations they learned the techniques of direct political action. Centralia was featured in reports by national news media and government officials began to take greater notice of its plight. But the confrontational tactics of Concerned Citizens did not meet with the approval of many fellow citizens in Centralia. The latter believed that publicity was a ploy to force the government to buy homes and relocate their occupants. To these people, the spectre of relocation was more frightening than the fire, because it portended destruction of the community they loved more surely than an uncertain fire.

The outcome of these differences was a two-year period of intense intracommunity conflict. Town meetings ended in shouting or fist fights. Telephone threats were made, car tyres slashed, and at least one fire-bombing occurred. Many neighbours – and even some family members – no longer spoke to one another. The atmosphere of the period was graphically recounted by one resident:

Centralia is like someone you know who is dying of cancer; I mean, every time you turn around there is another part of the town that's infected. If we would get together we could fight this cancer. But people around here are more concerned with themselves than with their neighbors. Rumors, hostileness, prejudice, backbiting ... this town's more sick than the fire. (Kroll-Smith and Couch 1990: 5)

The breakdown of communality in Centralia illustrates an important point. *Direct action may be helpful in moving a larger political system to act on the grievances of a particular community. At the same time, it may be extremely divisive within the community, sapping some of the strength that would be available for a response to the problem that threatens.* Time and again, representatives of the state and federal governments asked Centralians to come to some kind of agreement about what they wanted the government to do. That consensus never developed: government agencies and leaders were left to deal with several factions, each with its own proposed solutions to the problem.

Finally, in July 1983, a government-financed engineering study concluded that the fire was much worse than anyone had thought. Then burning under about 200 acres of land, it had the potential to spread under 3,700 acres, including all of the borough of Centralia. Swiftly, the US Congress passed a bill that authorized US$42 million to pay for the voluntary relocation of residents and businesses. This action opened a wider split in the community. On one side, a grass-roots Homeowners' Association formed to help residents get a fair settlement price from the government. But an opposing group, the Citizens to Save Our Borough, also formed, with the objective of keeping Centralia a viable corporate community.

Voluntary relocation began in early 1984 amid an atmosphere of tense coexistence between the contending groups. It also took place out of the spotlight of the mass media because neither group actively sought to attract their attention. Most Centralians who chose relocation were pleased with their financial settlements. As agreements were reached with government agencies, families moved, mainly to other communities within the region, near where friends and relatives lived. One by one the vacated homes were boarded up and then demolished. Grass and trees were planted on the empty building lots but they became expensive to maintain and were eventually replaced by wild flowers. Each year during the late spring and summer, Centralia displayed a tranquil and colourful mantle that belied the fire below. Meanwhile, nothing further was done about the mine fire itself.

By 1991, all who wanted to relocate had gone, leaving 58 people who wished to remain. Many of those had been active in Citizens to Save the Borough and had now become leaders of Centralia's normal political structure. In their new role they sought to maintain Centralia's viability despite the handicaps of a tiny population, virtually no local tax revenue, and diminished social services. At least now they could act with the full backing of their community, for those who remained in Centralia shared both a common experience and a common outlook on the future. They would stay and accept the consequences!

In early 1992, however, their efforts received a severe setback when state agencies ordered the remaining citizens to depart. Residents were given one final opportunity to participate in the long-standing relocation plan, with the alternative of having their property seized by the government under its power of eminent domain. At the time of writing, Centralia's remaining citizens are engaged in a legal battle to prevent the state-mandated extinction of their depleted town.

The Centralia case presents an instructive example of social devastation wrought by a chronic technological disaster (Couch and Kroll-Smith 1985). In this case, different interpretations of the environmental threat led to severe intracommunity conflict and fragmentation. As a consequence, the social community died long before most of the physical community of Centralia was relocated. As Mitchell (ch. 1) suggests, the experience of many modern industrial disasters is one of "surprise." Here the victims were not surprised by the mine fire; they were astonished by the unsympathetic, hostile, and divisive reactions of their neighbours. This was the unprecedented aspect of their disaster. About the only thing most Centralians agree upon is that they have received a "dirty deal" from the government that was supposed to protect them; this heightened their alienation and diminished their ability to cope with the problems facing them (Couch and Kroll-Smith 1991).

A stage model of industrial contamination

What is it about the experience of industrial contamination that results in such destructive social and psychological consequences? In addition to some of the case-specific factors mentioned above, recent research highlights a number of more general factors, including the psychological and emotional experience of contamination itself (Couch and Kroll-Smith 1985; Erikson 1991; Kroll-Smith and Couch 1991), the assignment of blame (Baum 1987: 38–41; Baum, Fleming, and Davidson 1983; Couch and Kroll-Smith 1985; Davidson and Baum 1991; Gill 1986; Levine 1982), problems of technical controllability (Berren, Biegel, and Ghertner 1980; Couch and Kroll-Smith 1992), ambiguity of cause and effect (Brown 1991; Kasperson and Pijawka 1985; Kroll-Smith and Couch 1990; Vyner 1988), and social stigma (Edelstein 1988, 1991; Reich 1983).

Another factor that deserves close attention is time (Baum, Fleming, and Singer 1983; Couch and Kroll-Smith 1985; Gill 1986; Shrivastava 1987). Industrial contamination extends over a long period, and therefore the stages of industrial contamination disasters differ in some very important ways from those that accompany natural disasters. Using the Centralia mine fire as an illustrative case, I propose a stage model for industrial contamination, a model that helps to explain the social breakdown that generally occurs in these situations and that has important implications for long-term recovery.

Let us begin by considering the stage model for natural disasters, as it has been presented in the disaster literature (Chapman 1962) (see fig. 3.3). This model begins with the "warning" stage, the apprehension that calamity may be approaching. By the time a "threat" stage emerges, there are unequivocal signs of impending trouble. During "impact," the threat becomes a reality, generating a maelstrom of flying debris, or raging floods, or towering walls of fire, ripping apart the last vestiges of "business as usual" in the full force of nature's wrath. During the "inventory" and "rescue" stages, survivors begin to assess their losses and gradually piece together a picture of what has happened. Survivor groups emerge spontaneously to help treat the wounded, extinguish fires, or free trapped victims. With the onset of a "remedy" stage, outside agencies take control and impose a formal structure on the inventory and rescue activities. During the "recovery," there is a reconstitution of the old community structure, sometimes with a modified pattern of personal and collective life.

Note that, in this stage model, the interval between warning and rescue may be very brief – in some cases, only several minutes. Also note that the customary sequence of stages in a natural disaster moves from order, to chaos, to the reconstitution of order. In addition, the signs of danger and destruction are relatively clear – there is a high

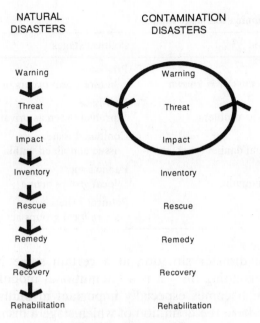

NATURAL
DISASTERS

CONTAMINATION
DISASTERS

Warning

Threat

Impact

Inventory

Rescue

Remedy

Recovery

Rehabilitation

Fig. 3.3 **Stage model**

level of agreement over what is taking place or has taken place. In this conceptualization, there is little trouble in placing a disaster situation at an appropriate disaster stage.

Industrial contamination disasters differ significantly from this model. Cases such as Centralia and Minamata involve a protracted, seemingly endless, period between warnings of possible danger and the belief that the worst is past. Indeed, people become trapped in the warning, threat, and impact stages, frozen in extended periods of apprehension and dread. Moreover, since the experience of contamination rarely involves an entire neighbourhood or community in the same way, it is not likely to become the occasion for communal action, or even for agreement about what stage the disaster is at. Multiple interpretations abound; here is the fertile soil for intense community conflict. And that conflict results in alienation, coping difficulties, and psychological distress for individuals, and social breakdown for communities (cf. Kroll-Smith and Couch 1990). In these circumstances, recovery – if it occurs at all – is likely to be very slow and incomplete.

Let us look in more detail at the stage model for contamination cases. And let us extend the model a little (see table 3.1). First, note

Table 3.1 **Contamination stage model**

Definitional stages	Political stages

Pre-event:
  before event occurs or is known
	Pre-issue:
	  before event occurs or is known

"No problem":
  event not seen as problem
	Non-issue:
	  problem seen as private trouble

Warning:
  signs of potential danger
	Contained issue:
	  issue contained within normal channels

Threat:
  danger seen as imminent
	Public issue:
	  local groups active

Impact:
  effects seen
	Political issue:
	  extra-local groups active

that placing a disaster situation at a certain stage is a matter of defining what is going on – it is a "definitional model." The definitional function becomes especially important in industrial contamination cases, where the definition of which stage a disaster is at often becomes a major bone of contention.

The "warning," "threat," and "impact" stages of industrial contamination disasters are similar to those of natural disasters. I have added a "no problem" stage in order to reflect the views of people who contend that contamination either does not exist or, if it does exist, poses no problem. I have also added a "pre-event" stage, representing a community's history before the contamination occurs or is discovered. This is an important addition because the precontamination structure and culture of a community affect its subsequent response (Kroll-Smith and Couch 1990: 13–28).

Because responses to industrial contamination are inherently political, I suggest that political stages overlie the (definitional) disaster stages. These political stages interact with the definitional stages in a complex web of changing social and political relationships. Such interactions shape the nature of conflict, the situation's outcome, and the possibility and nature of recovery.

In a recent book, Michael Reich fruitfully applies and extends a tripartite political stage model to the analysis of three toxic contamination cases. Reich deals in detail with how each stage differs in its implications for the political dynamics of the toxic disaster (Reich 1991). I have adapted Reich's three stages for use in my model. Here, the "non-issue" stage occurs when the problem is seen as a private trouble, not a public issue; the "public issue" stage begins when local activist groups become active; and the "political issue" stage occurs when interest groups from outside the community become involved in the struggle.

I have also added two newly identified stages. The "pre-issue" stage, like the "pre-event" stage, refers to the time before contamination occurs or is known. During this period, existing political structures and power relations set the stage for what will happen after contamination is discovered. The "contained issue" stage recognizes that an issue may be contained within normal political structures or institutions. Here, the issue has entered the political arena but has not led to the formation of emergent groups or the arrival of outside interest groups. Rather, the issue is being dealt with through "normal channels." Conflict may occur, and may be very intense, but the legitimacy of the public decision-making system is not questioned. Individuals and groups remain working within the system, rather than going outside or beyond it.

The nature of existing groups and political structures determines which political stage a given contamination situation will occupy, but there is no way of predicting when and how change to another stage will take place; that is governed by the dynamics of an individual controversy. Adding to the complexity, indeed the messiness, of contamination situations is that there is no obvious, dramatic "high point" of destruction, after which recovery begins. Rather, the community addresses itself to both the contamination problem and the recovery from its effects, simultaneously. This means that the kinds of social and political conflicts generally found during the recovery stage of a natural disaster are overlain by other conflicts that stem from the need to deal with continuing and substantial threats to life and health.

If there is no single "high point" in contamination disasters there is often a series of signal events – mini-disasters – that help to shape both definitions and political conflicts. For example, the discovery of a cancer cluster or a pattern of recurrent respiratory illnesses in a given population may persuade some residents that a contamination problem is more urgent and serious than previously thought, thus spurring them to new levels of action. But even signal events signal different things to different people: respiratory illnesses may be perceived as being due to the weather or a bad season for allergies; a cancer cluster may be judged to be due to coincidence or to a study's poor scientific methodology. Thus, signal events tend to shift conflict to new levels of intensity rather than to eliminate it.

Let us briefly illustrate how Centralia can be viewed through the

Table 3.2 **Centralia mine fire: Political stages**

Stage	Year	Events
Pre-issue	1855	First home built
	1866	Borough founded
	1869–1902	Boom–bust economy; violent coal and railroad strikes
	1920s	Coal production declines
	1950s	Coal production drops drastically
Contained issue	1962	Coal fire discovered in garbage dump
	1962–1981	Fire control efforts fail; fire has increasing human impacts
Political issue	1981	Boy falls in subsidence; elderly man overcome by carbon monoxide in home
	1981–1983	Emergent groups form; severe community conflict
	1983	Study leads to voluntary relocation plan
Public issue	1984–1986	Voluntary relocation takes place; 35 families elect to stay
Contained issue	1987–present	Borough Council fights to maintain Centralia
	1991	Voluntary relocation ended; 58 people remain
	1992	State orders Centralians to relocate; borough hires lawyer to try to remain in town

lens of the modified stage model (table 3.2). In this case, the time before the mine fire began in 1962 is the "pre-event/pre-issue" stage. During this period, Centralia's peripheral location and status as a declining coal town meant that it was not the sort of place to attract much attention from the world beyond its borders. Between 1962 and 1981, the mine fire can be categorized as a politically "contained" issue. Various outlays of public money were devoted to securing a technical solution to the problem. Definitional differences arose during these years. Originally, most residents believed the fire to be "no problem" or a "warning." However, as time passed, many defined the fire as a "threat" or as having a detrimental "impact," thereby increasing the probability that severe intracommunity conflict would develop.

As long as the issue was contained within the normal political structure, the potential severity of the conflict resulting from definitional differences remained unrecognized. But with the two near-death "signal events" of early 1981, the situation changed drastically.

In quick succession, grass-roots groups formed and outside interest group aid was sought and received; a "political issue" stage had arrived. Group formation and participation in direct action crystallized people's perceptions into one of the four definitional stages, thus making compromise and understanding more difficult and increasing the likelihood of conflict.

In 1984, the federally financed voluntary relocation plan got under way and began to seal the fate of Centralia. Sensing that the major decisions about the town's future had been made, national interest groups withdrew from involvement, and the Centralia case became a "public issue." Limited intracommunity conflict continued between the two remaining interest groups, but both of them sought to achieve some kind of settlement with the government rather than fighting each other.

With the end of voluntary relocation and the demise of the grass-roots interest groups, the mine fire once again became a "contained issue." Elected representatives of the borough's remaining population labelled the fire a non-problem and used official channels and resources to maintain the viability of their small community. Most recently, this has involved litigation in the face of the state's determination that the entire community must be abandoned because of fire-related dangers.

The stage model that is proposed helps to raise awareness of the social processes that occur in contamination situations. We can imagine a matrix in which different combinations of definitional and political stages result in different social responses. I will not attempt to develop a comprehensive list of propositions concerning responses here. However, the following are illustrative:

- If definitional differences are modest and the issue is "contained," conflict is likely between different factions and the government, but not at the community level itself.
- If definitional differences are great and the issue is "contained," there will be pressure for local emergent groups to form, moving the issue to the "public" stage.
- If definitional differences are great and the issue becomes "public" (i.e. with local emergent groups), intracommunity conflict is very likely.
- If definitional differences are great and outside interest groups become involved (i.e. the issue is "political"), intracommunity conflict is most likely to develop and be severe.

- If most in a community agree that the issue belongs to one definitional stage, intracommunity conflict will be minimal, regardless of the issue's political stage.
- To the extent that a strong faction in a community defines the issue as a "threat" or as having an "impact," it is likely to escalate toward "political issue" status, especially if there is no quick solution.

Conclusions

This brief account of Centralia's experience illustrates the importance of the time dimension in contamination cases.

- Unlike communities that are affected by natural disaster, contaminated communities become stuck in the "warning/threat/impact" stages. They are forced to confront a seemingly endless prospect of chronic apprehension and dread.
- Different people and groups interpret the situation differently over time (i.e. define the problem as being at different stages); this sows the seeds of intense and destructive intracommunity conflict, making recovery of the social community difficult, if not impossible.
- Disagreements over the definition of the situation take place within a political context; that context itself moves in and out of different political stages that shape the nature of the conflict and the outcomes.
- While chronic in nature, signal events do occur in contamination cases, but they are interpreted differently by different factions, tending to intensify rather than ameliorate the conflict.
- Recovery and emergency responses must take place simultaneously. This complicates recovery considerably.

This last point is particularly insidious. Modern society puts great faith in achieving technological solutions to its problems. Our customary response tends to be: "If it's broken, fix it; if it's contaminated, clean it; if it's burning, douse it." Clearly, the government agencies involved in Centralia defined the problem as technological, not social, in nature – as an engineering puzzle rather than a human problem (Couch and Kroll-Smith 1992). How to stop the fire was a dominant issue, whereas how to keep the community from unravelling was not. By focusing on technological failure, the question of blame was made central – whose fault is it that no technological solution has worked? Thus, the government set itself up to be blamed; it focused on technological problems which often (perhaps usually) cannot be solved, while it ignored human problems that may be able to be solved if attended to promptly and intelligently. The result was that Centralians displayed a high level of disillusion and mistrust of government. This is an outlook that is widely shared by residents of contaminated communities everywhere. It may be that high levels of alienation and mistrust in industrial contamination cases are also linked with high levels of psychological distress, including anxiety, depression, somaticism, paranoid ideation, and post-traumatic stress disorder (Couch and Kroll-Smith 1991; Couch, Kroll-Smith, and Wilson 1992).

In fact, concern over the controllability of contamination may call into question the very viability of recovery. This is very different from most cases of natural disaster, where recovery is assumed to be possible, albeit perhaps after the expenditure of much time, effort, and money. With contamination, even the possibility of recovery may be open to doubt, placing decisions about the community's viability squarely in the political arena. The intensity of intracommunity conflict in Centralia was partly caused by the high stakes as defined by the parties involved. For some, relocation was necessary in order to assure health and safety. But relocation meant the death of the community, something others fought vehemently against.

In the long run there are two main outcomes or "final stages" of identified industrial contamination situations. The first is relocation – people are moved away from the problem (see fig. 3.4). Personal safety is recovered, but at the loss of the community and of a certain geographical area or resource. The second category is the "techfix" – a technological solution is adopted that renders the community safe

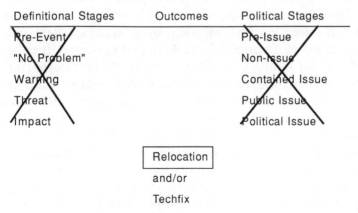

Fig. 3.4 **Relocation**

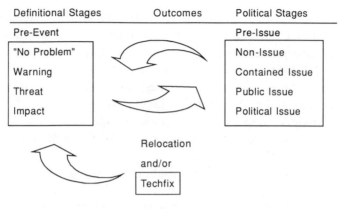

Definitional Stages	Outcomes	Political Stages

Pre-Event		Pre-Issue
"No Problem"		Non-Issue
Warning		Contained Issue
Threat		Public Issue
Impact		Political Issue

Relocation
and/or
Techfix

Fig. 3.5   **Techfix**

again and allows community-wide recovery to proceed (see fig. 3.5). Unfortunately, reliable technological solutions to contamination may not exist and are certain to be surrounded by disagreements about their adequacy. As a result, the problem is redefined as a "controversy" and there is a reversion to one of the model's other political stages. In other words, the battle goes on.

Centralia provides an example of a failed "techfix" that was followed by relocation. After trying to implement a "techfix" for nearly two decades, the government relocated most of the population but allowed those who defined the situation as "not dangerous" to remain. In the end, however, the government decided that a "techfix" to protect the remaining residents was not practical or financially feasible and it attempted to force relocation of the remaining residents.

In this regard it is interesting to contrast Centralia with Love Canal. The latter contamination case in New York State provided an example of relocation first, followed by a "techfix." Residents living near that toxic waste disposal site were first relocated, then remediation efforts got under way. Finally, most of the affected area was officially declared safe for habitation. Subsequently, some new residents moved into the neighbourhood. But many others disagreed with the government's contention that Love Canal was safe, and controversy continues over the adequacy of the "techfix".

In light of the history of Centralia and other contaminated communities it is clear that – unlike places affected by natural disasters – such communities rarely experience "amplified rebound" (disproportionately fast and altruistic recovery) after the event (Fritz 1961). In fact, even the concept of "recovery" is problematical. Recovery implies the regaining of something that was lost. At least on the community level, this seldom happens with industrial contamination. Social change is just too great, to talk of recovery in this sense. What happens is more akin to a transformation – a major change to something new, not a return to what had been. After a contamination disaster, people come to hold a very different view of the world, their community, and the roles played by various social institutions. New cultural norms develop that help people deal with the ongoing uncertainty that attends the breakdown of their physical and social environments. New community power structures are born and may become institutionalized. In some cases, such as Minamata, communities survive but in radically altered states. And in some cases, like Centralia, communities die.

Implications

Most models of post-disaster recovery are based on the aftermath of natural events. As Kliman and Kliman (1982) note: "We know a great deal about the strategies for crisis intervention that are most effective in helping individuals and communities deal with natural disasters. Much less is known through experience about what kinds of intervention strategies are most helpful when disasters are wrought by people." Thus, Centralia's experience has many implications for those who are interested in assisting communities to recover from industrial contamination.

Perhaps the most critical implication is that recovery (or transformation) is not a separate stage but is going on throughout a contamination situation. We need to be sensitive to where a situation falls on the stage model matrix at any particular time, in order to develop effective recovery (or transformation) strategies. For example, a community in which most perceive contamination as a "warning" and in which the issue is "contained," warrants a very different approach from one in which there is intense disagreement over the definitional stage and in which emergent grass-roots groups are plentiful. Public programmes to assist recovery may be more feasible in the first case than in the second.

Another implication is the importance of dealing with the social aspects of recovery. Most recovery strategies tend to be concerned mainly with technical, not social, issues. But dealing with the breakdown of trust and social cohesion within communities is critical to creating the possibility for survival and social reconstruction of the community. If there are too many deep wounds caused by social conflict, healing at the community level becomes impossible. For example, Kliman and Kliman described their experience as social workers at Love Canal as follows: "Our frustrating and saddening experience in consulting with United Way agencies ... was that the murkiness and pessimism of the situation resulted in divisions among victims ... Effective community organization was nearly impossible in an atmosphere of hopelessness and misplaced conflict" (Kliman and Kliman 1982: 267). Implementation of conflict-management strategies throughout the developing history of contamination cases could help keep deep social wounds to a minimum and might aid in finding common ground around which most in a community could unite, and through which the community could define and pursue its collective interests.

It is also important to consider the implications of the "pre-impact/ pre-issue" stage in terms of the resources and abilities of communities to deal with contamination disasters. Most such disasters are extremely expensive, calling for far more resources than the affected area can muster. Moreover, the risks of falling victim to a contamination disaster are distributed unequally among individuals, groups, communities, regions, and societies. The costs of living with, and recovering from, industrial contamination are borne disproportionately by those least equipped to manage them. There is a growing literature documenting the unequal distribution of technological hazards. For example, in 1983, the General Accounting Office reported on four hazardous waste sites threatening communities in one southern state: "At least 26% of the population in all four communities have income below the poverty level" (General Accounting Office 1983: 1). Similarly, the City of Houston pursued a policy of locating solid waste disposal sites in low-income, "predominantly black neighborhoods" (Bullard 1983: 285; see also Bullard and Wright 1986). Castleman (1979) looks at an international dimension to the question, arguing that "poverty and ignorance make communities in many parts of the world quite vulnerable to the exploitation implicit in hazardous export" (Castleman 1979: 570). Centralia is clearly a case in point, having a history of quasi-colonial exploitation while it was considered economically valuable and of neglect when it was not.

A further implication here is that contaminated communities are likely to have a history of economic and political dependence – a dependence that is exacerbated by the realization that vast resources are needed if contamination is to be tackled successfully. At the same

78

time, outside parties are usually reluctant to provide aid to such communities – the costs are great and there is little or nothing to gain. If they do become involved, corporations and government agencies are apt to put pressure on local residents to accept outsiders' definitions of the problem (e.g. Shrivastava 1991; Gephart 1992). And affected communities are unlikely to have sufficient "clout" to force adequate resolution of the problem through normal political channels. In such circumstances, a community's most effective weapon is often the mass media, and the probability of gaining media attention is higher if community groups decide to escalate their tactics to include rancorous confrontations with those in authority (e.g. demonstrations, marches, sit-ins). Therefore, there is a high probability that victims will seek help from outside the local political system – unless that system becomes more responsive to their needs.

If certain areas are more likely than others to be victimized by disasters, the existence of a disaster subculture may help them respond to the problem. Our experience with contamination disasters is too new to permit much more than speculation on this point, but the Centralia case suggests that a general disaster subculture (as opposed to one that is grounded only in chronic contamination) may hinder, rather than help, the development of effective responses to industrial contamination. We need to carry out additional research on the specific characteristics of disaster subcultures resulting from experience with various kinds of disasters, and on the relationship of those subcultures to community response and recovery.

Another implication for intervention, and another subject worthy of further research in its own right, is the importance of the territorial aspect of contamination. Feitelson (1991) suggests that one of the factors that make local environmental issues emotional and dissent-ridden is human attachment to specific places that are threatened by pollution or development. Clearly, in our culture, one's home is seen as a refuge from dangerous forces, as a safe haven from the risks of the outside world. And, while "community" may transcend one's local town or neighbourhood, the territorial basis of community is still seen as distinctive and important (Wilkinson 1991: 22–23). When that basis for community is threatened, when that safe haven becomes dangerous, or when one may be forced to relocate, people become very upset. The intensity of the reaction may be exacerbated by the fact that, in modern Western society, people generally have more choice over where they live (Fischer 1977: 192). Restraining that choice is seen as particularly loathsome, even as the violation of a person's rights. Any intervention should be especially sensitive to issues of attachment to place.

Finally, while contaminated communities are likely to be similar in the ways discussed above, they will also have vast cultural differences, differences that should be kept in mind when outside agencies seek to speed recovery. Intervention and recovery strategies that may work in a small mining community in the United States may not work in an industrial city in Japan or a farming region of Zimbabwe. Although much about the experience of contamination and its stages is remarkably similar across cultures, successful efforts at recovery will always be shaped by the specific culture of a community. This was clearly illustrated in Centralia, when government agents were shocked that their well-trained mining engineers were not believed or treated with much respect by local residents, most of whom had no college education. However, a person with knowledge of the local mining culture would not have been surprised – many townspeople had worked in the mines under the town and firmly believed that their first-hand knowledge was worth much more than that of any "book-trained" engineer.

Recommendations

It must be kept in mind that community recovery or transformation takes place within a larger sociopolitical context. Policy at the level of the nation or the state, prefecture, or province usually sets the boundaries of action. Where such policies exist at all, they are of recent vintage. And, in at least some of those places, policy is under-developed and contradictory. In the United States, for example, there is no formal policy on recovery from industrial contamination. Informally, relocation has been implemented with increasing frequency in recent years but without the benefit of adequate research about its effects and without a public debate that would come to grips with its implications. Will it result in the creation of geographic "sacrifice zones," where contaminated land is abandoned for ever? Would such zones draw waste from other areas? How much of an area can (or should) be sacrificed? What might be the implications for nearby settlements and for the physical and social environments? Would acceptance of relocation as a preferred policy cut down on the motivation of companies to reduce the production of hazardous chemicals and wastes?

Centralia is an example of what happens in this kind of policy vacuum. In the absence of a policy, and loath to take what might be seen as an authoritarian stand, the federal government allowed relocation to be voluntary when instituted in 1984. Now, the state government has decided that Centralia is too dangerous for human habitation and is forcing the remaining residents to leave. The result – almost everyone is unhappy with how the problem was handled. A policy on industrial contamination recovery would not, of course, eliminate conflict and satisfy everyone. But a policy might help define what recovery means in these cases and might provide guidelines for aiding impacted communities and individuals. In light of the growing number of industrial contamination cases, the need for policy is urgent.

All industrial countries, as well as all industrializing countries, should look towards the formulation of long-term industrial disaster policies. At this time it is not possible to provide guidelines for every country, so what follows highlights the United States. In order to facilitate the beginning of debate on a US national policy, I recommend the following:

1. Constitute a federally funded task force to recommend a policy and structure for overseeing community and individual recovery from long-term industrial disasters. The task force could be organized under the auspices of the National Academy of Sciences or a similar body. It would include a broad range of experts on industrial hazards and disasters, and experts on individual and community recovery from personal trauma and social disorganization.

2. The task force would be charged with addressing several kinds of public policy reform. These would include:

    (a) Centralized management of recovery. Much of the delay and confusion suffered in Centralia was due to the fact that no single agency had clear authority. Several existing federal agencies might be delegated this responsibility, though none is perfectly suited to the task. The Environmental Protection Agency is one possibility but it is a regulatory and enforcement body, not designed to assist with individual and community recovery (Zimmerman 1985). The Federal Emergency Management Agency was originally intended to oversee preparedness and recovery planning for one kind of technological disaster (i.e. nuclear warfare) but it has been more heavily committed to the arena of natural calamities. One of the federal agencies that is more directly concerned with community development might be appropriate, but these organizations seldom play a central role in disaster recovery. In any event,

81

wherever it is administratively located, the agency should have a clear mandate to focus on recovery issues.

(b) Federal policy should address not only environmental recovery but also human and community recovery. There is a prevailing tendency to focus on technological alternatives that are, at best, half measures. A successful policy would help individuals and communities to transform themselves.

(c) Many residents of affected communities will have to be empowered to effect the necessary transformations. Most do not have the resources to ensure their own recovery unaided, and many have a history of dependency that is deepened by industrial disasters. There is some risk that a centralized policy and a centralized agency might further increase dependency. Therefore, innovative efforts at community empowerment will probably be required. For example, Superfund (toxic waste) programmes that provide funds for communities to hire technical experts might be expanded to include other types of industrial hazards and to make available experts on social and psychological recovery. Moreover, since intracommunity conflict is such a devastating part of industrial contamination, people versed in facilitating or mediating such conflicts might be made available to communities.

(d) States should be encouraged to develop their own industrial contamination agencies and given responsibility for dealing with situations that fall outside the purview of the federal government or might be more appropriately addressed by state bodies.

While the shape, nature, and structure of a policy on industrial hazard recovery must be painted in broad strokes at this point, these recommendations provide points of departure for a debate on a national policy. It is clear that a response based on natural disaster precedents or on regulatory models is inadequate. Thanks to cases such as Centralia, we now have sufficient knowledge of the distinctive nature of responses to long-term industrial contamination to lay the groundwork for policies and strategies that will make possible successful recovery (or, better yet, transformation). Many of the appropriate measures that would be suitable for the United States might have broad applicability elsewhere. Therefore, the United Nations might well be involved in formulating an international system of industrial disaster recovery. In the name of past and present victims of these catastrophes, and in the hope of limiting the number of future victims, let the debate begin.

References

Aurand, Harold. 1971. *From the Molly Maguires to the United Mine Workers: The Social Ecology of an Industrial Union, 1869–1897.* Philadelphia: Temple University Press.

Baltzell, E. Digby. 1958. *Philadelphia Gentlemen: The Making of a National Upper Class.* Glencoe, Ill.: Free Press.

Baum, Andrew. 1987. "Toxins, technology and natural disasters." In: Gary Van den Bos and Brenda Bryant, eds. *Cataclysms, Crises and Catastrophes.* Washington, DC: American Psychological Association, pp. 5–54.

———, Raymond Fleming, and Laura M. Davidson. 1983. "Natural disaster and technological catastrophe." *Environment and Behavior* 15: 333–354.

———, ———, and Jerome E. Singer. 1983. "Coping with victimization by technological disaster." *Journal of Social Issues* 39: 122.

Berren, Michael R., Allan Biegel, and Stuart Ghertner. 1980. "A typology for the classification of disasters." *Mental Health Journal* 16: 103–110.

Bertoff, Rowland. 1965. "The social order of the Anthracite Region, 1825–1902." *The Pennsylvania Magazine of History and Biography* (July).

Brown, Phil. 1991. "The popular epidemiology approach to toxic waste contamination." In: Stephen R. Couch and J. Stephen Kroll-Smith, eds. *Communities At Risk: Collective Responses to Technological Hazards.* New York: Peter Lang, pp. 133–156.

Bullard, Robert D. 1983. "Solid waste sites and the black Houston community." *Sociological Inquiry* 53: 273–288.

———, and Beverly Hendrix Wright. 1986. "The politics of pollution: Implications for the black community." *Phylon* XLVII: 71–78.

Castleman, Barry I. 1979. "The export of hazardous factories to developing nations." *International Journal of Health Services* 9: 569–606.

Caudill, Henry. 1963. *Night Comes to the Cumberlands.* Boston: Little, Brown.

Chapman, Dwight W. 1962. "A brief introduction to contemporary disaster research." In: George W. Baker and Dwight W. Chapman, eds. *Man and Society in Disaster.* New York: Basic Books, pp. 3–22.

Couch, Stephen R. 1984. "The coal and iron police in anthracite country." In: David L. Salay, ed. *Hard Coal, Hard Times: Ethnicity and Labor in the Anthracite Region.* Scranton, Pa.: Anthracite Museum Press, pp. 100–119.

———, and J. Stephen Kroll-Smith. 1985. "The chronic technical disaster: Toward a social scientific perspective." *Social Science Quarterly* 66(3): 564–575.

———, and ———. 1991. "Alienation and toxic contamination." Paper presented at the Annual Meeting of the Society for the Study of Social Problems, Cincinnati (August).

———, and ———. 1992. "Controllability, social breakdown, and the Centralia mine fire." In: S.K. Majumdar, E.W. Miller, G.S. Forbes, and R.F. Schmalz, eds. *Natural and Technological Disasters: Causes, Effects and Preventive Measures.* Easton, Pa.: Pennsylvania Academy of Sciences.

———, ———, and John P. Wilson. 1992. "The psychosocial impact of toxic exposure at Brookhurst: Final report." Prepared for Spence, Moriarity, and Schuster, Jackson, Wyoming.

Davidson, Laura M., and Andrew Baum. 1991. "Victimization and self-blame following a technological disaster." In: Stephen R. Couch and J. Stephen Kroll-Smith, eds. *Communities At Risk: Collective Responses to Technological Hazards*. New York: Peter Lang, pp. 33–52.

Eavenson, Howard N. 1942. *The First Century and a Quarter of the American Coal Industry*. Baltimore: Waverly Press, p. 378.

Edelstein, Michael R. 1988. *Contaminated Communities: The Social and Psychological Impacts of Residential Toxic Exposure*. Boulder: Westview.

———. 1991. "Ecological threats and spoiled identities: Radon gas and environmental stigma." In: Stephen R. Couch and J. Stephen Kroll-Smith, eds. *Communities At Risk: Collective Responses to Technological Hazards*. New York: Peter Lang, pp. 205–226.

Erikson, Kai. 1991. "A new species of trouble." In Stephen R. Couch and J. Stephen Kroll-Smith, eds. *Communities At Risk: Collective Responses to Technological Hazards*. New York: Peter Lang, pp. 11–30.

Feitelson, E. 1991. "Sharing the globe: The role of attachment to place." *Global Environmental Change* 1: 396–406.

Fischer, Claude S. 1977. "Comments on the history and study of 'Community'." In: Claude S. Fischer et al., eds. *Networks and Places: Social Relations in the Urban Setting*. New York: Free Press, pp. 189–204.

Fritz, Charles E. 1961. "Disaster." In: Robert K. Merton and Robert A. Nisbet, eds. *Contemporary Social Problems*. New York: Harcourt, pp. 651–694.

General Accounting Office. 1983. "Siting of hazardous waste landfills and their correlation with racial and economic status of surrounding communities." Washington, DC: General Accounting Office, Resources, Community and Economic Development Division.

Gephart, R.P., Jr. 1992. "Sensemaking, communicative distortion and the logic of public inquiry legitimation." *Industrial Crisis Quarterly* 6: 115–136.

Geschwindt, John. 1984. Letter to the author, 27 March. State Library of Pennsylvania.

Gill, Duane A. 1986. "A disaster impact assessment model: An empirical study of a technological disaster." Ph.D. dissertation, Department of Sociology, Texas A & M University.

Gonzales-Casanova, Pablo. 1965. "Internal colonialism and national development." *Studies in Comparative International Development* 1: 27–37.

Hechter, Michael. 1975. *Internal Colonialism: The Celtic Fringe in British National Development, 1536–1966*. Berkeley: University of California Press.

History of Schuylkill County. 1881. New York: W.W. Munsell, pp. 53–54.

Homrighaus, Barbara K., Stephen R. Couch, and J. Stephen Kroll-Smith. 1985. "Building a town but preventing a community: A social history of Centralia, Pennsylvania." In: Lance E. Metz, ed. *Proceedings of the Canal History and Technology Symposium*. Easton: Center for Canal History and Technology, pp. 69–91.

Kasperson, Roger E., and K. David Pijawka. 1985. "Societal response to hazards and major hazard events: Comparing natural and technological hazards." *Public Administration Review* 45: 7–18.

Kliman, Jodie, and Gilbert Kliman. 1982. "Natural and human made disasters: Some therapeutic and epidemiological implications for crisis intervention." In: V. Rueveni, Ross U. Speck, and Joan L. Speck, eds. *Therapeutic Intervention*. New York: Human Science Press.

Kroll-Smith, J. Stephen, and Stephen Robert Couch. 1990. *The Real Disaster Is Above Ground: A Mine Fire and Social Conflict*. Lexington: University Press of Kentucky.

———, and ———. 1991. "What is a disaster? An ecological–symbolic approach to resolving the definitional debate." *International Journal of Mass Emergencies and Disasters* 9(3): 355–366.

Levine, Adeline G. 1982. *Love Canal: Science, Politics and People*. Lexington, Mass.: Lexington Books.

Nyden, Paul. 1979. "An internal colony: Labor conflict and capitalism in Appalachian coal." *Insurgent Sociologist* 8: 33–43.

Raphael, Beverley. 1986. *When Disaster Strikes: How Individuals and Communities Cope with Catastrophe*. New York: Basic Books.

Reich, Michael. 1983. "Environmental politics and science: The case of PBB contamination in Michigan." *American Journal of Public Health* 73(3): 302–313.

———. 1991. *Toxic Politics: Responding to Chemical Disasters*. Ithaca, New York: Cornell University Press, pp. 140–253.

Schalek, Adolf W., and D.C. Henning (eds.). 1907. *History of Schuylkill County, Pa. Vol. 1*. Harrisburg: State Historical Society.

Shrivastava, Paul. 1987. *Bhopal: Anatomy of a Crisis*. Cambridge, Mass.: Ballinger.

———. 1991. "Organizational myths in industrial crises: Obfuscating revelations." In: Stephen Robert Couch and J. Stephen Kroll-Smith, eds. *Communities At Risk: Collective Responses to Technological Hazards*. New York: Peter Lang, pp. 263–290.

Vyner, Henry. 1988. *Invisible Trauma*. Lexington, Mass.: Lexington Books.

Wallace, Anthony F.C. 1981. *St. Clair: A Nineteenth-Century Coal Town's Experience with a Disaster-Prone Industry*. Ithaca, New York: Cornell University Press.

Wilkinson, Kenneth P. 1991. *The Community in Rural America*. New York: Greenwood Press.

Zimmerman, Rae. 1985. "The relationship of emergency management to governmental policies on man-made technological disasters." *Public Administration Review* 45: 29–39.

4

Seveso: A paradoxical classic disaster

B. De Marchi, S. Funtowicz, and J. Ravetz

Introduction

For some people the name Seveso is tied to the experience of a seriously mismanaged toxic chemical release (Conti 1977; Hay 1982; Pocchiari, Silano, and Zapponi 1987); for others it is firmly and positively linked with a set of innovative public policies for managing industrial disasters. These contradictory characterizations make the interpretation of this industrial disaster both paradoxical and ambiguous. The Seveso experience illustrates many different types of uncertainty that are mobilized by industrial disasters and suggests a new interpretive model.

Overview

The chemical release

Around midday on Saturday 10 July 1976, an explosion occurred in a TCP (2,4,5-trichlorophenol) reactor of the ICMESA chemical plant on the outskirts of Meda, a small town about 20 kilometres north of Milan, Italy.[1] A toxic cloud containing TCDD (2,3,7,8-tetrachloro-dibenzo-p-dioxin), then widely believed to be one of the most toxic man-made chemicals (Mocarelli et al. 1991), was accidentally released into the atmosphere. The dioxin cloud contaminated a densely populated area about six kilometres long and one kilometre wide, lying

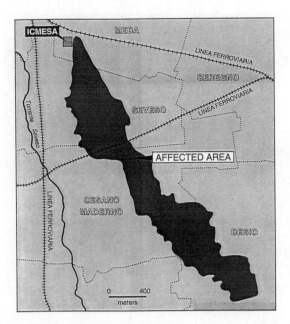

Fig. 4.1   **Area affected by the Seveso dioxin release (Source: *Roche Magazin* 1986)**

downwind from the site (fig. 4.1). This event became internationally known as the Seveso disaster, after the name of a neighbouring municipality that was most severely affected (Hay 1982; Pocchiari, Silano, and Zapponi 1987).

Eleven communities in the rolling countryside between Milan and Lake Como were directly involved in the toxic release and its aftermath. The four most impacted municipalities included Seveso (1976 population 17,000), Meda (19,000), Desio (33,000), and Cesano Maderno (34,000). Two other municipalities were subject to post-accident restrictions: Barlassina (6,000) and Bovisio Masciago (11,000). Health monitoring was extended to a further five munici-palities. The entire affected area is part of the Brianza, a prosperous district of Lombardy, itself one of the wealthiest and most indus-trialized regions of Italy (fig. 4.2). Though originally agricultural, the economy of this area depended on a cluster of small workshops and industries, mainly engaged in manufacturing furniture.

The Seveso disaster had a particularly traumatic effect on exposed local populations because its seriousness was recognized only gradu-ally. The community was divided by rancorous conflicts. People in other countries also experienced much heightened concern about

Fig. 4.2 **Location of Seveso**

industrial risks and the need for tighter regulation of hazardous chemical installations. In these respects Seveso resembled Bhopal (1984) and Chernobyl (1986), which have both come to be regarded as international symbols of industrial pathology.

But as we shall see, Seveso is a paradoxical symbol, because human health effects of the disaster have been obscure and the process of recovery has been unusual. Victims have been compensated, workers have been redeployed, a substantial programme of long-term health monitoring is in operation, and the site itself has been made into a park. Though initially slow and conflicted, responses to the accident may eventually have showed high-technology society working at its best. Recovery was therefore a process of overcoming initial traumas (e.g. chloracne, fear of genetic impairments, evacuation, animal deaths) and re-establishing customary patterns of societal, economic, and institutional life.

For some, the main lesson of Seveso might be that a reasonably prompt, effective, and generous response by public and private agencies is the key to community recovery. But, to a significant degree, local recovery was achieved by *exporting* parts of the problem. Seriously contaminated materials were disposed of abroad in an atmosphere of confusion and scandal; their ultimate fate is still unravelling (Gambino, Gumpel, and Novelli 1993; see also Chronology items

December 1992 and November 1993). This, too, is part of the style of high-technology industry: consumer satisfaction is often sustained by "externalizing" environmental costs and attendant social problems. In other words, the burdens of technology are often transferred away from producers and immediate consumers into a universally shared but unprotected natural environment or into specific poor communities (local or overseas) that are treated as sweatshops and dumps.[2]

Dioxin

The Seveso experience was essentially about dread – an emotion mobilized by involvement of the chemical dioxin. Dioxin first came to widespread public notice during the Viet Nam War, when it was identified as a component of the defoliant Agent Orange (Hay 1982). Previously, campaigns on behalf of agricultural and forestry workers had been mounted to have TCP banned because of its alleged toxic effects on humans. These frequently met with scientific disapproval, partly because the evidence was only "anecdotal." The United Kingdom's regulatory system was particularly unsympathetic to such claims (Wynne 1989).

Before the Seveso release, several industrial accidents involving TCP were known to have occurred. Among others, these affected the following firms and countries:
- 1949 Monsanto (USA);
- 1953 BASF (Germany);
- 1960 Dow Chemical (USA);
- 1963 Phillips Duphar (Netherlands);
- 1968 Coalite Chemical Productions (UK).

These accidents precipitated acute illness among affected workers and added to the burden of existing chronic sickness caused by prolonged exposure to the same chemicals under unsanitary conditions (Hay 1982: 138–140). After the BASF accident, production of TCP was stopped at that site. The same occurred at Phillips Duphar, where the plant was closed and subsequently dismantled; its pieces were swathed in concrete and dumped in the Atlantic Ocean. Similar procedures were adopted at the Coalite site near Bolsover. After the Dow Chemical accident, new installations were constructed there. The reactor was enclosed by a supplemental safety vessel, whose purpose was to collect and cool any toxic material that might leak if reactor valves ruptured (Otway and Amendola 1989). Similar "containment vessels" have been widely employed in nuclear power stations that house pressurized water-cooled reactors. Had there been such a vessel at ICMESA, there would probably have been no Seveso disaster.

Dioxin was known to be an extremely dangerous substance, partly because of these industrial experiences and partly because experimental evidence indicated that it was unprecedentedly toxic to some species of laboratory animals. In many ways the image of dioxin was similar to that of radioactivity: it was invisible, it poisoned at microscopic dose levels, and it was implicated in war. Moreover, because dioxin was carried by people and things, it took on the appearance of a dread disease – a plague. In particular, it was the sense of being gravely contaminated that increased personal, social, and economic distress among the affected population. Products of dioxin-impacted areas were rejected because of feared contamination, thus imposing a stigma on whole communities.

The Seveso Directive

The best-known consequence of the Seveso disaster was the impulse that it gave to the creation of the European Community's Seveso Directive, a new system of industrial regulation. Within the EC, each country previously followed its own rules for managing industrial safety. Urgent discussions about a new EC-wide regulatory framework for ensuring the safety of hazardous installations started after an explosion of cyclohexane in the Nypro Ltd. plant at Flixborough (United Kingdom, 1974).[3] During the next two years, three additional serious chemical accidents occurred within the European Community: these were at Beek (the Netherlands 1975), Manfredonia (Italy 1976), and finally Seveso (Otway and Amendola 1989; Drogaris 1991).

One of the most remarkable features of the Seveso experience was that neither the residents nor the local and regional authorities suspected that the ICMESA plant was a source of risk. They did not even know much about the type of production processes and chemical substances that occurred there. As the Mayor reported (Rocca 1992, personal communication), the factory had been in existence for 30 years and the only occasional complaints from nearby residents concerned some unpleasant smells. Moreover, at Seveso as well as Flixborough, "changes had been made in plant or processes which compromised the safety of the facilities but were not communicated to authorities responsible for public health and safety" (Otway and Amendola 1989: 507).

In light of these disastrous accidents it was clear that new legislation was needed to improve the safety of industrial sites, to plan for off-site emergencies, and to cope with broader regional and transboundary aspects of industrial safety. The Seveso Directive, adopted by the Council of Ministers of the European Communities in June 1982 (Directive 82/501/EEC), is the result of those efforts. A central part of the Directive is a requirement for public information about major industrial hazards and appropriate safety measures in the event of an accident. It is based on recognition that industrial workers and the general public need to know about hazards that threaten them and about safety procedures. This is the first time that the principle of "need to know" has been enshrined in European Community legislation. The "need to know" principle is not as strong as the "right to know" principle that is widely applied in the United States. The status of "need" is determined by the authorities; it is not a right of citizens (Baram 1991; Royal Society Study Group 1992).

Although the Seveso Directive grew out of deficiencies in the existing system of industrial regulation, it is not simply intended to provide protection against hazards: it is also designed to equalize the burden of regulation on industry. The creation of a single hazardous industry code ensures a "level playing field" for trade within the European Community by depriving unscrupulous industrial operators of competitive advantages that might flow from exploiting differences among varied national regulations. Moreover, adoption of the "need to know" principle increases the political equity of decision-making and adds a valuable new tool to the regulatory process. The next section examines this institutional response in greater detail.

The European Community's institutional response to Seveso

Directives are one type of legislation issued by the European Community. Others include regulations, decisions, recommendations, and opinions. Some of these are binding on the 12 European states that make up the Community,[4] while others are not. Several different units of the Community are involved in the process of legislating a directive (table 4.1).

The path for adopting a directive is as follows.[5] The Commission presents a proposal to the Council. After consultation with the Euro-

Table 4.1 **Units of the European Community involved in legislating a directive**

European Community Unit	Characteristics
Commission	Seventeen members appointed by 12 Member State governments for four years.
Council	Twelve representatives, one from each Member State government; presidency rotates among countries every six months.
European Parliament	Elected by peoples of the EC for five-year term according to each Member State's electoral system (518 members in 1992).
European Court of Justice	Thirteen judges appointed by agreement among Member State governments for six-year terms. Assisted by six advocates-general.
Economic and Social Committee	Assists the Council and the Commission with European Economic Community and European Atomic Energy Community matters; 189 members from various economic and social sectors.

pean Parliament and the Economic and Social Committee (whose opinions must be heard even if they are not strictly binding), the Council may formally adopt the proposal. After adoption, an EC directive is not immediately applicable to a Member State. Individual states must incorporate the directive into national legislation and take all the necessary measures for compliance within a specified period. Such a procedure allows for effective implementation, while respecting different juridical and administrative traditions. If a Member State fails to comply, the Commission may bring a case before the European Court of Justice.

In practice, the process of arriving at the directive on major accident hazards was long and complex. Technical and political problems required extended consultations among different parties and institutions. A proposal was finally presented by the Commission to the Council in July 1979. The required opinions of the European Parliament and the Economic and Social Committee were expressed in 1980 and it took two more years of further consulting and discussion before a directive was finally adopted, on 24 June 1982, 8 January 1984 being the anticipated deadline for implementation by the 10 EC Member States of that time. Directive 82/501/EEC soon became known as the Seveso Directive, despite opposition from Seveso residents, who formally complained to EC authorities in Brussels about what they perceived as an implied insult.

Before the Seveso Directive, manufacturers in different Member States were subject to obligations of varying stringency. For example, the submission of a safety report by the manufacturer responsible for a hazardous installation was not mandatory in all countries. Therefore, the Directive's main purpose was to ensure harmonization of regulations among different countries. This was achieved by establishing minimal EC requirements and permitting Member States to enforce stricter regulations. Such a general purpose is consistent with the overall EC policy on environmental health and safety matters. It is instructive to review the Directive's major components.

The Directive and its annexes

The Seveso Directive is addressed to EC Member States, and holds them responsible for ensuring that the relevant national institutions accomplish what is required for adequate risk management. The entire Directive is also shaped by a concern for prevention, even those parts that relate to post-accident activities. The first article defines relevant terms such as "industrial activity, manufacturer, major accident, and dangerous substances." It also makes reference to four annexes that identify types of production, operations, and storage activities that are subject to regulation, and dangers that are anticipated.

Articles 3 and 4 require Member States to ensure that manufacturers identify existing major accident hazards and adopt all appropriate safety measures, including information, training, and equipment for workers. They must also provide competent authorities with a notification containing detailed and updated information on safety precautions and other matters (Article 5). Moreover, Member States must set up competent authorities that will take responsibility for receiving such a notification, examining the information provided, organizing inspections or other measures of control, and ensuring that off-site emergency plans are prepared (Article 7). Furthermore, Member States are held responsible for assuring that "persons liable to be affected by a major accident ... are informed in an appropriate manner of the safety measures and of the correct behaviour to adopt in the event of an accident" (Article 8).

Article 8 is a very innovative feature in safety legislation. For the first time in Europe, the safety of people outside hazardous installations is taken into account; previously, only workers might have the right to be informed. The public's right to know was recognized on both pragmatic and ethical grounds. Not surprisingly, this article met with strong resistance and was subject to long delays in implementation (Wynne 1987; De Marchi 1991a, 1991b). Despite these initial difficulties, the Directive proved to be a watershed event. Matters that had previously been considered suitable "for experts alone" were now opened to inspection by – and input from – the general public.

Article 10 requires that Member States shall take the necessary measures to ensure that the manufacturer immediately provides full and detailed information about an accident to the competent authorities; they must in turn ensure that all necessary measures are taken and that full analysis of the accident is accomplished whenever possible. It is a specific obligation of Member States, to report any accident to the EC Commission (Article 11). The Commission is in charge of setting up a register containing a summary of major accidents that occur within the EC, including an analysis of causes, experience gained, and measures taken to enable Member States to use this information for prevention purposes (Article 12). Annex VI to the Directive lists the items of information that the Member States must report to the Commission in the event of a major accident.

The Directive includes provisions for ensuring effective implementation and for updating in light of technological change. Article 15 provides for the creation of a committee composed of representatives of the Member States and chaired by a representative of the Commission. The Member States and the Commission are expected to exchange information about the experiences acquired regarding the prevention of major accidents and the limitation of their consequences. Such information covers the operation of measures stipulated in the Directive (Article 18). Moreover, the Commission is required to make proposals for revising the technical annexes as new technologies are adopted.

Procedures for updating and revision include regular meetings of the Committee of Competent Authorities. Such meetings have produced two amendments to the original Directive that grew out of experience with major industrial disasters in Bhopal, Mexico City, and Basle during the early 1980s. The first amendment, Directive 87/216/EEC, adopted by the Council on 19 March 1987, modifies Annexes I, II, and III by lowering the threshold quantities of certain substances and including additional industrial activities in the category that requires notification under Article 5.

During the revision process, between 1979 and 1987, there was a continuous exchange of correspondence between the Special Bureau for Seveso (Ufficio Speciale), which had been set up by the Lombardy Region in June 1977 (see Chronology), and various institutions of the EC (Regione Lombardia 1992). In 1984, a report was prepared by the Ufficio Speciale for a meeting of a committee of the European Parliament which was held in Seveso (Meazza 1992, personal communication). The second amendment, Directive 88/610/EEC issued by the Council on 24 November 1988, further revised Annex II to include more types of storage activities. It also substantially revised Article 8, stating that information shall be made publicly available as well as actively provided in an appropriate manner. Such information shall be periodically repeated and updated as necessary. A new annex, Annex VII, was added, which specifies the information that shall be provided to the public.[6]

The official deadline for compliance of Member States with Directive 88/610/EEC was 1 June 1990. Meetings of the Competent Authorities have continued after the adoption of the second amendment, and further revision of the Seveso Directive is being discussed.

Other institutional effects of the Seveso Directive

In order to meet the Seveso Directive's requirements, the Major Accident Reporting System (MARS) data bank has been established to store and retrieve accident information reported by the Member States (Drogaris 1993). It is located at the Commission's Joint Research Centre, Institute of Systems Engineering and Informatics in Ispra, Italy. To promote safety-related knowledge further, a Community Documentation Centre on Industrial Risk (CDCIR) has also been established at the same site. This Centre collects, classifies, and reviews materials relevant to industrial risks and safety.

The effects of the Seveso Directive were not confined to improvements in the management of industrial accidents. The Directive also opened the floodgates for similar initiatives on a variety of other issues, particularly in the fields of environmental management and public health. Among these are the following: Directive 89/391/EEC, which mandates the introduction of measures to encourage improvements in occupational safety and health; Directive 89/654/EEC, which addresses minimum safety and health requirements for the workplace; Directive 90/219/EEC, which relates to biotechnology; Directive 90/313/EEC, on the freedom of access to environmental information; and Directive 89/618/Euratom, which concerns public information about radioactive emergencies. The European Single Act and the Maastricht Treaty also call for greater participation of citizens in EC decision-making and this has expanded the scope of public information programmes. Indeed, recent reluctance by Danish voters and others to approve the Maastricht Treaty has led to further broadening of the commitment to provide information in support of public policy within the EC.

Beyond the European Community, the Directive has relevance for many international organizations. Those that are concerned with industrial hazards include the World Bank, the United Nations Environment Programme, the Council of Europe, the International Atomic Energy Agency (IAEA), the Office of the UN Disaster Relief Co-ordinator (UNDRO), the World Health Organization (WHO), and the International Labour Organization (ILO). In particular, the OECD (Organisation for Economic Co-operation and Development) has devoted much attention to accident prevention and response and has published a number of recommendations, some of which are specifically addressed to public information and public participation in decision-making (OECD 1989, 1990, 1992).

The lessons of Seveso

A model for managing uncertainty

Many students of disaster have concluded that uncertainty and communication are key factors in the management of emergencies. During emergencies, uncertainty increases and formerly dominant consensual views of problems and solutions often break down; different parties tend to evaluate the same evidence differently and, at times, tend to perceive different sorts of evidence. Such divergent interpretations create antagonisms and mistrust, which persist after the acute phase of an emergency has ended and complicate the tasks of recovery (Quarantelli 1988; Otway and Wynne 1989).

Our study of Seveso and other disasters (De Marchi, Funtowicz, and Ravetz 1993) suggests that there are six basic types of uncertainty (table 4.2) and eight distinctive strategies for managing the communication of uncertainty (table 4.3). Together, these two sets of variables provide the basis for a model of uncertainty management that has broad applicability.

Situational uncertainty involves a poor match between the deci-

Table 4.2 **Types of uncertainty**

Type	Description
Situational	Inadequacy of available information in relation to necessary decisions
Legal/moral	Possibility of future liability or guilt for actions or inactions
Societal	Absence or scarcity of integration of publics and institutions
Institutional	Withholding of information by agencies for bureaucratic reasons
Proprietary	Contested rights to know, to warn, or to conceal
Scientific	Difficulty of risk assessment or of forecasts of emergencies

Table 4.3 **Strategies for communication of uncertainty**

Interpretations	Policies
Suppression	Secrecy
Discounting	Confidentiality
Recognition	Publicity
Amplification	Sharing

sions that must be taken and the information at hand. It is normally the most salient type of uncertainty because information is central to decision-making. It is also a very common type of uncertainty because complete high-quality information about major hazards is usually lacking. Moreover, interagency collaboration in decision-making is usually required and knowledge about the capabilities of such agencies is often incomplete.

In an ideal world, *legal/moral* uncertainty would not be salient because decisions would always be made in the public interest with due consideration of social justice; decision makers would be held free of liability. But few public decisions about industrial hazards meet these exacting criteria, so decision makers cannot ignore the possibility that they will be subject to legal action or moral censure. Concern about legal/moral uncertainty often leads to indecisiveness and defensiveness about the release of information.

Societal uncertainty occurs when institutions and the publics that they are intended to serve are not well integrated. Decisions that are subject to high degrees of legal/moral uncertainty also tend to be affected by societal uncertainty. Such uncertainty is most marked where every action is scrutinized by lawyers who represent other stakeholders. But societal uncertainty can be manifested in other ways. For example, respect for government agencies may be low, or individualism may be carried to extremes, either among the public or among leaders in major institutions.

Institutional uncertainty is brought about when agencies withhold information for bureaucratic reasons. It is most likely to be high in circumstances where there are difficulties about informal communication, acquaintance, and trust among personnel of agencies with different traditions and missions. This ensures that the necessary channels of understanding and confidence are absent during a crisis. Institutional uncertainty can be high even in relatively consensual societies, if there happens to be a tradition of bureaucratic secrecy.

When the parameters of confidentiality are strained, *proprietary* uncertainty becomes salient. Thus, in the midst of an emergency there may be a debate about the rights of persons to know, to warn, or to conceal.

Scientific uncertainty is the last (but by no means the least important) type of uncertainty. It is mobilized at various phases of hazard including before, during, and after emergencies. For example, (scientific) risk assessments that are undertaken well in advance of a crisis may employ long-established techniques to evaluate industrial plants and equipment but may have to depend on less-seasoned methodologies to analyse the transport of environmental pollutants (Funtowicz and Ravetz 1990). When a hazard is in the acute (emergency) phase, the possibility of effective forecasting may be either good or poor, depending on the circumstances (which themselves cannot always be predicted). Thus, scientific uncertainty can vary from low to very high.

Two sets of strategies (table 4.3) are available for communication of uncertainty, one of which is an attribute of people or agencies that make decisions; the other refers to the way in which communication is accomplished. Some people may decide to *suppress* information about uncertainty entirely, even from themselves. This may translate into a refusal to admit that uncertainty exists or a failure to notice it. It is an extreme form of *discounting*. Ordinary discounting will recognize a possibility but (as with many events in the distant future) will assign such a low value to its salience that it can be neglected for policy purposes. *Recognition* of an uncertain contingency is a balanced appreciation. By contrast, *amplification* is an emphasis – perhaps even an overemphasis – of the significance of uncertainty.

Corresponding to the interpretations are the policies concerning communication of uncertainties. At one extreme lies *secrecy*, the extreme case of *confidentiality*; then comes *publicity*, with its own extreme form – *sharing*. There are many variations and nuances in any practical policy of communication. The utility of these classification schema can be illustrated with reference to the Seveso disaster, the Seveso Directive, and the *Karin B* incident.

Modelling the Seveso disaster

At the time of the Seveso disaster, the complexity of communication problems under conditions of severe uncertainty was recognized, if not fully managed. Before the gas release, no one outside the plant – neither residents nor political or health authorities – had any idea that there was a hazard of such magnitude. The explosion and release were greeted by incredulity, followed by alarm and dismay. The firm's initial behaviour led to subsequent suspicion about their motives; various instructions for precautionary measures were issued almost immediately, but the firm denied knowledge of the toxic substances involved (Rocca 1980; Rocca 1992, personal communication). Ten days passed before the firm confirmed that dioxin had been released (Pocchiari, Silano, and Zapponi 1987). Only then did the governmental authorities and the public learn that there was a grave risk. Even so, it was impossible to assess the danger with any precision. There was an onset of genuine dread, about illness in general and about malformed babies in particular. The widespread illness and deaths of animals of many species was an ominous sign. The authorities had their own severe problems of decision-making under uncertainty, including the definition of different polluted zones, programmes of evacuation of endangered residents, and disposal of contaminated material.

From the very beginning of the disaster, situational uncertainty was salient; decisions had to be taken, sometimes under conditions of great urgency, in the nearly complete absence of information that might guide actions. Scientific uncertainty was salient, as shown by the fact that local investigating magistrates closed off the site within eight days of the accident. Societal uncertainty was severe because there had been no previous institutional preparation or consultation for the accident. Legal/moral uncertainty was also severe. For example, the (Swiss) Technical Director of ICMESA found himself under arrest when he attended a works meeting 12 days after the accident (the Director of Production was also placed under arrest at that time, and was assassinated by terrorists four years later). One of the few relatively straightforward aspects of the accident was the low level of proprietary uncertainty. Although the provision of relevant information did not proceed as quickly or smoothly as desired by all, at least there was no need for the government authorities to use legal means to force the firm to divulge information. The fact that the ICMESA factory was already sequestered would have made it highly imprudent for its owners to withhold information about the contaminants, and it was noted at the time that the dioxin threat had already been publicized by the media before it was officially confirmed. Later, and off the Seveso site, proprietary uncertainty was not as low, particularly in connection with the disposal of barrels containing toxic materials. From 1982 onwards, stories of concealment and blunders began to circulate and these have not yet ended (see Chronology).

Modelling the Seveso Directive

Our model of uncertainty management is also reflected in the regulations of the Seveso Directive. The main concern here is with communication:

Member States shall ensure that information on safety measures and on the correct behaviour to adopt in the case of an accident is supplied in an appropriate manner, and without their having to request it, to persons liable to be affected by the major accident originating in a notified industrial activity within the meaning of Article 5. The information should be repeated and updated at appropriate intervals. It shall also be made publicly available. Such information shall contain that laid down in Annex VII. (Article 8 of Directive 88/610/EEC, amending Directive 82/501/EEC)

This portion of the Directive reflects concerns about several sorts of uncertainty. First, there is an attempt to institute progressive reduction of scientific uncertainty via updating requirements. Second, the various phrases that call for effective implementation of the public's right to know show clear awareness of the need to confront problems of institutional uncertainty and proprietary uncertainty. Moreover, the very existence of the Directive, particularly Article 8, underscores heightened awareness of legal/moral uncertainty, for the Seveso event showed that simple "accidents," or "acts of God," are not the most important problems affecting the safety of industrial installations and surrounding communities.

When we consider the implementation of the hazard communication requirements of Article 8, we find that the model illuminates practice. First, actual EC regulations seem to assume that societal and institutional uncertainties are not salient or severe. Nor do they deal with the possibility of situational uncertainty (i.e. less than complete competence of available official expertise for prediction, prevention, or control). The contrast between European and American practice is noteworthy. In the United States, provision is often made for the inclusion of alternative expertise via environmental legislation that permits the use of public funds for the incorporation of local citizens' knowledge into the policy discourse on the grounds of due process or fairness.

Modelling the *Karin B* incident

Finally, the model can also be applied to the *Karin B* incident. Some 12 years after the Seveso gas release, a shipload of Italian industrial toxic wastes was first dumped in Nigeria and then reloaded after protests. In the full glare of publicity and widespread public dread, the regions of Emilia-Romagna and Tuscany undertook the final task of disposal, in the process showing how a large quantity of mixed toxic wastes could be managed, with full satisfaction of technical requirements and local concerns.

Between the time that the *Karin B* was discovered to be carrying a toxic cargo and the eventual agreement on destruction of the wastes, all uncertainties were effectively out of control. Whoever knew about such shipments had previously kept them secret; when they were discovered, therefore, all the issues of knowledge, uncertainty, and responsibility came into play simultaneously. However, when the regional authorities of Emilia-Romagna and Tuscany – together with several local authorities – finally took physical possession of the wastes, the change was dramatic. Acting in cooperation with each other and with the media, and creating opportunities for the participation of interested communities, they were able to reduce salient uncertainties, starting with the scientific ones and then proceeding to others, such as institutional uncertainties. The societal uncertainties became less severe and less salient, and the clean-up operation proceeded peacefully to a successful conclusion in all respects (Centro Informativo Karin B 1992; Egidi 1993).

A moral paradox

Health and safety have recently joined goodness, truth and justice among the pantheon of Western culture's root ideals. Moreover, better health and safety have become prominent public goals, precisely because there seem to be real possibilities for achieving them. Unfortunately, none of these ideals is unambiguous: all are characterized by internal contradictions that may generate either fruitful or destructive outcomes.

In the debates on risks in the 1970s, it gradually emerged that "safe" does not mean zero-risk. Just as an empirical proposition may be accepted as true and later proven false (e.g. the Ptolemaic system of the world), or an action apparently good later becomes judged to be bad, similarly an installation accepted as safe may later explode. But the reverse does not hold: if there is an explosion, it is not a simple refutation of the judgement "safe." This is an example of the principle that allows people to continue believing that flying in airplanes is "safe," even though there are occasional crashes.

These and similar contradictions associated with the concept of safety are managed pragmatically by a variety of devices. One of these is linguistic interpretation. "Safe" can mean that risk is variously "negligible," "acceptable," "tolerable," "in accordance with best (or even standard) practice," or "unavoidable." Many of these interpretations are equivalent to the legal meaning of "non-culpable" risks. The pragmatic interpretation that is invoked will depend on circumstances.

In spite of the fact that many experts and critics are aware of the dialectical character of safety, most public discussions reflect the belief that an objective condition of safety is obtainable with just a little more application and honest effort. When such expectations are disappointed, critics seek explanations in simplistic theories that usually involve misguided or malevolent parties. Academics are just as prone to this behaviour as others. An important recent example was the use of "cultural theory" by certain social scientists to explain why Americans apparently considered that environmental safety had declined during the 1970s despite considerable progress in pollution control. This explanation was based on a fourfold model of social psychological ideal types of people, in relation to their social groups. For example, environmentalists of all sorts were labelled "sectarians" and were said to possess a romantic cosmology that derived from the psychological contradictions of supposedly closed and egalitarian millenarian groups (Douglas and Wildavsky 1982). In our terms, Douglas and Wildavsky had become partially aware of the contradictions in the ideal of safety, and realized that it is not reducible to numbers. Yet they could not move on to accommodate the contradictions by means of practical measures for realizing safety in the face of real hazards (Funtowicz and Ravetz 1985).

The Seveso Directive provides an important and relevant example of the contradictory character of safety. Article 8 of the Directive is based on the assumption that openness on the part of firms and authorities is good for safety. Clearly, policies of concealment can be very bad for safety. But it is questionable that perfect openness leads to perfect safety. Let us consider what might have happened if the Seveso Directive had been in place in 1976; this is an imaginary, counterfactual case, which cannot be used for the logical proof of a thesis but which can be a useful heuristic device.

The Directive as a whole demands certain sorts of institutional behaviour, in return for which it provides a certification of quality of performance. In simple terms, if an installation meets the Directive's criteria it is deemed "safe." Suppose, now, that the Seveso regulations had been in force in July 1976. Then the ICMESA factory would have previously submitted its safety report and we suppose, further, that there would have been no objections to it. The local population and the authorities would have been provided with some information about the chemical processes and their hazards. Presumably, knowledge of the earlier accidents involving TCP would have been in the public domain. Also, there would have been some emergency procedures in place. Now, supposing that, in spite of all the available information, the explosion had still happened, what would have ensued? First, it is likely that there would not have been a delay of 10 days before dioxin was publicly identified, nor another 10 days lost before there was any clarity about what to do. Would it have helped the community response, for this information to have been known instantly?

There would doubtless have been a more speedy evacuation and, therefore, probably less exposure of the affected human population. But would there have been less trauma (Conti 1977; Edelstein 1988) resulting from the sight of dead and dying animals and from the evacuation, or less dread from the unknown consequences of the invisible poison, or less of a stigma associated with Seveso and its population and products (see Chronology, July 1977)? Probably not.

However, as we have remarked, it was the relatively successful recovery from the accident that enabled Seveso to become an uncomplicated symbol of successful response to industrial disasters. The contrast with Bhopal and Chernobyl is striking. Of course, there was an early period characterized by the recriminations and accusations of incompetence and cover-up that commonly afflict such victim communities. This aggravation reached its height about six months after the Seveso gas release, when little remedial work was under way and the regional government proposed to install an incinerator in the district. Since then there have been periods of lesser and greater tension, mainly associated with the use by others of Seveso as a symbol; but suspicions about the behaviour of the company and the authorities seem never to go away.

In the context of such heightened tensions, Seveso became a microcosm where all the existing conflicts within society (political, institutional, religious, industrial) were reflected. However, within a relatively short time such conflicts abated and the recovery of the community proceeded. For, in Seveso, blame was never at issue: the responsible party was known from the outset and soon offered reparation. Moreover, the eventual disappearance of the offending factory itself and the physical exportation of the toxic substances and polluted soil enabled the community to feel cleansed. The resolution of the emotional after-effects of the trauma, so necessary for the recovery of a community, was facilitated by these favourable circumstances.

All these achievements, which made Seveso a symbolic example of recovery from industrial disaster, depended on the construction of a working relationship between the community, the government agencies, and the firm. This was accomplished through open and sometimes bitter struggle among the various parties, but the common interest in a reasonable outcome was never in question. The victims knew that they would receive assistance. Had there been uncertainty and strife about the source, amount, and timing of *compensation*, the communities would not have been able to pull themselves together as they did within a year and a half, once the threat of malformed babies receded and evacuees were returned to their homes. Instead, we can imagine a permanent state of mistrust between the different governmental agencies and companies and, indeed, within the communities themselves, where the processes of recovery would have been seriously inhibited. Histories of recovery from other disasters, both natural and man-made, show how important are these factors in the political and moral spheres (Barton 1969; Erikson 1976; Couch and Kroll-Smith 1991).

Now we must ask, if a firm had already been in compliance with safety regulations of the kind later required by the Seveso Directive, would its response have been different? Suppose that a firm's legal advice was that its prior compliance with all regulations decreased its responsibility for the accident and hence its liability for compensation. It is a commonplace of the theory of regulation that the submission of firms to the financial costs of external regulation is compensated by the legal protection they receive for compliance.

All we need to imagine is a case where a firm's top management would have decided against total acquiescence in the picture of the disaster and its aftermath as presented by the local community and authorities. That would have been enough to slow down the reparations. But it was the unprecedented speed of compensation offers, along with acceptance of blame and contribution to rehabilitation, that made all the difference to the recovery of Seveso. Otherwise, there could have been the protracted litigation that occurs in so many such cases and which causes psychological and moral harm, ultimately inhibiting the healing processes of recovery.

Thus, we encounter a moral paradox illuminated by Seveso: *more effective prior safety regulation could conceivably have prevented the achievement of the best path to the subsequent recovery of a community.* Once an accident has occurred, the cleansing of resentment and guilt, which are experienced by agents and victims each in their own way, could be inhibited by a denial of moral liability. The paradox can be expressed as an ill effect of a good principle: *prior regulation, with openness of information, could lead to a confusion concerning responsibility after the event.* Such paradoxes are familiar to those managing hazards of various sorts in the insurance field; thus "moral hazard" refers to the tendency of people to take chances once they know that the insurers will pay; and the "no fault" principle for common accidents, while seeming to exculpate the responsible persons, is promoted as being useful in preventing the expenses and injustices of litigation.

A scientific paradox

Seveso also produced a paradox about the use of scientific knowledge in the policy process. Although there was undoubted physical and psychological illness among people, together with the deaths of many animals, dread consequences for human health have been elusive (Mastroiacovo et al. 1988; Regione Lombardia 1989; Mocarelli et al. 1991). In this respect it could be said that Seveso is a disaster that has not yet produced identifiable disastrous consequences. Even the most recent epidemiological results, while showing an increase in some

105

sorts of rare cancers, do not provide firm evidence for a generally increased cancer risk to the monitored population (Bertazzi et al. 1993)

In the Seveso case, dread was associated with the perceived toxicity of dioxin. Once it was realized that the population had been subjected to dioxin contamination, the accident became, by definition, a disaster with severe psychological, social, and economic effects. However, in this case, scientific certainty about the extreme toxicity of dioxin gradually dissipated. No established scientists have argued that Seveso's population continues to suffer significant health effects.[7] So the recent accusations (Chronology 1992, 1993) that dioxin was a component of the factory's production would, paradoxically again, amount to evidence that the substance was less toxic to humans than was initially believed.

A visitor to Seveso now finds a park where the factory once stood; some say that Seveso is now the least polluted place in Italy. Of course, the history of illness, dread, and disruption cannot be undone. But the recovery of the community proceeded smoothly; only the stigma of the town's name survives as a present source of harm. So Seveso has become, simultaneously, a symbol of an industrial disaster and a monument to relevant ignorance in science (Keynes 1921). But such ignorance is not absolute and it need not be paralysing for decision-making. At Seveso, monitoring continues, and the lessons of this relevant ignorance are being assimilated into our understanding of the place of science in the modern world.

Seveso now functions partly as an experiment, along with other monitored disaster sites such as Hiroshima. Data from the affected Seveso population are used as evidence in other, less straightforward, pollution cases and also for the ongoing review of regulations. Every experiment exists in a particular context, and inferences from its data depend on an assumption of similarity between the experimental set-up and that of the other case in question (Funtowicz, MacGill, and Ravetz 1989a, 1989b, 1989c). The extent to which Seveso, with its single event of atmospheric contamination (and later contact with contaminated objects), is an appropriate model for situations of long and continuous contamination will be debated among scientists and policy makers.

Toxicology necessarily makes inferential leaps – from animals to humans, from large doses to small, and from acute to chronic doses. In turn, these inferences underlie the dose–response models that are used to define "safe limits." Thus, toxicological models have large inherent uncertainties, and large-scale accidents with good subsequent monitoring can provide less unrealistic sources of data (Funtowicz and Ravetz 1995).[8]

The very classic status of Seveso as a dioxin disaster could possibly lead to the use of its data in a paradoxical way. As we have seen, Seveso was an immediately perceived disaster, but one where the long-term health consequences have up to now been accepted as far from disastrous. We may be tempted to make a simple inference: Seveso was a harmless dioxin disaster; therefore, other dioxin releases need not be harmful. Such an argument was recently made in Arkansas, where the evidence of Seveso has been used in arguments supporting the safety of a proposed toxic waste incinerator that would emit dioxin in a similar quantity to that estimated for Seveso (Schneider 1992). Thus, we have the scientific paradox of Seveso: *an event at first accepted as a disaster (with great consequences for regulatory policy) is now being used as evidence for safety.* The symbol of Seveso may now be becoming increasingly complex: its original connotation of dread is challenged by one of reassurance. Paradoxically, the excellence of the recovery of Seveso could be used for the assertion of limited liability, with possible consequences for litigation and impeded recovery elsewhere.

However, as scientists know, it needs only a single long-delayed pathological condition to appear in the monitoring process for the original negative resonance of Seveso to be restored. And then the recovery of Seveso, apparently so complete at this time, could suddenly be thrown into question. Even the complete absence of conclusive evidence of cancer among chloracne victims and others in the most exposed zone A might be explained in terms of "the small population size, youth of the subjects, and short follow-up period" (Bertazzi et al. 1993)

Industrial accidents, industrial society, and recovery

Since the 1970s, a number of serious industrial accidents have provoked a reappraisal of safety issues. First, it was realized that even apparently unique industrial disasters have regular causes; in one sense they are all "man-made" (Turner 1978) because of the way they occur through failure of systems for prevention. A more radical interpretation, derived from a study of Three Mile Island, is that they are actually "normal accidents" (Perrow 1984). The affected industries, while not planning such accidents, accept them as a normal aspect of operations. We can even consider industrial systems as "accident generating systems" (Haastrup and Funtowicz 1992), routinely producing unwanted outputs along with their intended products; these include continuous pollution and wastes, along with occasional incidents of different intensities. When an incident goes beyond a certain threshold (defined conventionally by the terms of relevant regulations) it is deemed to be an "accident," and some accidents eventually become disasters. But, as the Seveso case shows, even a "disaster" has strongly conventional elements in its definition and response (Susman, O'Keefe, and Wisner 1983; Quarantelli 1987). Thus, our comprehension of industrial risks has moved completely away from the acausal or "acts of God" approach; they are creations of the industrial system as much as its intended products.

This new awareness about industrial risks has coincided with an increasing concern for the perceived loss of environmental quality due to the synergistic effects of technological development and environmental processes, as in the cases of acid rain and global warming. We now appreciate that the technological system is global, complex, and rather tightly coupled. The dividing line between the "goods" and the "bads" produced by the system is sinuous and indistinct. Implementation of this ecological awareness in industrial and regulatory practice is now under way.

The new ecological awareness includes an appreciation not only of the interconnectedness of the effects of the "bads" of the industrial system but also of the conventional character of the traditional distinction between "man-made" and "natural." Industrial accidents, and recovery from them, cannot be seen in isolation from the pathologies of the total industrial system, itself a subsystem of the planet. Contradictions within that subsystem, and between it and other components of the total system, are the key to its comprehension. Thus, famine and floods (for example) may now be no different in kind from the sudden events called industrial accidents and disasters.

To understand the processes of recovery from such unwanted events we must conceive of them as occurring within that total system. In the case of industrial disasters, the recovery of a community takes place not only in the societal sphere but also in its moral dimensions and, equally importantly, in its ecological aspects as well. Thus, community recovery exists as part of a wider process, involving all the elements of the total ecosystem.

Seveso's recovery was dependent on the special character of the incident itself and especially on the response of the firm and the authorities. Seveso was especially fortunate, not merely because the damage occurred over a short time rather than a protracted period but also because the factory at Meda could be dispensed with. Other classic industrial disasters, such as Chernobyl and Bhopal, involved installations which, although themselves taken out of service, belong to a class that is kept in operation – even in the same locality. In such cases the hazard is chronic and there is no escape from the relevant pathologies of the industrial system.

Conclusion: "Seveso" – A paradoxical symbol

"Seveso" (the event as it has passed into myth) contains paradox and contradiction. At the outset, the dominating factor was dread, because of the possibility of economic and personal devastation caused by an unclean invisible agent – the dioxin that had defoliated Viet Nam. But, as the possibility of malformed babies subsided, dread gave way to a reassertion of community. In spite of this local success, Seveso remained a symbol of calamity: the European Community Directive is known by it, and even the notifiable sites are informally named after it. Thus, the symbol remains potent, figuratively and legally, outside Seveso itself while, inside, the visible traces of the accident have been disappearing.

But, as the recovery continues, the paradoxes of Seveso provide new lessons for reflection about future policy. The moral paradox relates to the institutional aspects of the accident: had there been some regulatory framework, whereby the firm's liability for the accident could have been absolved, there is a chance that the firm's response would not have been so appropriate. The moral basis of recovery could then have been severely impaired and the subsequent history not so encouraging. However, if it turns out that the parent company was actually confessing to a lesser sin (an avoidable accident) in order to conceal a greater one (production of chemical weapons), then the paradoxes in the Seveso experience will have become very complex indeed.

The scientific paradox continues to have its effects, through uncertainty about the effects of dioxin. With the continued absence of conclusive evidence of illness, almost twenty years afterwards, the lesson of the Seveso disaster has been reversed. Now a new message is conveyed by Seveso – one of reassurance that low-level dioxin contamination is, after all, innocuous. Of course, this optimism will last only as long as there is an absence of recorded health effects, and it is susceptible to modification in light of periodic reports from the ongoing monitoring programme.

It would be incorrect to interpret these paradoxes simplistically and then to write off Seveso as yet another notorious disaster that did not really happen. There is now a powerful reaction against the prophets of imminent ecological doom: apparent false alarms are being used as proof that our high-technology culture can absorb and recover from all sorts of disasters, industrial as well as natural.

An ecological awareness that connects industry with its environment – societal as much as natural – teaches that "disaster" and "recovery" are each total events. It is no longer possible to "externalize" the costs of consumer society. The various traditional "sinks" have become finite and reactive. There is now nothing "outside" the global industrial system, which predominantly serves a fortunate fraction of the world's people. Seveso is truly a paradoxical and contradictory symbol; to interpret it simplistically, either for alarm or for reassurance, would be a serious error, for history and for policy.

Acknowledgements

We wish to thank the persons listed below for providing very useful insights, information, and materials regarding their participation in the Seveso case: C. Galbiati, L. Meazza, P. Mocarelli, L. Noè, F. Rocca, N. Sbrissa, R. Vannucci. Also R. Peckham of the JRC-Ispra for figure 4.2.

Chronology

1976

Saturday 10 July. In building B of the ICMESA factory located in Meda, an increase in pressure due to an exothermic reaction in the TCP vessel causes the rupture disk of the safety valve to burst. As a consequence, a toxic cloud escapes into the air.

Sunday 11 July (accident day +1). ICMESA managers inform local authorities of the escape of a "cloud of herbicide that causes harm to agriculture" (Ufficio speciale ... 1984). They state that "in all likelihood the aerosol mixture which escaped consists of sodium trichlorphenate, caustic soda and solvent, but possibly other toxic substances as well" (*Roche Magazin* 1986) and they request the authorities to warn the population. Samples are sent by courier for examination in Switzerland.

12 July (+2). Nearby residents are warned not to eat any vegetables from their gardens.

14 July (+4). First symptoms on skin of children, and deaths of small animals. According to Roche (*Roche Magazin* 1986: 10), Dr. Sambeth, the Technical Director of Givaudan in Geneva, informs von Zwehl, the Technical Director of ICMESA, that the samples contain traces of TCDD. Authorities will be informed only much later.

15 July (+5). The factory workers are examined by the factory doctor. The Mayor of Seveso issues "Ordinanza 43," on the basis of indications by the Deputy Health Officer, declaring as contaminated the area to the south of the ICMESA factory (about 12 hectares and 200 residents). Warning signs and fences are to be erected. The Mayor of Meda issues a similar decree. Dr. Giuseppe Reggiani, Director of Clinical Research at Roche Basle, is instructed by the management of Roche to investigate the possible effects of the accident on workers and population and to take necessary measures. During a first meeting in the Municipio (Town Hall), ICMESA managers show maps, but are generally reticent.

16 July (+6). Increasing skin reactions: 13 children hospitalized. The LPIP (Laboratorio provinciale di igiene e profilassi) begins to collect vegetable samples for analysis. The Mayor of Seveso informs *Il Giorno*, a national newspaper. During a meeting in the Municipio, the ICMESA managers show new maps, indicating concentrations which they judge below the danger threshold for humans (Rocca 1980). They claim ignorance of the substance involved. Factory workers mobilize and accuse authorities of hiding facts. The local prefecture (representing the national government) is called in by the Mayor; they support his actions.

17 July (+7). First articles in the national press based in Milan (*Il Giorno, Corriere della Sera*). According to Roche accounts, the ICMESA Technical Director announces the release of dioxin (*Roche Magazin* 1986: 12). According to other sources, this information was delivered a few days later (see below, Pocchiari, Silano, and Zapponi 1987).

18 July (+8). The investigating magistrates seal building B of ICMESA, where the accident occurred. The Mayor of Meda orders that all other buildings are sealed as well. First news of the accident on television.

19 July (+9). For the first time, Givaudan admits that TCDD was found, in notification to local authorities (Pocchiari, Silano, and Zapponi 1987).

20 July (+10). In Geneva, Givaudan makes a public statement on the accident and the Givaudan chemists confirm, to the public health doctors caring for the children, that TCDD was found; they send a map showing where dioxin was found. The Mayor of Seveso hears for the first time that dioxin may be involved. This comes from a television journalist who was informed by a doctor at a research institute in Milan. In the evening this was confirmed by the Health Officer, who had gone to Zurich to get information. He decides not to release this information at the meeting that same evening in the Municipio (Rocca 1980).

21 July (+11). Banner headlines in the newspapers. The Technical Director and the Director of Production of ICMESA are arrested. The public health doctors inform the prefecture of Milan, who call a meeting with the Regional Health Department for 24 July. According to *Roche Magazin* (1986: 12), Dr. Reggiani contacts other companies that had accidents with dioxin and recommends evacuation to the Italian authorities. The Head of the Regional Health Department is reluctant. First official press release from the Lombardy Region. The Milan Province offers assistance; subsequently they are put in charge of decontamination.

22 July (+12). Eighty children from Seveso are sent away to a holiday camp belonging to the province. A census of all dead animals is ordered. A dermatological clinic is opened in Seveso to monitor exposed people.

23 July (+13). Dr. Reggiani has the first meeting with the authorities, including the Head of the Regional Health Department. With the Mayor of Seveso, he insists on an evacuation (*Roche Magazin* 1986: 12). For the first time, the mayors of Desio and Cesano Maderno are involved (Rocca 1980).

24 July (third week). First meeting at the Lombardy regional government office, chaired by the Head of the Regional Health Department, with experts, civil servants, and scientists of the Region, along with those of the LPIP, the national Ministry of Health, the ISS (Istituto Superiore della Sanità), and a representative of Givaudan. The so-called zone A (more than 50 micrograms of TCDD per square metre), about 15 hectares, was defined for evacuation, fencing-off, and prohibited entry. (Later, zone A was further divided into seven subzones according to the severity of contamination. The evacuated people often violated the zone, and on two occasions, in October and December, reoccupied their homes.) First public meeting.

26 July. Local authorities with the aid of armed forces accomplish the evacuation of 225 people (170 from Seveso, 55 from Meda). Following new laboratory results, it was decided to extend the evacuation zone, enlarging the area to 71.8 hectares. Approximately 3,300 animals died. Many others will eventually be slaughtered, a total of 81,000.

28 July. The Regional Health Department establishes four committees of scientific and technical experts to investigate different aspects of the accident. Their tasks are to define health problems and define measures for protection of public health; to define procedures for data, sampling, and interpretation; to study decontamination measures; and to investigate causes of animal deaths.

29 July. The contamination zone is further extended to 108 hectares and a total of 730 people are evacuated; 198 families are temporarily housed in two "residences" in the suburbs of Milan and in hotels and private houses in the vicinity of the affected area.

2 August (fourth week). Following further tests, a second zone (B) is defined (between 5 and 50 micrograms per square metre), comprising about 270 hectares in the municipalities of Cesano Maderno and Desio. Regional authorities decree that children under 12 and pregnant women within the third month should not stay in the affected area during the day. Strict rules are issued on food and water consumption. All productive activities are suspended in zone B. Health authorities give consent to abortion, in spite of its illegality at the time. Therapeutic abortion was allowed in special cases, including pregnancies that would be psychologically traumatic for the mother, following the judgement of the Constitutional Court no. 27 of 18 February 1975. (This case was later used politically in the debate that resulted in the law 194 of 1988, which legalized abortion, later confirmed by a popular referendum in 1981.)

4 August. The President of the Italian Council of Ministers nominates a governmental technical–scientific commission, to explore possible decontamination measures. It will be known as "Commissione Cimmino," after its Chairman.

5 August. First regional legislation to aid the affected population.

10 August (second month). The Italian government grants a loan of 40 billion liras to the region to finance necessary measures (it was raised to 115 billion in 1978).

11 August. In a press conference in Geneva, Roche commits itself to cover the costs of the damage.

13 August. The regional government sets up the Giovanardi Commission, which is to implement the proposals of the national Cimmino Commission.

14 August. The Cimmino Commission recommends the establishment of a third zone (R; 1400 hectares), where levels of contamination are below 5 micrograms per square metre.

15 August. The Regional Health Department completes the mapping of the affected zones. The epidemiological monitoring was extended to five more municipalities (Lentate sul Seveso, Seregno, Varedo, Muggiò, Nova Milanese), for a total of 220,000 inhabitants. First cases of chloracne (there would eventually be 193, some very serious, taking years to clear, with permanent scars).

August–December. Several measures for decontamination are suggested and attempted (e.g. spreading of olive oil preparations on contaminated lots). The region studies the possibility of constructing a high-temperature incinerator in the area. The affected communities react angrily: the region joins Givaudan as the enemies to be fought by local residents. An agreement is reached between Lombardy and Givaudan for removal and disposal of chemicals and raw materials from the factory. The ICMESA workers are re-employed in the area.

1977

January (six months after disaster). Decontamination work begun, to enable resumption of productive activities: removal of leaves, grass, and agricultural produce. Decontamination of schools. Hydrological studies; studies of incineration plant. Experimental studies for rehabilitation of buildings in zones furthest from ICMESA. Holidays and financial aid for special classes: children, pregnant women, elderly people.

February. First compensation payments made by ICMESA to private individuals.

Spring. Public protest about unorthodox methods of cleaning adopted by Milan Province; much pressure on President of province (Rocca 1980).

June. The region sets up the Ufficio Speciale di Seveso (Special Bureau for Seveso), located first in Seveso, then in Milan. It is responsible for putting the five action programmes into practice. (Closed in 1987, archive established in 1992.)

July (one year after disaster). Official promulgation of special legislation for Seveso (Regione Lombardia 1977), articulating five operational programmes: (1) analysis of soil, water, and vegetation plus measures for reclamation; (2) aid and medical monitoring programmes in the health sector; (3) social and educational aid; (4) rehabilitation of buildings; (5) aid for trade and industry.

Epidemiological monitoring programmes established as follows (with termination dates): abortions (1982); malformations (1982); tumours (1997); deaths (1997). Health monitoring of workers at ICMESA and on decontamination projects, and chloracne sufferers (1985).

Laboratory research undertaken, to improve knowledge of metabolic and toxic effects, for later development of health monitoring programmes.

Ghetti, Head of the Seveso Health Department, shot in the legs in a terrorist attack.

September. International Steering Committee established to assess toxicological and epidemiological data and findings of the monitoring programme. This was officially named "comitato dei garanti," as it represented international scientific authority and probity. Parliamentary Committee of Enquiry established.

October. Decontamination of zone A; return of first 511 evacuated persons.

Decision to demolish most heavily contaminated houses and to rebuild. Start of decontamination of zone B

1978

July (two years after disaster). Report by Parliamentary Committee of Enquiry, criticizing ICMESA and regional authorities. Settlements of private claims, the majority amicably, out of court.

1980

Decontamination continues. Zone R released for agricultural use. After long negotiations, an agreement between ICMESA, the Italian Government, and the Lombardy Region on the settlement of claims is signed. Poletti, the Director of Production at ICMESA at the time of the accident, is shot and killed in a terrorist attack. Disposal site in zone A approved by the Cimino Committee.

1981 (five years after disaster)

Out-of-court settlement with the municipalities of Desio and Cesano Maderno: ICMESA pays 1.45 and 2.85 billion liras, respectively. Preparation of plan for disposal of contaminated building B of ICMESA by ENEA (Italian state energy agency).

1982

June. Start of the mystery of the lost barrels of contaminated materials. According to *Roche Magazin* (1986: 18), they were eventually discovered in a barn in France.

September. Reactor where explosion occurred, emptied. Out-of-court settlement with Meda (ICMESA pays 1.3 billion liras).

1983

Out-of-court settlement with Seveso (ICMESA pays 15 billion liras).

1984

Health Report of the International Steering Committee: no human effects other than 193 cases of chloracne. Decontamination of zone A totally completed; zone B authorized for construction. Incineration of barrels begins in Switzerland; in the following year, officially said to be completed (see December 1992).

1985

Court of Appeals in Milan confirms criminal convictions of two of the five accused – the Director of ICMESA and the Technical Director of Givaudan. Demolition of the ICMESA premises, converted to a public park and community facilities.

1991 (15 years after disaster)

September. The newspaper *La Repubblica* (1991) reports a judgement by the civil court of Milan, requiring Givaudan to pay 2 million lira to each of 21 inhabitants of the zones B and R, for their material and psychological injuries. The plaintiffs belonged to a committee called "5d," composed of 300 citizens who were initially excluded by the courts from the civil suit for damages because they had not suffered material harm. They were disappointed by the amount awarded and will appeal. But they are satisfied by the court's acceptance of the principle that any exposed person is potentially entitled to damages. The court's judgement states: "The exposure to an unknown quantity of dioxin, the restrictions on liberty of actions and of life, the oppressive public-health measures, all constitute causes for disturbance and moral damage." Their advocate had argued that they had suffered inconvenience and distress caused by the discrimination they had experienced merely because they were from Seveso.

1992

December. The newspaper *Il Corriere della Sera* (1992) reports on a documentary on German television channel "Ard." They spoke of 150 tons (336,000 lb) of dioxin-contaminated material that had been put in a dump in Schoenberg, in the former East Germany, by the Italian firm Mannesmann, and which were described in the documents as "sodium chloride," or salt. According to the German television programme, the supposed destruction in Switzerland was only a diversion. The region of Mecklenburgh-Pomerania, where Schoenberg is located, has started an enquiry, requesting the participation of the Italian and French authorities.

1993

March. The newspaper *Il Corriere della Sera* (Magni 1993) reports that 850 citizens of the contaminated area have started legal procedures against Givaudan in order to be compensated for "moral and biological" damage.

November. On the initiative of the regional Director for the Environment, the Lombardy regional government nominates a Commission of Enquiry, with powers to re-examine the Seveso archives, with special reference to three issues. The first is the amount of dioxin released: it was generally accepted that some 200–300 grams were emitted, but even at the time some experts spoke of much higher quantities, even 40 kg or more. The second point concerns the 41 barrels: the official story that they had been burned in Basle has been questioned by the discovery of a stock of similar barrels in a site in Schoenberg. Third, what was ICMESA really producing? This question may be very difficult to answer.

Notes

1. ICMESA (Industrie Chimiche Meridionali Società Azionaria) was originally established in Naples during 1921, but its plant there was destroyed during World War II. In 1946 a new plant was opened in Meda, and the company's name was changed to "Industrie Chimiche Meda Società Azionaria" (thereby preserving the old acronym). At the time of the gas release, ICMESA employed 163 people. It was believed that the factory produced "intermediates" – chemicals used in the production of perfumes, flavourings, cosmetics, and pharmaceutical products. Recently, however, some doubt has been cast on whether production was exclusively in the civilian sector; the Region of Lombardy has set up a commission to investigate this and other obscure aspects of the Seveso case (see Chronology, November

1993). Givaudan SA, one of ICMESA's main customers, became a major shareholder in 1965 and took over the firm entirely four years later. From 1963, Givaudan's parent company was Hoffman-La Roche, a Basle-based multinational group. This group was founded in 1896 as a pharmaceutical concern, transformed in 1919 into a joint stock company, and eventually expanded its activities to include production of chemicals, perfumes, diagnostic instruments, and plant-protection products (*Roche Magazin* 1986).

2. As shown by the *Karin B* incident (see below), externalization of waste disposal is not inevitable in Italy or elsewhere.

3. The Flixborough explosion occurred on a rural site and resulted in 28 deaths and 36 injuries among the workforce. Outside the plant, 53 members of the public received major injuries and hundreds more sustained minor injuries. The plant was destroyed and close to two thousand houses, shops, and factories were damaged (Perrow 1984: 111). The legal frame for the implementation of the Seveso Directive in the UK (the so-called CIMAH regulations) is based on acts and actions taken according to the recommendations of the Flixborough accident investigations (Drogaris 1991: 1–2; see also Myers and Read 1992).

4. The Treaty of Paris (1951) established the European Coal and Steel Community (ECSC). The first Treaty of Rome (1957) established the European Economic Community (EEC), and the second Treaty of Rome (1957) set up the European Atomic Energy Community (Euratom). These three treaties, which are the legal basis of the European Community (EC), were originally signed by six countries – the Federal Republic of Germany (West Germany), Belgium, France, Italy, Luxembourg, and the Netherlands. Denmark, the United Kingdom, and Ireland joined the Community in 1973; Greece joined in 1981; and Portugal and Spain in 1986. The three original Communities (ECSC, EEC, Euratom) have been governed by a single Commission and a single Council since 1967. The European Parliament (originally called the Assembly) and the Court of Justice have been common to all three communities since 1958. In recent years, there have been moves toward converting what is now an economic union into a political one (e.g. the Maastricht Treaty), and the term European Community has been replaced by European Union.

5. New provisions for issuing and administering EC regulations have come into force since the Seveso Directive was adopted. In 1987, the European Single Act, which had been signed by the 12 Member States in the previous year, came into force, extending the Community's range of competencies and introducing changes in the relationships between EC institutions. In February 1992 the Member States signed the Maastricht Treaty on European Union, which "marks a new stage in the process of creating an ever closer union among the peoples of Europe, in which decisions are taken as closely as possible to the citizen" (*Treaty on European Union* 1992: Title I Common Provisions, article A). This new treaty substantially revised the Paris and Rome treaties, expanded their provisions on a number of matters, and redefined some of the tasks and relationships of the European institutions. The treaty includes a number of protocols, some establishing special conditions for particular countries.

6. Information that shall be provided to the public now includes the following:
   – full identification of the company and person giving the information;
   – explanation of industrial activities undertaken;
   – names and dangerous characteristics of substances and preparations;
   – nature of major accident hazards;
   – potential consequences of accidents on people and the physical environment;
   – existing safety measures and emergency plans, both on site and off site;
   – notice about the ways in which people will be warned and kept informed about accidents;
   – guidance about actions that should be taken in the event of an accident;
   – location of additional available information.

7. A recent anonymous news report in *Science* (10 September 1993, 261: 1383) indicates that elevated rates of several types of cancer have been found in the contaminated regions around Seveso. The researcher who uncovered this information intends to release the results of a 20-year follow-up study of Seveso residents that will, it is hoped, shed additional light on

these findings. The US Environmental Protection Agency has also issued an extensive review of evidence about dioxin that questions whether cancer is the main associated hazard but suggests that foetal harm and other effects may be much more prevalent. The overall conclusion is that part of dioxin's deadly reputation may no longer be justified but that there is increasing evidence for a "cascade" of non-cancerous health effects in people, possibly connected with trace contaminants in food (*New York Times*, 11 May 1994).
8. However, their interpretation is not unproblematic; the history of the Hiroshima data is an example of serious re-evaluation of basic parameters (Marshall 1992).

References

Baram, M. 1991. "Rights and duties concerning the availability of environmental risk information to the public." In: R.E. Kasperson and P.J.M. Stallen, eds. *Communicating Risks to the Public*. Dordrecht: Kluwer.

Barton, A.H. 1969. *Communities in Disaster: A Sociological Analysis of Collective Stress Situations*. Garden City, New York: Doubleday.

Bertazzi, P.A., A.C. Pesatori, D. Consonni, A. Tironi, M.T. Landi, and C. Zocchetti. 1993. "Cancer incidence in a population accidentally exposed to 2,3,7,8-tetra-chlorodibenzo-para-dioxin." *Epidemiology* 4(5): 398–406.

Centro Informativo Karin B. 1992. *Videotape* (T. Tartari director). Servizio Protezione Civile della Regione Emilia-Romagna.

Conti, L. 1977. *Visto da Seveso*. Milan: Feltrinelli.

Corriere della Sera 1992. "Diossina di Seveso ritrovata nell'ex Rdt." 12 December.

Couch S.R., and J.S. Kroll-Smith (eds.). 1991. *Communities at Risk*. New York: Peter Lang.

Council Directive of 24 June 1982 on the major accident hazards of certain industrial activities (82/501/EEC). *Official Journal of the European Communities* L 230, 5 August 1982.

Council Directive of 19 March 1987 amending Directive 82/501/EEC on the major accident hazards of certain industrial activities (87/216/EEC). *Official Journal of the European Communities* L 85, 28 March 1987.

Council Directive of 24 November 1988 amending Directive 82/501/EEC on the major accident hazards of certain industrial activities (88/610/EEC). *Official Journal of the European Communities* L 336, 7 December 1988.

Council Directive of 12 June 1989 concerning the introduction of measures to encourage improvements in the safety and health of workers at work (89/391/EEC). *Official Journal of the European Communities* L 183, 29 June 1989.

Council Directive of 27 November 1989 on information to the public concerning health protection measures and the behaviour to adopt in the event of a radioactive emergency (89/618/Euratom). *Official Journal of the European Communities* L 357, 7 December 1989.

Council Directive on the minimum safety and health requirements for the workplace (89/654/EEC). *Official Journal of the European Communities* L 393, 30 December 1989.

Council Directive of 23 April 1990 on the contained use of genetically modified micro-organisms (90/219/EEC). *Official Journal of the European Communities* L 117, 8 May 1990.

Council Directive of 7 June 1990 on the freedom of access to information of the environment (90/313/EEC). *Official Journal of the European Communities* L 158, 23 June 1990.

De Marchi, B. 1991a. "Public information about major accident-hazards: Legal requirements and practical implementation." *Industrial Crisis Quarterly* 5: 239–251.

———. 1991b. "The Seveso Directive: An Italian pilot study in enabling communication." *Risk Analysis* 11 (2): 207–215.

———, S.O. Funtowicz, and J.R. Ravetz. 1993. *The Management of Uncertainty in the Communication of Major Hazards.* EUR Report, Office for Official Publications of the European Communities, Luxembourg.

Douglas, M., and A. Wildavsky. 1982. *Risk and Culture: An Essay on the Selection of Technological and Environmental Dangers.* Berkeley: University of California.

Drogaris, G. 1991. "Controlling run-away reaction hazards within the framework of the Seveso Directive." *Technical Note* No. I.91.02, ISEI/SER 1977/91.

———. 1993. *Major Accident Reporting System. Lessons Learned from Accident Notified.* CDCIR, JRC, Commission of the European Communities, EUR 13385 EN, Office for Official Publications of the EC, Luxembourg.

Edelstein, M.R. 1988. *Contaminated Communities: The Social and Psychological Impacts of Residential Toxic Exposure.* Boulder: Westview.

Egidi, D. 1993. "Aspetti tecnici ed organizzativi della gestione commissariale dell'emergenza navi." In: *Proceedings of the National Conference Dall'emergenza navi al governo del ciclo dei rifiuti industriali,* Bologna, 11–13 June 1992.

Erikson, K. 1976. *Everything in Its Path. Destruction of Community in the Buffalo Creek Flood.* New York: Simon and Schuster.

Funtowicz, S.O., and J.R. Ravetz. 1985. "Three types of risk assessment." In: C. Whipple and V.T. Covello, eds. *Risk Analysis in the Private Sector.* New York: Plenum Press, pp. 217–231.

———, and ———. 1990. *Uncertainty and Quality in Science for Policy.* Dordrecht, Netherlands: Kluwer.

———, and ———. 1996. "Global risk, uncertainty, and ignorance." In: J.X. Kasperson and R.E. Kasperson, eds. *Global Environmental Risk.* Tokyo: United Nations University Press, forthcoming.

———, S.M. MacGill, and J.R. Ravetz. 1989a. "Quality assessment for radiological model parameters." *Journal of Radiological Protection* 9(4): 263–270.

———, ———, and ———. 1989b. "The management of uncertainty in radiological data." *Journal of Radiological Protection* 9(4): 257–261.

———, ———, and ———. 1989c. "The propagation of parameter uncertainties in radiological assessment models." *Journal of Radiological Protection* 9(4): 271–280.

Gambino, M., U. Gumpel, and S. Novelli. 1993. "L'nganno di Seveso. Che cosa c'era nel reattore. Inchiesta/Documenti su una catastrofe." *Avvenimenti* 20: 7–14.

Haastrup, P., and S.O. Funtowicz. 1992. "Accident generating systems and chaos: a dynamic study of accident time series." *Reliability Engineering and System Safety* 35: 31–37.

Hay, A. 1982. *The Chemical Scythe.* New York: Plenum.

Keynes, J.M. 1921. *A Treatise on Probability.* New York: St. Martin's Press, reprinted 1952.

Magni, V. 1993. "Seveso chiama giustizia." *Il Corriere della Sera,* 29 March.

Marshall, E. 1992. "Study casts doubt on Hiroshima data." *Science* 258: 394.

Mastroiacovo, P., A. Spagnolo, E. Marni, L. Meazza, R. Bertolini, and G. Segni. 1988. "Birth defects in the Seveso area after TCDD contamination." *Journal of the American Medical Association* 259: 1668–1672.

Mocarelli, P., A. Marocchi, P. Brambilla, P.M. Gerthoux, L. Colombo, A. Mondonico, and L. Meazza. 1991. "Effects of dioxin exposure in humans at Seveso, Italy." In: Banbury Report 35: *Biological Basis for Risk Assessment of Dioxin and Related Compounds*. Cold Spring Harbor, New York: Cold Spring Harbor Laboratory Press.

Myers, B., and P. Read. 1992. "Emergency planning and pollution." In: Malcolm Newson, Jeremy Barnes, Alan Davison, Terry Douglas, Ian Fells, David Harte, Mark Macklin, Bill Myers, Stan Openshaw, Paul Read, and Anthony Stevenson, eds. *Managing the Human Impact on the Natural Environment: Patterns and Processes*. London: Belhaven Press, pp. 196–210.

Organisation for Economic Co-operation and Development. 1989. *Accidents Involving Hazardous Substances*. *Environmental Monographs* No. 24. Paris: Organization for Economic Co-operation and Development.

———. 1990. *Atelier sur la Communication d'Informations au Public et le Rôle des Travailleurs dans la Prévention des Accidents et l'Intervention*. *Environmental Monographs* No. 29. Paris: Organization for Economic Co-operation and Development.

———. 1992. *Guiding Principles for Chemical Accident Prevention, Preparedness and Response*. *Environmental Monograph* No. 51. Paris: Organization for Economic Co-operation and Development.

Otway, H.H., and A. Amendola. 1989. "Major hazard information policy in the European Community: Implications for risk analysis." *Risk Analysis* 9: 505–512.

———, and B. Wynne. 1989. "Risk communication: Paradigm and paradox." *Risk Analysis* 9: 141–145.

Perrow, C. 1984. *Normal Accidents. Living with High-Risk Technologies*. New York: Basic Books.

Pocchiari, F., V. Silano, and G. Zapponi. 1987. "The Seveso accident and its aftermath." In: P. Kleindorfer and H. Kunreuther, eds. *Insuring and Managing Hazardous Risks: From Seveso to Bhopal and Beyond*. Berlin: Springer-Verlag, pp. 60–78.

Quarantelli, H.L. 1987. "What should we study? Questions and suggestions for researchers about the concept of disaster." *International Journal of Mass Emergencies and Disasters* 5: 7–32.

———. 1988. "Disaster crisis management: A summary of research findings." *Journal of Management Studies* 25: 373–385.

Regione Lombardia. 1977. *Bollettino Ufficiale* Anno VI, Supplemento straordinario al no. 28. Provvedimenti per Seveso 14 July 1977.

———. 1989. "Nota sui primi risulatati dello studio di Mortalità nell'area interessata dall'evento Icmesa." Settore Sanità e Igiene. Milan, 5 May (*Mimeo.*)

———. 1992. *Inventario dell'archivio dell' Ufficio speciale di Seveso*. Vols. 1 and 2. Milan.

Repubblica. 1991. "Vale due milioni l'incubo diossina." 19 September.

Rocca, F. 1980. *I giorni della diossina*. Supplemento a 'Quaderni Bianchi' no. 2/1980. Milan: Centro studi 'A. Grandi'.

Roche Magazin. 1986. *Ten Years After*. No. 27 (May).

Royal Society Study Group. 1992. *Risk Analysis Perception Management.* London: Royal Society.

Schneider, K. 1992. "Decision to burn dioxin divides Arkansas town." *New York Times*, 28 October.

Susman, P., P. O'Keefe, and B. Wisner. 1983. "Global disasters, a radical interpretation." In: K. Hewitt, ed. *Interpretations of Calamity*. Boston: Allen and Unwin, pp. 263–283.

Treaty on European Union. 1992. Luxembourg: Office for Official Publications of the European Communities.

Turner, B.A. 1978. *Man-Made Disasters*. London: Wykeham.

Ufficio speciale per i programmi della L.R. 17.01. 1977 no. 2, 1984. "L'evento Seveso al gennaio 1984." (*Mimeo.*)

Wynne, B. 1987. *Implementation of Article 8 of the Directive 82/501/EEC: A Study of Public Information*. Commission of the European Communities contract 86-B-6641-11-006-11N, Final Report.

Wynne, B. 1989. "Frameworks of rationality in risk management: Towards the testing of naïve sociology." In: J. Brown, ed. *Environmental Threats. Perception, Analysis and Management*. London: Belhaven Press, pp. 33–47.

5

Long-term recovery from the Bhopal crisis

Paul Shrivastava

Introduction

On the night of 2/3 December 1984, a major accident occurred in Bhopal, India, at a pesticide plant owned by the Union Carbide Corporation (Bogard 1989). This accident triggered a long-term industrial *crisis* for the entire population of Bhopal, for government agencies in India, and for the Union Carbide Corporation. Industrial crises are processes of severe disruption and harm that originate in industrial activities and technological systems. They affect people, property, and the natural environment. Communities, corporations, and government agencies are sometimes restructured in the wake of these crises.[1]

This chapter begins with a brief description of the Bhopal crisis. The second section discusses causes of the crisis in terms of antecedent conditions and accident-related failures. The third section describes a multiple-perspectives framework for understanding crisis recovery issues. In the subsequent three sections, crisis recovery is described from the perspectives of the primary stakeholders – the community and its victims, Union Carbide Corporation, and the Government of India. The final section includes speculations about long-term recovery from crisis and examines policy implications.

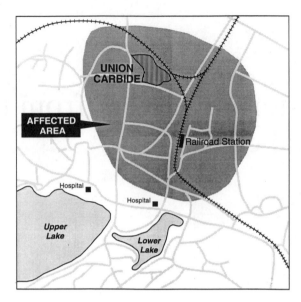

Fig. 5.1 **Bhopal, showing the area affected by the leakage of toxic gas (not to scale)**

The Bhopal toxic gas leak crisis

The Bhopal crisis was triggered by a technological accident: 45 tons (100,800 lb) of methyl isocyanate (MIC) gas escaped from two underground storage tanks at a Union Carbide pesticide plant. The accident occurred between 10 p.m. (2 December) and 1.30 a.m. (3 December) when the plant was on second shift and the surrounding population was asleep in slum "hutments" that are densely packed together in this part of Bhopal (fig. 5.1).

Leaked gases were trapped under a nocturnal temperature inversion in a shallow bubble that blanketed the city within five miles of the plant. Next morning, over 2,000 people were dead and 300,000 were injured. Another 1,500 people died in subsequent months owing to injuries caused by the accident. At least 7,000 animals perished but damage to the natural environment remains largely unassessed (Prasad and Pandey 1985).

Emergency services were completely overwhelmed and confusion was rampant in the affected neighbourhoods. Police instructed people to run away from the area, but many of those who did so inhaled large amounts of toxic MIC and succumbed to its effects. Residents were unaware that the simple act of covering their faces with wet cloths and lying indoors on the floor provided effective protection against the gas. That night, and in the days that followed, nearly 400,000 people fled the city in a haphazard and uncontrolled evacuation. Two weeks later, during government attempts to neutralize the plant's remaining MIC, another wave of mass flight involved 200,000 people (Shrivastava 1992; Diamond 1985; Morehouse and Subramaniam 1988).

To understand the causes of the larger crisis it is necessary to examine the antecedent conditions that set the stage for it, and the more proximate failures that directly caused the accident. Hazardous antecedent conditions and proximate failures occurred both inside Union Carbide and outside the company, in its social, economic, and political environments.

Antecedents and failures

Inside the plant

In 1934, Union Carbide Corporation set up a subsidiary company in India, known as Union Carbide (India) Ltd. (UCIL) (table 5.1a). This company's Bhopal facility was originally designed to formulate pesticides. The procedure involved buying stable ingredients locally, mixing them, and packaging them for sale to the government for use in an anti-malaria campaign.

In 1974, UCIL received a government licence to manufacture 50,000 tons of MIC-based pesticides each year; however, the market for these products was declining at the time, both because malaria was under control and because over 300 small manufacturing firms were now competing vigorously with UCIL (Dhingra 1978). Therefore, in a measure aimed at cutting costs, UCIL decided to manufacture key ingredients in its own plant instead of buying them from suppliers. In 1981 it established a plant to make MIC – a highly toxic and unstable chemical. In the next few years the agricultural pesticides market declined further because of poor weather and meagre crops.

By 1984, UCIL was ranked twenty-first in size among companies operating in India. It had revenues of Rs 2 billion (then equivalent to US$170 million). Fifty-one per cent of UCIL was owned by the parent company; remaining shares were held by 24,000 stockholders. Ten thousand people were employed in five operating divisions that manufactured batteries, carbon products, welding equipment, plastics, industrial chemicals, pesticides, and marine products.

The accident that is discussed here began when a large volume of

123

Shrivastava

Table 5.1

(a) Chronology of events leading to the accident	
Inside Union Carbide	Outside the company
	1100: Bhopal established
	Until 1860: undeveloped
	1860–1945: community dependent on agriculture for tax revenue
1934: UCIL[a]	
	1947: independence
	1950: population 70,000
1950s: UCIL expands into chemicals	
	1956: Bhopal becomes state capital
	1965: government pesticide market
1969: Agri Products Division	Booming pesticides market
	Mid 1970s: heavy competition
1978: licensed to make MIC[b]	
1981: MIC plant	
	1980–1982: bad weather
1981–1984: cut-backs	
	1984: population 695,000; lack of infrastructure
1982: safety defects (OSS)[c]	
1984: Oct, tank loses pressure; Nov, second tank loses pressure; 2 Dec, 11 p.m.: pipe washing; 3 Dec, 1 a.m.: accident	
	18 December: elections

(b) Failures	
Failures inside the plant	Failures outside the plant
Defective plant design	Haphazard urbanization
Faulty pipe washing	Inadequate housing
Lax safety procedures	Plant in densely populated area
MIC[b] tanks poorly maintained	Lack of infrastructure
Contaminants in the tank	Failure of government to identify hazard
Storage of contaminated MIC	Unprepared community
Failure of four safety devices	
Lack of on-site emergency plan	
OSS[c] findings not implemented	
Lack of investment in plant safety	
Management neglect	
Cut-back in personnel	
Lack of safety computers	
Cost-cutting erodes safety	
Lack of crisis management plans	
Top management ignorant of hazards	

a. Union Carbide (India) Ltd.
b. Methyl isocyanate.
c. Operational Safety Survey.

124

water entered the MIC storage tanks and triggered a violent exo-thermic chain reaction. Normally, water and MIC were kept sepa-rated, even when supply pipes were flushed with water during routine cleaning. However, on this occasion metal barriers known as slip blinds were not inserted and the cleaning water passed directly into the MIC tanks (table 5.1b). Additional water may have entered later during a mistaken effort to control the reaction by drenching it with water. The tanks' pressure systems had also been reported defective in October and November 1984. Within a few minutes of the intro-duction of water, temperatures and pressures in the tanks increased to the point of explosion (International Confederation of Free Trade Unions 1985).

Four safety devices that were meant to keep toxic gases from escaping into the atmosphere failed to function: lack of coolant in the MIC tank refrigerator prevented it from operating properly; the vent gas scrubber could not neutralize the gases because it lacked sodium hydroxide; a pipe leading to the flare tower had been dismantled for repairs, so the flare could not be used to burn escaping gases; finally, water sprays could not be used to douse the gases because they lacked sufficient pressure to reach the height from which the gases were spewing. As a result, 45 tons of MIC escaped from the tanks (Union Carbide Corporation 1982, 1985).

Outside the plant

Problems that occurred outside the plant were rooted in the historical underdevelopment of the surrounding region and its sudden indus-trialization after Indian independence. Bhopal was founded around 1100 A.D. near two large lakes that provided a reliable water supply for agriculture on a semi-arid plateau. Control over water in this area was a central issue that precipitated continuous battles among the Hindu kings and Moslem nawabs. Indeed, continuous feuding kept Bhopal politically unstable and economically underdeveloped for most of its history. Even during the more peaceful years of British colonial administration the region did not develop an industrial base.

After Indian independence (1947), Bhopal became the capital of Madhya Pradesh – a large, poor, unindustrialized, agricultural state in the centre of the country. As the seat of state government, Bhopal attracted new government offices, service jobs, commerce, and in-dustry. In 1956, Asia's largest heavy electrical manufacturing plant was established in the city. Throughout the 1960s, Bhopal continued to attract new industries and government institutions. With this sudden development came surging population growth and haphazard urbanization. From a base of 50,000 people in the mid-1950s, the city grew to 102,000 in 1961, to 385,000 in 1971, to 670,000 in 1981, and surpassed 1 million by 1991 (Bhopal Municipal Corporation 1975; Minocha 1981).

One clear result of rapid growth was an acute shortage of infrastructural services at the time of the accident. Housing, water supply, electricity, transportation, communication, and medical services were all inadequate. Nearly 20 per cent of the city's population lived in 156 slum colonies, many of which were located alongside various hazardous facilities. Throughout the city, water was available for only a few hours a day. There was no sewage treatment system. Cuts and reductions in electrical power were a continuing problem. Bhopal's antiquated and highly unreliable telephone system included only 10,000 lines to serve more than 1 million people. The medical system was even more inadequate: there were 1800 hospital beds and 300 doctors. When the accident occurred, this poor infrastructure limited the city's ability to mitigate damage (Bidwai 1984; Morehouse and Subramaniam 1988; Shrivastava 1992).

A multiple-perspectives understanding of crises

This chapter employs a multiple-perspectives analysis of Bhopal (Shrivastava 1992). This approach seeks to understand the crisis from the perspectives of all key stakeholders. Stakeholders are individuals and organizations that influence, or are influenced by, the crisis. The key stakeholders in the Bhopal crisis included victims (i.e. the community in Bhopal), Union Carbide Corporation, and the Government of India.

A multiple-perspectives approach also acknowledges the complexity of causes and the importance of contextual factors. It interprets causes in systemic terms (Mitchell, Devine, and Jagger 1989). Technological, organizational, and societal systems are susceptible to multiple, simultaneous, and interacting failures. A main limitation of the traditional systems view of causation is that it does not indicate which causes are more or less important, and from whose point of view. The multiple-perspectives approach addresses this limitation and accepts the impossibility of unambiguously fixing blame for industrial crises. Attempts to affix blame are reductionist: they merely divert analysts from proper understanding of the events. Finally, the multiple-perspectives approach regards controversies and conflicts as an integral part of crises. Such conflicts cannot be denied or brushed away: they are the central defining features of crises.

The most controversial elements of crises are their impacts or consequences. Consequences are difficult to ascertain because they are many, diverse, and difficult to measure. Some consequences are indirect, some are unknown, some are trans-generational, and some extend in space to unforeseeable areas. In the Bhopal case, victims saw the crisis largely in terms of personal losses: they lost their lives or faculties, their health, their sources of income, and their sense of community. An army of lawyers, government officials, activists, reporters, and researchers invaded Bhopal. The lives of residents have already been disrupted for months and years, and will continue to be disrupted for a long time to come. In these circumstances, recovery has involved efforts to rebound from multifaceted losses.

Officials at Union Carbide viewed this crisis as an unfortunate technological "incident." Because of its long history in the chemical industry, the company was familiar with the types of losses such incidents generate. These include legal liability for damages, financial losses, and bad reputation. Union Carbide's main concern was to protect its financial assets and reputation. It embarked on an elaborate strategy of legal defence, financial restructuring, and public relations (Union Carbide Corporation 1985).

For the Government of India, the crisis was a socio-economic and political disaster. As the institution responsible for safeguarding public safety, the government had failed abysmally. It needed to redeem itself in the eyes of the public, by deflecting responsibility for its role in the disaster. It was also saddled with the far more difficult task of managing recovery and rehabilitation of victims.

Recovery of the victims and their community

As used here, the term "recovery" refers to the period after the gas had dissipated and the victims were attempting to come to terms with its consequences. This does not mean that there was a return to a pre-accident state of normalcy or an overall improvement in the status of victims. In that sense, recovery may never have taken place for a majority of those who were affected by this crisis.

Medical recovery

In the immediate aftermath of the accident, most attention was devoted to medical recovery. MIC caused damage to lung tissue and respiratory functions. Victims suffered from breathlessness, cough, nausea, vomiting, chest pains, dry eyes, poor sight, photophobia, and loss of appetite. They also manifested psychological trauma symptoms: these included anxiety, depression, phobias, and nightmares.

Women in the affected area appear to have suffered a variety of medical problems. Studies of limited population samples showed that up to 50 per cent of women experienced irregular menstruation, and there was a failure of lactation in nursing mothers. The number of spontaneous abortions rose sharply. Women also bore a disproportionately large burden of economic and social losses: they lost earning members of their family and had no alternative source of income; they were socially ostracized and victimized by loan sharks.

Local doctors had no information on the toxicity and epidemiology of MIC poisoning. Even the publicly available scientific data on MIC did not reach doctors in Bhopal until several days after the accident. Hence, the only medical treatment provided was limited to symptomatic treatment of injuries. The medical system was simply overwhelmed by the large number of injured victims that rushed to hospitals. The coroner's office was unable to provide death certificates to victims' relatives. Many bodies were buried or cremated before official registration of death. Voluntary organizations set up makeshift clinics in the affected neighbourhoods to supplement the government's efforts: these included the Indian Red Cross, Voluntary Health Association of India, Medico Friends Circle, and several religious charitable organizations. In 1987 the state government converted one of its local clinics into a 150-bed hospital for gas victims.

The lack of medical documentation of injuries proved to be a major hindrance to the delivery of medical relief and the provision of compensation. But it was not the only problem: without baseline data on community health it was also difficult to identify specific medical consequences of MIC exposure and to develop focused treatment protocols. Poor health information is common in many disasters, especially those that affect developing countries. It has important implications for disaster-management strategies. Several epidemiological and medical surveillance studies were initiated by the Indian Council of Medical Research and the local medical college. They found that a large population (possibly 300,000 people) had been affected by the gas. Unfortunately, government-sponsored studies were not made fully public for several years, because they were to be used in the court case against Union Carbide.

Managing the health effects of MIC exposure was confounded by two other factors. First, most of the affected people were poor and malnourished; they suffered many of the post-exposure symptoms even before exposure to MIC. Second, it was not clear what gases besides MIC may have been implicated in the accident. Some doctors felt that cyanide may have been one of the by-products of the accident. They detected cyanide poisoning symptoms among the victims, though this was never proved or disproved.

Economic recovery

Economic losses from the accident included loss of jobs, loss of earning capacity of victims, business disruptions, cost of compensation and rehabilitation, and legal costs. The UCIL plant, a $25 million investment, was shut down immediately after the accident, and 650 permanent jobs were lost. A few months later the Union Carbide Research and Development Center, located in another part of Bhopal, was also cut back to a skeleton staff. Local businesses and state government offices were shut down for three weeks, losing business and tax revenues. The two mass evacuations disrupted commercial activities for several weeks, with resulting business losses of $8–65 million. Loss of work in government offices was not included in these estimates (Morehouse and Subramaniam 1988; Shrivastava 1992).

In the year after the accident, the government took many well-intentioned steps to provide economic relief to victims. Compensation of about $800 per fatality was paid to relatives of dead persons. Smaller cash compensation awards (less than $100) were distributed to 20,000 victims and 3,000 more victims were provided with part-time employment. New schools were also opened in the affected neighbourhoods. Unfortunately, in proportion to the tremendous relief needs these early (1985–1987) efforts were miniscule. Government relief failed to alleviate the misery of victims; it was simply too small in scale and limited in scope. But, given the many competing demands for government support, this was all that the government could manage at the time.

Beginning in March 1991, new interim relief payments were made to victims. Sums of Rs 200 (about $8) per month were paid to all victims who lived in 37 of the city's 54 wards that were officially classified as "gas affected." A total of $260 million was disbursed, but the money was given to all people who lived in the affected wards, not just the victims. In fact, many of the people who lived in these 37 wards were not victims at all: they had moved in after the accident. As cash relief payments flowed into the city, the local inflation rate jumped to between 15 and 20 per cent per annum. Most people pinned their hopes of long-term recovery on anticipated compensation from Union Carbide.

Struggle for compensation

Union Carbide paid $470 million of a compensation settlement in January 1989. This money remained in a court-administered account until 1992, while claims were sorted out. By early 1993 there were 630,000 claims, of which only 350,000 had been substantiated on the basis of medical records. Hundreds of victims continued to die during the prolonged politico-legal and bureaucratic battles over compensation.

The compensation that victims sought in mid-1985 was modest and reasonable. They asked that compensation for dead victims be paid according to the standards of death compensation then prevailing in India: seriously injured victims were to be paid $100–150 per month, to meet their food and medical needs; victims with minor injuries were to be paid a one-time compensation for medical costs and economic hardship (Morehouse and Subramaniam 1988). It was estimated that the total cost of all compensation would be between $600 million and $1.2 billion. The victims' quest for compensation took formal shape in a lawsuit filed by the Government of India against Union Carbide Corporation in New York, in March 1985. Table 5.2 summarizes the main legal events since the accident.

US-based cases were consolidated under Judge Keenan (Federal District Court of New York), and Union Carbide then asked that the case be moved to India, on the grounds that the United States was not a convenient venue for trial (Adler 1985). It was argued that the accident occurred in India and most of the evidence lay in India. Keenan sent the case to India under condition that "due process" of law would be followed there. The case went to the Bhopal District Court – the lowest-level court that could hear such a case. For the next four years it wound its way through the maze of legal bureau-

Table 5.2 **Chronology of legal events**

Date	Event
December 1984 to March 1985	Multiple lawsuits filed against Union Carbide Corporation (UCC) in India and the USA
March 1985	Bhopal Gas Leak Disaster Ordinance enacted in India. Government of India sues Union Carbide in New York
July 1985	UCC asks court to dismiss the case on grounds of *forum non conveniens*
November 1985	Court orders UCC to pay $5 million for interim relief
May 1986	Judge Keenan sends case to be tried in India
1987–1988	Out-of-court negotiations continue between UCC and Government of India. The case moves from Bhopal District Court to the State High Court, to the Supreme Court
January 1989	Supreme Court mediates a settlement for $470 million. Victims' lawyers challenge the settlement
October 1991	Supreme Court upholds settlement amount, but cancels immunity for UCC, opening up old suits
January 1992	Criminal cases reopened against UCC. Top UCC executives subpoenaed
January 1993	Compensation distribution initiated

cracy, via the State High Court, up to the Supreme Court of India. The Government of India did not want to expedite the case by appointing a special court. That might constitute lack of due process and thereby provide grounds for appeal by Union Carbide.

The two main legal disputes were over the amount of compensation and the exoneration of Union Carbide from future liabilities. But these disputes were complicated by lack of reliable information about causes and consequences. More importantly, the Government of India's Bhopal Gas Leak Disaster Ordinance – a law that appointed the government as sole representative of the victims – was challenged by victim activists. Victims were usually not consulted about legal matters or settlement possibilities. In the bureaucratic and political maze that constituted "the government," victims had no meaningful representation. This, in effect, dissolved the victims' identity as a constituency separate and differing from the government. This unintentional disempowerment of victims seems to occur in other disasters, too, especially where victims are poor and cannot afford independent legal help (Reich 1991).

The solution to costly and time-consuming litigation lay in reaching an out-of-court settlement. However, any settlement was fraught with many political dangers. A settlement with Union Carbide could back-fire on the government. It could be seen as capitulation to pressures from a multinational corporation and the United States. This meant that a viable settlement could be made only after the case reached the Supreme Court, beyond which level it could not be appealed, at least in India. It also required correct political timing, when the settle-ment could go through parliamentary approval with minimal political opposition. The national parliamentary elections of 1989 presented a good political opportunity to settle the case and win support from voters. Five years had passed since the accident; the legal case had reached the Supreme Court; victims were fed up with waiting. In any event, hundreds of victims had died and thousands had moved out of the gas-affected neighbourhoods. The level of organization among victims was at the lowest point and their ability to protest was mini-mal. In January 1989, the Supreme Court brokered a settlement of $470 million in compensation that gave Union Carbide immunity from future prosecution.

Victims and activists challenged the settlement in the Supreme Court. They argued that the settlement amount was inadequate and claimed that granting Union Carbide immunity from criminal prose-cution was unconstitutional. In October 1991, the Supreme Court ruled on this challenge: it upheld the compensation amount and ordered the government to distribute the compensation funds imme-diately. However, it also cancelled Union Carbide's immunity from further prosecution.

Victims remain victims

By 1991, seven years after the accident and two years after the settle-ment, victims were poised to receive compensation payments. But bureaucratic procedures delayed the initiation of payments until 1993. What had happened in the interim? The population of Bhopal had nearly doubled since the accident. Conflicts had politicized the definition of victims. The government was in the process of setting up 17 administrative courts for validating claims and distributing funds. It lacked good medico-legal documentation of damages to sort out valid claims: there were 13,000 death claims, whereas government figures showed 4,000 deaths. Of the 630,000 claimants, 280,000 failed to appear before officials to validate their claims.

At the beginning of 1993, distribution of compensation money was started. Union Carbide's original $470 million had accumulated considerable interest and now totalled $700 million. By March of that year, 700 victims had received $2 million. This included relatives of the dead, who received $3,200 per fatality (more for multiple bereavements in the same family). Those who suffered serious injuries received $3,000 each; people with minor injuries were to receive much less (Hazarika 1993).

Bhopal has been in a chronic crisis since the accident. Only the parameters of the crisis have changed with time. At the time of the accident, medical and ecological damages were most salient; today, the economic and social damages are more important. The city has also experienced a steady transformation of social and cultural attitudes towards the disaster. For people not affected by it, the disaster became a nuisance. It was a source of political conflicts and economic decline of the city. This segment of Bhopal viewed gas victims as a burden on the city's limited resources. They preferred to forget about the accident and get on with their lives.

The precarious and explosive situation in Bhopal was apparent during the Hindu–Muslim riots of December 1992 and early 1993. Bhopal was among the three worst-affected cities in India and incurred 150 deaths; 1,300 gas victims had their homes and compensation documents destroyed in fires.

Recovery of Union Carbide

Financial restructuring

The accident threatened Union Carbide's financial survival (Union Carbide Corporation 1985–1990). It faced multibillion-dollar liability suits and bad publicity at a time when its stock price had fallen dramatically. Before the disaster, UCC stock traded at between $50 and $58; in the months immediately following the accident it traded at $32–$40. Speculators bought a large number of stocks from financial institutions seeking to unload them. Then, in the latter half of 1985, the GAF Corporation of New York made a hostile bid to take over Union Carbide. This battle and speculative stock trading ran up the UCC stock price to $96 and forced it into financial restructuring.

To respond to the GAF attack, Union Carbide sold the consumer products division, which was its most profitable business. Commodity chemicals were retained, although this was a business the company had originally wanted to divest itself of. In 1986, Union Carbide sold assets worth over $3.3 billion and repurchased 38.8 million of the shares to protect the company from further threats of take-over. Stockholders were given $1.1 billion in cash and a three-for-one stock split. The company also took on nearly $3 billion in debt. The 1987 *Annual Report* called this restructuring a "true come back story." Throughout 1987 the company consolidated its new structure. The new Union Carbide now has three divisions – Chemicals and Plastics, Industrial Gases, and Carbon Products.

In addition to company restructuring, there were many changes in personnel and business activities. Key top managers at the time of the accident were transferred, or retired, or left the company. At the parent company, Warren Anderson (the Chief Executive Officer), Ronald Wishart (Executive Vice President for Public and Government Relations), and Jackson Browning (Vice President for Environment, Safety, and Health), have retired. At the Indian subsidiary, the Chairman, Keshub Mahindra, and the Bhopal Factory Manager, J. Mukund, moved on to new positions. Most of the Bhopal plant managers left the company after the plant closed.

The departure of employees directly involved with the accident was convenient for Union Carbide. It allowed the company to distance itself psychologically from the disaster. Under the new Chief Executive, Robert Kennedy, a campaign was begun to rebuild a business decimated by the 1985 hostile take-over attempt. GAF's take-over bid forced UCC to reverse its corporate strategy and move counter to industry trends. Other large chemical companies, such as Du Pont and Monsanto, were diversifying away from commodity chemicals into new glamorous areas of biotechnology and pharmaceuticals. Union Carbide, too, wanted to balance its business portfolio by reducing dependence on cyclical commodity chemicals and expanding consumer products. In 1984, UCC tried unsuccessfully to sell its commodity chemicals business. However, to fend off the GAF attack, UCC sold its most profitable consumer products business units. It took on additional debt to buy back stock. There were few resources left with which to diversify. UCC cut back operations and emerged a much smaller, yet profitable, firm. According to company spokespeople, 1988 was "the best year in the 71 year history of Union Carbide." Earnings per share were $4.88, including a charge of $0.43 per share for resolution of the Bhopal litigation. By now, the Bhopal accident was exclusively in the hands of the company's legal department and outside attorneys.

After the compensation settlement of 1989, Union Carbide believed that the crisis was over. Its leaders embarked on the task of aggressively rebuilding their various businesses. The company returned to the strategy it was considering in pre-Bhopal days, i.e. reducing dependence on heavy chemicals while diversifying into pharmaceuticals and consumer products. Therefore, in 1990, Union Carbide bought Vitaphore Corporation, a maker of medical devices. Joint ventures in dermatological products and plant genetics were also begun with other companies (Lepkowski 1993).

The crushing debt burden, acquired in the process of fending off GAF's threatened take-over, hampered the company's financial recovery. At the end of 1986, debt accounted for a staggering 80 per cent of capitalization. At the end of 1991, debt still remained at 50 per cent of capitalization and sales were $7.35 billion. In 1992, UCC sold its Linde Gas Division for $2.4 billion, leaving the company at less than half its pre-Bhopal size.

It is clear that the Bhopal disaster slowly but steadily sapped the financial strength of Union Carbide and adversely affected its morale and productivity. Pre-tax profits per employee were just $16,700. In comparison, its competitor and industry leader Dow Chemicals had pre-tax profits per employee of $41,200. Some financial analysts point to Union Carbide's reduced size, low profitability, lack of diversification, lack of competitive edge, and low employee morale as major liabilities (McMurray 1992).

The Indian subsidiary, Union Carbide India Ltd., maintained a low profile in the post-Bhopal period. It steered clear of lawsuits between the parent company and the Government of India, and concentrated on managing other businesses in India. UCIL closed the pesticide plant and reduced the Research and Development Center in Bhopal to a skeleton staff. Top management personnel from the Bhopal plant moved to other parts of the company. Apart from the fact that UCIL was denied permits that would have permitted expansion, it remained largely unaffected by the Bhopal accident.

Legal battles and the "sabotage" defence

For Union Carbide, the legal battle with the Government of India was a major long-term effect of the Bhopal disaster. The company's legal defence was built around the claim that it was not liable for damages from the accident, because they were the result of "sabotage" by a disgruntled worker. UCC claimed it knew the saboteur's identity, and the firm of Arthur D. Little, Inc. was hired to verify and publicize this viewpoint (Kalelkar 1988). The company also circulated videos about the sabotage claim to the media and other interested observers.

How was sabotage supposed to have occurred? It was alleged that water could not have entered the MIC tanks during pipe-washing operations: pipes leading to the tanks were simply too long; passages were too complex and blocked with closed valves. These factors would have presented an insuperable physical barrier to water. The only way that so much water could get into the MIC storage tanks was through deliberate action by an individual. According to UCC, a disgruntled worker wanted to spoil the MIC in tank 610. The main evidence was a hose connected to a water main beside an open inlet pipe leading to the tank.

The UCC sabotage theory did not explain how several other simultaneous failures contributed to the accident. In addition to water entry, there were failures in four safety devices – the vent gas scrubber, the flare tower, the refrigeration system, and the water spray. There were failures in design, operating procedures, and staffing, as described earlier. The positive-pressure systems in the MIC tanks had failed, four to eight weeks before the accident.

Union Carbide's information about the sabotage came from interviews with unnamed witnesses conducted several years after the accident, in unreliable conditions. The interviews were held neither under oath nor in the presence of legal authorities or any independent (not paid by Union Carbide) observers. UCC did not reveal the name of the saboteur so that legal action could be initiated.

The sabotage claim did not explain why a disgruntled worker would want to destroy a batch of MIC. Far greater financial damage could have been inflicted on the company by smashing expensive equipment or pouring water on finished goods. Without convincing evidence, the sabotage claim remains just that – a claim.

The deliberate introduction of water into MIC storage tanks might have taken place without any intention to commit sabotage. A small quantity of water from pipe washing could have initiated the accident. Operators on duty might have been alarmed by the sight of a rumbling hot tank and could have introduced water to cool it. Such a scenario was hinted at by some witnesses and it accommodates most of the claims raised in the sabotage defence.

Recovery of the government

Political management of the crisis

The Bhopal crisis presented a major political problem for the Madhya Pradesh state government and the central government of India, both of which were controlled by the Congress Party. The accident occurred three weeks before national parliamentary elections, and the Congress Party stood to lose heavily if its partners in the state government were seen to be implicated, or did not deal firmly with Union Carbide.

Initially, the state government tried to place all the blame squarely on Union Carbide Corporation. It sued UCC for damages on behalf of victims. In a largely symbolic gesture against the company, UCC's Chief Executive, Warren Anderson, was arrested on his arrival in Bhopal. The government thwarted several efforts by UCC to provide relief to victims, in an attempt to prevent the company from earning goodwill among the public. This early political management was very effective. In nationwide elections that took place four weeks after the accident, the Congress Party won both the state legislative assembly and the national parliament seats from Madhya Pradesh by wide margins (table 5.3).

The combination of a successful political containment strategy and an ongoing legal case shifted political attention from Bhopal, and the issue did not receive high priority for four years. It resurfaced in 1989 at the time of the next elections and a few months after the Congress-dominated government of Rajiv Gandhi reached an out-of-court settlement on compensation with UCC.

Key political events related to Bhopal are shown in table 5.3. The Congress Party lost the 1989 elections and were replaced by a National Front coalition government, led by Mr. V.P. Singh of the Janata Dal Party and supported by several minority parties (Bharatiya Janata Party [BJP] and Communist parties). Singh had campaigned on a social justice platform that appealed to the weakest economic segments and lowest castes in society (which included Bhopal gas victims). His government decided to appeal the compensation settlement reached by the previous government. It reinstated civil and criminal cases against Union Carbide and supported victim activist lawyers who had challenged the Bhopal Ordinance.

In a populist move, V.P. Singh announced that interim compensation of Rs 200 per month would be paid to all victims from govern-

Table 5.3 **Political changes during the Bhopal crisis**

Date	Event
December 1984	National and state parliamentary elections held. Congress Party wins both at the centre and in Madhya Pradesh (M.P.) state
1985–1988	Government provides relief to victims, and fights legal case
January 1989	Rajiv Gandhi's Congress Party government settles compensation suit with UCC
May 1989	National and local parliamentary elections held. Congress Party loses. V.P. Singh of Janata Dal becomes Prime Minister of a coalition government. M.P. state government controlled by Bharatiya Janata Party
December 1989	V.P. Singh declares interim relief and supports victims' demand for reconsidering the compensation settlement
May 1990–1991	V.P. Singh government replaced by another coalition government. Political turmoil and constitutional crisis lead to mid-term elections
March 1991	Interim relief payments started in 37 wards of the city
May 1991	Rajiv Gandhi assassinated. Congress Party wins mid-term elections
October 1991	Suprement Court upholds the settlement partially, and ratifies the Bhopal Ordinance
December 1991	The government constitutes a committee to oversee compensation distribution
1992–1993	Religous strife and riots dominate politics. Gas victims suffer riot losses

ment funds (not from UCC settlement money). A total of US$260 million was to be used for these payments, which were to be deducted from the final compensation settlement. Owing to the lack of good medico-legal documentation, it was impossible to decide exactly who should receive the compensation. Therefore, the government chose 37 wards of the city as "gas affected areas." Everyone within these wards was eligible for compensation. The population of Bhopal had virtually doubled over the seven years since the disaster. Therefore, many people who applied for, and got, interim compensation (starting in March 1991) were not victims of the accident.

Interim compensation provided much-needed economic help to some genuine victims. However, it was also a clever political ploy by the V.P. Singh government (which was not expected to last long). By gaining the sympathies of victims, the government hoped to pick up votes in the coming mid-term elections. Local politicians extended the ploy by arguing that a larger area of the city should be declared "gas affected." This action made real victims irrelevant, and completely politicized the definition of "victims." As a result, the nature of the Bhopal crisis was profoundly changed. Victims were no longer defined by scientific standards or medico-legal documentation, but by political considerations. They became an economically advantaged category, instead of aggrieved and injured individuals. Everyone wanted to be counted as a gas victim, so that they could collect money from the interim relief programme. By the end of 1991, several local leaders and ministers of the state government were agitating to have their own wards and constituents declared as "gas affected."

Singh's National Front government eventually fell from power and new elections for the National Parliament took place in May 1991. The Congress Party returned to power in New Delhi under the leadership of Prime Minister P.V. Narasimha Rao. In Madhya Pradesh, the previous BJP government retained power, thereby diminishing the political significance of Bhopal for central government leaders.

In October 1991, India's Supreme Court upheld the compensation settlement but cancelled Union Carbide's immunity from criminal prosecution. The Court instructed the government to distribute the available $470 million compensation money to victims immediately. This ruling also allowed further prosecution of criminal cases against key Union Carbide executives (including UCC's former Chief Executive Officer, Warren Anderson). In March 1992, the Bhopal District Court asked for extradition of Warren Anderson to stand trial in this case.

Learning by government institutions

Although the Bhopal compensation case dominated the Indian government's attention, actions were also taken to prevent similar accidents in the future. A variety of legislative, legal, and administrative changes were aimed at improving institutional risk-management capacity. Three key acts that dealt with industrial hazards were amended, i.e. the Factories Act (1948), the Water Act (1974 and 1977), and the Air Act (1981). The Environmental Protection Act of 1986 was also enacted. This comprehensive new law vastly improved regulatory coverage of hazardous technologies and substances. It empowered government inspectors to enter, inspect, and test any equipment at plants. Inspectors can now conduct searches, seize equipment, and shut down high-risk operations. Citizens and public interest groups can approach the government or the courts directly to seek redress against violations of these laws. Top management of companies are also now liable for offences under the act. Cumulatively, the regulatory changes have considerably strengthened statutory control over all aspects of industrial risks: these include safety standards, worker health standards, maintenance standards, emission standards, factory inspection procedures, emergency planning, liability for damages, early warning systems, citizen rights to information, and penalties for violation (Bowonder, Kasperson, and Kasperson 1994).

The spirit of the regulatory changes was reinforced by the judiciary in several landmark cases. In December 1985, the Supreme Court of India established the principle of "strict and absolute liability" in the Shriram Food and Fertilizer Industries oleum leak case. This means that owners of hazardous plants are strictly and absolutely liable for damage originating from their activities, regardless of who is at fault. The Supreme Court also established the principle of "vicarious liability" in another important case involving Modi Industries. According to this principle, top executives are responsible for implementing the provisions of the Water Act, unless violations were committed without their knowledge. In a tannery pollution case, the Supreme Court ruled that lack of financial capacity cannot be used by smaller companies as an excuse for not treating polluting effluents.

Besides creating these new legal principles and doctrines, the Supreme Court began taking public interest litigation for environmental protection very seriously. Specific judges encouraged such litigation and took an activist stand in many cases. The overall effect of these actions was positive. The judiciary that historically was unresponsive, bureaucratic, and inefficient began to be viewed as an ally in environmental protection.

The government also initiated several administrative changes that put teeth into the laws. Inspection and enforcement efforts were intensified. New administrative units were set up at the state level to monitor compliance of laws. New multidisciplinary task forces were created to analyse existing hazardous facilities, to review emergency plans, and to improve safety practices. A national Disaster Training College was also set up in Bhopal. Factory inspection procedures were revised in accordance with a new hazard priority classification system that focused inspection efforts on high-risk facilities.

Despite these seemingly extensive changes, the institutional capacity to identify hazards and deal with emergency incidents has not changed much. In two major incidents that took place since Bhopal, emergency planning and systematic evacuation were still deficient. Failure is partly due to inadequate implementation of new policies. There are severe shortages of resources, toxicological information, and skilled personnel, and the poor quality of the industrial infrastructure makes it all but impossible to bring about real changes (Bowonder, Kasperson, and Kasperson 1994).

Implications for long-term disaster recovery

The Bhopal crisis was a landmark event. It was the worst-ever industrial disaster, as measured by the number of direct immediate fatalities. Its impacts were international in scope and extended in time. It raised many issues for disaster recovery theory and practice, including the burgeoning hazardousness of third world cities. For these and other reasons, Bhopal opened a new discourse on industrial crises, crisis management, technology–environment relationships, and technology–society relationships. It set into motion new research studies and new curricular programmes in crisis prevention and management (Shrivastava 1993; Jasanoff 1992). Here I want to examine only a few of the main theoretical issues raised by Bhopal and to suggest propositions about future disasters whose empirical verification must await the test of time.

Crisis morphology

Industrial crises do not end. They simply change form and content.
   In existing theory, crises and disasters are typically viewed as events or processes that are clearly delineated in time and space. Every crisis has an end that is usually treated as a return to some form of normality (Morin 1993; Perrow 1984). But the Bhopal crisis has lingered on for nine years. Criminal lawsuits are still pending in courts, and victims still face economic disaster. Certainly, the form, content, and focus of the crisis have shifted: it was once mainly a medical and ecological crisis; then it became primarily a legal and corporate crisis; now it has become predominantly an economic and political crisis. Moreover, with each change in form, the spatial reach of the crisis also extended: at first it was a local crisis confined to Bhopal; then it became an international social crisis and an industry-wide financial crisis. Drawing on US examples, Edelstein (1988) came to similar conclusions

141

about the continuous spreading of crises. He remarked that the changing forms of crisis often go unnoticed because impacts are unevenly distributed and mixed in with impacts attributable to other economic, social, and political processes.

The morphology of crises is poorly understood. We do not know how or why one type of crisis evolves into another. If recovery is to be improved it will be necessary to undertake studies that trace and analyse such changes.

The permanence of victims

Victims are permanently victimized because of their socially structured position of disadvantage.

The sorry history of Bhopal's victims leads me to question why victims are unable to fare better in industrial crises. In the struggle for redress, victims of major crises possess some important advantages: these include publicity, the sympathy of interested publics, and the presumption of innocence. World media attention is focused on them. They have the sympathy of important people and organizations. But, though widely deemed to be innocent, they are still not able to get the justice they deserve. Typically, appropriate compensation for damages is denied or delayed. Even when compensation money is made available, it is often misused or misdirected to the wrong people. Why is this so?

In poor developing countries, most victims are themselves drawn from the poorest socio-economic groups. Their structural position in a society puts them at special disadvantage. They do not have access to instruments of justice or to political power. They usually lack sufficient information to establish a strong legal claim for the restitution of loss. In any event, they cannot afford to hire high-powered lawyers. As they pursue damage claims with meagre resources they must continue a daily struggle for survival. Delays and denial of just compensation are a frequent result (Couch and Kroll-Smith 1991; Reich 1991).

Proposition two opens up a host of empirical questions. What part does social structure play in recovery? How, for example, do socially advantaged victims, such as those involved in airplane accidents, fare in comparison to victims of industrial accidents? If the salience of social structure is borne out empirically, it would have important implications for long-term recovery. Recovery efforts would need to be sensitive to the socio-economic class characteristics of victims (Kreps 1989).

Revising stage models of disasters

The seeds of crisis are sowed many years prior to a triggering event. Study of antecedent conditions may hold the key to crisis prevention.

Stage models of disasters are in need of modification (Turner 1978). According to conventional wisdom, a disaster is initiated by an event that triggers an impact and then gives rise to a series of stages that include emergency response, post-disaster recovery, and return to normality. Although the pre-disaster period is crucial for improving crisis prevention, what happens before the disaster occurs is generally not well understood.

Many of the factors that cause crises become embedded in organizational and societal systems many years before the crisis emerges. They weaken such systems and make them more prone to crises. Organizations prone to crises have been found to go through a cycle of expansion, contraction, and uncertainty (boom, bust, and chaos). This cycle can occur over several years. During expansion, they recklessly overbuild capacity; during contraction they cut back expenditure. Many of the cut-backs (such as in personnel, maintenance schedules, and inventories) have deleterious effects on safety (Shrivastava, Miller, and Miglani 1991).

Policy implications

Crises are double-edged phenomena: they wreak havoc but they also provide opportunities for change. Change becomes feasible, even desirable, because crises unfreeze past behaviour patterns, question past assumptions, and present a clear impetus for change.

Bhopal provided a stimulus for major changes around the world. It helped to usher in new regulations for chemical industries and other hazardous industries. It changed the structure of the overseas liability insurance industry. Chemical companies made voluntary organizational improvements and new investments to avoid Bhopal-type disasters. Communities in many parts of the world changed their perceptions of local technological and industrial risks. They initiated programmes of risk assessment, risk communication, and emergency preparedness (Shrivastava 1992).

The three propositions stated above in italics underline both the importance and the potential of crisis-prevention strategies. Numerous and frequent early warnings are emitted from hazard systems. Unfortunately, industrial managers tend to focus heavily on technological early warning signals that come from safety and monitoring equipment. All too often, they ignore more subtle, if ambiguous, organizational clues that could signal impending disasters. For example, among the organizational behaviours that may indicate systemic problems are the following: lax security of operations, indiscriminate cost cutting, lapsed maintenance, frequent minor incidents, and increases in routine repairs or equipment down time. If these problems are analysed quickly they can point to the potential for deeper-seated failures that may cause system breakdown. Policy makers and corporate managers need to expand their notion of "early warnings" to include both technological and organizational sources of error.

Bhopal also teaches several important lessons about disaster management in a developing-country context. First is the importance of good medical information that can be used in legal actions. The lack of adequate medico-legal documentation is a major hindrance to assessment of health consequences and development of appropriate medical treatments. It also complicates conflict resolution over compensation. Lack of accurate assessment of losses precludes identification of real victims. With the passage of time, there is often no way of distinguishing real victims from economically motivated fake victims. The victim compensation system can be abused severely, with injustice to the needy. Disaster management can benefit from development of baseline health data and medical surveillance infrastructure to document health effects of disasters.

Another disaster-management lesson involves the need to empower victims and encourage their independence. Industrial disasters often involve many poor victims. Charitable and social institutions help victims with material support. They also represent victims in their struggle for just compensation. Despite the good intentions underlying such representational arrangements, victims lose their voices as the struggle unfolds. Victims' representatives (such as government, lawyers, public leaders, voluntary groups) inadvertently usurp the right of victims to control the terms of debate. In Bhopal, the Government of India did this through the Bhopal Ordinance.

From the victims' perspective, it is important to maintain the identity and independence of their representatives. They should also be allowed to participate directly in any conflict-resolution processes.

This can be done in several ways: victims may be permitted to pursue private avenues of redress that complement the work of formal representational groups; advisory structures, consisting of victims, can be created to give substantive inputs to representative groups.

For corporate managers, the challenge of Bhopal is the challenge of grappling with fundamental systemic sources of industrial disasters. Corporations can minimize the likelihood of failures by directing strategic attention and resources to issues of safety, environmental protection, and public health. They can minimize their company's vulnerability to disasters by changing the technologies that they use. It is both possible and wise to forego inherently hazardous technologies and to replace them with technologies that are environment friendly and safe.

Risk cannot be completely eliminated from industrial operations. Therefore, companies need to be prepared for crisis management. They should develop crisis-management teams and emergency plans, and should educate customers and the public about product safety and environment-protection measures. Finally, companies operating in developing countries cannot count on existing infrastructure and public services. It may be necessary for companies to supplement local infrastructure by investing in electric power, water supply, sewage treatment, waste disposal, and communications services. Risk can also be reduced by locating industrial plants away from population centres. In developing countries, special attention must be paid to keeping people away from hazardous facilities after they have been established.

The lingering nature of industrial crises requires government and corporations to be engaged in disaster recovery over an extended period. The Bhopal crisis has lasted for 10 years and continues; the Minamata crisis has evolved over 40 years and still remains partially unresolved. These long time frames suggest that ad hoc and temporary organization of disaster recovery is not adequate. As a society, we need more carefully thought-out strategies and permanent institutions in charge of the recovery from industrial crises.

Note

1. Use of the terms "disaster" and "crisis" partly reflects the development of specialized language in two different research traditions. Students of disaster have focused on natural or technological events that overwhelm human coping capabilities (e.g. earthquakes, industrial explosions). Students of business management have concentrated on economic shocks to firms and public institutions (e.g. market failures, hostile take-overs). When a combination of

145

physical events and economic shocks occurs simultaneously, a complex concatenation of impacts may follow. It is the latter process that is addressed in this chapter.

References

Adler, S. 1985. "Carbide plays hardball in court." *American Lawyer*, November.

Bhopal Municipal Corporation, 1975. *Bhopal Development Plan*. Bhopal: Bhopal Municipal Corporation, Town and Country Planning Department.

Bidwai, P. 1984. "Plant design badly flawed." *The Times of India*, 27 December.

Bogard, William P. 1989. *The Bhopal Tragedy: Language, Logic, and Politics in the Production of a Hazard*. Boulder, Col.: Westview Press.

Bowonder, B., R. Kasperson, and J.X. Kasperson. 1994. In: S. Jasanoff, ed. *Learning from Disaster: Risk Management after Bhopal*. Philadelphia: University of Pennsylvania Press.

Couch, S.J., and S. Kroll-Smith. 1991. *Communities at Risk*. New York: Peter Lang.

Dhingra, K.C. 1978. *The Pesticides Handbook*. New Delhi: Small Industries Research Institute.

Diamond, S. 1985. "The Bhopal disaster: How it happened." *New York Times*, 28 January.

Edelstein, M.R. 1988. *Contaminated Communities: The Social and Psychological Impacts of Residential Toxic Exposure*. Boulder: Westview Press.

Hazarika, S. 1993. "Settlement slow in India gas disaster claims." *New York Times*, 25 March, A6.

International Confederation of Free Trade Unions. 1985. *The Trade Union Report on Bhopal*. Geneva: ICFTU.

Jasanoff, S. (ed.). 1994. *Learning from Disaster: Risk Management after Bhopal*. Philadelphia: University of Pennsylvania Press.

Kalelkar, A.S. 1988. "Investigation of large-magnitude incidents: Bhopal as a case study." Paper presented at the Institution of Engineers Conference on Preventing Major Chemical Accidents, in London, May.

Kreps, G. 1989. *Social Structure and Disaster*. Newark: University of Delaware Press.

Lepkowski, Will. 1994. "The restructuring of Union Carbide since Bhopal." In: S. Jasanoff, ed. *Learning from Disaster: Risk Management after Bhopal*. Philadelphia: University of Pennsylvania Press.

McMurray, S. 1992. "Union Carbide offers some sober lessons in crisis management." *Wall Street Journal*, 28 January.

Minocha, A.C. 1981. "Changing industrial structure of Madhya Pradesh, 1960–1975." *Margin* 4(1): 46–61.

Mitchell, J.K., N. Devine, and K. Jagger. 1989. "A contextual model of natural hazard." *Geographical Review* 89(4): 391–409.

Morehouse, Ward, and Arun Subramaniam. 1988. *The Bhopal Tragedy*. New York: Council on International and Public Affairs.

Morin, E. 1993. "Towards a crisiology." *Industrial and Environmental Crisis Quarterly* 7(1).

Perrow, C. 1984. *Normal Accidents: Living with High Risk Technologies*. New York: Basic Books.

Prasad, R., and R.K. Pandey. 1985. "Methyl isocyanate (MIC) hazard to the vegetation in Bhopal." *Journal of Tropical Forestry* 1(1): 40–50.

Reich, M.R. 1991. *Toxic Politics: Responding to Chemical Disasters.* Ithaca: Cornell University Press.

Shrivastava, P. 1992. *Bhopal: Anatomy of a Crisis.* 2nd edn. London: Paul Chapman.

———. 1993. "Crisis theory/practice: towards sustainable development." *Industrial and Environmental Crisis Quarterly* 7(1): 23–42.

———, D. Miller, and A. Miglani. 1991. The evolution of crises: Crisis precursors. *International Journal of Mass Emergencies and Disasters* 9.

Turner, B.A. 1978. *Man Made Disasters.* London: Wykenham Publications.

Union Carbide Corporation. 1982. *Operational Safety Survey.* Danbury, Conn.: Union Carbide Corporation.

———. 1985. *Bhopal Methyl Isocyanate Incident Investigation Team Report*, Danbury, Conn: Union Carbide Corporation, March.

———. 1985–1990. *Annual Report.* Danbury, Conn.: Union Carbide Corporation.

6

Iranian recovery from industrial devastation during war with Iraq

Hooshang Amirahmadi

Introduction

Mainstream literature about industrial disasters hardly recognizes the relevance of war. Yet war is a major destroyer of industrial facilities. Ongoing wars in the former Yugoslavia and the former USSR not only have killed tens of thousands of people but also have destroyed important industrial plants in places such as Sarajevo, Groznyy, and Sukhumi – with far-reaching consequences for the economic survival of those cities. The Persian Gulf War of 1990–1991 devastated the industrial bases of Iraq and Kuwait, caused substantial harm to humans, and damaged the natural environment (El-Baz and Makharita 1994). Obviously, war may trigger the same kinds of industrial disasters that occur during peacetime (e.g. fires, explosions). It can also add some new dimensions to industrial disasters (e.g. systematic, deliberate, and repeated destruction of the same facilities; contamination of industrial plants by chemical weapons). Finally, the influence of war on industrial disasters may be indirect, as in the threat of pollution from weapons-manufacturing plants, weapon-testing sites, and weapons dumps (Stockholm International Peace Research Institute [SIPRI] 1977, 1980).

War is a more complex and pervasive phenomenon than industrial disaster, so planning for – and recovering from – war-related industrial disasters is likely to be a complicated business. Explanations of

148

the origins of the war touch on many different deep-seated and wide-ranging attributes of society. Wars themselves are repetitive phenomena but every war is unique. Wars are also semi-continuous and more or less all-embracing. Compared with conventional industrial hazards, the period of active threat is usually prolonged during wars and a larger proportion of the citizenry are affected. Because wars leave a more complex and pervasive imprint on society, they make post-war reconstruction more challenging than restoration in the wake of industrial disasters.

The changing nature of contemporary war signals a possibility of more war-related industrial disasters in the future as well as a wider range of other threats to the environment and human health (Winnefeld and Morris 1994). This is an outcome of trends in three factors – the technical sophistication of weaponry, the strategic logic of targeting a nation's industrial capacity during war, and the increasingly regional nature of conflict. Advances in war-making technologies such as methods of surveillance, precision-guided short-range missiles, chemical and biological warfare, helicopters, and all-weather and night vision systems, among others, ensure increased destructive capabilities. A nation's industrial capacity and associated civilian populations are increasingly favoured targets because they generate income and materials needed to maintain the war effort. Regional conflict is unquestionably on the rise (e.g. Bosnia, Armenia, Azerbaijan, Somalia, Afghanistan, Rwanda, Philippines, Sri Lanka). During such conflicts, damage is usually restricted to small areas, which sustain repeated attacks and disproportionately heavy losses.

What follows is a case-study of industrial hazards associated with Iran's eight-year war against Iraq (1980–1988). Many of the communities in Iran's oil- and gas-producing regions were affected by this conflict. The war's impact on industry was merely one facet of the wider conflict, so the case-study is discussed in the larger context of the conflict's socio-economic impact on Iranian society (Cordesman 1990). Because neither an accurate nor a first-hand account of Iraq's experience with this war is readily available, the perspective is consciously Iranian.[1] Although the account may be incomplete, the information is nevertheless believed to be accurate.

By delineating Iran's experience with the war and reconstruction, it is intended not only to analyse the relationship of war, community destruction, and industrial disaster but also to show how particular issues of recovery from industrial disasters can become caught up in broader concerns about recovery from other events that inflict more

149

encompassing types of damage. Further, this chapter explores inter-connections among local-level reconstruction priorities, national-level goals, and intervention by the international community in the post-war peace and reconstruction efforts. It is hoped that the case-study will also provide insights that lead toward creation of models of industrial disaster impact assessment and recovery for war-damaged societies and will identify obstacles to reconstruction and ways of improving implementation.

Military and strategic context

Iraq invaded Iran in September 1980 and initiated a protracted land, sea, and air conflict that lasted until August 1988, when it was brought to an end by United Nations Security Council Resolution 598. The invasion followed Saddam Hussein's unilateral abrogation of the Treaty of Algiers, which he had himself negotiated with the then Shah of Iran in 1975.[2]

Five Iranian provinces that border Iraq – Khuzestan, Ilam, Kermanshahan, Kurdestan, and West Azerbaijan – became active theatres of air and ground conflicts, while another 11 provinces suffered sustained aerial bombardment (fig. 6.1). These five provinces account for 10.8 per cent of Iran's land area and include the country's most heavily populated and developed region. In 1980, the war-torn region's population density was 35.4 per square mile, compared with 23.2 for the national average (Amirahmadi 1990b). Before the war, Khuzestan boasted major economic establishments, including port facilities, steel factories, oil wells and refineries, petrochemical complexes, and a major hydroelectric dam and irrigation project. Kermanshahan was considered an important centre for agriculture and traditional industry. Nearly 14,000 square kilometres of Iranian territory were occupied by Iraqi forces for most of the war.

The Iran–Iraq war was unusual for a number of reasons. Though it was the longest conventional war of the twentieth century, it was confined to a relatively small land area. A mixture of ancient and modern tactics were employed, including intensive "human wave" assaults (i.e. the simultaneous convergence of thousands of armed troops on one target) and a "war on cities" that included the use of technologically advanced artillery to target distant industries precisely (Shemirani 1993). Iraq used direct missile attacks as part of an explicit strategy to depopulate settlements and strangle the Iranian economy. The Iraqi army also used chemical and biological weapons

Fig. 6.1 Front-line provinces of Iran, 1980–1988 (Source: Amirahmadi 1987: 136) (redrawn)

in significant numbers, though precise figures are difficult to determine. One source lists 20 chemical rocket attacks, 284 chemical air attacks, and 74 chemical artillery attacks, which killed over 5,700 people, mostly civilians living in urban areas (Shemirani 1993). The Iraqi Kurdish town of Halabcheh was almost totally destroyed by a chemical bombardment undertaken by Iraq to prevent it falling into the hands of Iranian troops. Even now, many years after the end of open hostilities, both countries still retain stockpiles of chemical weapons.

151

Impacts of the war on human health and long-term habitability of the region

Human losses

Eight years of intense conflict exacted heavy tolls on the population of Iran. There were approximately 300,000 Iranian casualties, including 61,000 missing in action and 5,000 in Iraqi prisons. The relief and reconstruction process was further complicated by the fact that another 2.5 million Iranians have become homeless, have lost their jobs, or are displaced. Most of these have taken sanctuary in refugee camps, makeshift shacks, and temporary shelters in major urban centres or in peripheral areas of war zones (Amirahmadi 1990b: 63). A government survey taken after the end of hostilities revealed that 593,000 civilians were physically and/or mentally disabled by the war (United Nations Secretary-General 1991a: 48).

The future productivity of Iran has been permanently altered; the energy and capacity of millions of productive working people who served in the war have been irretrievably lost. Almost all of them were young and dedicated to the Iranian revolution. Human development – including education – has been grievously affected. In the war region alone, more than 20 per cent (9,300) of the pre-war classrooms (44,300) were damaged or destroyed. Over a third (450,000) of the region's 1.25 million students fled elsewhere. This placed great strains on receiving school systems, which were forced to teach pupils in continuous shifts (United Nations Secretary-General 1991a: 45). The provision of health care was similarly interrupted: "... a total of 102 'health houses', 84 rural health centers, 80 urban health centers and 12 provincial and/or district health centers were destroyed" (United Nations Secretary-General 1991a: 48). Water and sewerage systems in the area were also heavily damaged.

The demographic profile of Iran has been greatly altered since the beginning of the war. Many of the changes are a direct consequence of government policy to increase the national population. During the war years, population grew at more than 3.7 per cent annually; by 1988, total numbers were about 50 per cent greater than in 1976. In 1976, 17.2 per cent of Iran's population lived in the five war-affected provinces; by 1986, the proportion had fallen to 15 per cent. At present, 45 per cent of the national population are under the age of 14. Concomitant demands for social services and educational facilities pose a challenge for authorities engaged in the allocation of resources for reconstruction (United Nations Secretary-General 1991a: 29). More recently, the government has acted to slow population growth. The new policy seems to be having some effect, but the country's population is still growing fast enough (3.2 per cent in 1992) to cause serious alarm.

Environmental damage

Information about environmental damage inflicted by the war is scattered and inconclusive. This is primarily because the Iranian authorities who were charged with reconstruction focused attention on immediate relief efforts and on rebuilding both the economy and the military. Moreover, in contrast to the Gulf War of 1990, the international community did not monitor environmental effects of the Iran–Iraq war. This is attributable both to difficulties that the mass media experienced in reporting the war and to the fact that Iran had fallen out of favour with Western governments that might otherwise have taken an interest.

Despite the lack of reliable data on environmental impacts, some effects are known (Hawley 1992; Jochnick and Normand n.d.). For example, it is known that extensive minefields and unexploded war materials in all of Iran's five war-affected provinces have posed daily hazards to local populations. Reza Malekzadeh, representative of the Iranian Ministry of Health, reported in 1991 that at least 10 people a day were wounded, maimed, or killed by live war munitions (United Nations Secretary-General 1991a: 29). It is also known that ground battles and aerial bombardments caused extensive destruction of forests – a process that was exacerbated by people searching for cooking fuel to replace normal supplies; run-off and erosion have increased as a result. During the conflict, more than 3 million date palms and 5,000 hectares of orchards were destroyed. Some 130,000 hectares of natural forests and 753,000 hectares of pasture land in the war-afflicted provinces were also rendered unusable.

The impact of war on farmland was equally significant. In Khuzestan, Ilam, and Kermanshahan, "... reconstruction of the farming sub-sector involves land-leveling and grading of about 251,000 ha of irrigated farmland and rough leveling of 53,700 ha of rain-fed land" (United Nations Secretary-General 1991a: 40–41). Farmlands in the five war-impacted provinces appear to be contaminated by toxic materials emanating from chemical and biological weapons. During the war, produce from southern Iran was considered unhealthy and could not be marketed, thereby driving up prices and creating shortages.

The situation was not simply one of direct destruction and contamination. The problems of warfare were compounded by other problems, including removal of topsoil, compaction and flooding of agricultural lands, modifications of river flows, interruption of irrigation water supplies, and waterlogging and salinization due to salt water flowing onto agricultural land when irrigation canals were destroyed. Finally, study of contamination in rural areas is hampered by the presence of unidentified minefields (United Nations Secretary-General 1991a: 28–48).

Levels of environmental intoxication are much more difficult to ascertain than direct destruction, particularly because of the lack of records mentioned above but also because intoxication assessment requires fairly sophisticated technology that has been neither available in Iran nor supplied by the international environmental community. None the less, it is possible to provide a general overview of the impacts on a region-by-region basis.

The south-western provinces have experienced extreme environmental damage, particularly in the coastal strip and along main inland waterways. The Karoun River, once the mainstay of economic activity, is now heavily polluted and unusable. Among the rural population, a high incidence of diseases, especially eye infections, stomach illnesses, and skin ailments, has been reported (United Nations Secretary-General 1991a: 28–48). The exact cause of these ailments is not known, but health officials note that the rate of incidence is much higher than in areas unaffected by the war. Since the war's end there has been an alarming increase in health-threatening insects and pests. There has also been an increased incidence of acute respiratory disease, possibly as a result of war-induced toxins in the environment, as well as an increase in the number of those afflicted by severe diarrhoea, which can be more directly linked to the disruption of the provision of fresh water supplies.

The coastal region between Abadan and the Strait of Hormuz, encompassing approximately 250 square kilometres of beach, was covered in tar and asphalt. These substances posed a grave threat to already endangered species and protective vegetation. Leaks from oil tankers attacked in the Gulf are believed to be the cause (Walker 1989). Oil-related pollution is also attributed to the bombing of oil platforms in the Gulf. Capping these oil wells has taken years of effort. The territory of Iran includes many islands in the Gulf, 20 of which have been adversely affected by oil pollution and oil spills. The prawn-fishing industry has been severely threatened, owing to the destruction of mangrove and sea-grass cultures in the coastal regions of the Gulf. Sea grasses are affected by toxic hydrocarbons and contamination of sediments; oils penetrate the stomata and kill entire sea-grass communities that provide nursery grounds for prawns (United Nations Secretary-General 1991b: 29). In addition, the destruction of all or part of the prawn year class has cumulative effects on subsequent catches.

Another source of contaminants is the sunken ships and wrecks that still lie in and along the Shatt-al-Arab waterway. The magnitude of the problem increases with time because currents carry contaminant cargoes throughout the waterway system and out to the Gulf. This poses a distinct threat to the fishing industry as well as to the ecology of the area, and quite possibly to the adjacent water-table. The nature of the cargo in these ships is unknown and only a substantial investigation would reveal the exact contaminants. The estimated cost of clean-up has been put by various sources at $2 billion to $4 billion. No less than two years of continuous work is needed to rehabilitate the river.

Further destabilization of the environment in southern Iran has resulted from disturbances in the Gulf region during the US-led Persian Gulf War of 1990–1991. Some of the environmental effects that are now observed in southern Iran may be traceable in part to that war.[3]

Damage to human settlements and the economy

Damage to settlements in Iran was enormous. The war wiped out 4,000 villages, damaged 52 cities, and destroyed about 120,000 houses; 6 of the cities were completely levelled while another 15 sustained damage of 30–80 per cent. The city of Khorramshahr (1980 population 300,000) was Iran's most important port on the Gulf. It now lies in near-total ruin, having sustained destruction of 80 per cent of its buildings. Impacts in rural areas were equally great: over 30 per cent of the villages in the five most war-torn provinces were completely destroyed; others sustained severe damage. The monetary value of damage to human settlements was estimated at $13 billion for the period September 1980 to September 1985. For the entire war, human settlements damage may have exceeded $18 billion (Amirahmadi 1992a: 82).

Three types of *direct* economic damage resulting from the war were distinguished by the Iranian government – buildings and installations, machinery and equipment, and materials and goods (see table 6.1). The government also calculated a separate *indirect* economic damage category that includes opportunity costs but excludes damage to the defence sector and human losses; a value-added approach was used within a national income-accounting framework. The seven economic sectors for which data are available include agriculture, mining, manufacturing, oil, electricity/gas/water, construction and housing, and services.[4]

By the time that Iran and Iraq agreed to a cease-fire, Iran's industry was operating at only 20–30 per cent of capacity. Direct economic damage (i.e. physical destruction) inflicted on Iran amounted to a yearly average of 23.35 per cent of the country's gross domestic product (GDP). The UN Security Council estimates that the cost of direct economic damage, excluding military damage and loss of human life, amounted to $97.3 billion. Using a different exchange rate, the Iranian government puts the figure much higher, at over $300 billion. Military damage was estimated at $50 billion. Some observers estimate that the total cost of damage is in the neighbourhood of US$1,000 billion (Athari 1991).

Of all the productive sectors, the oil sector sustained by far the most damage (table 6.2; fig. 6.2). This sector accounted for 23.96 per cent of the total direct economic damage and 59.45 per cent of the damage inflicted on all productive sectors. In these sectors, nearly 86 per cent of all the damage inflicted on buildings and installations was borne by the oil industry.

Oil installations in the Gulf region were a primary attack target. The main Iranian loading terminal, located in Kharg Island, was badly damaged in August 1982, effectively halving Iranian oil exports. Before the attacks, Kharg had an offloading capacity of 14 million barrels of oil per day at 14 berthing facilities; its 1993 capacity was just 2 million barrels per day. Of 39 crude oil storage tanks, 21 were completely destroyed by fires resulting from attacks; assuming full capacity, oil spills into the Gulf from the Kharg facility alone amounted to 12 million barrels (United Nations Secretary-General 1991a: 29)

The oil industry was, and is, extremely important to the economic viability of Iran. Oil revenues accounted for 51 per cent of total government revenues in 1983–1984 and 44 per cent of total government revenues in 1986–1987. In fact, oil revenues generally account for over 95 per cent of Iran's foreign exchange earnings and pay for the

Table 6.1 **Direct economic damage (DED) of the war, 1980–1988, from the beginning to the cease-fire (million rials, current prices)**

Year	Buildings and installations	Machinery and equipment	Materials and goods	Total annual DED	Annual DED as percentage of grand total	Current price GDP[a]	Total annual DED as percentage of annual GDP
1980	297,039	236,707	304,400	838,146	2.72	6,758,900	12.40
1981	343,791	448,918	244,507	1,037,216	3.37	8,218,500	12.62
1982	50,738	97,654	3,580,140	3,728,532	12.10	10,621,500	35.10
1983	1,021,087	1,203,698	2,296,948	4,521,733	14.68	13,471,300	33.57
1984	238,545	1,130,960	568,747	1,938,252	6.29	14,600,700	13.28
1985	558,119	1,056,650	2,129,796	3,744,565	12.15	15,948,200	23.48
1986	6,671,457	960,222	763,890	8,395,569	27.25	17,512,600	47.94
1987	621,670	1,330,533	1,320,906	3,273,109	10.62	20,605,400	15.88
1988	125,852	3,086,606	121,843	3,334,301	10.82	24,244,400	13.75
Grand total	9,928,298	9,551,948	11,331,177	30,811,423	100.00	131,981,500	23.35
Percentage of total	32.22	31.00	36.78	100.00			

Source: Amirahmadi (1992b: 70).
a. Gross domestic product.

Table 6.2 **Sectoral distribution of direct and indirect damage of the war, 1980–1988 (million rials, current prices)**

Sectors	Direct economic damage					Indirect economic damage	Total direct and indirect damage	Share of direct damage in total damage (%)
	Buildings and installations	Machinery and equipment	Materials and goods	Total	Share in total (%)			
A Productive sectors (total)	7,915,822	2,436,932	2,065,121	12,417,875	40.30	30,108,007	42,525,882	29.20
1 Agriculture	644,544	557,013	581,820	1,783,377	5.79	14,173,955	15,957,332	11.18
2 Mining	19,209	10,074	6,507	35,790	0.12	23,410	59,200	60.46
3 Manufacturing	154,597	1,441,900	30,363	1,626,860	5.28	851,859	2,478,719	65.63
4 Oil	6,802,044	250,786	329,795	7,382,625	23.96	13,416,915	20,799,540	35.49
5 Electricity, gas, and water	115,013	175,019	1,023,703	1,313,735	4.26	1,634,922	2,948,657	44.55
6 Construction and housing	180,415	2,140	92,933	275,488	0.89	6,946	282,434	97.54
B Service sectors (total)	2,012,476	7,115,017	9,266,055	18,393,548	59.70	4,434,319	22,827,867	80.57
1 Trade, restaurants, and hotels	682,782	35,434	8,538	726,754	2.36	15,436	742,190	97.92
2 Transportation, communication, and storage	96,528	1,027,239	106,721	1,230,488	3.99	632,059	1,862,547	66.06
3 Fiscal and monetary institutions	120,026	772	20,532	141,330	0.46	870,511	1,011,841	13.97
4 Public services	644,380	6,028,398	9,098,642	15,771,420	51.19	1,690,972	17,462,392	90.32
5 Social, personal, and household services	468,760	23,174	31,622	523,556	1.70	1,225,341	1,748,897	29.94
Grand total (A and B)	9,928,298	9,551,949	11,331,176	30,811,423	100.00	34,542,326	65,353,749	47.15

Source: Amirahmadi (1992b: 75).

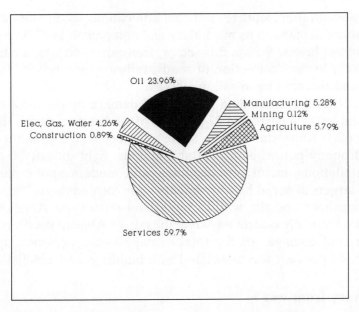

Fig. 6.2 **Direct economic losses by sector (Source: Plan and Budget Organization, Islamic Republic of Iran 1991: 50)**

bulk of Iran's industrial inputs, food imports, and military needs. Iranian industries depend on foreign markets for over 65 per cent of their raw materials, 75 per cent of their intermediate inputs, and over 90 per cent of their capital goods. One analyst estimated that the cost of the war absorbed 60 per cent of Iran's gross national product (GNP) during the 1980–1988 period (Mofid 1990).

Further breakdown of sectoral damage reveals that the manufacturing sector suffered most heavily in terms of machinery and equipment, namely, loss of capital stock: it accounts for the largest share of damage in this category, at 59.17 per cent, with agriculture a distant second at 22.86 per cent. Electricity, gas, and water incurred the most damage in terms of materials and goods – constituting 49.57 per cent of the total losses to materials and goods, while agriculture accounts for 28.17 per cent of this type of damage. Within agriculture, farming suffered the most damage, followed by forestry, animal husbandry, hunting, and fisheries. Most damage in the construction sector was to buildings and installations, which constituted 65.49 per cent of the damage to that sector. Direct economic damage to the nation's public services alone accounts for 51.19 per cent of the total and 85.74 per cent of the damage sustained by the service sector as a whole.

The transportation, storage, and communications sector sustained the
majority of damage to its machinery and equipment, at 83.48 per cent
of its direct losses. Within this sector, transportation was the hardest
hit, owing to the destruction of roads, railways, and private vehicles
(Plan and Budget Organization 1991).

A breakdown of the data for sectoral damage by province reveals
that Khuzestan incurred 34.27 per cent of all direct economic damage
(table 6.3). Khuzestan's large share of the damage was not unexpected: many petrochemical establishments, light industry facilities,
oil installations, major port facilities, and modern agribusinesses –
prime targets of aerial bombardments – are located there. The city of
Khorramshahr and the world's largest oil refinery at Abadan were
almost completely destroyed, while the city of Abadan itself sustained
50 per cent damage. Of the total damage to the province, approximately 40 per cent was associated with buildings and installations.

Recovery from war

Defining priorities for reconstruction became a fulcrum for partisan
debate and political contest in the Iranian government. This is an
experience common to many societies that have experienced widespread destruction from disaster, whether it is war, industrial calamity,
or natural disaster. In Iran, different political groups sought to have
their own social and economic agendas reflected in the reconstruction
strategy. Debate centred around four issues – rebuilding the military,
reinvigorating the national economy, promoting the economic well-
being of the poor, and reconstructing war-damaged areas. Only the
most radical faction of the government was concerned with equity
and social justice. Conservative and pragmatist factions believed that
economic growth and efficiency should guide reconstruction, and it is
these views that came to dominate official policy. As a result, most
reconstruction efforts are devoted to strengthening market mechanisms, privatization, and liberalization of trade.

Imports are an essential component of the Iranian economy, and
reconstruction of both the civilian and military sectors cannot be
accomplished without them. But imports must be paid for with hard
currency and most of this is obtained in exchange for Iranian oil.
Unfortunately, Iran's oil revenues have been insufficient for the task
and government leaders are preoccupied with finding alternative
sources of hard currency. Conservative factions – which are currently
in power – favour opening the Iranian economy to foreign investors,

Table 6.3 **Distribution of direct economic damage of the war by province, 1980–1988 (million rials, current prices)**

Province	Buildings and installations	Machinery and equipment	Materials and goods	Total	Percentage of total
Khuzestan	7,523,721	1,449,719	1,585,219	10,558,659	34.27
Lorestan	10,689	1,007,378	34,737	1,052,804	3.42
Ilam	637,761	6,453	82,721	726,935	2.36
Bakhtaran	275,065	36,059	271,764	582,888	1.89
Sistan and Baluchestan	0	315,074	3	315,077	1.02
W. Azerbaijan	11,113	264,763	31,691	307,567	1.00
Total of the six most-damaged provinces	8,458,349	3,079,446	2,006,135	13,543,930	43.96
Other provinces	1,469,949	6,472,502	9,325,041	17,267,492	56.04
Total	9,928,298	9,551,948	11,331,176	30,811,422	100.00
Share of the six most-damaged provinces in total damage (%)	85.19	32.24	17.70	43.96	

Source: Amirahmadi (1992b: 80).

161

limiting state intervention, and allowing the market and the private sector to stimulate rapid economic growth. More radical factions have argued for growth at a slower pace and for government investment in domestic industries that will supply cement, steel, and other commodities to meet the basic needs of reconstruction. The radicals have also favoured a welfare relief programme that targets the neediest. While domestic investment and relief are included in the government's reconstruction plan, conservative policies are clearly dominant.

Since 1989, President Ali Akbar Hashemi Rafsanjani, a political pragmatist, has tried to accommodate public, private, and cooperative sectors in the reconstruction process. His government has relied on a blend of domestic resources and capabilities; international trade, investment and borrowing; expansion of the role of the private sector; and utilization of public planning and market mechanisms. Following recommendations of the World Bank and the International Monetary Fund (IMF), the government has implemented economic stabilization and structural adjustment programmes that are designed to put the economy on a peacetime footing that emphasizes increased growth and greater efficiency. Most price controls have been lifted; nationalized industries are being sold to the private sector; subsidies have largely been eliminated; a single exchange rate has been introduced; the Iranian rial has been devalued and made convertible, and the government's budget deficit has been brought under control. The Iranian government has also taken a series of other steps: it has borrowed upwards of $30 billion from foreign governments and financial and industrial institutions; it has encouraged – with less success – foreign investment; and it has created free economic zones in the Persian Gulf islands and elsewhere in the country. The immediate impacts of this macroeconomic policy have been higher inflation, a wider gap between the incomes of rich and poor, and a larger international debt; meanwhile, its long-term success remains in doubt while the US government opposes the government in Teheran and there is uncertainty about political changes following the end of Rafsanjani's term in 1997. However, from the perspective of economic growth, the policy has already been successful because the growth rate has averaged about 8 per cent per year between 1989 and 1992. None the less, most of the benefits of this growth have been eroded by a population increase rate of around 3.2 per cent per year (1992).

National reconstruction plans

The First Socio-Economic and Cultural Development Plan of the Islamic Republic provided for three, more or less distinct, stages of economic reconstruction. Industrial recovery is an important objective. In the first stage, efforts are directed toward full use of existing productive capacities (particularly in oil and gas), infrastructure, and human resources. Strong emphasis is also placed on agriculture and rural development. The goal at this stage is the restoration of the economy to its normal functioning level and the increase of oil exports to generate as much foreign exchange as possible. Structural adjustment and stabilization, as prescribed by the World Bank and IMF, and investment in the oil sector are the major government programmes at present.

The next plan (1994–1998) will focus on using oil revenue to achieve economic growth and increased per capita income by expanding productive capacities and job-generating investments. The third and final plan will attempt to consolidate the growth process and make it independent of the oil sector. This is a stage far into the future. Iranian leaders believe that only then will the country be able to achieve goals of social justice and economic self-sufficiency.

While economic normalization is the focus of the first national plan, the government has also been making progress toward the physical reconstruction of war-damaged areas and the establishment of new economic activities. Before authorities could plan for rebuilding urban and industrial areas, they needed to know how many people would be returning to pre-war settlements; hence population projections were undertaken. Second, the government studied the functions of various cities in anticipation of changing their pre-war roles. Third, authorities adopted a regional view of development according to which, cities and villages were regarded as integral parts of provinces that were themselves part of an integrated national state.

The National Spatial Planning Strategy requires that reconstruction of rural settlements will precede that of the cities. The intent is to prevent unwanted migration of rural people to the cities. This strategy is consistent with the government's earlier plan to make agriculture an axis of development and to resettle rural areas. The government's plan calls for gradual reconstruction of towns and villages so that people will return to their previous settlements as essential public and private activities are taking shape. Planning, cultural matters, and other human dimensions of reconstruction are said to have received particular attention. It is judged that, as ravaged areas are revitalized, war migrants will return and help to rebuild damaged structures. Housing reconstruction has remained a major parameter in the overall plan for normalization of conditions (*tabi'i sazi*) in the damaged areas.

During the war, reconstruction was an emergency or replacement activity that focused largely on housing. Now it includes upgrading building quality, infrastructure, and economic productivity. The Supreme Council for Reconstruction and Renovation of War-Damaged Areas is the highest-level body responsible for reconstruction. It makes strategic decisions and oversees efforts to promote public financial contributions. Another body, the Central Headquarters for Reconstruction, sets priorities, makes policies, supervises implementation of projects, and coordinates the work of other organizations. The various sectoral reconstruction headquarters coordinate reconstruction works with the sectoral planning committees and supervise projects being implemented by contractors. Finally, the provincial and county reconstruction headquarters are responsible for a variety of tasks, including prioritizing the reconstruction projects for implementation. These governmental institutions are assisted by other public and private organizations including the Housing Foundation, the Ministry of Reconstruction Crusade, the Endowment for the Eighth Imam, *Setadha-ye Mo'in* (supporting centres for particular projects or cities such as Khorramshahr's *Setad*), philanthropic organizations, and revolutionary foundations (*baseej* and *komiteh*).

Where possible, the Iranian government does not relocate or attempt to combine damaged settlements. Rather, the policy is to rebuild them on their original sites (*darja sazi*). This is intended to minimize cost, save time, and prevent unnecessary conflict between the people and the government. The government also avoids certain actions such as reconstructing apartment complexes, building houses before the owners have returned to the settlements, and using prefabrication techniques. Experience in Iran indicates that previously those actions were not popular with the people. Rather, endogenous techniques and ones that use more local or national resources are preferred: they are said to reduce the nation's technological dependency. A flexible planning approach is adopted so that feedback and inputs from people are easily incorporated to improve the quality of operations. In reconstructing population centres, the order of priority is, first, residential and commercial units and factories producing construction materials, followed by other employment-generating activities, particularly in agriculture and small industries. Provision of heat, water, electricity, roads, infrastructures, educational and health services, communication links, and urban amenities are also given high priority. At the national level, special priority has been attached to reconstruction of large industrial units such as petrochemical complexes, oil refineries, and power plants.

There are three levels of reconstruction plans. "National sector" plans (*bakhsh-e melli*) include large industrial and infrastructural projects that are implemented by ministries. "Popular sector" plans (*bakhsh-e mardomi*) deal with reconstruction of residential and commercial units by their owners. "Regional sector" plans (*bakhsh-e mantaqehei*) encompass regional development programmes and urban or rural service projects. They are implemented by reconstruction offices in the damaged areas. The role of government is limited to investing in job-generating productive units, supervision of reconstruction processes, provision of technical services, and financial assistance. In all cases, site preparation is a public responsibility. The government is also responsible for equipping public offices with adequate equipment and skilled labour, as well as for delivering basic construction materials to the project sites.

Financially, the public sector assists reconstruction by investing in infrastructure; providing technical and managerial personnel; reimbursing the public for part of the war-related losses; and granting credits, loans, and other banking services. For rebuilding urban residential units (from 60 to 120 square metres), the government pays up to 6 million rials, plus the cost of construction materials.

Support from international organizations and local communities

International economic and diplomatic communities are playing a limited but direct role in reconstruction, to some degree reversing the "hands-off" approach adopted by other countries during the war. Firms from Western Europe, Japan, Russia, and the United States (as subcontractors) are currently involved in rebuilding oil installations and have joined in other major industrial and infrastructural projects. The United Nations Security Council (December 1991) has made unsuccessful overtures to the West for technical and financial assistance to Iran.[5]

The support of local citizens has been crucial to fighting the war and rebuilding ravaged communities. During the war's early years there was great popular enthusiasm for the Iranian revolution, and citizens were willing to take the lead in reconstructing houses and public facilities. This spirit continues even after the war's end: it is reflected in recommendations of the Council of Policy Making for Reconstruction. In 1988, the Council, acting on recommendations from the late Ayatollah Khomeini, outlined its Directive on the Comprehensive National Reconstruction Plan. The Directive called for a reconstruction strategy that is founded on the capabilities of people in war-torn areas, and that stresses the importance of "observing the cultural, traditional, and psychological characteristics of the people in each area...." (Amirahmadi 1990b: 247). Despite the emphasis on local initiatives, the government and social systems of Iran are centralized. The national government is wholly responsible for all reconstruction plans. It decides which productive centres are to be rebuilt, the pace of rebuilding, and land-use patterns.

Local participation was intended to be institutionalized by means of expanded provincial and municipal authorities, as well as town councils. However, there is no autonomous non-governmental agency that encourages grass-roots inputs. The national government's call for citizen participation in the rebuilding is a top-down management strategy, wherein the central authority makes the important decisions about a wide range of matters, including how to refashion cities, reinvigorate local industry, and create post-war local administrations. Over time, the government has also redefined local participation in terms of increasing privatization of the public sector by means of various incentive packages. Consequently, the claim that residents of war-afflicted areas will be involved in the rebuilding process has a hollow ring, except in the case of private housing reconstruction. With the adoption of free market mechanisms as the ultimate arbiters of reconstruction, community members become involved in the process only to the extent that they provide the human capital necessary for economic growth and restructuring. The government does, however, continue to provide materials to individuals wishing to rebuild. Compensation of victims for losses incurred during the war is viewed as essential for maintaining popular support of the regime.

Owners are responsible for the design and reconstruction of their own units. The Director of the Provincial Reconstruction Office may, at his discretion, assist an owner with up to 180 square metres of roof coverage. An owner may be also assisted by bank loans. For urban commercial establishments, the government pays up to 1.5 million

rials and assists the owner with bank loans. For rebuilding and reno-
vating production units, the government pays up to 6 million rials and
provides construction materials at official prices. Other government
assistance includes bank loans and provision of foreign exchange to
be used for purchase of machinery and equipment. The government
also reimburses private victims for a long list of damaged items,
ranging from agricultural products and palm trees to animals and
private vehicles. Building permits and access to water and electricity
are also provided free of charge. The Reconstruction Organization is
responsible for clearing and removal of debris at no cost to owners.
Finally, the government sells the following seven "basic" household
items to war migrants who are returning to villages: machine-made
carpet; refrigerator; black and white television; stove; kitchen ware
and plates; sewing machine, and fan.

Urban reconstruction

Cities are being reconstructed on their previous sites and with an eye
toward modernization. While mixed land uses are maintained in most
cases, industrial and commercial zones are separated from residential
areas. This has led to significant changes in landholding patterns
within reconstructed urban settlements. Attempts are being made
to enforce Islamic building codes and architecture, but without much
success. A new urban strategy is now in place. It focuses first on the
reconstruction of productive sectors of the economy and then on
infrastructure, housing, and services as bottlenecks develop in those
areas. The new strategy is intended to bring about a gradual repopu-
lation of damaged settlements, adjusted to the rate at which housing
and jobs are available.

In many places reconstruction has proceeded slowly and with considerable debate. For example, the rebuilding of Khorramshahr was
slowed by disagreement about whether the city had lost its justification as a major port. Alternative ports had been developed elsewhere
during the war, some on more strategically secure sites. When reconstruction began in some parts of Khorramshahr, original foundations
were excavated in an attempt to confirm land ownership with survivors. The effort required to carry out such painstaking reconstruction
was judged to be warranted by the psychological, social, and economic
benefits that accrued from working closely with local residents (Zargar
and Poor 1991).

Implementation of reconstruction plans begins when the Ministry of Health and the Red Crescent Society have finished disinfecting a war-damaged area. At that time an area manager is appointed to oversee the rebuilding of houses. He (invariably male) is the sole representative of the Housing Foundation in the locality and his decision may not be overturned by other public officials. However, the area manager must work within the framework of the relevant provincial development plan and coordinate his activities with provincial officials and activities. In addition to area managers, other agents involved in the task of housing reconstruction include owners of houses, Islamic Councils, auxiliary work groups, and provincial representatives of the Housing Foundation.

Housing reconstruction

The national government puts little money into the reconstruction of damaged houses. Most government funds are invested in public services, site preparation, employment-generating productive activities, provision of construction materials, architectural design, technical supervision, and builder training. The government has adopted a "new town" development strategy and employs the "site and service provision" approach advocated by the World Bank. In rural areas, the Housing Foundation is primarily responsible for the quality of the construction materials and buildings.

Some financial assistance is available to home-builders: it can take the form of grants, credit, or bank loans. But the emphasis on self-help makes home-owners responsible for design and construction and encourages them to rely on local technology and resources.

Industrial reconstruction

Major economic enterprises and industries are responsible for reconstructing their respective facilities under the direction of the Ministry of Heavy Industries, the Ministry of (Light) Industries or the Ministry of Mines and Metals. Oil, gas, petrochemical industries, basic industries, firms producing construction materials, metal products, and basic needs consumer goods have been given top priority.

A committee first determines if a specific firm should be scrapped or rebuilt and whether its facilities warrant repair, replacement, or upgrading. Units that are unlikely to be rebuilt include those with more than 30 per cent damage, those technically too obsolete or too dependent, and units with little prospect for significant value-added capability. Attention is also paid to labour and financial markets, capital markets, production technology, inputs–outputs markets, trade prospects, management requirements and capabilities, and other necessary institutional arrangements. While these activities have been followed in the case of industrial rebuilding, the nation as yet does not have a clear industrial policy or a policy of industrial security in case of another war.

What this overview of post-war reconstruction shows is that industrial redevelopment is a priority of the Iranian government, but that there is little explicit concern for industrial safety as a planning criterion, for adding improved accident-prevention systems to the rebuilt industrial facilities, or for making other attempts to mitigate potential industrial disasters. Whereas peacetime industrial disasters have sometimes stimulated hazard-reduction legislation and other initiatives, one lesson of Iran's experience is that war-related industrial disasters are not followed by such changes.

Conceptual framework for a model of post-war reconstruction and industrial hazard recovery

The best way to prevent war-related industrial disasters is to prevent wars from occurring in the first place. Obviously, it is too late to prevent the outbreak of hostilities between Iran and Iraq: the damage has already been done. Regrettably, similar situations are likely to arise in the future and there will continue to be a need for reconstruction in the wake of armed conflict. Figure 6.3 summarizes a framework for post-war reconstruction that is based on the Iranian experience. In the pages that follow, the most important elements of the framework are explained, with special attention to the recovery of industrial facilities that have been destroyed or damaged and of adjacent areas and populations that have been polluted.

A reconstruction strategy

The formulation of a post-war reconstruction strategy is bound to become the centre of fierce debate, for it must satisfy and cut across varying ideologies, social groups, time periods, and cultures. The chosen strategy will depend in large measure on the nature of the war itself and the extent of damage. Each nation must fashion its own national reconstruction strategy, but the Iranian experience can serve as a guide to issues and alternatives.

169

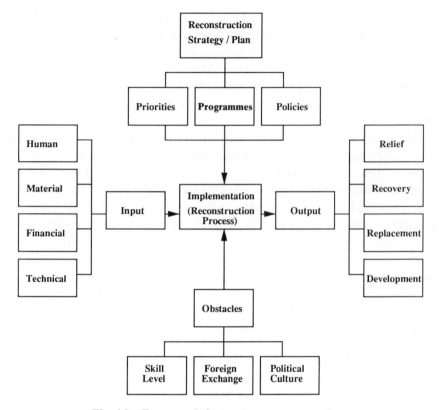

Fig. 6.3   **Framework for post-war reconstruction**

First and foremost, a reconstruction strategy must be versatile and flexible. This means that it must be broad enough to be usable by different sectors and different levels of political administration, and able to accommodate the changing mix of problems that arise at different stages of the reconstruction process. It must also be able to respond to the needs of different socio-economic groups and to focus resources on urgent problems that demand quick action (e.g. industrial hazards and associated contamination). The strategy must also strike a balance between competing demands for the immediate relief of destruction and the need to invest in activities that will eventually restore the country's long-term economic base. Typically, in the post-war atmosphere of economic austerity, many forces compete for scarce resources, and governments can be drawn into wasteful social projects that are attractive on political grounds.

In addition to these general principles, a reconstruction strategy should incorporate clear long-term goals. To ensure success, goals must be translated into clearly defined objectives that realistically take into account the society's resources, expectations, constraints, and capabilities. After an evaluation of these factors, a hierarchy of goals must be formed, based on a set of national priorities. In postwar societies these goals generally include restoration of human health and long-term habitability, reconstruction of the economy, rebuilding of national defence, rehabilitation of war-damaged areas, and the correction of social imbalances caused by war.[6]

National planning is based on an assumption that "the details" can be left to regional, local, or sectoral plans. But what happens when there is widespread localized destruction of industrial facilities that have the potential to create pervasive, long-running hazards for regions, countries, or the entire earth? Perhaps it will be necessary to devise new forms of national planning or to conceptualize local–national–global events and strategies in new ways. For the more focused task of industrial revival, such procedural approaches have to become even more specific, allowing for implementation of tasks relating to various resources and commodity markets, and organizational arrangements within and outside the industries. Participation of employees in the revival of industries is a critical need that may be met by organizing them in various consultative and executive bodies.

Implementation is better achieved if accompanied by well-defined and specific policies concerning environmental, economic, social, political, ideological, cultural, infrastructural, territorial, educational, technical, and legal changes. Environmental policies not only must take into consideration existing problems but also must address the future security of industrial plants and surrounding populations against internal and external hazards. Economic policies need to account for budget deficits incurred in a war effort, which generate inflation, unemployment, and poverty. The government must also be responsible for generating incentive packages that will induce the private sector to invest in productive activities, while at the same time curbing non-productive uses of capital through selective measures such as taxes and cumbersome licensing requirements. The government could also seek out direct foreign investment for revitalizing industries.

Social policies must be directed toward the provision of basic needs in such areas as health, education, housing, and recreation, with explicit emphasis on services for those who were physically or mentally traumatized during the war. Housing policy is the most critical component of the government's social policy during reconstruction after the war: the housing sector normally receives the most damage and suffers from shortages even in peacetime. Implementing a policy that allows for a sustainable housing process is the most important aspect of a more effective social policy. Here, income generation should become the primary goal. Education policy plays a very significant role in reconstruction, particularly in the third world where professional and technical education levels remain low. A more effective education programme should be specifically directed at training policy makers, planners, managers, and local leaders, as well as toward transforming fighters into producers and polluters into environmentalists! Cultural policies are needed to maintain diversity and unity during the highly disruptive and transformative process of reconstruction.

After housing, infrastructure is the sector of society that is most severely affected by war. Therefore, the success of a reconstruction strategy hinges on well-designed infrastructural policies that take into account future needs of communities and strengthen linkages between them. Infrastructural policies are best implemented in conjunction with settlement policies. These can benefit from an integrated regional approach in which a hierarchy of rural and urban areas are linked together functionally, as well as by transportation and communication networks. Targeting specific cities as market centres or other functional centres may require restructuring of the pre-war urban system. Small-scale rural industries that stimulate the agricultural sector (e.g. food processing) could be linked to industries at higher levels of the territorial hierarchy.

An essential part of the implementation process is the codification of all the policies mentioned above, in the form of an appropriate legal framework. The reconstruction plan itself must be made into law if its implementation is truly to be carried out. Last, but by no means least, reconstruction strategy must deal with political issues that permeate every aspect of reconstruction: there is a great deal of potentially destructive ambiguity about the roles of post-war military forces, about factionalism, and about state–society relations. While democratization and public participation are the only means for creating political legitimacy, most post-war states are too fragile and unstable to allow for their implementation in the short term if they were not firmly entrenched in the political system before war began. Most post-war societies are characterized by political discord and national conflicts. In spite of this, there simply is no alternative to national reconciliation if reconstruction is to be implemented successfully.

The reconstruction process

To some degree, the reconstruction process exhibits predictable characteristics. These include the tendency for damaged cities and industries to be rebuilt on the same sites, continuation of pre-war trends in population growth and urban expansion, continuation of predominance of certain industries, and continuation of previous social stratification patterns (Haas, Kates, and Bowden 1977). The tendency for a society to return to the *status quo ante* after war can be explained by two powerful forces – fear of change (particularly in a society that has already seen so much negative transformation) and the desire of those who control existing institutions to hold onto power. If market mechanisms are relied upon too heavily during post-war reconstruction, class cleavages may become even more pronounced than before the war. Underprivileged members of society are the most vulnerable in a disaster: they are the least likely to live in well-constructed shelters that may survive attacks, and the least likely to have savings to fall back on for the replacement of destroyed possessions. Some owners and merchants, on the other hand, are able to benefit from the business booms generated by the flood of resources into the reconstruction effort. These circumstances must be borne in mind at every stage of the planning process.

An acceptable reconstruction process – much like an appropriate reconstruction strategy – will, of course, vary from case to case. Further research into the critically important properties of post-war reconstruction will provide societies with better information for decision-making. The following set of hypotheses is based on existing literature and the author's experience with disaster planning and post-war reconstruction, and is offered as a framework for further analysis.

1. *Reconstruction tends to become politicized and factionalism tends to delay the reconstruction of war-damaged areas.* War simultaneously places demands on a country's resources and increases public expectations of post-war economic improvements. The shortages that occur generate societal tension and intensify pressure on the state to implement immediate corrective measures. Factions struggle over reconstruction strategy (planned versus market approach) and there is reduced political will for recon-

struction of war-damaged areas. Although there is general agreement about the need to resolve economic crises, political factionalism may prevent specific measures from being implemented.
Environmental disasters – including those that are connected
with industries – are, however, a more serious matter that cannot
long be ignored. As a result, they tend to require expenditure of
national resources in the post-war period.

2. *Reconstruction is essential therapy for a wounded society.* Social
therapy centres on people rebuilding their communities, both
physically and emotionally, and this process can succeed only if
there is a national commitment to healing. Long-term habitability
must become a priority and the guiding goal of the reconstruction.

3. *Enforcement of legal safety codes and provision of social insurance are essential to reconstruction.* This is particularly true when
industrial hazards are pervasive and environmental degradation
has become threatening. The immediate post-war period gener-
ates high emotions and pressures for rapid response, and there is
an understandable tendency toward quick fixes. However, quick
fixes may ultimately be much more costly than more comprehensive repairs. Unsafe industrial sites and poorly reconstructed
buildings pose dangerous hazards for reconstruction workers and
residents, with both moral and material consequences.

4. *Just as reconstruction after natural disaster must be used to pre-
pare for or mitigate the effects of the next disaster, so must post-
war reconstruction be used to reduce the risk of another war and
its consequent industrial hazards by incorporating the causes of
the war into the strategy itself.* In addition to war-reduction strategies, a nation must also adopt preventive strategies that reduce
industrial hazard. Therefore, national and industrial security
schemes, and defensive and preventive measures, become major
components of the post-war reconstruction. These measures are
best achieved by emphasizing peace and by renouncing war as a
means to settle dispute. Several strategies can be used to oper-
ationalize this goal. First, there must be wide recognition of the
fact that a good defence policy must be based on diplomacy, as
well as on the fact that maintaining an offensive force at the
expense of economic development does little toward increasing a
nation's share of the international balance of power. Second,
people's attitudes toward the enemy as well as toward the war
and environmental safety must be transformed. This may prove
difficult, particularly after a defeat, but reconstructionists can

play an important role as peace activists, as well as environmentalists, and education can be targeted toward reducing the
country's zeal for war and increasing its appreciation of ecological safety. Realistic defensive measures that are designed to
improve a nation's perception of security can be built into the
reconstruction process, as can preventive measures that improve
industrial security. Border areas must be repopulated and physically reconstructed with the explicit goal of security, while strategic economic activities and industrial plants can be relocated
to safer places. Regional government and military installations
must be reforged with an eye to territorial balance and cultural
integration.

5. *War damage, industrial hazards, and reconstruction needs must be
carefully determined and assessed.* An assessment of war damage
and industrial hazards requires an interdisciplinary approach, for
damage and hazard situations differ in terms of their physical and
chemical nature, the social consequences they generate, and the
economic feasibility of their repair and clean-ups. Skilled professionals in all disciplines, as well as the population at large,
must join together to form a consensus on rebuilding priorities.
Record keeping of damage and hazards is essential. Among other
things, carefully kept records of damage avoid confusion over
ownership and provide help in determining compensation for war
victims, targeting priority reconstruction projects, and locating
resources.

6. *Existing and potential resources for reconstruction and clean-
ups must be quickly identified and mobilized.* The mobilization
of resources must begin with an identification of their type,
quality, amount, distribution, costs, function, ease of use, and
impact. Indigenous resources must be distinguished from external resources, and these resources must be weighed in terms
of their potential to cause dependency, unwanted control over
development, and uneven development. After resources are
identified and analysed, they must be mobilized. Mobilization
will depend largely on government action, but can effectively be
augmented through the utilization of grass-roots organizations
such as self-help projects, women's groups, and cooperatives
designed to train people and provide materials for rebuilding.
Military personnel can become clean-up crews and rebuilders.
Public and private initiatives, such as the selling of war bonds and
self-financing, will help the government tap personal wealth for

mobilization. Material resources can be mobilized by expanding mineral exploration and by relying on local materials for building. Effective communication and transportation systems are vital for resource mobilization.

7. *Successful reconstruction and hazard reduction depend on accurate timing.* Speed is essential in harnessing political will and public enthusiasm before allocation of dwindling resources induces pessimism. The first step in post-disaster planning is an analysis to determine the cause and consequences of the disaster. The optimal time for reconstruction and clean-ups is after the war, when people are returning to war-damaged areas and can be involved in the process. The best time to plan, however, is during the war so that the nation is ready to rebuild as soon as the war is over. It is doubtful if the existing industrial disaster response plans (like a US Superfund-style programme) intended for peacetime use will work during or after a war.

8. *Reconstruction should be defined, planned, and implemented in stages.* According to existing literature about disaster planning, the main stages are emergency, restoration, replacement, and developmental reconstruction (Amirahmadi 1990b: 268). These stages are not necessarily chronological, nor are they mutually exclusive. The duration of each stage will vary according to the scale of the disaster, the level of commitment to clean-up and reconstruction, and the ability of a society to cope with the disaster and to formulate strategies. Other factors include availability of resources and the government's ability to mobilize them, quality of leadership, the speed at which decisions are made and implemented, existence of popular and humanitarian organizations, and international cooperation.

The goal of the emergency stage is to cope with the disaster and to help victims survive. The urgency of this stage precludes any real planning; in this case the planning must come before the disaster. It includes such activities as search, rescue, mass feeding, clearance of debris, paramedical help, and provision of shelter and other basic needs for the victim. The primary resources for the emergency stage are community emergency services and self-help, although international relief agencies often may provide assistance. The emergency stage overlaps with the restoration, or recovery, stage, in which the goal is to make the community at least partially functional. Damaged structures are patched up or retrofitted and made usable again. This stage obviously involves more comprehensive planning, as well as greater need for resources, particularly construction materials. Investments and expenditures during this stage are by nature temporary, and repairs generally require a second, more permanent investment.

The goal of the replacement stage is to return the community to its pre-disaster state through the creation of permanent housing, the return of displaced persons, resumption of public services, revival of industries, and the creation of jobs. This stage requires substantial comprehensive planning as well as massive resources. It should be followed – or even accompanied – by a fourth stage, developmental reconstruction, in which the goal is to develop the community beyond the pre-disaster level. Combining policy and resources for the replacement and development stages may mitigate the tendency to patch things quickly, which often leads to double investment and waste. The development reconstruction stage is very difficult in a war-torn society, for wars do not simply destroy part of what exists: they also prevent society from making new investments, from utilizing production capacity and resources, and from developing skills and technical capabilities.

9. *Reconstruction and hazard removal must be properly and efficiently managed.* The government must, of course, assume ultimate responsibility for management, yet certain local functions could be assumed by grass-roots organizations. A comprehensive management system can be embodied in one of three forms of government bureaucracy – establishment of a specialized new ministry for reconstruction and disaster planning, creation of reconstruction and disaster-management offices within the existing ministries, or formation of a headquarters within the executive office for the jobs.

10. *Progress made toward reconstruction and clean-up must be documented and evaluated.* Results should be periodically published in academic and professional, as well as popular, media. Evaluation of reconstruction and hazard-removal activities should be undertaken by independent agencies that have access to key governmental data and policies but remain outside the government's sphere of direct influence.

Improving recovery and policy implications

This chapter has analysed the relationship of war, community destruction, and industrial disaster in terms of Iran's experience.

It has shown how particular issues of recovery from industrial disasters became caught up in broader concerns of recovery from more encompassing damage to the community, and it has highlighted the role of macroeconomic planning issues. Further, the chapter has explored interconnections among local-level reconstruction priorities and national-level goals, demonstrating how – in Iran's case – the latter became dominant in the course of post-war reconstruction. This trend, in turn, led to a lower priority for hazard clean-up and for rebuilding industries with low value-added attributes. Intervention by the international community in the post-war peace and reconstruction efforts was shown to have been minimal because of Iran's fractured image in the West. This may not, however, be the case in other situations where the national leadership maintains good contacts with the international community.

Iran's experience suggests that the process of planning for industrial hazards must take into consideration the context of wartime economic damage. After a war, the knowledge that destruction was the intent of an aggressor puts recovery and reconstruction initiatives in a special light. Perceptions of military and diplomatic security become crucial to the process of national rehabilitation. Demoralization that accompanies war has the potential to thwart the industrial rebuilding process, particularly if such efforts are already hampered by an absence of sufficient resources, or if the frontier of impact is subject to possible repeated attacks. In cases such as these, the disaster cycle of emergency relief, restoration, replacement, and reconstruction is undertaken again and again, each time progressively eroding the resilience and resources of the affected population.

Moreover, because the impact of war is more complex and pervasive than that of natural disasters or peacetime industrial disasters, post-war reconstruction is an especially challenging task. For example, after an industrial disaster, affected facilities are usually either repaired and reopened – with or without improvements – or are closed down, abandoned, or removed. In either case, explicit and swift decisions about the future of these facilities are generally taken by owners and governments. During wars, the same facilities may continue to operate in an impaired state for long periods, after partial and temporary repairs have been made, or they may remain inoperable until such times as formal decisions about their future can be taken at the conclusion of hostilities. In short, the course of recovery from a war-induced industrial disaster is likely to differ from that which occurs in peacetime.

The process of maintaining a war effort and the process of post-war reconstruction are links in the same chain, and that chain is forged of materials and money. Wars cost phenomenal amounts of money, while war damage is precisely calculated to reduce an enemy's capacity to finance a war. The war effort often absorbs so much government revenue that there are few reserves left for reconstruction or clean-up work. Lack of funding for relief, hazard reduction, and reconstruction becomes particularly severe if the nations engaged in war continue to feel threatened and subsequently feel compelled to channel the few remaining funds into the military. A government's time and labour may be spent in evaluating the future potential of its own armed forces, instead of first analysing the impact of war destruction and associated industrial hazards and then determining the best plan for healing society and reinvigorating economic productivity.

Iran's experience provides insights about the components of a model of disaster-impact assessment and recovery for war-damaged societies, helps to specify possible obstacles to reconstruction, and suggests ways of improving implementation. However, if the conceptual framework developed in this chapter were to be applied to Iran, it would force the government to become more concerned with industrial hazards and ways of recovering from them than has been the case so far. Unfortunately, Iran's relative neglect of industrial hazards in the larger recovery process is not at all unique. In most developing nations, where resources are scarce and macroeconomic distortions tend to destabilize regimes, economic matters take precedence over environmental concerns. This is as true of nations that have gone through a war as it is of nations that have been at peace for decades. Therefore, the model proposed in this chapter may be considered equally applicable to many developing nations that face economic decline and recovery from man-made or natural disasters.

Notes

1. Some overviews of the war provide sketchy information about the war's impact on Iraq's population and environment. See, for example, Kubba (1993).
2. That treaty had been based on principles of "territorial integrity, the inviolability of borders, and non-interference in internal affairs." It was intended to settle political and territorial disputes between the two governments and to ensure shared sovereignty over the Shatt-al-Arab waterway, which provides both countries with vital access to the Persian Gulf. President Hussein proclaimed that he had ample justification for annulling the treaty because Iran had allegedly broken it by refusing to relinquish territorial rights and by interfering in Iraq's internal affairs. In retrospect, evidence suggests that President Hussein was also motivated by other interests including the prospect of gaining full sovereignty over the Shatt-al-Arab,

179

control of Khuzestan province (where over 90 per cent of Iran's oil reserves are located), the possibility of installing a pro-Iraq government in Iran, and the prospect of securing a new regional leadership role for Iraq in the aftermath of the Shah's overthrow.
3. The Persian Gulf is a long, shallow, relatively narrow, semi-enclosed sea that receives only limited freshwater inputs from rivers and possesses weak flushing currents. The entire system is readily disrupted by pollutants. The weak tidal currents prevent rapid dissipation of contaminants, which remain in the water – the non-volatile components of oil falling to the bottom and continuing to cause damage for many years. The food chain, which normally sustains 250 species of fish and approximately 140 species of migrating birds, is severely threatened. High temperatures, shallow waters, and high winds, which characterize the Gulf, cause rapid evaporation, increasing the salinity of the water and contributing to the stress of organisms living there. Contamination by oil and heavy metals stresses the ecosystem even further. Crude oil contains such heavy metals as mercury, cadmium, and vanadium, as well as other carcinogenic chemical agents. Commercial fishing in the area is severely restricted, and replenishment of Gulf stocks from the ocean will be very slow. For Iran, as well as for other countries that depend on Gulf fish for daily protein requirements, the destruction of the fishing industry means increased food imports, further exacerbating foreign currency reserves and fostering dependencies on other countries for basic foodstuffs.
4. The tally of direct economic damage may be slightly inflated because the government's immediate concern was to provide compensation. Any inflation attributable to this cause is likely to be offset by the absence of some types of real economic costs, such as environmental consequences, concessions given to regional allies, increased insurance costs, and the psychological and sociocultural costs of the war (Amirahmadi 1992a: 69).
5. The World Bank responded by giving a few small loans to Iran for reconstruction of earthquake-damaged areas ($250 million) and for improving urban infrastructure ($67 million). In 1993, another loan for $162 million was approved for the expansion of a power-generating plant in Qum city. IMF and the Bank have helped the Iranian government to formulate an economic stabilization programme but have not as yet responded to requests for a major loan. Regional authorities, such as the Organization of Islamic Conference, the Arab League, and the Gulf Cooperation Council, have largely remained inactive (Amirahmadi 1992a: 277). By identifying Iraq as the aggressor state, the United Nations Security Council has provided an implicit basis for restitution by the Iraqi government. It is likely that Iran would have regained international respectability among the community of nations and been the beneficiary of increased international assistance if it was not for continued opposition by the United States.
6. Ecological restoration should guide the other goals and take priority because it underpins human health; in other words, restoration of human health and long-term environmental habitability are preconditions for the general revival of society. Plans and projects must be drawn up for environmental clean-up and removal of hazardous situations in various economic sectors, industries in particular, where such hazards tend to pose health problems and create obstacles for rebuilding. Achieving economic vitality is a two-part process which hinges, first, on making the most of available resources and removing supply bottlenecks (e.g. in foreign exchange and skilled labour) and, second, on achieving economic growth.

References

Amirahmadi, Hooshang. 1987. "Destruction and reconstruction: A strategy for the war damaged areas of Iran." *International Journal of Disaster Studies and Practice* 11(2): 134–147.
———. 1990a. "Economic reconstruction of Iran: Costing the war damage." *Third World Quarterly* 12(1): 26–47.

————. 1990b. *Revolution and Economic Transition.* Albany, New York: State University of New York Press.

————. 1992a. "Economic costs of the war and the reconstruction in Iran." In: Cyrus Bina and Hamid Zangeneh, eds. *Modern Capitalism and Islamic Ideology in Iran.* New York: St. Martin's Press.

————. 1992b. "Economic destruction and imbalances in post-revolutionary Iran." In: H. Amirahmadi and N. Entessar, eds. *Reconstruction and Regional Diplomacy in the Persian Gulf.* London: Routledge.

Athari, Djamal. 1991. "Revolutionary changes and post-war reconstruction in Iran." In: *Reviving War Damaged Settlements.* A Report and Charter prepared in connection with the Third International York Workshop on Settlement Reconstruction Post-War, 22–24 July 1991. York: University of York, Institute of Advanced Architectural Studies, Post-War Reconstruction and Development Unit, p. 14.

Cordesman, Anthony H. 1990. *The Lessons of Modern War.* Boulder: Westview Press.

El-Baz, Farouk, and R.M. Makharita. 1994. *The Gulf War and the Environment.* New York: Gordon and Breach Science Publishers.

Haas, J. Eugene, Robert W. Kates, and Martyn J. Bowden (eds.). 1977. *Reconstruction Following Disaster.* Cambridge, Mass.: Massachusetts Institute of Technology Press.

Hawley, T.M. 1992. *Against the Fires of Hell: The Environmental Disaster of the Gulf War.* New York: Harcourt Brace Jovanovich.

Jochnick, Chris A.F., and Roger Normand. "A critical look at the law of war: Lessons from the Persian Gulf war." Unpublished paper in file with the author. Authors of the article are Co-Editor in Chief and Executive Editor of the *Harvard Human Rights Journal.*

Kubba, Laith. 1993. "The war's impact on Iraq." In: Farhang Rajaee, ed. *The Iran–Iraq War: The Politics of Aggression.* Gainesville: University of Florida Press, pp. 47–54.

Mofid, Kamran. 1990. "Iran: War, destruction and reconstruction." In: Charles Davies, ed. *After the War: Iran, Iraq and the Arab Gulf.* Chichester: Carden Publications, pp. 117–141.

Plan and Budget Organization, Islamic Republic of Iran. 1991. *Final Report on the Assessment of the Economic Damages of the War Imposed by Iraq on the Islamic Republic of Iran (1980–1988).* Teheran: Centre for Socio-Economic Documentation and Publications.

Shemirani, Taheri. 1993. "The war of the cities." In: Farhang Rajaee, ed. *The Iran–Iraq War: The Politics of Aggression.* Gainesville: University of Florida Press, pp. 32–40.

SIPRI (Stockholm International Peace Research Institute). 1977. *Weapons of Mass Destruction and the Environment.* New York: Crane, Russak, and Company.

————. 1980. *Warfare in a Fragile World: Military Impact on the Human Environment.* London: Taylor and Francis.

United Nations Secretary-General. 1991a. "Report on Iran's reconstruction efforts in the wake of the conflict between the Islamic Republic of Iran and Iraq." 24 December.

————. 1991b. "Report on the scope and nature of damage inflicted on the Kuwaiti infrastructure during the Iraqi occupation." 26 April.

181

Walker, A.R. 1989. "Recessional and Gulf War impacts on port development and shipping in the Gulf states in the 1980s." *GeoJournal* 18(3): 273–284.

Winnefeld, James A., and Mary E. Morris. 1994. *Where Environmental Concerns and Security Strategies Meet: Green Conflict in Asia and the Middle East*. Santa Monica: Rand.

Zargar, Akbar, and Mohsen Poor. 1991. "City reconstruction: The case of Khoramshar, Iran." In: *Reviving War Damaged Settlements*. A Report and Charter prepared in connection with the Third International York Workshop on Settlement Reconstruction Post-War, 22–24 July 1991. York: University of York, Institute of Advanced Architectural Studies, Post-War Reconstruction and Development Unit, p. 10.

7

The Chernobyl disaster: Its effect on Belarus and Ukraine

David R. Marples

Introduction

The Chernobyl disaster began at 1.23 a.m. on Saturday 26 April 1986, in a civilian nuclear power station of Kiev[1] Oblast (province) in the (then) Ukrainian SSR (Soviet Socialist Republic). A chemical explosion at the station's fourth reactor and an uncontrolled graphite fire that followed led to the release of more than 450 radionuclides, comprising about 3.5 per cent of the fuel stored in the reactor core. Official reports put the immediate death toll at 31, but it is widely believed that many more died in the first hours and weeks after the explosion. The Ukrainian government has estimated the number of deaths among clean-up workers alone as 7,000–8,000. Total civilian casualties are not known and may never be known. Although nuclear radiation is no longer leaking from the damaged reactor into the atmosphere, this event is far from over. Its repercussions will continue well into the next century, sometimes in places far distant from the point of origin. There are those who believe that this was a unique occurrence in the history of civilian nuclear power. However, it is difficult to judge such a claim because the context in which it occurred was highly unusual. The disaster took place in a country on the brink of social upheaval, with a political administration that was to undertake major reforms under a new leader. These factors strongly affected the way the event was reported and the subsequent responses.

This chapter opens with an account of the background to Chernobyl and a summary of the immediate responses. The early dominant role of the Soviet Union's governmental apparatus is emphasized, including the limitations of President Mikhail Gorbachev's glasnost policy. The process of longer-term regeneration and recovery is then discussed in the context of the breakup of the Soviet system and the emergence of two of the new independent republics – Belarus and Ukraine. Similarities and differences among the approaches of various institutional actors and post-Soviet regimes are noted. Theoretical issues are the focus of the third section of the chapter. An outline model of nuclear power disasters is proposed, based on the experience of other disasters in the Soviet Union and the global nuclear power industry as well as Chernobyl.

Finally, I offer a series of recommendations for improving recovery from nuclear accidents and other industrial emergencies. These include the creation of registries for populations in the vicinity of hazardous facilities, and an international system for providing expertise and material assistance in the event of disasters that involve advanced industrial technologies whose effects exceed existing national coping capacities. While there may be no adequate way to avoid surprises like Chernobyl, it is clear that the Chernobyl experience was made much worse by failures of the government and the ruling political party in the weeks and months after the accident, and by broader economic and political changes that began in the period 1986–1991 and continue into the severe economic crisis of the post-Soviet era.

The accident and its immediate aftermath

The town of Chernobyl is situated about 110 miles north of Kiev, the modern capital of Ukraine, and just to the west of Chernigov Oblast, the site of the original seventeenth-century Ukrainian state (fig. 7.1).[2] It was founded in the twelfth century and remained small for most of the next 800 years. By 1986, Chernobyl's population had reached 10,000 and the town was officially classified as a raion (district) in northern Kiev Oblast.

A paved road connects Kiev with Chernobyl and runs through a series of small peasant villages. The nuclear power station is located about 12 miles north of Chernobyl. Two miles further on lies the town of Pripyat, one of several "nuclear" communities built in the 1970s for employees of the station, their families, service personnel,

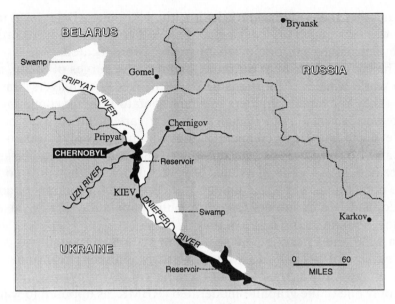

Fig. 7.1 **The regional setting of Chernobyl**

and fire crews. Like most Soviet towns, Pripyat consists of high-rise apartment blocks. It possesses a fairground and two soccer pitches, but no church. At the time of the accident, Pripyat's population was estimated at 45,000 and growing. Eight miles north of Pripyat stands the border between Ukraine and the Gomel Oblast of the Republic of Belarus (then the Byelorussian SSR). To the north-east lies the Bryansk Oblast of Russia.

This is an area of small towns and villages. The nearest large settlements within a hundred miles are Chernigov (Ukraine, population 270,000) and Gomel (Belarus, population 500,000).[3] They lie near the junction of the Pripyat and Uzh rivers, both of which feed the massive Kiev Reservoir. It is from this reservoir that the Dnieper River winds southward to the Black Sea, neatly bisecting the Republic of Ukraine. Nearby also are the Poles'ye (Pripyat Marshes), an area of sparsely inhabited, unproductive agricultural land and sandy podzolic soil that was once considered a natural barrier against invasion of the USSR from the west.[4] The area's population speaks a native patois that combines Russian, Belarusian, and Ukrainian. Families that lived in these settlements in early 1986 were also of mixed origin and rarely saw themselves as one nationality or another. Indeed, for most purposes other than political jurisdiction, the Ukrainian–Belarusian border was very much an irrelevance. People's connections were rather with their villages of origin, wherever they were located.

The collectivization of Soviet agriculture, the purges of Stalin, and two world wars had not fundamentally changed the villagers' way of life. They remained members of simple potato-farming communities who were suspicious of outsiders. Health care facilities were negligible, doctors few, and communications with major centres were often impaired by poor roads and rail links. Since the 1970s, in Ukraine, there had been a general exodus of young people to the cities, so village populations were predominantly elderly and the amount of cultivated land was shrinking. In contrast, the population of Pripyat was young, with an average age of only 27 years.

In 1986, the Chernobyl nuclear power station contained two completed sets of twin reactors and a third (unfinished) set, some 400 metres away. It was the oldest of Ukraine's nuclear power plants, and the only one of the graphite-moderated (RBMK, as opposed to water-pressurized – VVER) design.[5] The RBMK's original function was the production of materials for the Soviet nuclear weapons programme, but it was adapted to civilian usage by the 1970s. Other Soviet RBMKs were located in Russia – at Kursk (a twin of Chernobyl), St. Petersburg (the first reactor of this type in the USSR), and Smolensk – and in Lithuania at Ignalina. Except for Ignalina (1500 megawatts), all had a standard 1,000 megawatts capacity. Although the Soviet authorities planned to phase out the RBMK reactor in favour of the more widely used VVER type, it still generated the majority of the USSR's nuclear-produced electricity at the time of the Chernobyl disaster.

The Chernobyl station was part of a programme for rapid expansion of nuclear energy production in the Soviet Union. This was centred on Ukraine, partly because of available water supplies. To the west of Chernobyl were located the Rovno and Khmelnitsky stations, to the south-east were Zaporozhye and Nikolaev (South Ukraine), all of which were to be expanded to accommodate VVER-1000 reactors during the period covered by the 1986–1990 plan. Several other power stations were under construction, including one in the Crimea and another at Chigirin. Both of the latter had caused public concern – Crimea because the station was located on the Kerch Peninsula (a seismically active region), and Chigirin because the station was located on the already overused Dnieper River in an area of Ukrainian national heritage off limits to the public.

Most of the problems associated with the Chernobyl station before

186

April 1986 were related to construction or labour. Recent revelations suggest that these were serious enough to constitute a danger to the environment. For example, as early as 1979, a KGB report outlined various defects in construction of the first reactor unit, as follows:

Deputy head of the Construction Directorate, Comrade V.T. Gora, gave instructions for backfilling the foundation in many places where vertical waterproofing was damaged. Similar violations were permitted in other sections with the knowledge of Comrade V.T. Gora and the head of the construction group, Comrade IU. L. Matveev. Damage to the waterproofing can lead to ground water seepage into the station and radioactive contamination of the environment. (USSR Committee for State Security [KGB] 1979)

The document from which this quote is taken remained secret until 1992, but numerous other construction flaws and accidents have been revealed by a variety of sources, from the critical Ukrainian newspaper, *Literaturna Ukraina*, to the former Soviet dissident scientist, Zhores Medvedev.[6] The construction defects were a sign of the erratic way in which Soviet industry generally operated and they show that even buildings of military significance were not immune to problems. In order to comprehend the initial Soviet reaction to Chernobyl, it is necessary to outline briefly the operation of the Soviet bureaucracy in this sphere.

Although the Chernobyl station is located in Ukraine, it was completely subordinate to ministries based in Moscow. In theory, the most important of these was the USSR Ministry of Power and Electrification, which also possessed a Ukrainian "branch." The Ministry of Power was responsible for energy-producing industries, and for meeting the demands of the Five-Year Plan in the energy sector. Its control therefore extended to the three main types of power stations – thermal, hydroelectric, and atomic. Initially, its key concern was with thermal power stations, that were predominantly coal fired. As late as 1975, these supplied 86 per cent of all electricity generated in the Soviet Union (*Energetika SSSR v 1976–1980 godakh* 1977: 11). The ministry's control was limited, however, in those sectors of nuclear energy that were connected with the military (i.e. stations that were, or had at one time been, part of the atomic weapons programme). Such stations were administered by the USSR Ministry of Medium Machine Building. Even today, while it is obvious that the machine ministry had some control over Chernobyl, the division of responsibilities with the Ministry of Power is unclear. Most of the significant

187

political dismissals resulting from Chernobyl occurred in these two ministries.

According to Soviet propaganda, the country's nuclear industry was "accident-free." Moreover, it was assumed that, unlike in the West, an accident could not happen. Hence, accident preparation was minimal. The station, like its counterparts elsewhere in the Soviet Union, lacked protective clothing, Geiger counters to monitor radiation, and a code of conduct that could be followed in the event of a serious accident. There appear to have been adequate preparations only for "incidents" such as the outbreak of a fire at the station or minor injuries to work personnel. Such laxity also extended to the regime within the station. Individual operators clearly were permitted to dismantle vital safety devices. The roof of the station was overlain with inflammable bitumen. Only the key managerial personnel, such as the Station Director and Chief Engineer, appear to have had adequate training for work in this dangerous facility.

Safety problems were exacerbated by the Soviet Union's penchant for centralized command systems. In this case, reactors were designed around a single central turbine hall so that they could be installed and brought on line in quick succession. Yet the close juxtaposition of the reactors was to constitute a grave danger after the accident. One of the very first tasks of the fire crews was to prevent the graphite fire spreading from the first two reactor units to the third (only achieved at high cost in human lives). The lives of more personnel were in jeopardy than would have been the case had reactors been sited in individual buildings with separate protective containments.

For over a decade the Ukrainian government had been run by Party Chief Volodymyr Shcherbytsky and Premier Oleksandr Lyashko. Shcherbytsky took over as party leader in 1972, and had shown himself to be a ruthless *apparatchik*, completely loyal to USSR President Brezhnev. The latter had Russified the Ukrainian government and public institutions systematically, and had clamped down on the dissident movement in the republic. Many observers were surprised that Shcherbytsky remained in the Politburo after Gorbachev became General Secretary, for he appeared to be an anachronism in a basically new leadership team (see, for example, Solchanyk 1986). That he did so was significant in the official Ukrainian reaction to Chernobyl: Shcherbytsky visited Chernobyl (very briefly) only three times and issued no statements of importance on the subject. With a few individual exceptions, his party members on the spot at Pripyat and

Chernobyl were confused and frightened, and unable to respond to the emergency. As in the past, the Shcherbytsky regime decided to await guidance from Moscow about how to act in this unprecedented situation.

Thus, in the immediate aftermath of the disaster, the most notable feature was confusion. According to eyewitnesses, personnel at the station did not comprehend the significance of the accident when it first occurred. The Station Director did not realize that the explosion was in the reactor unit itself. No public warnings were issued. Although 26 April was a Saturday, children still attended school. A wedding and an outdoor soccer game were also held in Pripyat. Men went fishing as usual, and one of the most popular fishing spots was the cooling pond of the Chernobyl nuclear station!

After the explosion, fire crews succumbed quickly to the effects of intense radiation. Helicopter pilots who attempted to blanket the fire with sand and chemicals also died, usually weeks or months later. The weight of these dumped materials forced the reactor downward and necessitated a period of hectic tunnelling to permit the installation of supports intended to prevent it from sinking further into the water-table. Because there were no nearby hospitals that could treat radiation patients, some were taken to one hospital in Kiev, and the most severely burned were transported by plane to Moscow's Hospital No. 6 – the only one in the country adequately prepared for such an emergency. Thus, in most respects, Chernobyl was an object lesson in spontaneous and disorganized response to a major crisis.

By 28 April, a formal announcement about the accident had been made by the Soviet government in Moscow. This reported the establishment of a government commission that was charged – in the stilted euphemisms of the Soviet bureaucracy – to "liquidate the consequences of the accident."[7] The first chairman was Boris Shcherbina, a deputy chairman of the USSR Council of Ministers.

The two-day delay in publicly acknowledging the accident and the 40 hours that were taken to organize the evacuation of Pripyat suggest that Moscow remained ignorant of events at Chernobyl for some time after they occurred. However, as early as 27 April, the editors of the government newspaper *Izvestiya* were ordered to suppress a story providing more details of the event.[8] In brief, it appears that Kiev informed Moscow about the fire promptly, but that there was no immediate reaction from the Soviet authorities. The probability is that, like most observers on the spot, Soviet officials did not realize the seriousness or full implications of the event. At the same time, neither the Ukrainian nor the Belarusian governments were willing to take independent initiatives in response to the crisis.

On 2 May, two representatives of the Politburo, Nikolai Ryzhkov and Yegor Ligachev, arrived in Chernobyl. They discussed the problems of Chernobyl with Shcherbina, Shcherbytsky, Lyashko, and the Party Chief of the Kiev Oblast, Grigorii Revenko. Measures were immediately implemented for the evacuation of all areas within 30 kilometres of the stricken power station, including the town of Chernobyl. The distance of 30 kilometres was a purely arbitrary choice. As later revealed, it did not encompass a majority of the areas affected by Chernobyl. But, at the time, it seemed justified for a number of reasons. First, the Soviet authorities had to have houses and apartments available for evacuees and most of these were located more than 30 kilometres from the reactor site. Further, there are indications that Ryzhkov and Ligachev were unaware of the real levels of leaking radiation. The officially reported "average" figure in the evacuation zone was 1 rem (=0.01 Sv) per hour in the first days after the accident. It was later revealed that, 40 miles to the west, in Narodichi Raion of Zhitomir Oblast, local civil defence officials had recorded levels as high as 3 rem per hour on 27 April. The figure of 1 rem per hour was as randomly selected as the designation of a 30 kilometre evacuation zone. It gave no indication of the very high radiation levels in the immediate vicinity of the damaged reactor.

It was reported that 135,000 persons were evacuated between 27 April and 31 May, but the evacuees were not taken immediately to safety. About 45,000 people were unwittingly transported from the southern part of Gomel Oblast (Belarus) to the north of the oblast, an area that was later shown to be highly contaminated. In Ukraine also, the first evacuees were removed to nearby Polesskoe Raion, which later became affected by the radioactive plume as it moved across Europe. Thus, most evacuees had to be moved again from their new places of residence. Finally, the evacuations encompassed only a fraction of the people living in contaminated zones, though this was not apparent at the time.

In contrast to the hesitant and uneven physical response to the accident, Soviet propaganda agencies were much more decisive. By and large, there were three different types of response – public reassurance, deflection of criticism, and selective cooperation with external agencies.

The accident is "under control"

First came measures designed to reassure the Soviet public that the situation was not dangerous and was basically "under control." Reports that the accident at Chernobyl was less serious than first feared began as early as 30 April 1986 and continued into 1987. On 30 April, for example, Radio Moscow reported (without any knowledge of the actual situation) that the quality of the drinking water in rivers and reservoirs had not been affected. Radio Kiev also began inauspiciously with the statement that "only two" people had been killed, as though the loss of two lives did not indicate a serious accident. Major newspapers in Moscow, Minsk, and Kiev featured the May Day celebrations in their 1 May editions, relegating the events at Chernobyl to the inside or back pages. The radiation background level, according to Radio Kiev, had fallen a further "1.5 to 2 times" from the time of the accident on 26 April 1986 – it was not stated, however, what the initial levels had been.[9] In addition to the May Day events, Kiev also featured the start of a bicycle race and the streets were filled with children in national costumes. The impression given to the outside world was one of normality.

Statements about victims were similarly circumspect, conforming to a USSR Ministry of Health decision not to release pertinent information immediately after the disaster. However, because Chernobyl quickly became an event of international significance, foreign governments and scientists soon began to offer aid. The roles of the International Atomic Energy Agency (IAEA) and foreign physicians are discussed below. In these circumstances, the Soviet authorities were obliged to disclose some of the casualty figures, though they were limited to people in the public eye – in hospitals, among fire crews, and among first-aid workers who tended to the fire-fighters.

Moreover, at the accident scene itself, the desire to ensure an atmosphere of normality was taken to extremes. The first evacuees were informed that they would be moved for a period of only three days; this may have been in part to discourage them from taking belongings from their residences and to reduce the time required for evacuation. Though reactor number four had been destroyed, and reactor three was in serious danger of catching fire, reactors one and two were left in service for a full 24 hours after the accident. On 9 May, Ukrainian Health Minister Anatolii Romanenko was heard on Radio Kiev, assuring listeners that radiation levels at Chernobyl were now within both national and international norms. On the same day, however, there was a "sudden new eruption of radioactive material" from the damaged reactor, which was not officially acknowledged by Soviet authorities until June 1989. Areas up to 40 miles from the reactor were affected![10] This new release of radioactivity was not mentioned in the Soviet report to the IAEA (August 1986) – a report that outsider observers heralded as a sign of new openness among the USSR's leaders.

Similarly, on 11 May 1986, scientists who had visited the disaster site held a press conference in Moscow and announced that the situation at Chernobyl "is stabilizing." It was reported that peak levels of radiation in the 30 kilometre zone had at first been 10–15 milliroentgens per hour; by 5 May they had fallen to 2–3 milliroentgens and by 8 May to 0.15 (*Sovetskaya Belorussiya*, 11 May 1986).[11] Hans Blix, the Director-General of the IAEA, was inducted into the campaign of reassurance. At the press conference after his visit to Kiev, he noted that life near Chernobyl was proceeding normally. Schools were open and there were many foreign tourists in the streets. He said that, before long, the neighbouring fields would again be cultivated, and the "settlements around the nuclear power plant will be safe for residence."[12]

The optimistic (and quite unrealistic) tone continued for several weeks. On 13 May, for example, the news agency Novosti cited a 10 May report from the USSR Council of Ministers, that employed data from the USSR State Committee for Hydrometeorology and Environmental Control. It stated that, 60 kilometres from the station, radiation levels were 0.33 milliroentgens per hour, only slightly above those in Kiev (0.32) and "completely safe for the health of the people."[13] In the western borderlands of the USSR, the situation was reported to be "normal." In Ukraine and Belarus, levels of radiation remained "the same as before the accident" (*Sovetskaya Belorussiya*, 13 May 1986). Not until three years later, when independent researchers tested radiation in rural areas of Ukraine and Belarus, was it recognized that these reports were, at best, incomplete and, at worst, fallacious.

In his memoirs, Andrei Sakharov recalls that he was at first taken in by the publication of such figures: "To my shame, I at first pretended that nothing much had happened." Observing that an early May 1986 report in the Soviet press had stated that radiation levels around the reactor were 10–15 milliroentgens per hour, he believed that there would be no significant fallout. However, "I had, in fact made a serious mistake. The radiation levels published in the Soviet press were one percent or less of the true figure ... " Sakharov goes on to point out that he was ignorant of whether the publication of erroneous figures was a deliberate deception (Sakharov 1992: 608).

That an eminent scientist such as Sakharov could have been reassured by the publication of such figures is testimony to the effectiveness of the Soviet campaign to assure the public that the consequences of Chernobyl were limited in scope and firmly under control. It was left to the scrutiny of Evgenii Velikhov, Vice-President of the Soviet Academy of Sciences, to produce a more realistic picture that finally convinced Sakharov something was amiss.

On 14 May, the USSR Council of Ministers entered a new realm of surrealism when it declared that "the radiation situation in Byelorussia and in Ukraine, including Kiev, is improving" (*Sovetskaya Belorussiya*, 14 May 1993). Though the trend was reported accurately, the statement gave no indication of what the original levels had been. People were left with the misleading implication that the accident was over and life was proceeding in conditions of safety. Regions on the edge of the 30 kilometre zone were supposedly conducting agricultural work, industrial enterprises were functioning as normal, and the "usual tourist trips" were being carried out. Of the casualties from Chernobyl, 35 people were declared to be in a "serious condition," and six had died (ibid.). The toll rose to 31 by the summer of 1986, and there it remained. None of the many officially corroborated direct victims of Chernobyl were ever added to this list: their deaths were attributed to other causes.

Focus on the West

The second strand of the Soviet propaganda strategy aimed at deflecting criticism by focusing on sensational reports in Western media and purported flaws in the Western nuclear power industry.

Some might argue that sensational accounts about Chernobyl in the Western media invited a repudiation by the USSR. But the Soviet response went much further: relatively innocuous errors and exaggerations were quickly seized upon like a lifeline. On 6 May 1986, Tass denounced people "of base motives" who were propagating rumours of thousands of deaths, instilling panic among the population.[14] On the previous day, the government newspaper *Izvestiya* ran an article that took up an entire inside page, under the title "Accidents at Nuclear Power Plants." The main focus was on accidents in the United States, and even the most minor "incidents" were characterized as full-blown accidents. A second article targeted the United Kingdom's nuclear industry. The aim of both pieces was clearly to divert attention from Chernobyl and to demonstrate that major industrialized nations of the West regularly suffered accidents in the nuclear industry, whereas there had been only one such accident in the USSR. Appearing on Soviet television on 14 May, Mikhail Gorbachev also began his first public statement on Chernobyl by lambasting the "mountains of lies" issued in the West about the event.

The practice of deflecting criticism of flaws in one nation's industrial hazard management system by appealing to the existence of supposedly greater flaws in other nations' systems is a highly unusual one. In this case it took advantage of a long-established defence mechanism in Soviet governing circles, that is, a willingness to portray the West and other capitalist states as intrinsically malevolent. Parochialism in the leadership ranks of the USSR – especially in Russia – was reminiscent of World War II. At a time of crisis, it was important for the country to be united! In this climate of opinion it was hardly surprising that reports of heroism at Chernobyl took priority over accounts of real hazards (Marples 1988: 148–155). A secretive state that had been close to totalitarian was faced with a major international crisis – a crisis, moreover, in which through silence and lack of concerted action it appeared to be the guilty party. The international community was giving the issue almost unprecedented publicity. Under such conditions, the state reacted by withdrawing into its shell, so to speak, and defending itself with denunciations of the accusers. This reaction was relatively short lived. Indeed, it soon became unnecessary because international governments and media began to give Soviet authorities the benefit of the doubt in issues about the adequacy of responses to disaster.

International cooperation

When it became clear that an accident of major proportions had indeed occurred at Chernobyl, the Soviet propaganda campaign switched tactics and underscored the country's alleged support for global nuclear disarmament and international controls on the peaceful uses of atomic energy. This explains the publicity given to Soviet cooperation with institutions such as the IAEA. Embedded in these manoeuvres was the implication that Chernobyl was a minor event hardly comparable to the destruction that would follow military use of atomic weapons.

Mikhail Gorbachev had been in office only 13 months when Chernobyl occurred. He had arrived to a warm response from Western political leaders. Much younger and more active than his predecessors, he appeared to herald a time of change in the USSR. In 1986, however, he inherited an ossified Soviet state that was Leonid Brezhnev's legacy. Gorbachev's reaction to Chernobyl was very cautious but, in addition to the defensive posture adopted by his government initially, he also indicated a willingness to cooperate with the IAEA. It should be noted that in 1985 the USSR had agreed to IAEA inspections of some of its nuclear reactors, and thus this policy was not necessarily a new departure. Similarly, aid offered from long-established "friends of the USSR" abroad was also accepted, while that of individual governments was turned down.

On 14 May, Gorbachev declared his desire for "serious cooperation" with the IAEA, with respect to four specific proposals:
1. The creation of an international regime for safe development of nuclear energy involving close cooperation among all nuclear energy-using states;
2. A highly authoritative special international conference in Vienna under the aegis of the IAEA to discuss these "complex questions";
3. An increased role and scope for IAEA;
4. Safe development of "peaceful nuclear activities," involving the United Nations and its specialized departments, such as the World Health Organization (WHO) and the United Nations Environmental Program (UNEP) (*Sovetskaya Belorussiya*, 15 May 1986).

These proposals suggested that Gorbachev was broadening the scope of the accident to one of international concern, but at the same time he was implying that such accidents were common enough to warrant the establishment of a global regime to deal with them. Despite frequent IAEA visits to the Soviet Union after Chernobyl, the August conference did not live up to its promise as an open forum. The report on the accident was prepared exclusively by a Soviet team under the leadership of Valery Legasov of the Kurchatov Institute. It focused less on inherent reactor flaws, such as the positive void coefficient and the faulty manufacture of the control rods used on the RBMK,[15] and more on operator error. In retrospect, the greatest concern about the continuing operation of former Soviet RBMKs recently has come from leaders of the world's strongest economies – the so-called G7 countries – rather than the IAEA.

Gorbachev was also prepared to cooperate with known friends of the Soviet Union, such as Armand Hammer, the prominent US industrialist and director of Occidental Petroleum. When Robert Gale, a bone marrow specialist from the University of California at Los Angeles (UCLA), expressed a desire to go to the USSR to aid Chernobyl victims, he arranged the visit through the auspices of Dr. Hammer. The latter was also actively involved, and both Hammer and Gale were granted an audience with Gorbachev on 17 May.[16] There are also indications that, in the period 1986–1989, the Soviet nuclear establishment was prepared to cooperate with international scientists who were known to be sympathetic to the development of nuclear energy.[17] One should thus add to the initial Soviet reactions of calming the public and denouncing Western propaganda, one of careful, guarded, but visible cooperation with international agencies or individuals who were known to be sympathetic to the regime or to nuclear energy in particular.

The affected community

How clearly can the community affected by Chernobyl be identified? Initially, it was confined to evacuees from a zone within 30 kilometres around the damaged reactor, as well as people who worked to decontaminate the area. As more information has been acquired, the sizes of the impact zone and the impacted population have increased. If one includes all the 1993 population living in the territory contaminated with over 1 curie ($=3.7 \times 10^{10}$ Bq) of caesium per kilometre in the soil (the figure most commonly used to indicate a serious problem), the size of the impacted community has been estimated at 2.2 million in Belarus, 1.6 million in Ukraine, and 700,000 in Russia (*Charnobylski sled na Belarusi* 1992: 7), i.e. a total of 4.5 million persons.

The clean-up crews, whose numbers have been estimated at around 600,000, may have been the group most affected physically by Chernobyl but, strictly speaking they cannot be considered part of the local community. Many were young military reservists, often from distant regions, and very few had any ties with the places in which they worked. It is also important to distinguish among several other groups: these comprise those who were evacuated initially; those who were evacuated but chose to return to their homes (mainly the elderly); the workers of the Chernobyl nuclear power plant; those who were evacuated in subsequent waves; and – by far the largest group today – those who are living in areas that are designated as con-taminated zones.

Among people who were initially removed, the largest single group was the population of Pripyat. Despite official optimism and state-ments such as that of Hans Blix, by late 1986 it was clear that the city of Pripyat could not be repopulated. Soviet authorities therefore ordered the construction of a new city for plant employees and their families, about 65 kilometres to the north-east of the Chernobyl plant, in Chernigov Oblast, to be called Slavutich.[18] By 1989, the only remaining activity in Pripyat was at a hothouse (which had been transformed into an experiment station for comparing the growth of non-irradiated and irradiated plants) and a swimming pool, which was used by the hothouse workers and by officials at the Kombinat Association (later Pripyat Industrial and Research Association) based at Chernobyl to coordinate the clean-up operation.

Residents of Pripyat were moved in different directions: some nuclear plant operators were transferred to other Soviet nuclear power stations; others were moved to apartment blocks in Kiev or Chernigov that were made available for them on a priority basis; others were eventually transferred to Slavutich. Pripyat thus remains today a ghost town, its buildings intact but without a population. By contrast, there are still some personnel at Chernobyl itself. The former Kombinat Association was disbanded by the independent Ukrainian government after decontamination efforts in the 30 kilo-metre zone had ended, but personnel were still required to monitor the state of the covered fourth reactor, and especially to check the concrete covering (the "sarcophagus"), which by 1992 was revealed as unstable (Marples 1992a: 57).

Evacuees from the 30 kilometre zone are also unlikely to return to their former homes in the foreseeable future. Some have been employed on collective and state farms in other regions. The radio-active isotope caesium-137 has been the most damaging to livelihood. At first, scientists were optimistic about the ability of humans to withstand increased radiation, but the question soon gave rise to furious disputes between the central authorities in Moscow and non-government organizations and critics in Kiev. What may have dis-tinguished Chernobyl from other international accidents was the complete rift that occurred as a result of conflicting interpretations of the event in Moscow (the centre) and the two (periphery) republics most affected – Belarus and Ukraine. This conflict culminated in a ferocious argument about radiation tolerance (Marples 1993c).

The details of this conflict have been covered elsewhere (Marples 1989). Suffice it to say that, by the early 1990s, both the Ukrainian and Belarusian governments had lowered the tolerance limits for those living in zones affected by Chernobyl from 35 additional rems over a natural life-span (cited as 70 years), or an additional 0.5 rems annually, to only 7 rems, or 0.1 annually. As radiation levels in the atmosphere have decreased significantly since the accident, this tolerance is monitored through the amount of caesium, strontium, and plutonium that is contained in the soil. It should be added that the most harmful and plentiful element released initially was iodine-131, which was especially damaging in a region of iodine deficiency. Radioactive iodine was quickly ingested by the thyroid glands of the population, and of the children in particular. But the half-life of iodine-131 is only 8 days; that of caesium-137 is 30 years.

Concern was initially expressed about places with a caesium uptake in the soil of over 15 curies per square kilometre. The reduction of tolerance levels, however, meant that even at 1–5 curies per square kilometre the ground should be subject to constant monitoring.[19] At 5–15 curies, the population, in theory, had the right to be evacuated. New laws were issued after the publication of maps in the early spring of 1989, which indicated that areas of radiation fallout were much more extensive than had at first been revealed.[20] They also indicated that the Republic of Belarus was the most severely contaminated as a result of the accident, while the most extensive – but not the most dangerous – fallout had occurred in the Russian Republic. The communities most affected lay in the oblasts of Gomel and Mogilev (Belarus); in Bryansk (Russia); and in Kiev, Chernigov, and Zhitomir (Ukraine).

It should be stressed, however, that the pattern of fallout was uneven. Not all regions of the oblasts were contaminated. Radiation levels could vary by 10–100 times merely on crossing a street or a field. Areas of peat and sandy soil and of woodland, such as those prevalent in southern Belarus, proved to be particularly susceptible to radiation penetration. Many remote villages could not be provided with clean supplies of food and water by the respective governments. In some cases, especially among elderly people, families continued to live off the products of the land long after the accident and even after the publication of the radiation maps in 1989. Further, the psychological impacts of Chernobyl were much more difficult to define than the medical impacts.

Since 1986, local residents have become increasingly mistrustful of the central authorities. An initial period of governmental silence, followed by reassuring comments, appears to have had the opposite effect to that which was intended. In 1989, for example, individual investigators in the Narodichi Raion of Zhitomir Oblast (Ukraine) discovered that radiation levels there were higher than in most areas of the evacuated zone. The discovery fuelled existing fears of radiation and prompted an acute distrust of the Soviet government among all sectors of society, from local doctors to party officials.[21] In the Ukrainian case, events in Narodichi provided a further incentive to activists in Kiev, who considered that the central government had concealed the real effects of Chernobyl. In Belarus, which did not possess the same degree of national consciousness as Ukraine, popular reaction to the secrecy that surrounded Chernobyl was much slower to develop.

As a result of the collapse of the Soviet Union towards the end of 1991, the republics inherited the responsibility of dealing with communities affected by Chernobyl. This herculean task was beyond the capabilities of the Soviet government, but the newly emerged independent states were additionally hampered by severe financial and economic problems. The USSR Ministry of Nuclear Power and Industry, which operated the Chernobyl station, was replaced by a Ukrainian Nuclear Safety Inspectorate, under the leadership of the director of the Chernobyl nuclear power plant, Mikhail Umanets. The USSR Ministry of Health was replaced by Ukrainian and Belarusian equivalents. After Ukraine's declaration of sovereignty on 16 July 1990, the Ukrainian health authorities took over the Centre for Radiation Medicine in Kiev, which had formerly been administered by the Soviet Academy of Medical Sciences. Essentially, the dismantling of the USSR had both a positive and negative side. Beneficially, the republics' governments could now formulate their own plans for the affected communities without constant interference from Moscow. But now there were three separate state campaigns to deal with the effects of Chernobyl, rather than one, and none took account of the fact that radiation did not stop at state borders.

The dissolution of the USSR also has complicated the task of international organizations that offered aid to the impacted communities through a single set of authorities in Moscow. Further, local republics have faced a shortage of expertise – of qualified doctors and scientists to deal with Chernobyl victims. The Soviet system, with its

Russocentric and Moscow-dominated professional class, is being replaced only piecemeal, in stages. The situation has been further complicated by the role of the respective governments. Both Belarus and Ukraine are drastically short of funds and increasingly reliant on international aid to deal with the effects of Chernobyl.[22] Both are authoritarian states with strong tendencies toward apathy and corruption. In addition, the immediate problems of statehood have taken priority over those of an apparently receding disaster, despite the fact that the real impact of that disaster began to materialize only in the early 1990s. In the spring of 1993, for example, the governments of Belarus and Ukraine were both facing new political crises. In Belarus, the Chairman of the Supreme Soviet, Stanislav Shushkevich, was involved in a bitter dispute with his rival, Premier Vyacheslav Kebich, after the latter precipitated a parliamentary vote on the notion of a military union that would unite Belarus with Russia and Kazakhstan on security issues (see, for example, *Narodnaya hazeta*, 7 April 1993; *Zvyazda*, 15 April 1993). In Ukraine, both the Prime Minister and President sought an increase of power over the parliament in order to press forward with privatization of the ailing economy (Reuters, 23 May 1993; UPI, 23 May 1993).

It has been estimated that 2.2 million people are living in contaminated zones of Belarus, including more than 660,000 children.[23] Twenty-two settlements with an aggregate population of 77,000 currently have radiation levels in excess of 40 curies of caesium per square kilometre of soil. There are no similarly affected settlements in Ukraine, and only eight in the Bryansk Oblast of Russia. A further 373 Belarus communities are located in areas with soil contamination of over 5 curies of caesium per square kilometre. People who live in these areas can be assumed to have consumed contaminated food and to have inhaled radioactive particles shortly after the accident (Konoplya 1992a). Today, the major community of concern is located to the north and north-east of the damaged reactor, for this is the area where fallout, soils, hydrology, and vegetation have combined to produce the most serious hazards. Poorly coordinated and belated action on the part of the government of Belarus has also hindered recovery (see below).

The number of casualties from Chernobyl has become a question of intense debate. Official determination to stick with a death toll of 31 people has aroused the ire of many citizens in affected communities. They are convinced that a surge in unusual sicknesses, especially among children, is connected with the Chernobyl accident (Belarusian Charitable Fund for the Children of Chernobyl 1992; Konoplya 1992b). One Chernobyl official, questioned in September 1990 by the author about direct casualties of the disaster, stated the following:

Last year, when the Chernobyl' Union[24] convened for its inaugural conference, some information was revealed about this question. The figure of 256 was announced for the first time. We at Chernobyl' did not know the precise number of deaths, though from my own experience I know many people whose friends died subsequently, mostly from heart attacks. These men were in their late twenties or thirties ... The most recent figure was cited by Shcherbak at a session of "Zelenyi svit" (Green World); he declared that 5,000 people had now died. The figure is not corroborated and is considered to be unofficial, but I admit that it is not unrealistic. More than 500,000 people were exposed to radiation, so it is a plausible percentage. (Marples 1992b: 148)

According to Ukraine's Minister for Chernobyl, Georgii Gotovchits, by April 1992 between 6,000 and 8,000 people had died in Ukraine as a result of the Chernobyl disaster, i.e. six years after the event (Itar–Tass, 22 April 1992). Individual spokespersons have maintained that the actual number is even higher.[25] These figures pertain only to Ukraine. In Belarus, the health consequences from Chernobyl not only are serious but are directly linked with the areas of radiation fallout. In particular, the radioactive iodine that pervaded the republic in the first days after the accident has resulted in an unprecedented rise in thyroid tumours among children (Belarusian Charitable Fund for the Children of Chernobyl 1992). This has occurred predominantly in Gomel Oblast and to a lesser extent in Brest Oblast. Figures compiled by Dr. E.P. Demidchik, Head of the Thyroid Tumour Clinic in Minsk, are illustrative. In 1986, only two cases of thyroid tumours among children were diagnosed in the entire republic; in 1988, the figure was five, rising to eight in 1989. According to Demidchik, none of these figures caused undue alarm. Rather, they reflected a gradual rise in cases throughout Europe, including among adults. In 1990, however, the total among children was 29 and in 1991, 59. In April 1993, the clinic was dealing with over 200 such cases. One child had died, and the tumours were reported to be aggressive, requiring very early detection and surgery.[26] Of the 200, more than 50 per cent occurred in the Gomel region and 17 per cent in Brest. Mogilev Oblast, the other area contaminated seriously after Chernobyl, had produced only 3.5 per cent of the total thyroid cancers among children. Demidchik noted that, in Mogilev, a grass-roots campaign had been mounted to provide potassium iodide tablets for children; elsewhere, this was not done.

Research on the health effects of Chernobyl is only in its infancy. Increased numbers of leukaemias were being detected during the spring of 1993 in Belarus, but not at catastrophic levels.[27] It will be some time yet before the significance of these trends can be established. A host of ostensibly unrelated diseases have seen marked rises. For example, diabetes among children was being detected as early as 10 months of age and, once again, was most prevalent in areas of high contamination.[28] A Minsk doctor pointed out that, often, although a disease appears to be linked to the accident at Chernobyl, it is also necessary to take account of other factors that may have exacerbated its penetration (e.g. poor nutrition, stress, an unhealthy lifestyle, lack of drugs).[29]

Regeneration and recovery

What are the possibilities that the affected population will recover during the next 10–15 years? Can the stricken communities of Belarus and Ukraine absorb the effects of Chernobyl? The answer is difficult to provide because of the scope of recent societal changes and the uncertainties that pervade the region's future. Many observers have pointed to the resilience of these same communities during and after the German invasion of 1941–1944: within 10 years of the war's end, the region had fully recovered from massive losses. But Chernobyl raises a different type of challenge. As was pointed out by the authorities, politicians, and journalists, the invisible threat posed by radiation was more dangerous than the average German soldier. Moreover, it was the now-defunct Soviet community, led ostensibly by the Communist Party,[30] which mounted the recovery campaign against the nuclear disaster. The future of its successors is cloudy.

Moreover, no country and no industry in history has experienced anything similar to Chernobyl, an accident whose principal effects will occur in the future. Comparisons with previous events are difficult and may be specious. The psychological impact is particularly hard to evaluate because it must be measured against a background of fundamental political and economic upheaval. The resolution of Chernobyl-related problems now involves three governments rather than one, and each state is lacking in political stability. Nevertheless, some trends can be postulated.

First, the locally resident community is likely to shrink because of out-migration. A substantial outflow of population from the villages to the towns was evident since the early 1970s throughout the USSR, and that movement is unlikely to cease during the present period of economic hardship. This will increase the difficulty of monitoring people affected by Chernobyl. It may lead to the creation of ghost towns in rural Belarus and Ukraine. Moreover, the demographic make-up of village communities is generally older than that of the towns, so the loss of younger village residents will soon impose severe burdens on rural areas. There has already been an alarming drop in the birth rates of Belarus and Ukraine, to levels below the replacement rate. In other words, the national populations are declining. Moreover, the mortality rate in Belarus is rising. Total deaths in 1992 rose to 106,040, compared with 104,910 in 1991, while the birth rate dropped from 122,952 (1991) to 116,943 (Mikhaylov 1993: 6).[31] Similar trends have been evident in all three Slavic republics of the former Soviet Union. Medical equipment is also decades out of date, compared with Western Europe (see *Moscow News* No. 5, 1993; Marples 1993a).

These problems were evident before the Chernobyl accident occurred and are not necessarily related to its effects. They exist in other former Soviet areas that were not contaminated by radio-activity. Nevertheless, they exacerbate the region's predicament.

What is being done to cope with the impacts of Chernobyl? Officially, the Ukrainian and Belarusian governments gave high priority to the elimination of Chernobyl's consequences. Ukraine, for example, created a Ministry specifically for such a mission, while both the Ukrainians and Belarusians established State Chernobyl Committees. There was also a plethora of other bodies at lower governmental levels, including Children of Chernobyl organizations (the largest of these is based in Moscow). In Belarus, the Ministry of Foreign Affairs set up a special section for Chernobyl. The governments of all three states also put forward very similar programmes to deal with the disaster and to ensure the safety of those citizens compelled or resolved to live in areas that had been contaminated. Largely as a result of financial problems, such programmes proved much easier to design than to put into practice.

The initial actions taken by Belarusian authorities provide a clear picture of the efforts and limitations of government aid. Seven types of emergency actions occurred:
1. Evacuation of up to 24,700 people from the worst-affected regions

(Bragin, Narovlia, and Khoiniki of Gomel Oblast) and rapid re-settlement, complete with compensation funds and new careers.
2. Construction of new apartments, and service and cultural facilities for the evacuees. Eventually this included secondary schools, kindergartens, and day-care centres for 8,500 children.
3. Construction of roads and upgrading of existing roads.
4. Decontamination of settlements, including 450 in Gomel region, 189 in Mogilev region, 214 cattle-breeding farms and 96 machine stations. About 4,600 dilapidated buildings were destroyed, and 254,000 hectares of land "were subject to double-dose high hydro-lithic acidity liming" to prevent the spread of radiation.
5. Dispatch of "clean" food to contaminated areas by various trading organizations.
6. Purification of the water supply in May–June 1986 by cleaning over 3,000 pit wells, connecting some artesian pools to city networks, and building new pumping stations.
7. Creation of an all-Union (later National) Register, which by 1990 had 173,000 names of people under regular care from health establishments (*Chernobylskaya katastrofa i tragediya Belorussii* 1990: 6–10). These figures pertain only to those areas of Belarus that were designated as badly contaminated. In fact, they encompassed only a small fraction of the total areas and numbers of people affected.

In 1991, on the fifth anniversary of Chernobyl, Konstantin Masyk, then the first Deputy Premier of Ukraine, issued an impassioned appeal for international aid for the victims of Chernobyl, because the government of Ukraine was unable to provide funds.[32] The situation was no better in Belarus, where the government was believed to have disbursed only a fraction of the funds originally allocated for Chernobyl, because these were needed to meet the general economic and financial crisis that beset the country in late 1992 (*Gomelskaya pravda*, 3 December 1992). According to the Belarusian Minister of Finance, Stepan Yanchuk, the laws adopted by the government to deal with Chernobyl in early 1993 anticipated an expenditure of US$865 million, of which only $450 million could be raised (IPS, 3 February 1993). In short, the unforeseen effects of the disintegration of the Soviet Union have left the new governments financially incapable of dealing with the consequences of a major disaster. As a result, two other categories of response have became important – victim action groups and international humanitarian aid.

Victim action groups

The appearance of victim action groups in the USSR was a much slower process than it would have been in the West, because there was no established tradition of citizen organizations unrelated to either the government or the Communist Party. By and large, such groups were more successful in the Ukraine than in Belarus because nascent opposition movements already existed in Ukraine. Ukrainian opposition began with the Writers' Union, members of which were largely responsible for the establishment of the Popular Movement for Perestroika (Rukh) early in 1989. One facet of the Rukh, which eventually operated as an independent force, was the Green World ecological association (*Zelenyi Svit*), founded by Chernobyl activists under the leadership of Yurii Nikolaevich Shcherbak, a writer and doctor. Shcherbak had visited Chernobyl shortly after the accident and interviewed many of the leading figures involved in the aftermath. The Green World began as a non-political association committed to the cessation of Ukraine's nuclear power programme, especially the Chernobyl station.

Chernobyl was featured at the First Congress of the Rukh in 1989. Indeed, the founders of Rukh were the most eloquent in drawing attention to the secrecy surrounding the event and the reported failure of central authorities to take effective action. The leadership of the organization in this period was dominated by former Communists – Ivan Drach, its Chairman; Volodymyr Yavorivsky, another student of the Chernobyl event and renowned writer; and Dmytro Pavlychko, a poet and Chairman of the Shevchenko Ukrainian Language Society. Disaffected Communists were effective because they were acquainted with the old power structure from the first, and maintained contacts within the Communist Party of Ukraine and with the more radical sections of Rukh. Shcherbak, a non-Communist, maintained close ties with the Rukh leaders.

Political events in Ukraine since 1989 cannot be dealt with in detail here.[33] Suffice it to say that the victim action programme in Ukraine was effective in drawing attention to the plight of Ukrainians who suffered from Chernobyl. In 1989–1991, many of its leaders visited the West and stimulated the creation of new organizations that channelled aid to Chernobyl victims in Ukraine. By 1990, the existing ruling structure in Ukraine was being eroded. Shcherbytsky, the old party leader, was retired with honour in September 1989, and died the following January. His successor, Volodymyr Ivashko, remained in office for only a few months before accepting an offer to become a deputy vice-president to Mikhail Gorbachev in Moscow, an action that was regarded as a betrayal in Ukrainian political circles. Ivashko's replacement, Stanislav Hurenko, was a hard-line Communist leader in the Shcherbytsky mould. Consequently, the effective leadership of Ukrainian Communists devolved on the parliamentary group, led by Leonid Kravchuk, a politician who was ultra-sensitive to the vacillations of public opinion.

For our purposes, the significance of these events is that, once the country's leadership and impetus had devolved on the parliament, the voice of the opposition was always heard and became influential. Long discussions on Chernobyl occurred in sessions; laws were enacted; demonstrations were held outside the parliament; and the opposition deputies – albeit a small group of 87 out of 400 – were very vocal. Yet the main impact of the Rukh and Green World was to curtail the Ukrainian nuclear power programme and to focus on questions of environmental degradation rather than to resolve questions relating to Chernobyl. The Rukh had a strong voice but was not a political party and did not attempt to take power for itself. In 1992, the Green World and the newly created Green Party was "beheaded" when Shcherbak (Ukraine's Minister of the Environment) took on ambassadorial duties in Israel.

In Belarus, the Popular Front (BPF) had placed Chernobyl at the very top of its agenda, but found it much more difficult to make progress because the government and parliament in 1992–1993 were dominated by Communists. After BPF was founded in the fall of 1988, the authorities tried to suppress its activities with a combination of force and harassment. They were incensed with BPF's campaign to boycott spring elections to the Congress of People's Deputies (*Vechernii Minsk*, 22 March 1989). They also resorted to the crudest of propaganda to brand the members of the Front Nazi as collaborators.[34] In June 1989, the BPF held its founding congress outside the republic, in Vilnius, Lithuania, and advocated a multi-party system in the republic as well as full sovereignty (*Zvyazda*, 14 July 1989). However, the organization did not match the progress of the Sajudis in Lithuania or the Popular Front of Estonia. It remained relatively small and, in 1993, possessed only 32 deputies in the Belarusian parliament under the leadership of archaeologist Zenon Poznyak.

Late in 1992, Poznyak, an outspoken nationalist, declared that the BPF has been the only impediment to complete domination by the old "nomenklatura" in the republic. In his view, this latter group has "appropriated" private property. Prime Minister Kebich has, he states, relied on the former-ruling élite in a close alliance with Russia. In fact, in the fall of 1992, all strategic forces on Belarusian territory had been transferred to the jurisdiction of Russia, but without compensation for the use of Belarus as a testing ground and for its airfields. The picture provided is a bleak one, of a centralized and very authoritarian regime and one, moreover, without any national leaders of the stature of Ukraine's Leonid Kravchuk (*Moscow News* No. 48, 29 November–6 December 1992: 8). The BPF has remained an isolated voice in support of democracy. The importance of such intransigence in the republic that faces the most acute consequences of Chernobyl cannot be underestimated.[35]

Some of the BPF members have been active in the Belarusian Charitable Fund for the Children of Chernobyl, which is led by Deputy Gennadii Grushevoi. The Fund was the most effective of the various non-government organizations in Ukraine that sought to aid young victims. It has cooperated particularly closely with German organizations (see, for example, *Znamya yunosti*, 27 July 1991). By late 1992, the scope of the Fund went well beyond its initial role, which was to send children from the contaminated regions for periods of recuperation abroad. Instead, it had taken on the role of disseminator of information about Belarus and Belarusian culture, and published two journals – a magazine called *Demos*, which appeared in Germany and Russia, and an independent women's newspaper, *Milo*. It had also created an International Humanitarian Association, oriented to resolving problems associated with Chernobyl.[36]

The Fund and Association, while only at the beginning of their operations, represent singular examples of how victim action groups responded to a disaster, not merely without government aid but in the face of constant government harassment.[37] They have continued to highlight inadequacies of the official programme for dealing with Chernobyl and they have focused on individuals within the government – rather than ministries – who might offer aid on a personal basis. At the same time, their leadership is realistic enough to recognize the limitations of operating within Belarus, and they have developed particularly close relations with charitable groups in Germany. Herein lies a general lesson for victim action groups. In a totalitarian or authoritarian state, such groups can develop a wide network of contacts and pursue goals that go beyond those of simply aiding the victims: they can become foci for quasi-opposition movements. In Minsk during

1992–1993, the Children of Chernobyl Fund was a unique example of an operation that was both effective and thriving and, through its actions, supplementing official aid.

International aid

The Chernobyl disaster has resulted in a substantial campaign of international aid to the former Slavic republics of the USSR. Aid has been offered by foreign governments; the international scientific community; independent activist groups, such as Greenpeace International; the International Red Cross; and scores of individual organizations of a humanitarian nature, some of which developed in the Ukrainian diaspora. Most of the funding that is currently used to deal with effects of Chernobyl comes from such sources. Though enduring and vital, this kind of support suffers from certain drawbacks and restrictions that are discussed below.

Organizational constraints
The question has often been raised by external humanitarian groups: with whom should we deal in offering aid? Between 1986 and 1990, the most substantial assistance was offered through the central authorities (and, correspondingly, the Soviet Bank) in Moscow. This development was resented in the republics, especially by those people who were trying to divert attention from the centre of the USSR to their own areas. It signified that, after the surprising collapse of the USSR, many aid groups were left without a known contact when administration of Chernobyl problems was transferred from Moscow to the republics. Russia, though widely affected by Chernobyl, was not as seriously damaged as Belarus and Ukraine, and yet most of the central ministries were readapted as purely Russian variants. Conversely, many international groups had no wish to deal with organizations based in the republics that, before 1991, had little or no decision-making experience or authority.

International aid groups
In both Ukraine and Belarus, the ending of Soviet hegemony has not made it easier for grass-roots organizations to aid Chernobyl's victims. True, the dominant political systems are less oppressive than in the past, but they are often staffed by the same individuals. Moreover, independent associations face severe financial handicaps that preclude large-scale action. A plethora of such groups vies for public

support and the ear of decision makers. In Belarus, it has been speculated that the government has deliberately tried to organize groups with independent-sounding names to facilitate the diversion of funds away from charitable associations. In mid-1991, for example, there were 13 officially registered charitable Chernobyl funds (as listed in *Narodnaya hazeta*, 20 July 1991), namely:

1. The Belarusian Social–Ecological Union "Chernobyl," founded on 16 November 1990 to protect the rights of citizens suffering from the catastrophe;
2. The Belarusian–Japanese Society "Chernobyl–Hiroshima," formed on 19 November 1990 as a technological provision programme for the "liquidation of the accident";
3. The Charitable Center "Otklik" (Response), founded on 19 November 1990 to offer charitable aid to those "suffering from the catastrophe";
4. The Belarusian Charitable Fund for the Children of Chernobyl, registered on 20 November 1990 and described above;
5. The Belarusian Committee "Children of Chernobyl," founded on 21 November 1990 to give aid to those suffering from the disaster;
6. The Belarusian Action Committee "Echo of Chernobyl," formed on 23 November 1990 for the same purpose;
7. The Belarusian Union of Participants in the Liquidation of the Consequences of the Catastrophe at Chernobyl Nuclear Power Plant, created on 6 December 1990 to provide social, material, and medical aid to those in need;
8. The Fund of International Cooperation for Social Protection "Byelorussian," founded on 20 December 1990, whose mission is described in its title;
9. The Belarusian Union of the Participants in the Liquidation of the Consequences of the Chernobyl Catastrophe "Pripyat," formed on 24 December 1990 to protect the interests of the clean-up crews;
10. The "Chernobyl" Union of the Belarusian SSR, founded on 6 February 1991 – a state and government organization aimed at protecting the rights of those affected by Chernobyl;
11. The Young Ecological Movement of the Belarusian SSR "Belarus," formed on 30 April 1991, which was involved in the state programme to eliminate Chernobyl's consequences;
12. The Belarusian Society of Radiobiologists, created on 30 April 1991 to study the results of the disaster;

13. The Belarusian Homeopathic Association, which dates from 28 March 1991 and was devoted to medical assistance for the victims of Chernobyl.

With so many apparently praiseworthy competitors it has been difficult for any single fund to receive the scale of aid that is required to make real inroads on the problems engendered by Chernobyl. Moreover, the fact that the government itself has organized several of the associations named above may have precluded "fair competition" between them. Almost all newspapers in the republic are funded by state and government organs and can draw attention to official rather than to privately run charitable bodies.

Information problems

A third problem, and perhaps the major one to date, has been the lack of accurate information about radiation fallout and the health effects of the disaster. We have seen that the first maps of the fallout were released only in the spring of 1989, and the overall picture has emerged only since that time. It is still not clearly defined. There is not even an accurate tally of deaths. There is no single and complete data bank that encompasses those affected by Chernobyl, and may never be.[38] The effects of low-level radiation on the population are not known. On the one hand, some scientists maintain that there have been no discernible effects; others state that the results are already being seen and that even very small rises in background radiation can cause changes to the human organism. We do not know the precise area of all radiation fallout, particularly hotspots of plutonium, caesium, and strontium fallout in parts of Russia and the Baltic republics. Ultimately establishing the effects of Chernobyl radiation may come down to mundane questions (such as what people were doing at the time of the accident) and to matters of general health (such as how healthy were such people in April 1986; did they smoke; did they have access to clean food?). All these factors render Chernobyl one of the most difficult disasters about which to offer definitive statements.

Towards a model for nuclear and industrial accidents

In the paragraphs that follow I have endeavoured to construct a general model of large-scale industrial accidents with international implications that is based on the Chernobyl experience. This might be a useful explanatory tool for several different types of accidents – those whose effects transcend national boundaries (e.g. spillage of chemicals into transnational rivers like the Rhine or the Danube); accidents whose effects are restricted to one country but involve one or more international actors (e.g. Bhopal 1984); and accidents with localized effects that are the responsibility of a national (governmental) actor (e.g. Three Mile Island 1979; Kyshtym 1957; Windscale/Sellafield 1957). As befits a historian of institutional behaviour, I have placed the emphasis of this model on organizational responses of a predominantly political and legal nature.

Stages of crisis management

Various stages of crisis management are dependent on the specific nature of the accident. The essential variable is not, however, the magnitude of the crisis but the nature of "responsible" organizations involved. The management of a crisis that involves corporate responsibility will be essentially *legal* in nature, assuming that the corporate entity does not enjoy political (i.e. governmental) support. If, however, the "responsible" party is a government-controlled body, then the management of the crisis will be primarily, though not exclusively, *political* in nature. In simple terms, it is relatively easy to litigate against a corporate entity but far more difficult to sue a government.

Surprisingly, the character of the extant political system (e.g. democratic, totalitarian) probably has little impact on crisis management. The fact that the Chernobyl disaster occurred in the Soviet Union, a quasi-totalitarian state with a lengthy record of abuse of human rights, may not have been especially significant. The democratic government of the United States has proved notoriously capricious in similar cases, and the results of the Windscale disaster in Britain were classified for 30 years by order of the British government on the pretext that revelations about the accident might prejudice the US–UK alliance. It is also extremely difficult to achieve a legal settlement that pins blame on a government.

The political and legal responses of governments faced with crises like Chernobyl are remarkably similar. Typically, they deny the magnitude of the crisis and attempt to conceal or classify pertinent data, particularly that which relates to the short- and long-term health effects of that crisis. Governments do not willingly accept either legal or operational culpability for a disaster. In the case of Chernobyl, it is only within the past few years that the governments of Belarus and Ukraine have issued legal documents about compensation for residents of contaminated communities. The Soviet government never

211

accepted full responsibility for the consequences of Chernobyl, especially its international aspects, which included a radioactive cloud that crossed Europe and caused extensive harm to communities in northern Scandinavia, southern Germany, and the uplands of Britain. In refusing to take the blame, the Soviet regime was following a path trodden by previous national governments.

Victims also have a role to play in crisis management. "Victim action" is a recurrent theme here, in both political and legal terms. Victim action can involve everything from a single individual all the way up to large-scale non-governmental organizations such as the OECD (Organisation for Economic Co-operation and Development) or IAEA. But the same dynamic of interest groups and action is at work here also. In the case of Chernobyl, it is hardly surprising that the Ukrainian Green World environmental association took a far dimmer view of the accident than did the IAEA, whose mandate includes not only the international regulation of the nuclear power and nuclear weapons industries, but also the promotion of nuclear power.

In the same way, the response of the Ukrainian government to Chernobyl is best explained by political motives, or else by response to the existing political realities. Although the ramifications of Chernobyl were felt first in Ukraine, rather than in distant Moscow, the "victim" government chose not only to side with the responsible government (USSR), which ran the ministries responsible for construction of nuclear plants and nuclear energy production, but declined to take any significant form of independent action, including the prompt evacuation of villages and settlements near the damaged reactor. Perception plays a crucial role in the management of a crisis by victims as well as perpetrators.

Though not truly independent, the mass media comprise another important factor in crisis management. Despite suggestions to the contrary (e.g. the film *The China Syndrome*), the media rarely *uncover* a large-scale industrial accident. The media are mainly a reactive force, obliged to depend – often heavily – on information supplied by sources closely associated with the accident. As these situations are fast moving and rapidly changing, the media often report information which, under normal circumstances, they would reject as unsound or uncorroborated. During a rapidly unfolding crisis in which official information is severely restricted, the media may abdicate the editorial duties of weighing and assessing the value of information gained, preferring to resort to inflammatory headlines.[39]

How this occurred in the case of Chernobyl was illustrated by *Time* magazine:

A Dutch amateur radio enthusiast reported picking up a broadcast in which a distraught ham operator near Chernobyl announced that two units were ablaze and spoke of "many hundreds dead and wounded." In [this] account, the man cried, "We heard heavy explosions! You can't imagine what's happening here with all the deaths and fire.... I don't know if our leaders know what to do because this is a real disaster. Please tell the world to help us."

In the absence of any Soviet description of events at the time, this dramatic but unconfirmed account was seized on by the media and widely carried (*Time*, 12 May 1986: 28–29).

Sensational accounts sell copy, and few Western newspapers were immune to the tendency to indulge in hyperbolic descriptions of what was occurring at Chernobyl, as long as the authorities within the Soviet Union declined to present an alternative picture. The drab and censorious statement from Moscow – "Measures are being taken to eliminate the consequences of the accident" – was a further factor in catalysing the furore in the West, and was equally misleading.

It is, therefore, clear that a large-scale "model" industrial accident is impossible to quantify. Much depends on the actions of responsible parties and the reaction of the victims. The key question is not how an accident is managed, but why it is managed in a particular fashion. The interest groups involved in any industrial accident fall into three categories – those deemed responsible (operators, plant managers); those deemed affected (victims); and an uncertain group, the media. In most industrial accidents the actions of each group are remarkably consistent and follow an identifiable pattern of conflict and, it is hoped, resolution. This section briefly examines the actions of the three key groups in some industrial accidents, both within the Soviet Union and elsewhere.

Three Mile Island, 1979

The accident at the Three Mile Island (TMI) nuclear plant in Harrisburg, Pennsylvania, occurred at 4 a.m. on 28 March 1979. The company responsible for the plant's operation (Metropolitan Edison) released little information about the accident in the first hours and days after its occurrence. The evidence suggests that the company knew the accident was very serious, involving a partial core meltdown

213

and failure of the primary containment vessel, with subsequent leakage of radioactive material into the reactor building. They would also have been aware that the reactor building was unlikely to prevent further leakage into the outside atmosphere (Rubin 1982: 131–141). Indeed, it is widely believed that Metropolitan Edison already knew that radioactive particles were entering the atmosphere even as they held their first news conference about 12 hours after the accident. Yet they decided not to inform the public of this fact. Later, when pressed, an official of the company admitted that he had not mentioned any releases into the environment "because he had not been asked directly about them" (Rubin 1982: 133).

One critic has pointed out that this reticence broke the first rule of effective public relations: when the news is bad, it should be published in full as quickly as possible (Rubin 1982: 133). Nevertheless, the Metropolitan Edison company chose to withhold information that was perceived as being in the vital interests of the general public once it finally became available. This produced a cascade effect in the company's dealings with the media in particular and the public in general. Once people realized that they had been deceived, they were less inclined to accept any information subsequently released by the company. A confrontational stance was preferred.

A US government study released after the accident found that the situation worsened when some officials of the Nuclear Regulatory Commission (NRC) chose to support Metropolitan Edison's position and adopted an "optimistic tone," despite the fact that news about the seriousness of the accident was already surfacing in the media (President's Commission on the Accident at Three Mile Island 1979). With the credibility of both Metropolitan Edison and the NRC damaged, pro-nuclear interest groups suffered a major public relations setback from which they never recovered. Anti-nuclear sentiments could now be voiced in a more confident way. As David M. Rubin pointed out, "One way or another the reporters were going to get a story. If the utility was not going to provide facts (as it did not), reporters would turn to other sources" (Rubin 1982: 136).

Information about TMI that appeared in the media therefore consisted of "informed speculation," often from sources within the anti-nuclear movement and often of an alarmist character. Since the information was not printed with any qualification, the public was unable to determine its accuracy. Moreover, the media had not reported on nuclear accidents hitherto and so had little experience in evaluating the information they were disseminating. One result was widespread confusion and long-term distrust of the nuclear energy industry.

Despite the blunder committed by officials from both Metropolitan Edison and the NRC, the practice of downplaying accidents continues in the nuclear industry. As far as possible, spokespersons for nuclear installations tend to minimize the seriousness of accidents and maintain a "healthy optimism" about efforts to "remove (the) consequences." The TMI experience illustrated a problem involving the accurate communication of information in an emergency. This legacy soon had reverberations. In March 1981, when there was a serious leakage of radioactive waste water from a nuclear power plant in Tsuruga, Japan, the operating company did not disclose the seriousness of the accident until radiation was detected in a nearby bay six weeks later (*Time*, 12 May 1986).

The international nuclear energy industry's response to Chernobyl

The response of the international nuclear energy industry to Chernobyl is particularly instructive because it demonstrates how an embattled industry sought to minimize the repercussions of a disaster. The industry adopted three different interpretations of the accident and shifted among them as they became untenable. In every case, criticisms were launched against vocal groups opposed to nuclear energy, accusing them of scaremongering, alarmism, and a lack of expertise. These groups, for their part, labelled the nuclear industry's attempts to downplay the magnitude of the crisis as "chicanery" and "duplicity."

The first interpretive strategy appeared immediately after the accident at Chernobyl became known in the West. Technical analyses of the accident were extremely conservative. For example, the June 1986 issue of *Atom*, the magazine of the United Kingdom Atomic Energy Authority (UKAEA), reported that a "significant radiation release occurred" at Chernobyl. But, reassuringly, it was immediately stressed that the "reactor is of a unique design not found outside the USSR. Its safety and operating characteristics are quite unlike those of any UK reactor" (*Atom* No. 356, June 1986: 29). As if this was not calming enough, the subsequent issue of the magazine contained a report written by Dr. J.H. Gittus, the Director of the UKAEA's Safety and Reliability Directorate, that discussed the radioactive plume released from Chernobyl and carried by wind over Britain. Gittus concluded that:

The real difference between the [radiation] exposures from natural background and from the Chernobyl accident is that those from Chernobyl will cease in a relatively short time; those from background sources will continue forever and are part and parcel of man's natural environment. (*Atom* No. 357, July 1986: 17)

Again, this sort of response follows the pattern seen at TMI: optimistic predictions about the accident were made with the objective of defusing the issues.

A concomitant tactic in this sort of response is to denigrate authors of conflicting views. Thus, reviewers in *Atom* were busy excoriating some of the "instant books" on Chernobyl that appeared in the summer of 1986. One, written by a team of journalists from the London *Observer*, was reviewed as follows: "It would be nice to describe this book on the Chernobyl accident as the 'worst book in the world'. [A play on the book's title, *The Worst Accident in the World*.] But it is merely one in a long tradition of anti-nuclear 'horror' books that manipulates facts and superstition towards the writers' apparent end of ridding the world of nuclear power" (*Atom* No. 359, September 1986: 27). Professor Jovan Jovanovich of the University of Manitoba, the lone Canadian representative on an international advisory committee to the IAEA, referred to what he termed "horror stories" about the disaster as "trash" (*Winnipeg Free Press*, 23 May 1991). His concern was that the media had sensationalized the consequences of Chernobyl but, in making his allegations, he may have underestimated the extent of the effects of the disaster.

The second interpretive strategy adopted by UK nuclear authorities ignored the radioactive plume that had drifted overhead and turned instead to the issue of Soviet reactor design and safety procedures. It was emphasized repeatedly that such an accident could never occur in a British nuclear establishment. The same line was adopted by the US Council for Energy Awareness, and maintained until at least 1991. Its *Chernobyl Briefing Book* (1991) stressed:

... the Chernobyl-type design is not used anywhere except the Soviet Union, and could not be licensed to operate in the United States or other industrial nations in the West and Far East.... The Chernobyl accident was a unique event, on a scale by itself. It was the first and only time in the history of commercial nuclear energy that people were killed. (US Council for Energy Awareness 1991: 1)[40]

216

The third interpretive strategy adopted by Western officials and supporters of the nuclear power industry was derived from a Soviet report to the IAEA in Vienna (August 1986). This highlighted operator error as the cause of the Chernobyl accident and (correctly) pointed out that several safety features designed to prevent such an accident were disconnected intentionally at the time of the reactor test on 25–26 April 1986. Not only was this fact seized upon by industry analysts; comparisons were immediately made to show that it would be impossible for operators to disconnect such a wide array of safety devices on a Western reactor, which would shut down automatically if such actions were attempted (*Atom* No. 368, June 1987: 8).

Finally, the Soviet government, in its international response to Chernobyl, permitted the IAEA to take on an unprecedented supervisory role. Members of the agency and its advisors were given unique access to the Chernobyl area and allowed to carry out tests and inspections of local residents. Professor Jovanovich might have been typical of those who took an optimistic view of the disaster's consequences:

... initially the Soviet authorities were handling the accident pretty much in the same old way, in isolation, out of sight of the world community. Thanks to socio-political changes that have occurred in the Soviet Union since the accident, the Soviet scientists and politicians, using the good offices of the International Atomic Energy Agency, got together with the international professional community and said "let us work together." Thus the International Chernobyl Project was born. In my view the greatest benefit and success of the ICP has been the fact that an open and sincere international collaboration has been established among recent Cold War adversaries ... (Jovanovich 1991 [draft])

Once again, self-buttressing statements by supporters of the nuclear industry are apparent: witness the reference to an "international professional community." Within the industry, spokespersons are invariably referred to as "experts" or "professionals," while those outside the industry (who might be equally cognizant of the workings of nuclear plants or the effects of radiation) are dismissed as "non-specialists," "environmentalists," or representatives of the media looking for horror stories.[41]

Summary

It is apparent that the various "actors" involved in civilian nuclear accidents act in a remarkably consistent fashion when confronted with a crisis. Those responsible attempt, as far as possible, to conceal the extent of the accident and to promulgate an optimistic view of the situation. Such a reaction, therefore, was not unique to the Soviet government after Chernobyl. This author has stated elsewhere that, as a test of glasnost in the USSR, Chernobyl was a failure.[42] However, the reaction of the Soviet authorities – silence until confronted with incontrovertible proof that radiation had spread beyond the borders of the USSR – was not dissimilar to that of Metropolitan Edison in the case of TMI, or of the UKAEA after the fire at Windscale/Sellafield (President's Commission on the Accident at Three Mile Island 1979). This does not mean that any of these organizations were overtly callous or reckless. The individuals involved most probably believed that the consequences of the respective accidents could be contained in secret, free from the attentions of troublesome and irresponsible media. In all three cases cited, the evident secrecy surrounding the accidents served to decrease public trust of the industry and to inflame the media and other interest groups.

The media reacted to the lack of information in two different ways. First, reporters began to speculate what might have happened. Such speculations included two reactor explosions at Chernobyl, mass graves for thousands of victims, a nuclear meltdown, and similar stories. Apart from the differing scale of events, this development paralleled what had happened after TMI seven years earlier. There, an unrelated fire that broke out the day after the accident was quickly reported as a reactor fuel fire. Metropolitan Edison was also reported to be burning radioactive material at night, out of the public eye. Both of these reports were false, but they were partly a result of failure to provide timely and accurate information.

Why did the authorities react in such a fashion? There are several possible reasons. The one that is most often cited (and it was referred to with regularity after Chernobyl) is that they wished to avoid panic among the population.[43] Ivan Yemelyanov, one of the designers of the Chernobyl plant and a deputy director of the USSR Institute of Energy Technology, informed the Italian Communist Party newspaper, *Unita*, that selective information had been released about the accident in order to forestall panic (Marples 1986: 170). (Literature on human responses to disaster would suggest that generally confusion, shock, and trauma are more likely than outright panic, and the majority of the population in Pripyat appears to have conformed to this norm.) The most charitable explanation for holding May Day parades in Kiev and Minsk, only five days after the accident, is that the Ukrainian and Belarusian governments were anxious to portray life as "normal."

A second possibility is that such accidents trigger an inherent "self-protection" mechanism in an offending industry. Invidious comparisons with competing industries are often made. Thus, it was pointed out by nuclear advocates that human casualties in coal and oil production industries are consistently high. Four deaths per 1,000 tons of coal extracted is a often-cited toll for Soviet and post-Soviet coal industries (Marples 1991, ch. 7). In the same way, sympathizers of the nuclear industry also cite the damage caused to the environment by coal-fired power stations and note the comparative rarity of accidents in nuclear plants. The IAEA has been similarly protective, issuing a much-vaunted study of communities in Belarus and Ukraine in the summer of 1991 without examining the two most severely contaminated groups – clean-up crews and evacuees. Perhaps it is believed that accurate accounts would create a sensation in the media and that competing industries would escape similar scrutiny.

Third, there is the question of culpability. Few official spokespersons are willing to attribute a catastrophe to failed technology, because the public cannot be left with the perception that such sophisticated machines are fallible. Further, there is an understandable reluctance on the part of operators to take the blame for an accident. The greater the accident, the more likely it will result in dismissals, official inquiries, and shut-downs. If the accident, on the other hand, can be contained within a short period of time, with relatively few casualties, then the industry can still be considered competent and worthy of support. The culpability issue is one reason why the number of officially reported Chernobyl casualties remained at 31 long after even the most hard-boiled officials acknowledged that the real figure was in the thousands.[44] The reliance of Soviet authorities upon nuclear energy for future energy needs also depended on avoidance of culpability. Given the problems already being encountered in other energy resource industries, it was felt that the future of nuclear energy could not be compromised by providing a full account of what was then known about the Chernobyl accident.

Yet it should be reiterated that patterns of response are similar among all energy industries. Public affairs spokespersons are selected to provide assurances that the effects of an accident are limited and being eliminated. Radio and television reports from such people project an image of calm confidence. In this way the industry protects itself, like a mother sheltering her young. At Chernobyl, these various defence mechanisms were to be put to their severest test.

Suggestions for a general model of recovery from industrial accidents

In certain respects, Chernobyl was a unique accident that might have been avoided or mitigated by some precautionary measures. These include the use of less-combustible material on the roof of the reactor, immediate dispensation of potassium iodide tablets among population within a radius of at least 100 miles, provision of protective equipment at the reactor site, and establishment of dispensaries in nearby settlements. Suggestions for improving recovery are more difficult to make because many of Chernobyl's ramifications (e.g. tumours and leukaemias) still lie ahead. In light of these uncertainties the following remarks are tentative.

1. It would be useful to establish international safety norms for radiation and other consequences of industrial accidents, including contamination of soil and water. These would allow authorities to make prompt decisions about the evacuation of threatened communities. At Chernobyl, arguably, the initial area evacuated was much too small, while areas that at present have the right to be evacuated may be too large. An evacuation is an event of great stress that should be conducted only when absolutely necessary.[45]
2. It is necessary to provide facilities and personnel for accident response and evacuation in locations that are relatively close to the hazardous industrial enterprise (e.g. fire and first-aid crews; vehicular transportation). These resources should be provided before such an enterprise comes into operation. Such positioning requires answers to several questions: in the event of an emergency, how quickly could the entire workforce (and threatened others) be removed from the area; by what means; to which localities might they be moved? Scientists cannot possibly foresee every major accident, but planners can ensure that employees and local residents have a reliable means of swift removal from areas at risk.
3. All potentially hazardous facilities need a communications system linked to appropriate authorities. At Chernobyl, great confusion was caused by lack of communication among plant authorities, the local Communist Party organization, and the affected community. Releases of dangerous substances into the atmosphere must be

reported promptly, through the use of radio and television networks. The premise here is that delay does not reduce fear and may generate opposition. Ignorance and fear of the unknown are more harmful than secrecy.

4. Neighbouring states should be warned promptly in the event of an industrial accident whose consequences could transcend national boundaries.

5. If an accident has contaminated the zone around the industrial enterprise, then no further work should be conducted in the area. There should be a general shut-down of the affected enterprise; local farms, schools, and day-care centres; and general services. Forests and lakes should also be declared off limits. In order to ensure that such measures are put into practice, it may be necessary to use the armed forces as well as regular police.

6. Simple safety procedures should be emphasized before an evacuation and explained to communities that cannot be evacuated immediately. These include staying indoors as far as possible, not consuming food or water from the affected region, and the washing of steps and entrances to buildings. In the Chernobyl case, the situation was confusing. Such warnings were issued but at the same time there were reassuring statements that the water supply and other critical resources had not been affected.

7. A register of names of affected people should be established as quickly as possible. Presumably, such a document could be compiled for communities living in the vicinity of dangerous enterprises prior to start-up. All persons who enter a hazardous zone should also be registered. Addresses of new homes for evacuees must also be registered in order to monitor long-term effects of the accident upon human health. On no account should such information be classified, unless the enterprise in question is one that involves national security considerations.

8. Finally, there should be provision for development of an international aid system. This is, perhaps, the most controversial suggestion, especially for advanced industrial countries, which may decide such a system is superfluous. Yet the impact of a major nuclear disaster was well beyond the resources of the USSR, a country that withstood the loss of millions of people and 50 per cent of its industrial capacity during World War II. Moreover, Western nuclear stations are often located closer to major cities than are those of Eastern Europe and the former Soviet Union.[46] This system of aid could be jointly administered by United Nations

organizations, such as the IAEA, but it should also include groups that are not connected with the affected industries. These might be environmental groups, concerned scientists, and individual experts in specific industries.

This last point requires further emphasis. One of the paradoxes revealed by Chernobyl is the supervisory or advisory role of the IAEA, an organization whose member states are committed to advancing the cause of nuclear energy. On the national level, in the former Soviet Union, the nuclear industry was developed almost exclusively by ministries that sought its rapid expansion. Today, the Russian nuclear authorities have revised their planning methods for such enterprises: they must now be approved by both nuclear agencies and environmental agencies.[47] The last proposal noted above seeks to extend this reform to accident control: it is essential that the authorities placed in control of an accident are not supporters of the affected industrial enterprise or its products. At Chernobyl, organizations such as Greenpeace International and the International Red Cross were only belatedly involved in the response. As Mikhail Gorbachev noted in his 14 May 1986 address to the Soviet people, it is necessary to involve international organizations in the resolution of transnational problems. But those organizations should be broader in scope and more impartial than the ones that were called to Chernobyl.

In the contemporary world, unforeseen accidents will continue to happen. Their consequences may be unprecedented and may involve the rapid spread of hazardous materials. Humankind has made the decision that it is preferable to run certain risks in order to possess the material advantages of the modern world. When so much is at stake in major industrial accidents, secrecy and lack of accurate information are also commonplace.

Chernobyl remains an object lesson in human inability to deal with the consequences of its inventions. The accident's results were made worse by the reaction of the Soviet government and by the economic and political changes that have occurred in the area since 1986. On the other hand, even in the worst-affected areas, Chernobyl has not had a long-term effect on official energy policy. One of the most surprising events of 1993 was the decision of the government of Russia to begin a new, ambitious, nuclear power programme! At the time of writing there are strong indications that the governments of Ukraine, Belarus, Lithuania, and Armenia will soon follow suit (Marples 1993b). Chernobyl remains a major and pressing problem in all three

Slavic states as the number of related medical illnesses has risen dramatically. Seven years after the event, there are no obvious new measures for improving response. The best that can be done is to offer suggestions that may render a future major accident less cataclysmic.

Acknowledgement

I wish to thank David Freeland Duke, doctoral candidate in Soviet history at the University of Alberta, for his assistance with this chapter.

Chronology

1986

25–26 April. Safety test takes place at Chernobyl nuclear power plant, Ukraine.

26 April (1.38 a.m.). An explosion destroys the fourth reactor.

27 April (2.00 p.m.). Evacuation of Pripyat begins.

28 April. Tass announces the accident to the world.

29 April. First news item is published in the Soviet press.

1 May. May Day celebrations take place as planned in Kiev, Minsk, and other cities.

2 May. Politburo members Ryzhkov and Ligachev visit Chernobyl. A 30 kilometre zone around the reactor is designated for evacuation.

10 May. The fourth reactor is "capped" with sand and boron, and leakages of radiation end.

May–June. Military reservists brought to Chernobyl to lead the clean-up operation.

August. The Soviet Report on the causes of the accident is presented to the International Atomic Energy Agency in Vienna.

December. A concrete roof ("sarcophagus") is completed over the fourth reactor.

1987

July. Chernobyl director and five plant operators are found guilty of gross negligence at a trial held mostly in camera in the town of Chernobyl.

1989

February. The first maps highlighting radiation fallout from Chernobyl are published in the Soviet press.

1991

April. On the fifth anniversary of Chernobyl there are mass demonstrations in Kiev and Minsk. The world press focuses on the event, highlighting new evacuations, alleged sicknesses in contaminated zones, and the continuing operation of Soviet RBMK reactors, including those at Chernobyl.

1992

March. The Ukrainian government reports that cracks have appeared in the sarcophagus. An international competition is to be held for a design for a replacement roof.

Notes

1. All names used in this paper have been cited in the Russian version. While I have no wish to offend Ukrainians or Belarusians, I consider that this usage is pertinent here since the names are well known to the Western reader. Moreover, to use three different languages in one paper would only cause confusion. Hence I use Chernobyl (not Chornobyl), Kiev (not Kyyiv), and Minsk (rather than Miensk).

2. Of the numerous sources on the immediate aftermath to Chernobyl, see especially Grigorii Medvedev (1991), Shcherbak (1988), and Illesh and Pralnikov (1987). A photographic depiction, which includes excellent commentaries by Vladimir Yavorivsky, Andrei Illesh, and others is Eisymont (1988). The above account is also based on eyewitness statements made to the author during a visit to Chernobyl in June 1989.

3. The population figures are derived from State Committee of Statistics of the Ukrainian SSR 1984: 8 and State Committee of Statistics of the Belorussian SSR 1990: 15.

4. The area is described in Marples (1986: 115).

5. On the design of the RBMK reactor and its inherent problems, see Zhores Medvedev (1990: 3–7) and Marples (1986: 109–113).

6. The most famous criticism was that of journalist Lyubov Kovalevska, a reporter for the Pripyat newspaper, who published an article about the flaws in the construction of the fifth Chernobyl reactor in *Literaturna Ukraina*, 27 March 1986. See also Marples (1986: 118–124). Zhores Medvedev also notes that, for purely political reasons, the fourth reactor at Chernobyl was brought into operation well ahead of its official schedule and without adequate safety tests (Medvedev 1990: 12).

7. This imprecise phrase has an interesting history itself. As far as I can ascertain, it was first used by Stalin (or, at the least, widely used in public statements) during his first collectivization campaign, to eliminate alleged rich farmers or kulaks, to wit: "the liquidation of the kulaks as a class." Subsequently, it was used to designate a time of frantic and sustained activity, particularly in accident or wartime situations.

8. Interview with the editorial board of *Izvestiya*, 27 November 1987.

9. Radio Kiev, 1 May 1986.

10. Zhores Medvedev (1990: 65), citing the eyewitness testimony of his namesake (no relation), Grigorii Medvedev.

11. One roentgen of gamma rays is equivalent to one radiation absorbed dose (rad; 0.01 Gy) or one radiation dose equivalent (rem [acronym for radiation equivalent man]; 0.01 Sv).

12. Ibid.

13. The figure is, none the less, more than 30 times higher than the natural background.

14. In May 1986, incidentally, it was almost impossible to locate a current issue of a Western newspaper in Kiev, and such newspapers were never seen outside the major cities. Foreign radio broadcasts from the Voice of America and Radio Liberty were still being heavily jammed. Thus the accusation that such reports were causing panic seems far-fetched. The only possible means of such panic might emanate from telephone calls. According to many American and Canadian Ukrainians with whom I spoke, who tried during that period to call relatives and friends in Ukraine, it was extremely difficult to get a connection.

15. See the account of the accident by Victor G. Snell of Atomic Energy of Canada Limited (AECL) written as an introduction to Marples (1988: 1–24).

16. The meeting was publicized on the front page of some newspapers; see, for example, *Sovetskaya Belorussiya*, 17 May 1986.

17. Professor Jovan Jovanovich, for example, notes that his request to visit Chernobyl as a private citizen in 1988 was promptly granted, and the visit took place in February 1989 (Jovanovich 1991: 10). He was thus the first Canadian to visit the site as an individual. I was the second, but my request had taken three years to be accepted. While I was there, it was made clear that I was regarded initially (i.e. in 1986–1987) as a hostile observer.

18. The brief history of Slavutich is a miserable one. Billed as a twenty-first century city, it was belatedly discovered to be located in a radioactive "patch" and surrounding forests had to be cut down. Shortly after the completion of what was labelled as its first stage, the Ukrainian government announced the forthcoming permanent closure of the Chernobyl station in 1995. In December 1991, once Ukraine became independent, the ultimate fate of the station appeared more certain. Residents were reported to be depressed and unsure of their future. Its present population is estimated at 20,000, i.e. less than half that of Pripyat in early 1986. For an account of its construction, see Marples (1988: 225–238).
19. See *Zakon Respubliki Belarus* (1992), especially Article 3 on page 2.
20. Perhaps inevitably, this was taken to extremes. Thus, the Ukrainian government began in 1989 to publish maps of individual oblasts, some of which had received virtually no significant radiation fallout, but may have had a few isolated areas of radioactive caesium of more than one curie per square kilometre in the soil. The maps, without doubt, caused some unnecessary panic, though in such oblasts there were often other environmental hazards that constituted a far greater danger to the population but which were being ignored. The maps are still being published regularly. See, for example, the map of Vinnitsya Oblast, published in *Demokratychna Ukraina*, 12 May 1992.
21. It is symptomatic of the depth of concern manifested in Ukraine that the local party leader from Narodichi, G. Gotovchits, subsequently became Ukraine's first Minister for Chernobyl in the new government of 1992.
22. In March 1993, an estimate of the costs of the Chernobyl accident was provided by the Belarusian parliamentary deputy, Anatoly Volkov: in Russia, $174 billion; in Belarus, $171 billion; and in Ukraine, $138 billion. He estimated with regard to the "current republican budgets" that Russia would be able to raise the necessary funds within 8 years, Ukraine in 28 years, and Belarus in 171 years (*Minsk Business News*, March 1993: 7). I have reservations about the size of the bill for Russia, which had a broader area affected but at less intensive levels. The comment in any case precludes international aid, which thus far has proved vital in attempting to meet the problems engendered by Chernobyl, particularly in the medical sphere.
23. A statement by Boris Prister, First Deputy Minister for Protection of the Population from the consequences of the Chernobyl Accident, cites a figure of 420,000 people "directly affected by the accident" [IPS (Moscow), 3 February 1993]. There was no indication, however, of what was signified by "directly affected." In June 1992 at the United Nations conference on Environment and Development in Brazil, Yurii Shcherbak, then Ukrainian Minister of the Environment, declared that in the territories of Ukraine contaminated by Chernobyl there were living 2.4 million people, including 500,000 children under the age of 14. There was no indication of the level of radiation used to arrive at such figures, however (Radio Ukraina, 1 June 1992, 10.20 p.m.).
24. The informal association of clean-up workers involved in the decontamination process at Chernobyl and the immediate vicinity.
25. For example, Vladimir Chernousenko, a clean-up worker, who maintains that up to 10,000 "volunteers" have died to date. Cited in Marples (1993c).
26. Interview with Dr. E.P. Demidchik, Institute of Oncology, Minsk, Belarus, 17 April 1993.
27. Interview with Academician E.P. Konoplya, Institute of Radiobiology, Minsk, Belarus, 14 April 1993.
28. Interview with Drs. D. Chesnov and K. Radyuk, Minsk No. 3 Hospital for Sick Children, Minsk, Belarus, 20 April 1993. I was permitted to see and speak to the children suffering from diabetes, thyroid problems, and other illnesses.
29. Dmitrii Chesnov, 20 April 1993.
30. In reality, the role of the Communist Party at Chernobyl was a controversial and far from decisive one. Disaster control remained in the hands of the Soviet government (the Government Commission) and relevant ministries (such as Medium Machine Building, Power and Electrification, Internal Affairs, Coal). It was pointed out to me by one observer that

the spheres in which the party or Komsomol (Communist League of Youth) did take control were notable for widespread corruption. A prime example of this was said to be the administration of the Pripyat Industrial and Research Association, which administered the decontamination operation led by military reservists, which was run by the Komsomol.

31. For a more detailed look at birth and death rate trends in this republic in the period since 1970, see State Committee of Statistics of the Belorussian SSR (1990: 20).

32. The appeal was issued during the Eurochernobyl-2 Congress in Kiev, in April 1991, at which I was present. Ironically, Masyk has since been accused, by the Chairman of the Ukrainian State Committee for Chernobyl, Volodymyr Yavorivsky, of embezzling funds designated for Chernobyl children. See *Pravda Ukrainy*, 24 November 1992.

33. A complete history of these events has now been published (Solchanyk 1993). Periodic updates have been published by Solchanyk, Bohdan Nahaylo, Kathleen Mihalisko, and David Marples in Radio Liberty's *Report on the USSR*, which was renamed *RFE/RL Research Report* in 1992. An informative perspective is found in the diary of a Kiev intellectual; see Pavlychko (1992).

34. On 25 March 1990, the BPF intended to commemorate the seventy-second anniversary of the creation of the Belorussian Democratic Republic. This action was regarded with horror by the authorities, who tried to equate the political orientation of this short-lived government (it was eliminated by a Polish invasion) with the German National Socialists. In this way, the BPF leaders themselves were branded as extreme nationalists. See *Shag* (Minsk), special issue, No. 2, 23 March 1990.

35. I am here not simply taking Pozniak's statements at face value. Over the course of three visits to Minsk in 1992 and 1993 I have had ample opportunity to experience for myself the unchanged political climate in the republic. The main square and street in the capital city provide symbolic testimony to the maintenance of the status quo, with statues of Lenin and founder of the Cheka (KGB) Feliks Dzerzhinsky. It is recalled that after the failed putsch in Moscow in August 1991, Dzerzhinsky's statue outside KGB headquarters was the first to be dismantled. Belarus is also the only state to have retained a secret police under its original acronym of KGB.

36. Interview with Iryna Grushevaya, Minsk, Belarus, 13 October 1992 and ff.

37. In early 1992, the government declared that all the children being sent abroad must be registered with the Ministry of Education. Later in the year, it was ordered that children must also receive a personal letter of invitation from their host families, despite the fact that more than 20,000 children had already taken part in such visits (interview with Iryna Grushevaya, 13 October 1992). The purpose of such trips appears to be at least partly psychological – to remove children from a fairly wretched situation in the villages and divert their attention from medical and Chernobyl-related issues, while ensuring that their diet is both healthy and nutritious.

38. I was informed, however, by the Director of the Institute of Radiobiology, Belarusian Academy of Sciences, Academician Evgenii P. Konoplya, that the medical data on victims in Belarus was essentially complete (interview with E.P. Konoplya, Minsk, Belarus, 14 April 1993).

39. One example in the case of Chernobyl was that of a UPI reporter who stated that there were 2,000 immediate victims, evidently on the basis of a single telephone interview with a woman who later retracted her story. Similarly, the 2 May 1986 headline in the *New York Post* concerning Chernobyl was as follows: "Mass Grave for 15,000-N Victims."

40. Fatal accidents had occurred, however, in military nuclear stations. For example, a power surge occurred at the nuclear reactor experimental station at Deep River, six miles from Canada's first atomic plant at Chalk River on 12 December 1952, and it took two years to clean up the radioactive water that had spilled into the basement of the building (see Silver 1987: 89–90).

41. Thus, in his book on the effects of Chernobyl internationally, L. Ray Silver, a strong advo-

cate of nuclear power development in Canada, notes with pleasure how a national magazine that had at one time regarded an anti-nuclear spokesperson as an expert, cited this same person merely as a "critic" after the Chernobyl disaster. In his view, this was a sign that the magazine in question was becoming more professional in its response to nuclear accidents (Silver 1987: 152).

42. See Marples (1988). Other scientists have verified these comments. For example, the noted scientist Zhores Medvedev stated that: "For several months after the Chernobyl accident the Soviet nuclear establishment was generally successful in promoting a cover-up story about the test of an entirely new safety device" (Medvedev 1990: 33). See also Sakharov (1992: 608–609).

43. Thus, on 26 May 1986, the Novosti press agency reported in English with regard to Chernobyl that "There was a danger of scaring people into panic which could result [sic] from misinterpreted excessive information." In fact, the only panic seems to have occurred among party members in Pripyat, who were, perhaps, more aware of the scale of the disaster than ordinary citizens: 177 of them fled the scene (Marples 1986: 170).

44. The same figure was repeated as recently as February 1993 by Dr. Robert Gale, who returned to Moscow to check on some of the patients he had originally treated after the accident. This is an indication, perhaps, of the effectiveness of official propaganda, and the old dictum propagated by Hitler that, if a lie is repeated enough times, it will be regarded as the truth. See Associated Press, 4 February 1993. The real figure of immediate deaths is not known, though several prominent figures died in the summer of 1986 (including the Ukrainian film director Volodymyr Shevchenko and an official from the Ministry of Medium Machine Building) as a result of exposure to high levels of radiation at Chernobyl. There is ample evidence to indicate dozens of other cases. However, no precise figure has ever been determined, and the Ukrainian government's 1992–1993 citation of 8,000 Chernobyl casualties remains uncorroborated.

45. The question of the necessity for a large-scale evacuation after Chernobyl continues to be debated. It appears that evacuation has greatly increased trauma among evacuees. Therefore, some specialists advocate strongly that future evacuations should not take place until every possibility for reducing the dangers of increased radiation intake through food and water has been exhausted. See the comments of Professor of Biology Yakov Kenigsberg in *Katastrofa* (special publication of the Belarusian State Chernobyl Committee), 24 April 1993: 10.

46. For details on demographics of areas around nuclear power stations, see Mitchell (1983: 367–384).

47. This was outlined in the press conference of the Russian Ministry of Atomic Energy, Moscow, 21 January 1993. Reported by the Federal News Service, Washington, DC.

References

Belarusian Charitable Fund for the Children of Chernobyl. 1992. "Analysis of morbidity on children's endocrinology in Belarus." Unpublished paper.

Charnobylski sled na Belarusi. [*The Chernobyl Trace in Belarus.*] 1992. Minsk: Central Board of Hydrometeorology and Ministry of Foreign Affairs of the Republic of Belarus.

Chernobylskaya katastrofa i tragediya Belorussii. [*The Chernobyl Catastrophe and the Tragedy of Belorussia.*] 1990. Minsk: Polymya, pp. 6–10.

Eisymont, A.V. (ed). 1988. *Chernobylskyi reportazh.* [*Chernobyl Reportage.*] Moscow: Planeta.

Energetika SSSR v 1976–1980 godakh. 1977. Moscow: Energiya.

Illesh, A.B., and A.E. Pralnikov. 1987. *Reportazh iz Chernobylya.* [*Reportage from Chernobyl.*] Moscow: Mysl.

Jovanovich, Jovan V. 1991. "The Chernobyl accident: Five years after. Part II: Radioactive releases and consequences." *Physics in Canada* (July).

Konoplya, E.P. 1992a. "Globalno–ekologicheskie posledstviya katastrofy na Chernobylskoi AES." ["The global–ecological consequences of the catastrophe at the Chernobyl nuclear power plant."] Paper delivered at the International Congress, "The World After Chernobyl," Minsk, Belarus, 15 April 1992.

———. 1992b. "Otsenka posleavariinoi radioekologicheskoi obstanovki na territorii Belarusi i mediko-biologicheskie posledstviya dlya naseleniya." In: *Mir posle Chernobyla.* Minsk: Belarusian Charitable Fund for the Children of Chernobyl.

Marples, David R. 1986. *Chernobyl and Nuclear Power in the USSR.* New York: St. Martin's Press.

———. 1988. *The Social Impact of the Chernobyl Disaster.* New York: St. Martin's Press.

———. 1989. "The debate over radiation exposure in Ukraine." *Report on the USSR* 1(40): 20.

———. 1991. *Ukraine Under Perestroika: Ecology, Economics and the Workers' Revolt.* New York: St. Martin's Press.

———. 1992a. "Chernobyl and nuclear energy in post-Soviet Ukraine." *RFE/RL Research Report* 1(35): 54–58.

———. 1992b. "An insider's view of Chernobyl': An interview with Yurii Risovannyi." In: Roman Solchanyk, ed. *Ukraine from Chernobyl' to Sovereignty.* New York: St. Martin's Press, p. 148.

———. 1993a. "The legacy of Chernobyl' in Belarus." *RFE/RL Research Report* 2(5): 46–50.

———. 1993b. "The post-Soviet nuclear power program." *Post-Soviet Geography* (34): 172–184.

———. 1993c. "A correlation between radiation and health problems in Belarus?" *Post-Soviet Geography* 34(5): 281.

Medvedev, Grigorii. 1991. *The Truth About Chernobyl.* New York: Basic Books.

Medvedev, Zhores. 1990. *The Legacy of Chernobyl.* New York: W.W. Norton.

Mikhaylov, Mikhail. 1993. "Fewer born: more die." *Minsk Business News*, March.

Mitchell, James K. 1983. "Nuclear power station hazards in nonmetropolitan America." In: Rutherford Platt and George Macinko, eds. *Beyond the Urban Fringe: Land Use Issues of Nonmetropolitan America.* Minneapolis: University of Minnesota Press.

Pavlychko, Solomea. 1992. *Letters From Kiev.* Edmonton: Canadian Institute of Ukrainian Studies.

President's Commission on the Accident at Three Mile Island. 1979. *Report of the Public's Right to Information Task Force to the President's Commission on the Accident at Three Mile Island.* Washington, DC: Government Printing Office, p. 96.

Rubin, David M. 1982. "The public's right to know: The accident at Three Mile Island." In: David L. Sills, C.P. Wolf, and Vivien B. Shelanski, eds. *The Accident at Three Mile Island: The Human Dimensions.* Boulder: Westview Press, pp. 131–141.

Sakharov, Andrei. 1992. *Memoirs.* New York: Vintage Books.

Shcherbak, Yurii. 1988. *Chernobyl: A Documentary Story.* New York: St. Martin's Press.

Silver, L. Ray. 1987. *Fallout from Chernobyl.* Toronto: Deneau Publishers.

Solchanyk, Roman. 1986. "The perils of prognostication." *Soviet Analyst* 15(5), 5 March.

———. 1993. *Ukraine: The Road to Independence.* New York: St. Martin's Press.

State Committee of Statistics of the Belorussian SSR. 1990. *Narodnoe khozyaistvo Belorusskoi SSR v 1989g.* [*The Economy of the Belorussian SSR in 1989.*] Minsk, Belarus: State Committee of Statistics.

State Committee of Statistics of the Ukrainian SSR. 1984. *Narodnoe khozyaistvo Ukrainskoi SSR 1983: statisticheskii ezhegodnik.* [*The Economy of the Ukrainian SSR in 1983: A Statistical Compendium.*] Kiev: Tekhnika.

US Council for Energy Awareness. 1991. *Chernobyl Briefing Book.* Washington, DC, n.p.

USSR Committee for State Security (KGB). 1979. "Construction flaws at the Chernobyl nuclear power plant." Document No. 346-A, Moscow, 21 February. Document displayed at the Soviet archival exhibit of the Library of Congress, Washington, DC, 1992.

Zakon Respubliki Belarus. 1992. *Zakon Respubliki Belarus o sotsialnoi zashchite grazhdan postradavshykh ot katastrofy na Chernobylskoi AES.* [*Law of the Republic of Belarus about the Social Protection of Citizens Suffering from the Catastrophe at Chernobyl Nuclear Power Plant.*] Minsk, 9 June.

Media sources

Associated Press (agency, London).
Atom (London).
Demokratychyna Ukraina (newspaper, Kiev).
Federal News Service (Washington, DC).
Gomelskaya pravda (newspaper, Minsk).
IPS (news agency, Moscow).
Itar (news agency, Moscow).
Izvestiya (newspaper, Moscow).
Katastrofa (newspaper, Minsk).
Literaturna Ukraina (newspaper, Kiev).
Minsk Business News.
Moscow News.
Narodnaya hazeta (newspaper, Minsk).
New York Post.
Novosti (news agency, St. Petersburg).
Pravda Ukrainy (newspaper, Kiev).
Radio Kiev.
Radio Ukraina.
Reuters (news agency, London).
Shag (newspaper, Minsk).
Sovetskaya Belorussiya (newspaper, Minsk).

Tass (news agency, Moscow)
Time (New York).
UPI (news agency, New York).
Vechernii Minsk (newspaper, Minsk).
Winnipeg Free Press.
Znamya yunosti (newspaper, Minsk).
Zvyazda (newspaper, Minsk).

8

The *Exxon Valdez* oil spill, Alaska

Nancy Y. Davis

Introduction

Oil spills in the ocean epitomize the increasingly global nature of industrial disasters. All countries use oil and most import it by sea. As other industries expand, more oil is consumed and the volume of tanker traffic increases, linking risk upon risk, country by country. Moreover, oil transportation is a complex international undertaking that spreads moral – if not legal – responsibility for accidents among many states. This was well demonstrated in 1993 when the tanker *Braer* broke up in the Shetland Islands. As one Canadian transportation official noted, the *Braer* was "... constructed in Japan under Liberian registry ... owned by an American company ... chartered by a Canadian company with a crew from Greece, the Philippines and Poland, and ... went aground in England with oil from Norway" (Kizzia 1993a: 9).

If that oil had found its way around the North Sea, then six adjacent countries might have been added to the list of involved states – Sweden, Denmark, Germany, Netherlands, Belgium, and France. Fifteen countries potentially involved in only one oil spill! With 7,000 tankers transporting 10 billion barrels of oil by sea each year, the stage is set for increasingly complex disasters.

This chapter addresses the largest marine oil spill in North America.[1] It occurred when the *Exxon Valdez* ran aground and leaked

231

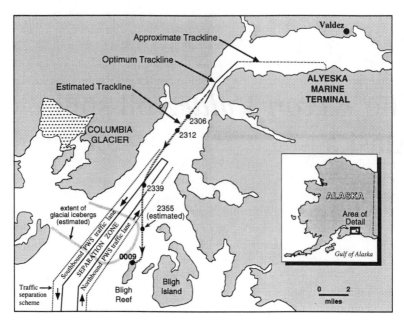

Fig. 8.1   **Location of the *Exxon Valdez* grounding**

oil into Alaska's Prince William Sound on 24 March 1989 (fig. 8.1).
About one-quarter of the cargo, 10.8 million (US) gallons, or 258,000
barrels (38,800 tons) of crude oil was spilled. Some ultimately coated
about 1,200 miles of coastline, up to 470 miles away from the site of
the accident. No human lives were lost, but 20 communities and a rich
natural environment were affected.

Characteristics of vulnerability to disaster in a culturally diverse
and spatially dispersed population provide an organizing theme for
this study. The coast of south-east Alaska is a setting where a giant oil
spill had the potential to bring rapid cultural change. Yet, while some
cultural patterns were modified, others seem to persist. In some cases,
predisaster changes accelerated, while in others they slowed. New
elements, new organizations, new positions, new leaders, new arenas
for conflict arose out of the confusing rubble. Do the new entities add
to the predisaster ones, or displace them? Some cultures welcome
new ideas; others resist them. Some survivors thrive with the new
challenges; others may never fully recover.

This chapter draws on anthropological concepts and understand-
ings of cultures, of community histories, their value systems, and relative amenability to modification. The *Exxon Valdez* disaster seems

to have generated considerable emotional energy; massive sums of money; a flurry of new jobs; a gaggle of regulations; and extensive, continuing litigation. But, because of legal constraints connected with class action lawsuits filed on behalf of fishermen and Native populations, few results of social science research on the recovery of communities have been published. What follows represents an attempt to summarize what is known and to raise new questions about the implications.

The oil industry and the spill

Oil was first discovered in Alaska in 1901, and commercial production began over 50 years later near the Kenai Peninsula in the southern part of the state. But the crude oil that leaked from the *Exxon Valdez* originated on Alaska's north coast (the so-called North Slope) near Prudhoe Bay. Following discovery of this field in 1968, the technology for transporting oil south across 800 miles of Arctic and subarctic terrain had to be engineered, a consortium of invest-ment and management companies organized, environmental issues considered, laws passed, land claims of Alaska Natives addressed, the pipeline built, and port facilities constructed. A need for speed was highlighted by the Middle East oil embargo of 1973–1974 and a growing awareness of the extent to which Americans might be dependent on Alaskan oil. The Trans-Alaskan Pipeline Authoriza-tion Act was passed in 1973, setting aside some of the requirements of the National Environmental Policy Act (1970) – a previously unheard-of action. Construction began on 29 April 1974, and the first oil flowed through a 48 inch pipe to the terminal in Valdez on 31 July 1977. At present, a volume of about 1.7 million barrels arrives in Valdez every day and, because of limited storage space, most of it must be transferred to tankers that navigate the narrow passage of Valdez Arm into the Gulf of Alaska. Between 1977 and 24 March 1989, from 700 to 1,100 tankers per year crossed Prince William Sound. Alaskan oil provides about 20 per cent of the 1991 US petro-leum production, and about 85 per cent of the State of Alaska's annual revenue. However, the North Slope fields appear to have reached the peak of production and now face an inexorable decline in output over the next several decades.

Gramling and Freudenberg (1992) place the *Exxon Valdez* spill in the historical context of national and international petroleum politics. They note that $11\frac{1}{2}$ years elapsed between the first major oil discovery on the North Slope and the beginning of oil transportation from Valdez, and that another $11\frac{1}{2}$ years passed before the first major oil spill occurred on Bligh Reef in 1989. As the North Slope oil industry grew, Alaskan citizens tended to associate it with ARCO, one major shareholder in the consortium of firms that made up the Alyeska Pipeline Company. Most Alaskans did not know that Exxon was one of seven companies sharing the facility. When the oil tanker accident occurred, there were only about 35 Exxon employees in the state, in contrast to 2,600 of ARCO's. That fact may have made a considerable difference to subsequent developments: lacking much contact with Alaska, Exxon's leaders did not know the cultural complexities and diversity present among the Alaskan population. Nor did Alaskans in the small communities along the North Pacific know much about Exxon or the complex business structures and cultural characteristics of its corporate world.

Because Arctic ecosystems were poorly known and assumed to be fragile, environmental concerns were an integral part of the negotiation and building phases of the Alaskan pipeline and associated facilities. Numerous safeguards were included in the project. But, over the years, an "atrophy of vigilance" had taken hold – many of the precautions had been relaxed, personnel had been cut back, and equipment had not been maintained (Gramling and Freudenburg 1992: 176). This falling away of concern was partly a result of the oil industry's safety record in Alaska. After years of more or less trouble-free operation, the pipeline did not seem as disruptive to the environment as originally anticipated, despite the fact that it crossed three mountain ranges, three active seismic zones, and hundreds of rivers and streams. Tankers had successfully passed through the Valdez Arm 8,700 times! In light of this record, even the hitherto sacrosanct Arctic National Wildlife Refuge was in danger of being opened to oil exploration and development. But the appearance of a riskless industry was deceptive. As Browning and Shetler (1993) suggest:

What we often fail to imagine as likely possibilities occur more normally and more frequently than expected. Such accidents seem to arrive as complete surprises, and only 20/20 hindsight reveals the systematically ignored potential risks that have been triggered by the coincidence of various causes, apparently unconnected and ordinarily insufficient, but accumulating enough critical mass of disaster when they unexpectedly reinforce each other.

And so it proved to be. The spill became "a benchmark event in the public perception of technological hazards" (Tierney and Quarantelli 1992: 167–173), highlighting how lax different organizations with fragmented responsibilities had become.

The accident

Exxon Valdez was a new ship, the largest vessel ever built on the US west coast at the time of its delivery in San Diego on 11 December 1986 by the National Steel and Ship Building Company to the world's largest oil company. It measured 987 feet long, 166 feet wide, and 88 feet deep from the main deck. With the aid of computerized equipment, the master, Joseph Hazelwood, and his crew of 20 could transport up to 1.48 million barrels of crude oil per voyage.

The ill-fated ship arrived in Valdez late on 22 March 1989, loaded 1,263,000 barrels of crude oil, and departed from Berth Five of the Alyeska Marine Terminal at 9.16 p.m. on 23 March. The following brief outline of subsequent events is based on several sources (Keeble 1991: 36–46; Richter 1990).

Icebergs, calved off the nearby Columbia glacier, had been reported in the Valdez Arm passage, and the crew were aware that evasive action might be necessary. As midnight neared, the tanker was heading down the Arm at full speed and those on board were preparing for the change of watch (fig. 8.1). Third mate Cousins was in charge on the bridge and able-bodied crew member (AB) Kagan was at the helm; Captain Hazelwood was in his quarters. AB Jones was assigned to the watch usually posted at the bow of the ship, but that night she was suffering from a cold and asked permission to stand watch outside the bridge. She reported a red light on the starboard (right) of the boat; it should have been to the left (port). Cousins was watching the radar looking for icebergs and the steering may have been on automatic pilot. In any case, Cousins registered the danger, and instructed Kagan to change course. The ship did not respond immediately, owing to either the shallow water or the fact that it was still on automatic pilot. Cousins called for Hazelwood but, before the Captain could respond, the tanker ran onto Bligh Reef.[2] The time was 12.04 a.m., 24 March 1989.

On shore in Valdez, staff at the Coast Guard Station who were charged with tracking the tankers were also changing watch. Only one person there was assigned to monitor the radar. The single radar that extended vision out of the Arm to Bligh Island was also out of order. Another one had been requested and funded but not yet installed. The *Exxon Valdez*'s imminent danger was not noticed.

The first day: American Good Friday

For many Alaskans, especially in the villages in Tatitlek, Chenega, and Old Harbor and the towns of Kodiak, Seward, and Valdez, the fact that it was Good Friday was significant. Twenty-five years before, on Good Friday, 27 March 1964, the largest earthquake in North America during modern times occurred. Its epicentre was 32 miles north-west of the *Exxon Valdez* grounding. Many of the same communities, and in some cases the same people, were affected by both events.

Richter (1990) provides the most comprehensive account of the first 40 days after the accident. A detailed report of agency responses and organizational turmoil can be found in Harrald, Cohn, and Wallace (1992).

During the first days, Exxon was concerned about offloading the remaining oil from the ship, and the fishermen were concerned about the oil already flowing. Boats and crews were ready to work but oil-containment and recovery equipment was not available. For several days, oil continued to pour out of the tanker. Debates about the use of chemical dispersants occurred throughout the first three days but, by the time they were resolved, a storm had begun to move the oil away from the vicinity of Bligh reef (see the Chronology of the first 10 days; Alaska Oil Spill Commission 1990).

Thereafter, marine life began to incur severe losses. Years later, damage assessment continues and the total impacts are not fully known (Baker, Clark and Kingston, 1991; Exxon Company 1992). One of the 51 loss studies that were undertaken shortly after the accident reported that the number of seabirds killed ranged from "260,000 to 580,000, with a best approximation of between 350,000 and 390,000" (US General Accounting Office [GAO] 1991c: 2). Other summary data estimated that perhaps 300,000 seabirds and up to 5,500 sea otters had been killed. The sea otter, in particular, became a focus of worldwide environmental and media concern. By 28 March, bird and otter rescue centres had opened. Restoration of 193 otters cost about $80,000 each.

Between April and 15 September, shoreline assessment teams surveyed about 3,400 miles and determined that around 1,300 miles had been impacted by oil (fig. 8.2). At the height of clean-up activity in

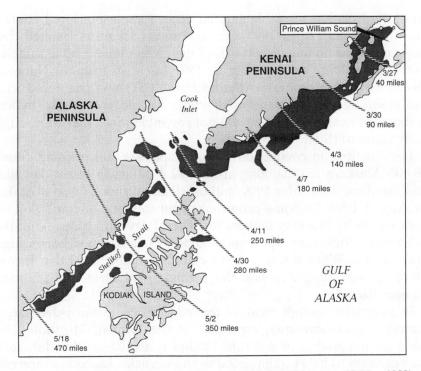

Fig. 8.2 **Movement of oil from the *Exxon Valdez* (24 March to 18 May 1989)**

1989 more than 11,000 workers, 1,400 vessels, and 80 aircraft were at work in the region. Clean-up techniques included cold-water washing, warm-water washing, bioremediation, mechanical treatment, and manual removal. The relative effectiveness of different methods continues to be debated.

During the first winter after the spill, monitoring programmes were put in place and, by May 1990, shoreline assessment teams were again sent out. More than 1,000 workers treated 600 shoreline sites during the summer of 1990. Federal and state oil spill legislation was also passed. Clean-up continued in 1991, albeit on a smaller scale: five teams treated 147 shoreline sites (Baker, Clark, and Kingston 1991). At this time an *Exxon Valdez* Oil Spill Trustee Council and a series of Regional Council Advisory committees were established. In May and June 1992, two teams checked 21 miles of shoreline and found traces of oil on 7 miles. By 12 June the US Coast Guard and the State of Alaska declared the clean-up complete.

Now, more than five years after the accident, there is no clear consensus on the spill's effects. Controversies about data, methods,

237

and interpretation were highlighted at an Exxon-sponsored conference in Atlanta (April 1993). Exxon-funded scientists claimed that
they could find no lingering traces of the *Exxon Valdez* oil in samples
of fish and wildlife collected during 1991; scientists from the National
Oceanic and Atmospheric Administration (NOAA) countered with
the observation that plants and animals could metabolize hydrocarbons into compounds that did not resemble those that were originally ingested (Stone 1993).

Legal actions in connection with the spill are still pending. Some
40,000 Alaskans are claiming around $2.4 billion in direct damages
and the disposition of a $900 million clean-up fund is also at stake.
In August 1993, 74 boats protested about the lack of resolution on
their claims by blocking tankers for several days in Valdez Arm; the
fishermen's frustration was compounded by failed runs of herring and
pink salmon. When it was announced in September 1993 that Exxon
Shipping was suing Alyeska, the pending settlement was reported
"jeopardized."

In summary, though most of the oil appears to have dissipated,
human impacts continue, especially in the form of litigation. The
need for integration of scientific studies is also clear; thus far, such
studies seem to be as fragmented as the agencies and other interests
that conducted them.

Historical and cultural contexts

To understand the various responses to the *Exxon Valdez* oil spill,
the affected area as a whole should be considered – its geology, cultures, communities, economies, and history, including its history of
previous disasters. This kind of analysis provides a regional approach,
with time depth. If we can better understand the significance of differences in community size, local cultures, and relative vulnerability
to "surprises," more appropriate prevention and mitigation plans for
the future can be made concerning industrial and natural hazards.

A topographical map of south-central Alaska reflects the wrinkling
effects of geological upheavals as the Pacific tectonic plate plunges
north under the North American plate. This area is a highly active
volcanic and earthquake zone. It is also a zone of active glaciation.
Most of the dramatic land-forms were carved out by Pleistocene gla-
ciers and their successors continue to advance and recede, sometimes
calving massive icebergs into adjacent waterways such as Valdez Arm.
Like the coasts of Hawaii and Japan, the Alaskan coasts are also

vulnerable to tsunamis generated elsewhere. In summary, this is a hazard-prone part of the planet.

Prehistoric evidence indicates that human settlement along the coasts began about 7000 B.P. (Clark 1984). The Alaska Native population now are referred to by their common linguistic affiliation, Alutiiq. This cultural region lies between the Tlingit Indians of south-east Alaska and the Aleuts of the Aleutian Islands to the west.

The Alutiiq Native population occupies 16 villages in four sub-regions and is affiliated with three different Native corporations that were formed in the 1970s to manage lands and natural resources according to provisions of the Alaska Native Land Claims Settlement Act. The villages are small, physically isolated, coastal, and oriented primarily to the fishing industry (Cultural Dynamics, Ltd. 1993; Davis 1977, 1984, 1986). All were affected in some way by the oil spill and subsequent events.

Native residents of the area also live in four regional towns, which are largely occupied by non-Natives. The towns are larger, more diversified, and historically linked to different resources – Cordova to copper development in 1906, Valdez to the gold fields in 1898, Seward to the railroad and seaport access to coal in 1903, and Kodiak to Russian access to sea otter in the early nineteenth century. Now, each of these towns continues to have a different economic mix: commercial fishing provides the primary support of Kodiak and Cordova; Valdez (the terminus of the oil pipeline) and Seward both have fish-processing companies and also are educational centres and tourist destinations.

Valdez and Seward are linked by road to Alaska's major city, Anchorage. The other two towns – Kodiak City and Cordova – and all 16 villages are connected to each other only by air, boat, and, for some, an occasional ferry on the Alaska Marine Highway system. Although these communities are relatively small, they represent considerable diversity in ethnicity, economies, and politics. In all, around 16,000 people live in the affected area, including about 2,000 in the small villages, which range in size from 50 to 300 residents (Fall 1993b).

Disaster experiences have further helped to give different communities distinctive histories. Three major disasters have occurred in this region during the twentieth century, each the largest of its kind in North America: these are the Katmai eruption in 1912, the great Alaskan earthquake of 1964, and the *Exxon Valdez* oil spill. Because the experiences and skills involved in coping with *Exxon Valdez* may have been affected by the legacy of the other disasters, a brief discussion of their impacts is in order.

The Katmai eruption

On 6 June 1912, three cubic miles of volcanic debris erupted from Mount Katmai on the Alaska Peninsula. The explosion was heard 750 miles away in Juneau. An ash cloud spread over 100,000 square miles and traces were discovered as far away as Algeria, giving rise to concern about possible climate changes. To the south of Katmai, ash and darkness fell over a band of sea and land for three days. Up to four feet of ash descended on Kodiak: roofs collapsed; fish streams became clogged; gardens were smothered.

Captain Perry, of the US Revenue Cutter *Manning*, took charge of rescue, evacuation, and survival efforts in Kodiak. He coordinated supplies, allocated resources, and brought frightened villagers on board. Further, he closed the two bars in the town. There was no question about his authority or the quality of his leadership. Many individuals wrote later about his efficiency and fairness. This experience stands in sharp contrast to the confusion about leadership and authority that surrounded the oil spill 77 years later.

Because an electrical storm associated with the eruption disabled the telegraph station on Woody Island near Kodiak, the area was without direct means for letting the world know what had happened. A flurry of telegrams was routed through the town of Seward to Washington, DC. Secretary of the Interior Walter L. Fisher tried to validate information with Alaska's Territorial Governor Walter E. Clark, who was also trying to assess what had happened and how serious conditions were.

Eventually, three Native villages on the Alaska Peninsula were relocated: the residents of Savinofsky moved to South Naknek in the Bristol Bay area; and the residents of Katmai and Cape Douglas were brought first to Afognak and then resettled at a new village site on the Peninsula, which they named Perryville after Captain Perry (Davis 1986; National Archives: Record Group 75, Bureau of Education; National Archives: Record Group 22, Bureau of Fisheries).

As with most disasters, there were dire predictions of severe and possibly irreversible negative impacts – ruined fish seasons; dead barnacles, mussels and kelp; destroyed streams; blind birds and animals; smothered gardens. But, to the amazement of the scientists who arrived later that summer, the rivers ran, the fish returned, mussels

240

and kelp grew, few animals died, and gardens thrived in the rich ash (Calahane 1959).

One of the benefits of the Katmai disaster was new information provided by a scientific expedition organized by the National Geographic Society to study the Valley of 10,000 Smokes (Griggs 1922; Martin 1913). The area was set aside as a national monument. Through a series of additions, it now encompasses 4.1 million acres called the Katmai National Park and Preserve.

The Native people of Katmai received one of the earliest village schools in Alaska at the new village of Perryville. Another unexpected, but temporary, benefit is mentioned by Martin (1913: 180): during the summer of 1912 there were no mosquitoes in the area. Also, the Katmai eruption left a more permanent marker, a special aid to future archaeological stratigraphy, by depositing a distinctive ash level, one of 14 identified.

In summary, the Katmai eruption of 1912 created a terrible, intense, but temporary fright for those in the path of the ash. No lives were lost. The government quickly came to the rescue; several villages were abandoned and new ones built. New scientific information was gained. Moreover, the event was remembered by a few people in spontaneous references 52 years later, during my research in the region following the next greatest disaster of its kind in North America – the 1964 earthquake.

The great Alaskan earthquake

At 5.36 p.m. on 27 March 1964, a shallow-focus earthquake measuring 9.2 on the Richter scale (revised from an earlier 8.4) wrenched 100,000 square miles of the earth's crust. The epicentre was 55 miles west of Valdez and 73 miles east of Anchorage. Whole islands in Prince William Sound were uplifted: Montague Island rose 23 feet; Latouche Island moved 60 feet south-east. The Portage area on Turnagain Arm of Cook Inlet subsided 9 feet. Earthquake damage in part of the city of Anchorage was extensive. Underwater avalanches caused tsunamis that destroyed three villages – Chenega in Prince William Sound, and Kaguyak and Old Harbor on Kodiak Island. Three towns (Valdez, Seward, Kodiak) and two villages (Afognak, Ouzinkie) were partly destroyed. Property damage was estimated to be $300–400 million in 1964 US dollars. Partly because of the time of day, and partly because of the low population density of the area, the death toll of 115 (in Alaska) was remarkably low: 9 deaths were from the earthquake and 106 from local waves generated by underwater landslides and tsunamis. The tsunami run-up was 30 feet at Seward, 90 feet at Chenega, and 220 feet at Valdez.

Physical destruction was great, and the initial fright was compounded by a series of major aftershocks (11 with magnitudes greater than 6.0 on the first day alone) and rumours of more tsunamis (Norton and Haas 1970; Davis 1970, 1971, 1987). As with other disasters, some people were relocated. Two villages were abandoned. The survivors from Kaguyak and Chenega were merged with two other villages, forming larger, more complex, communities receiving more services for all – and new problems. The social organizations of four separate villages do not combine easily into two, a phenomenon that probably has occurred periodically under similar circumstances throughout human history. Just as biotas meet, shift, and interchange species following rearrangement of the earth's crust and climate (Vermeij 1991), so also are populations of humans dislocated, relocated, and newly mixed under radically changed conditions (Workman 1979).

During the recovery period, new local skills were developed to manage agency involvement and new technology, such as community-wide generator systems that were installed in the villages. Valdez was relocated to a nearby site; the port at Seward was rebuilt; urban renewal projects were brought to downtown Kodiak and to Seldovia. The village of Afognak was moved to a new community, Port Lions. Survivors from Chenega were relocated to Tatitlek. Most of the residents of Kaguyak relocated at Akhiok. The village of Old Harbor was rebuilt at the same site, a few feet above high-tide level.

After the 1964 earthquake, the Alaska Regional Tsunami Warning System, later renamed the Alaska Tsunami Warning Center (ATWC), was installed in Palmer. It links Alaska with the Pacific Tsunami Warning Center in Honolulu, established in 1948. New regulations for building construction were adopted (and some later modified or abandoned). The National Academy of Sciences promptly organized an Earthquake Committee and by 1 June 1964 their first meeting was held. The multivolume study was published by 1970; it stands as a pathbreaking example of interdisciplinary cooperation in support of attempts to resolve a major public problem. As noted by Rogers (1970) and Dacy and Kunreuther (1969), the earthquake brought in federal funds just shortly after statehood (1959), a time when Alaska was just beginning to spring free of total federal control.

Displacement; new local skills; new technology; additional funds, knowledge and organizations; these all followed the 1964 earthquake. Did this also happen after *Exxon Valdez*?

The oil spill: Community impact

Like the earthquake that was followed by a series of tsunamis, the oil spill was followed by a series of metaphorical tsunamis of the emotions. It became a media event with powerful, disturbing images, especially of oiled birds and sea otters (Davis 1990).

The section that follows draws on many kinds of data: (a) community-specific accounts by sociologists and anthropologists (Araji 1990a, 1990b, 1991, 1993); (b) corporate, state, and federal reports (US GAO 1989, 1991b); (c) selected media coverage; as well as (d) my own research on the ferry *Tustemena* (7–14 May 1989) and in seven communities during July and August 1989 (Davis 1989b). Some conclusions are also based on observations made while living in Anchorage during most of the first four years following the oil spill.

Psychological, social, and cultural impacts

Studies that assess selected human impacts of the oil spill include the following: Araji (1992a, 1992b, 1993) on Homer, Seldovia, and Port Graham; Cohen (1992) and Mason (1993) on commercial fishing; Dyer, Gill, and Picou (1992) and Picou et al. (1992) on Cordova; Impact Assessment Inc. (1990), Palinkas et al. (1993), and Rodin et al. (1992), on the "Oiled Mayors" study; and Jorgensen (1993) and the US Department of the Interior (DOI) (1992, 1993a, 1993b) on the Social Indicators study that was extended to include communities involved in the oil spill. Theoretical analyses can be found in Gramling and Freudenburg (1992); Harrald, Cohn, and Wallace (1992); Browning and Shetler (1993); and Tierney and Quarantelli (1992). The most extensive research – and the only continuing investigation – of community response and recovery has been accomplished by a team in the Subsistence Division of the Alaska Department of Fish and Game. They have been documenting the changing utilization of fish and wildlife resources in all the affected communities since the oil spill, and in many cases have pre-spill data (Fall 1990, 1991a, 1991b, 1993a, 1993b). The DOI's Minerals Management Service (MMS) have contributed to the continuity of this research through a joint cooperative research plan and funds.

Emphases, community foci, methodologies, and timing differ among

these studies, but no effort is made here to analyse those variations. Rather, the basic outline and results of the two largest studies
(Impact Assessment, Inc. and US DOI, MMS) are briefly summarized.

Between 30 March and 15 May 1990, a population-based study by
a team of applied anthropologists under contract to Impact Assessment, Inc. (15 field workers) interviewed 594 men and women in 13
communities – 11 in the oil-affected region and 2 control communities
outside the area. The study considered everything – from relationships between exposure to the oil spill and the subsequent clean-up
efforts to social and psychological impacts. The following were the
major findings:

1. A decline in traditional social relations;
2. A decline in subsistence production and distribution;
3. Increases in drinking, drug abuse, and domestic violence;
4. A decline in health status;
5. An increase in reported medical conditions;
6. Increased post-spill anxiety disorder, post-traumatic stress disorder, and depression.

Alaska Natives, especially women, were found to be particularly
at risk for the (latter) three psychiatric disorders. Other findings
included the following: (a) money was the source of considerable
friction; (b) after the accident, people spent less time visiting with
friends and less time on community activities; and (c) there was concern about the safety of basic subsistence foods that might have been
affected by oil. In summary:

These results document the profound impact that exposure to the oil spill
had on social relations, traditional subsistence activities, the prevalence of
psychiatric disorders, community perceptions of alcohol and drug abuse
and domestic violence, and physical health of Alaskan Native and non-
Native residents of the affected communities. (Palinkas et al. 1993: 8)

Although the study focused on negative impacts, some positive
findings were also noted: "Positive changes resulting from the oil spill
and cleanup were indicated in some responses, and these often had
to do with either economic benefits or an increased sense of communities pulling together in times of adversity" (Palinkas et al. 1993:
6). Overall, the team concluded that "... the oil spill's impact on the
psychosocial environment was as significant as its impact on the
physical environment" (Palinkas et al. 1993: 1).

The second major study of communities affected by the *Exxon
Valdez* oil spill was an extension of the single most comprehensive

social and cultural study of contemporary life in Alaska, begun in 1986. It was funded by the DOI MMS and awarded to Joseph G. Jorgensen, as principal investigator, through the Human Relations Area Files, Inc. Thirty Alaskan coastal villages had already participated in the multimethod project. After the oil spill, new questions were designed and additional communities included in the study. In the summer of 1989, eight villages located in the *Exxon Valdez* spill area and two villages in adjacent control areas were added. Two communities, Kodiak City and Old Harbor, that had been included in the original study, provided pre-spill data. A total of 354 residents were interviewed (Jorgensen 1993).

Two volumes of the Social Indicators Study (Technical Report 155) provide post-spill key informant summaries: Part 1 includes Cordova, Tatitlek, and Valdez; and Part 2 includes Kenai, Tyonek, Seldovia, Kodiak City, Karluk, Old Harbor, and Chignik (US DOI 1993a, 1993b).

Impacts – not recovery – were the focus of these studies. However, they provide important data for comparative and diachronic studies in the future. Here, briefly, are a few selected findings:

Perceived declines in natural resources are most often registered in small communities, communities closest to the spill, and communities with relatively dominant fisheries economies.

Spill-related economic impacts (spill cleanup and related employment, job relocations, losses of employment, property damages, compensation for damages) tend to cluster in communities close to the spill, which are smaller, dominated by commercial-fisheries economies, and have the least diversified economies.

Structured inequality in spill consequences was revealed.

Relatively unstable households, such as single-parent households, are more likely to report relocation associated with spill-related work.

In summary, it was noted that

... the *Exxon Valdez* spill may be reproducing an existing or latent social reality – in a sense, replaying an "old script" – that now is characterized by underdevelopment in rural regions, dominance of urban centers that are able to mobilize great resources, and marginalization of Native and un- or underemployed residents who lack substantial political power. Because similar patterns have emerged in many of the accounts of great technological disasters (Bhopal, Chernobyl, etc.), this is not at all surprising. (McNabb 1993: 21–23)

These two major studies both indicate that greater disruption occurred in the smaller, Native, communities. That finding may have been the result of the timing of the research and the general orientation that anthropologists tend to have of concern for smaller Native communities. It may also be an artifact of questions that seem designed to understand kinds and degrees of impact. That was, after all, their charge.

However, what is missing is a sense of recovery. Do small, Native, culturally distinctive communities suffer longer or do they have the ingredients for rapid recovery and a philosophy of getting on with life? One small statement in the MMS report on Old Harbor at least suggests this latter possibility:

The Natives of Old Harbor are no strangers to tragedy. Following the destruction of their village in 1964, but bolstered by their religious faith, Old Harbor Natives rebuilt their homes and their lives. In the same way, Old Harbor residents will survive the effects of the 1989 *Exxon Valdez* oil spill. During the winter of 1991 the people of Old Harbor were concerned primarily with looking forward. (Rooks 1993: 808)

Preliminary studies by the Subsistence Division of the Alaska Department of Fish and Game suggest that the harvesting of natural resources is back to pre-spill levels and in several villages has risen above pre-spill levels, both in amount and in diversity. Perhaps the values of subsistence activities have been heightened because these resources were temporarily lost and there was great uncertainty about their safety and future availability.

Further publications are expected, based on these multi-year studies. Also, one publicly funded study for community research focuses on "what can be done to avoid or reduce (mitigate) the problems following future oil spills that would otherwise directly affect residents" (Institute of Social and Economic Research 1993: 1). The project was funded from Alyeska through the Regional Citizen's Advisory Council (RCAC) to the University of Alaska Anchorage for a three-year period beginning in 1992. It has a clear local community theme. The Alaska Department of Fish and Game in cooperation with the MMS is continuing research on subsistence harvesting. The results of these studies are not yet available.

Archaeological impact studies constitute another category of research. The Alaska State Department of Natural Resources has published a report on the effect of the oil on some archaeological sites (Reger, McMahan, and Holmes 1992). Exxon's Cultural Resource Program hired a total of 24 archaeologists and has published three large reports addressing archaeological sites (Betts et al. 1991; Haggarty et al. 1991; Mobley et al. 1990). A whole issue of the journal *Arctic Anthropology*, including 13 articles on maritime cultures of southern Alaska, was funded by Exxon (Moss and Erlandson 1992). The science of archaeology has clearly been enhanced. Further, two major studies have been funded by the Exxon Valdez Trustees Council – one in 1992 to protect archaeological resources ($160,000) and one in 1993 to assess injury to 24 archaeology sites and to begin restoration on some of them ($260,100) (Exxon Valdez Oil Spill Trustees 1992; Exxon Valdez Oil Spill Restoration Office 1993). Funds for a museum in Kodiak were approved by the Trustees Council for $1,500,000. Far more attention seems to be given to humans who are dead than to those still living!

Despite this apparent bias – and the far great attention given to the biological environment of the fish, birds, animals and beaches – 20 coastal communities of south-central Alaska were also affected. The following is a summary of some of those impacts.

The villages

Sixteen Alutiiq villages were included in studies following the oil spill. Their experience, disruption of their personal lives, participation in clean-up efforts, and general impacts varied significantly, in some areas as a result of relative proximity to the oil and in other areas as a result of economic inequities and other difficulties.

The kind and timing of community research shapes our understanding. The data are uneven and require careful scrutiny for quality. The methods and professional training of the researchers, the length of some of the questionnaires (up to 300 discrete items), and the mandates and funding sources of the studies superimpose upon the real local experience all kinds of variables, most of which are not easily identified.

In terms of proximity to the actual site of the spill, the distribution of the villages from the closest to furthest away is as follows: Tatitlek (5 miles), Chenega, English Bay (Nanwalek), Port Graham, Port Lions, Ouzinkie, Larsen Bay, Karluk, Old Harbor, Akhiok, Chignik Bay, Chignik Lagoon, Chignik Lake, Perryville, and Ivanof Bay (about 500 miles away). However, on the basis of relative disruptive impact, the order would be different. Chenega not only had oil (which did not hit Tatitlek) but this small village of 77 (1989 census) also served as a major centre for clean-up activities. Ouzinkie received little oil, but reacted with great fear to possible contamination of subsistence resources. Chignik Bay, centre of the highly valued red salmon run, received no perceptible oil but experienced intense hostilities within the community, centred on perceived inequities in the selection and allocation of lucrative boat charters.

Impacts on the villages were rarely the direct result of spilled oil. Rather, fear of the oil, fear of contamination, and uncertainty about how far and to what extent oil would affect the food chain concerned many, and for a long time (Fall 1993a). The continuing uncertainty of the actual distribution and effects of the oil over time became one of the single most disturbing factors during the first summer (Fall 1991a).

Another problem was the assignment of leadership positions to persons not from the local community. Such jobs paid well, and the organization hired by Exxon (VECO Inc.) did not know the residence status of the persons they were hiring. If someone looked Native, it was assumed that they were, and that they came from the local community. In fact, relatives of local residents sometimes arrived after many years of absence, took the available jobs and made a great deal of money. Because they may have appeared to have had more experience with the larger world and, sometimes, to be more educated, they were given responsible, and higher-paying, assignments. The hiring policies seemed not to take account of the local sense of fairness.

Need for extra child care was also a problem. Suddenly, parents had an opportunity to make a great deal of money in a relatively short time, especially if both worked. Young children were left to take care of other, younger children or – as in one village – a grandmother was placed in charge of 15 small children. This situation may have been of greater concern to the social workers than the parents, who were insulted by the suggestion that they were neglecting their families. Culturally distinctive characteristics of small, isolated Native villages include the relative flexibility of hours and freedom of children, especially during the summer time. However, in both towns and villages, parents expressed concern that there were so many strangers around that the usual sense of safety and security was threatened.

The flurry of meetings and media events was also disruptive, though some people thrived on the attention and the opportunities for recognition. Here, again, cultural differences were highlighted. Respected Native leaders would prefer not to call attention to themselves; however, after the oil spill, they were suddenly expected to be expert speakers, to attend all kinds of meetings, and to accept whole new categories of responsibility.

Itinerant Orthodox priests somewhat tempered the intensity of intrusion in the villages. Most of the villagers are Orthodox, a strong tradition established during the Russian America period, and recently revitalized through the establishment of a seminary in Kodiak in 1973. The Church has always played an important role in these communities. During the height of the eruption in 1912, Native residents in Kodiak went to the church and the bell was tolled. The role of the Orthodox Church after the earthquake and tsunamis of 1964 has been documented (Davis 1970). Now, with the emotional trauma of the oil spill, priests were requested to visit and to hold services. At times of environmental disaster, as at other stressful times, local communities have culturally shaped ways of managing crises.

The two large studies on village responses (Impact Assessment, Inc. and DOI MMS) both reflect a sense of social weakness in small communities – a lack of knowledge combined with different leadership styles. For example, according to these sources, "in practically all areas of impact the native communities were rendered more impotent than the non-native communities" (Rodin et al. 1992: 233). I am not persuaded that this is true. Native communities may be more capable of managing impacts and initiating recovery than the towns.

Town responses

The range of concerns, irritations, and benefits varied greatly among the affected towns during the summer of 1989. Polarizations, between those who worked for Exxon or its contracted service organization VECO Inc. and those who did not, set people against each other in new ways. Many looked favourably on opportunities to make large sums of money ($16.69 an hour) on clean-up activities, or to charter their boats (up to $6,000 a day), or to provide other well-paid services. Those not hired, or who spurned Exxon or VECO, scorned their neighbours who accepted the employment. If a fisherman or any local resident wanted to make money, the opportunity generally was available. If, on the other hand, a fisherman refused to work for the oil company that was perceived as being responsible for the mess, then he was doubly penalized – he lost the chance to make money from the clean-up and he also lost expected income from fishing areas that were closed because of fears about oil contamination. Disagreements among the fishermen were intense and painful. Lack of resolution, combined with a sudden decline in chum salmon during the summer of 1993, led frustrated fishermen to block tanker traffic on Valdez Arm in a desperate attempt to force a discussion with Exxon about their claims. Litigation, and decline in fish stocks, prices, and permit value, have unquestionably slowed recovery for this segment of the population.

As a community, Cordova appears to have suffered the greatest disruption for the longest time and gained the least. Before 1989 it was already a conflict-ridden town; the oil spill may just have offered a new arena for traditional hostilities and exacerbated some of the old problems. But this may also be a misreading of the evidence because more data have been gathered – and made available – on Cordova than on other towns (Picou et al. 1992; Dyer, Gill, and Picou 1992; Reynolds 1993).

Nevertheless, the sources of dispute in Cordova were many: they included the fishermen's willingness or unwillingness to help; inequities of hire by Exxon and Veco; closure of the fishing season; a sudden decline in the number and price of chum salmon, from 40 cents a pound in 1990 to 12 in 1991; decline of fish permit values; the suicide of Cordova's Mayor (Enge 1993); protracted litigation; the fishermen's boycott of oil tankers in August 1993; and the announcement, in September 1993, that 74 of the boycotting boats might face fines from the Coast Guard. Clearly, during 1993, the fishermen from Cordova had not recovered. For many, as reported by Reynolds (1993), "the 1989 oil spill was still an unfolding disaster. Spill-related problems, fears, and conflicts were widespread." And they still are.

Conditions were different in Valdez. Here, the community was inundated by people, goods, guards, media, and traffic. The oil industry had long been a mainstay of the community and most people had benefited directly or indirectly from the presence of the Alaska pipeline terminus. As the clean-up progressed, there was a massive convergence of people and materials on Valdez. Everyone who wanted to work, could. New bed and breakfast accommodations were opened. People rented their extra bedrooms; some even rented their whole houses and left the state. But, as the population climbed from 2,500 to 10,000, the strain was too much, even for a town that claimed to be accustomed to similar fluctuations. Local residents found they had to forego eating out in restaurants, baby sitters, visiting friends, and going to baseball games. Even the traditional Gold Rush Day celebrations were cancelled in 1989. By July 1990, local people were out of patience with the oil spill and its aftermath; the town had the exhausted feeling that comes with being in a war zone (Robbins, E. 1993).

Seward, like Valdez, was accustomed to increased traffic brought by seasonal tourism, but to nothing like that experienced during the summer of 1989. Unlike some other communities, people in Seward took control of the situation before oil actually approached the area (US DOI 1993a, 1993b).

Of all the impacts on Alaskan towns the uproar in Kodiak is perhaps the most thoroughly documented (Impact Assessment Inc. 1990; US DOI 1993a, 1993b; see, especially, Endter-Wada et al. 1993). Kodiak processes the third-largest volume of fish of any port in North America, and, although little oil reached the town, extensive disruption did.

In summary, the impacts of *Exxon Valdez* on the communities of southern Alaska varied greatly. Towns and villages experienced different levels of threat; different volumes of oil, and different degrees of contamination; different amounts of access to money and other clean-up benefits; and differences in the quantity and quality of research that was accomplished.

Recovery

It is impossible to give definitive answers about the recovery process because so much either is not known or remains unpublished. Nearly all of the research funded to date is concerned with the biology of Prince William Sound (Natural Resource Damage Assessments [NRDA] 1992; Oil Spill Public Information Center [OSPIC] 1992). But it is difficult to be sure just what the long-term effects of the spill on non-human life-forms have been. The situation is complicated by the fact that oil has been spilled here at several times in the past. For example, oil that was used in the Valdez asphalt plant was originally imported from California. Patches were found on two of eight beaches tested in Prince William Sound, distributed there by the massive tsunami that followed the 1964 earthquake (*Anchorage Daily News*, 16 September 1992). In a study of six major oil spills (not including *Exxon Valdez*), Mielke (1990) found that the ocean – unlike the mass media – was impressively forgiving in a relatively short time. But many questions remain to be answered, and one wonders about ocean recovery over time, in the face of accumulated pollution.

251

Obviously, much of the biota that was originally damaged has recovered in the sense of surviving in numbers similar to those of the past, but there is no clear understanding of what the word "recovery" might mean and hence no measure of what should be looked for. However, if the Alutiiq communities survived the 1912 Katmai eruption and the 1964 earthquake, it may be safe to assume that they will also survive the consequences of the oil spill. If the people of Valdez have managed to rebound from a gold rush, a fire, an earthquake, and a tsunami, we must assume that they will also survive *Exxon Valdez*, perhaps exceptionally well. But social scientists who want to analyse the human responses to this oil spill are severely handicapped because there are virtually no funds for understanding that process. Moreover, pending litigation has put a damper on scientific research of all kinds. The few investigators who might be in a position to offer informed assessments are discouraged from offering their views by the threat of legal penalties.

Litigation initiatives

On 4 April 1989, two weeks after the oil spill, the law firms of Sonosky, Chambers, Sachse, and Miller of Anchorage and Cohen, Milstein, and Hausfeld of Washington DC filed a class action suit against Exxon Corporation, Exxon Shipping Co., and Alyeska Pipeline Service Co. on behalf of plaintiffs. The latter included Native residents in the seven Chugach communities, six Native councils, nine individuals, and the non-profit Native Corporation (North Pacific Rim) that provides services to the Native residents in the Chugach region. That was only the beginning. By December 1989, more than 150 lawsuits had been filed. A year later, Exxon had committed more than $302 million to fund compensation of 12,300 damage claims, but many remained unresolved.

By September 1993, Exxon had settled claims with the State of Alaska and federal agencies for 1 billion dollars. However, approximately 55,000 claimants and about 50 law firms were still involved in continuing litigation; 115 expert witnesses had been hired for pending court cases. There may even be as many as 19,000 third-party legal cases still pending. Many years after the spill, original data of researchers were still being subpoenaed for use in court suits, including information from the Subsistence Division of the Alaska Department of Fish and Game, the one agency that has ongoing pre-spill and post-spill data about the impacted communities.

This wide-ranging and prolonged litigation "mania" must be considered as one of the more significant impacts of the oil spill. Scientific investigations have been paralysed, research funding has been slow to be released, and a strange kind of professional paranoia has set in, polarizing scientists and keeping them silent in the face of court-imposed gag rules. Others have reported that intimidation haunts research (Tierney and Quarantelli 1992: 167–173; Shaw 1992; Stone 1993; Roberts 1992; Wheelwright 1991). The research that was funded tended to be focused on short-term impacts for the purposes of documenting damage. A major set-back for social scientists occurred when Picou, a University of Southern Alabama sociologist, was requested by Exxon to release the original data from his team's three-year study in Cordova (*Anchorage Daily News*, 26 May 1993).

Among the many problems inhibiting creative research during the summer of 1990 was the question of boundaries. Who was responsible for studying which part of the environment – the federal agencies, the state agencies, Exxon, or the Native organizations? At what point on the beach did federal responsibility end and state jurisdiction begin? If the land was under Native control, who, then, was responsible? How did the tides affect the studies and the boundaries? Could different agencies at least coordinate research in the intertidal zones?

At fall 1989 meetings of the Arctic Division of the American Association for the Advancement of Science held in Fairbanks, no one could officially report anything about anything: all research had a strange (and unhealthy) constraint placed on it because all research was assumed to be potentially contentious in the decades of litigation that were anticipated.[3] The intrusion of litigation on research following this disaster may be a reflection of similar directions in other scientific fields, such as DNA studies (Roberts 1992).

If social science is going to be increasingly directed (and funded) by attorneys, especially after disasters, then appropriate steps must be taken to study vulnerable communities before a disaster strikes. Then at least some baseline – relatively independent – data will be available on the richness of local human cultures, including corporate and governmental ones.

Certainly, in the case of *Exxon Valdez*, many different cultures were involved. Most fishermen, business people, agency personnel, and Native residents had never before met employees of one of the world's largest corporations. And most Exxon employees were not accustomed to understanding the values and cultural complexes of people living in Alaska's small isolated communities. They were, lit-

253

erally, from markedly different worlds. Other distinctive perspectives separated seine fishermen from setnetters, and Native fishermen with small boats from non-Native fishermen with large ones. Inter-agency jurisdictional disputes and differences in outlook compounded cultural and historical differences between state agencies and federal ones. Federal mandates within the Department of the Interior, such as the National Park Service, Bureau of Indian Affairs, and Fish and Wildlife Service, differ quite markedly from the Forest Service in the Department of Agriculture (Clark and McCool 1985). The Alaska Department of Fish and Game have their own special divisions and sections devoted to different species. Added to this mix were the traditional feuds between one town and another, between one village and another. The diversity of cultures in this relatively small part of the world was magnified by the forcing action of the oil spill. It should have been a social anthropologist's heyday. And, in many ways, it was: here could be found sharp polarities between the good guys and the bad guys, the rich and the poor, the environmentalists and the capitalists, loggers and attorneys – the conflict of many cultures exacerbated for many years by one oil spill.

The communities

But, for the purposes of this paper a central question remains: at what point does negative impact cease and recovery begin? Many reports are available on the recovery of fauna and flora. Studies funded by the oil industry found it to be remarkably quick and complete (Jahns and Koons 1993), but others thought that reports about recovery were premature and highly questionable (Wolforth 1993). The results depend partly on what is being studied and partly on who is doing the research and the reporting. Public controversy concerning these studies has not helped to resolve the questions. Thus far, no study has specifically addressed recovery in the human communities. An underlying assumption in the community studies that have been undertaken is a lack of recovery, of long-term distress, and continuing mental problems related to the oil spill (Impact Assessments Inc. 1990; US DOI 1993a, 1993b). It is highly unlikely that any study will be funded to address the question of lingering problems, or the absence of them.

Studies directed toward documenting long-term disruption and mental distress of two categories of people – the Native people and fishermen – are generally not available, though some indication of continuing oil spill-related problems in Cordova is given by Keeble (1993), Picou et al. (1992), and Reynolds (1993). Studies that have been designed to address those issues are confidential and are being reserved for court on advice of attorneys. Nothing official can be reported without, presumably, jeopardizing the chances of Natives and fishermen for financial retribution in some distant future.

Unofficially, and as an independent scholar, I can report the following observations based on study of past recovery from other disasters. The Native villages have remarkable recovery capability. The residents in very small communities seem to have a philosophy of tolerance, a resiliency to disruptions, a sense of humour, and a traditional fisherman's perspective that if things are bad this year they probably will be better next year. This is an adaptive optimism for a people who live with great fluctuations in year-to-year economy. Also, village residents have family – they are rich in relatives – and they maintain a value system that does not dwell on past misery. The Alutiiq people, like the Yupik and Inupiat further north, prefer not to talk about bad things of the past; nor are they inclined to project plans long into the future. These traits, though wholesome for traditional community health, are difficult for resource agencies committed to the planning processes and to eliciting local ideas in the peculiar format called "public hearings."

Native adaptation strategies of creative accommodation to changes provide a challenge for attorneys, who seek evidence of social, mental, and economic damage linked to *Exxon Valdez* in order to win funds for their clients and fees for themselves. A classic example of coaching to say the politically correct thing in public occurred during the summer of 1989. A "chief," who was billed as a high subsistence resource user of a small village supposedly inundated with oil, was scheduled to read a speech at a meeting of international "oiled mayors." An attorney wrote a rather powerful, emotional, narrative, but the chief did not read it. Nor did he attend the meeting. The oil had not damaged his resources: he was a relatively wealthy man and no longer participated in the rigour of subsistence harvesting and processing; he bought his groceries in a store. Later that fall, his village had a hard time processing all the free fish that was shipped at great expense. The freezers were already full of store-bought goods. Furthermore, significant amounts of oil never reached this community. But social services and attorneys did. The chief was too kind to hurt their feelings and, for a while, simply accepted what others insisted on bringing – including a speech he is credited with but did not write.

After the 1964 earthquake, three Kodiak villages took specific actions to resolve various kinds of pre-disaster conflict before initiating steps for reconstruction. Resolving those arenas of conflict may be considered a kind of recovery. Also, one of the communities had experienced so much intrusion in the lives of its people that its residents wanted to "declare a three month vacation and none of your white people come" (Davis 1969). Similar responses were evident after the 1989 disaster. English Bay experienced so much intrusion upon the privacy of their village that the council declared a 90-day moratorium on visitors, beginning in November 1990. If any agency had business in the village, its representatives could request permission to come; if permission were granted, they could arrive only on Tuesday, would be met at the plane, accompanied by a community member until business was completed, and escorted back to the plane for departure on the same day. As further indication of the struggle to retrieve and reassert some autonomy, this community also changed its name to Nanwalek, an Alutiiq (Sugestun) place-name for the area. These may be considered steps of recovery.

Nearby, Port Graham residents were surprised to learn, in October 1991, that the American Indian Heritage Foundation, located in Falls Church, Virginia, was sending out "arrow-star telegrams" to solicit funds for the starving "Paiutes" (not Aleuts) of Port Graham. In December they were offered 1,000 pounds of liver, which they managed to decline in time, through threat of legal action. This episode was recalled with hilarity, but it was irritating at the time because this village is quite self-sufficient and certainly did not need, desire, or request liver. Later that year, the hefty women's volleyball team had T-shirts made which carried the slogan "The Starving Paiutes of Port Graham." Recovery was signalled even earlier by cartoons in the newspapers, and T-shirts which read: "Let's go to Naked Island and be Crude" and "We cleaned PWS rock, by rock, by rock, by rock, by rock ..."

So much free food was distributed out of Chenega, one fisherman reported he gained 28 pounds in weight by mid-July. Other well-fed residents also developed what was called "The Exxon Waddle." On Southern Kenai Peninsula the added pounds were called "The Port Chatham Roll."

Another village refused to respond to agency requests and offers of help. They just wanted to be left alone, which may be one quality of their former life they will never be able to reclaim. Through the media attention to the oil spill in 1989, Prince William Sound and all of the coastal areas of south-central Alaska have been discovered by the world. Privacy as they knew it before has been lost, probably irreversibly. But new skills, a new sense of ethnicity, and inter-regional awareness were also part of recovery.

Organizational responses

Over half a century ago, Sorokin suggested that calamities tend to strengthen public and social controls at the expense of private and individual ones:

The main uniform effect of calamities upon the political and social structure of society is an expansion of governmental regulation, regimentation, and control of social relationships and a decrease in the regulation and management of social relationships by individuals and private groups. (Sorokin 1943: 122)

The *Exxon Valdez* case reinforces Sorokin's view. After the initial confused flurry of activity (e.g. ill-directed action; bickering about jurisdiction and procedures; fighting over funds, mandates, and litigation), numerous organizations that are ostensibly involved in recovery have done remarkably well. As measured by new personnel, new agencies, new organizations, new legislation, more funds, additional monitoring devices and escort vessels, greater overall coordination and organizational complexity, and enhanced levels of corporate and public awareness of risks and responsibilities, the oil spill might be considered a great enduring boon to the people of southern Alaska. Much was learned and many precautionary preventive actions taken.

Two major laws warrant particular comment: these are the (federal) Oil Pollution Act of 1990, and the State of Alaska's oil spill prevention bill, House Bill 567. "OPA 90," as the first law has come to be known, is major oil spill legislation, 182 pages in length. This law established many new organizations and at least 40 new regulations. For example, regional advisory councils were mandated: the Cook Inlet Regional Citizens' Advisory Council and the Regional Citizens' Advisory Council of Prince William Sound are outgrowths of the bill. The latter, for example, is an independent non-profit organization formed in late 1989 to "promote environmentally safe operation of the crude oil terminal in Valdez, Alaska and the tankers it serves." This body has 18 member organizations, a staff of 14, four task forces, eight community response centres, and a publication called *The Observer*. The Prince William Sound Regional Citizens' Advisory Council (RCAC) is under contract with the Alyeska Pipeline Service Company to monitor and advise Alyeska about terminal operations, spill prevention, response planning, and other environmental issues (RCAC 1993). The funding level for 1992 was $2.224 million.

Also newly formed and mandated by OPA 90, the Marine Spill Response Corporation (MSRC) is an organization of 22 US oil transporters and producers, that was required to have 16 spill-response ships equipped, online and located in five regional centres in 1993. The cost of MSRC was about $900 million for equipment, facilities, and personnel (US GAO 1991a; Robbins, L. 1993: 476).

Another new organization is the Exxon Valdez Oil Spill Trustee Council established in October 1991 as a result of the civil settlement by Exxon Corporation with the State of Alaska and the Federal Government. Six trustees – three state and three federal – were appointed to administer $900 million to be received over a 10 year period. By July 1993 a total of $240 million had been paid by Exxon. The intent of the funds is to restore the resources and associated services injured by the spill. A fact sheet dated July 1993 identifies 49 projects funded in 1992 and 1993 for $37 million (Exxon Valdez Oil Spill Trustee Council 1993). These projects appear in four broad categories: General Restoration ($5,357,700), Habitat Protection ($23,017,770), Recovery Monitoring ($8,650,400), and projects to support restoration activities ($354,300). The studies funded include, for example, 18 of fish ($6,517,800), 8 of birds ($3,133,700), 5 of sea mammals ($939,900), 2 of shellfish ($1,278,800), and 2 of algae ($993,100). In addition there are administrative costs (the organization includes staff, a restoration team, work groups, and a public advisory group) and reimbursement costs for agencies that were participants in the original clean-up effort. A report by the US GAO concerning the use of the Exxon Valdez Oil Spill Settlement funds raised serious questions about the management and allocation of funds (US GAO 1993).

Part of community recovery may involve the allocation of Exxon Valdez Trust funds for the purchase of lands to protect natural resources from future developments, or for the replacement of resources lost or harmed by the oil spill. By September 1993, several steps had been taken (or were being considered) by the Trustees

Council that, at least indirectly, and eventually, may provide some "recovery" funds or benefits to the communities. For example, these included $7.5 million for the purchase of inholdings in Kachemak Bay, and a commitment to purchase lands in Seal Bay on Afognak Island. Negotiations were continuing in 1993 for the protection of threatened habitats in three additional locations. Also, the Trustees Council has approved $1.5 million for a Kodiak Museum. In these cases, at least, some direct benefit to the communities involved may occur. However, as stated in the GAO report (August 1993), much of the Trustees Council funds have thus far been allocated to staff and study costs. The studies that have been funded are primarily being done by state and federal agencies that are already involved in assessment and restoration of the habitat.

The Oil Spill Public Information Center (or "OSPIC"), a new library – with staff – has been created in Anchorage. New divisions in agencies include the Spill Prevention and Response Division in the Alaska Department of Environmental Conservation. Oil Spill Impact Assessment and Restoration is a new division within the Alaska Department of Fish and Game that was created in 1989. In 1992 it was merged with the Habitat Division and is now called the Habitat and Restoration Division. The National Park Service created a Coastal Program Division in 1990 that at one time had over 100 people involved. Now there are only eight people, and four of these are temporary employees. One result of the oil spill is that it highlighted how complex and overlapping the many agencies had become. The creation of a single research agency, the National Biological Survey, may serve to consolidate federal science projects in the future.

Oil companies have also added new personnel, equipment, and organization. For example, by February 1990, less than a year after the spill, Alyeska Pipeline Service Company had taken specific measures to minimize the risks that lead to oil spills, including more escort vessels; 24-hour duty crews; increased pilot requirements; enhanced and more frequent radio communications; establishment of a Navigation Committee; and other steps, including training, drug and alcohol screening, and equipment and personnel increases (Alyeska Corporate Affairs 1990).

The following is a brief list of some other changes that had occurred in response to the oil spill by late 1993 (RCAC 1993): the vessel traffic system now includes a watch supervisor, more radar coverage, and a navigation aid on Bligh Reef; speed restrictions and more escort vessels; weather restrictions; breath tests of all tanker captains an hour before sailing; tanker escorts; containment booms in Valdez while cargo is being transferred; double hulls for all tankers in US waters by 2015; tanker inspections; citizen involvement; more monitoring and oversight by regulatory agencies, especially the Alaska Department of Environmental Conservation and the US Coast Guard; and more training, equipment, inspection, maintenance, contingency plans, and clarification of who is responsible when. The Alyeska Ship Escort and Response Vessel System includes five escorts and three tugs. There are 33 miles of containment boom, 37 skimming systems and barges on line, and 300 boats and crews trained in basic oil-spill response. Spill containment and removal equipment is stockpiled at five fish hatcheries, and storage capacity for nearly 20 million gallons of recovered oil and water mixture is available. Now, drills are held as part of the training: in 1992, nine drills were held. As an example of the magnitude of these drills, in early October 1993, 90 boats and more than 300 people in Valdez participated. An Incident Command System has been worked out that integrates the party responsible for the spill, the State of Alaska, and the Coast Guard; it establishes a predetermined decision-making process and a common language that is intended to reduce significantly confusion and misunderstandings among personnel from different organizations (RCAC 1993: 17).

New risks

Unfortunately, sometimes "solutions" create new risks, in addition to new jobs, surveillance, and safety. For example, one of the new oil-spill response boats assigned to Cook Inlet, the 193-foot vessel *Sun Tide*, accidently struck a drilling rig, spilling 13,000 gallons of diesel fuel on 23 August 1993 (Kizzia 1993b). In this case the oil dissipated in about 12 hours, and no environmental damage occurred. This spill from an oil-spill watch boat gave other oil-spill response boats and crews an opportunity to respond and to hone their skills. With more boats and personnel involved, the chance of accidents may – ironically – be increased.

With the increase in jobs and departments, there is always a risk of downsizing, and merging of positions and divisions, surely stressful for those involved. This happened at the Native non-profit service organization North Pacific Rim (Chugachmiut), the National Park Service, and the Alaska Department of Fish and Game, for example.

The RCAC *Observer* (Summer 1993) also reports concern that the State of Alaska is going to cut back funding, surveillance – and jobs.

One of the unintended consequences of delivering oil to the United States now, as a result of OPA 90, is "increased liability insurance policies: from 49 cents per gross ton to $7.12." These increased costs forced oil companies to look for and develop fields elsewhere, increasing risks abroad and increasing costs at home (Browning and Shetler 1993). With all the new organizations that have been created, the response to future oil spills will probably be better organized and more expensive, if not more effective.

Other kinds of recovery activities

The first year after the oil spill was in some ways an exceptionally creative one for many individuals. Poems were written (O'Meara 1989), songs composed, museum exhibits prepared, books drafted, cartoons drawn, pictures painted, and emotional singing wakes held. The *Chugach Symphony*, composed by Philip Munger, was performed by the Anchorage Symphony Orchestra on 21 October 1989. Further, many new "words" have been added to the local lexicon – "Evos" for *Exxon Valdez* Oil Spill, "OPA 90" for the Oil Pollution Act of 1990, "OSPIC" for the Oil Spill Public Information Center and "RCAC," the Regional Citizens' Advisory Committee.

The oil spill brought out a human compassion for animals, especially the sea otters; it highlighted a national concern about environment. The attention challenged Exxon and other oil corporations into new precautionary efforts. OPA 90 and HB 567 insisted on it. Clean-up efforts brought $2 billion to the state during the first summer. If good things are measured by amounts of money, then, as one villager observed, "Santa Claus sure came the summer of 1989." But the Alaska Fish and Game Subsistence Division reported a marked decrease in subsistence harvest, processing, and consumption the year following the oil spill; it is assumed this was because people were afraid to eat anything from the sea. What need to be added to the equation are the amounts of cash (and free groceries) that were available. Some local conflict occurred over who got how much, and over the advice to several communities by attorneys to reject free food from Exxon because it would weaken their case for compensation later.

Indications of perceived positive results are reflected in the statement of a village chief who noted, "now we know more about our relatives in Prince William Sound." The sense of unified ethnicity was recognized, and encouraged, by a series of regional meetings and elders' conferences. The Native organization, North Pacific Rim, changed its named to Chugachmiut and, for several years, increased in funding and personnel hired from 55 (in 1989) to over 150 in 1992. However, when the funds declined and jobs were lost, regrouping was necessary. Perhaps this is an example of how a response to the original impact was so great that a new impact on the region was created when the jobs, services, and funds were subsequently reduced.

But, what is recovery?

At what point does "impact" of oil-related events shift toward "recovery"? Is there a threshold; is there a critical event that marks the change? How do we perceive recovery, and how do we measure and study it? In the case of *Exxon Valdez*, hundreds of studies of "impact" have been accomplished, some published. "Recovery" and "restoration" of the biological aspects of the ecology are being studied and debated. The sudden plunge in the numbers of pink salmon in the summer of 1993 is considered by the fisherman to be a continuation of the impact and, for some, it is clearly delaying their "recovery."

But, to date, no published study has addressed the recovery of the communities. And it is not likely any study will be funded for such consideration until after the litigation has been resolved. What recovery has occurred as of 1993 remains undocumented, unvoiced. To ask, to study, to document, and to publish evidence of recovery of communities or of the fishermen would be to jeopardize class action court cases against the corporate giant. For the time being, we must simply assume that at least the Alutiiq villagers are recovering with the strengths and the resilience documented from previous disasters.

Conclusions

The *Exxon Valdez* oil spill in Prince William Sound, Alaska, on 24 March 1989, was an industrial accident but a technological and organizational disaster. The biological impacts were spread by subsequent natural events (severe storms) – also unexpected. The movement of oil into vulnerable natural habitats and over great distances further highlighted the lack of preparedness to stop it. Even without the storms, neither technological knowledge nor the equipment then available could have contained the oil once it was released.

The physical problems were magnified by organizational confusion of responsibility, allocation of authority, and decision-making. Local community capacities to respond creatively were inhibited; instead, external plans and people were imposed. The subsequent social disruption for some communities was severe and, perhaps, long lasting. It would seem, in retrospect, that everything that might go wrong, did.

However, partly because of national and international attention to the series of embarrassing events and controversies, an array of constructive steps has been taken. New regulations are in place. Monitoring devices in many forms have been installed – radars, escort vessels, added personnel, and citizens' advisory groups. New positions, new organizations, and new publications have been funded, at least temporarily. Numerous scientific studies have been published and more are forthcoming. New knowledge, and a fuller sense of shared responsibility, has resulted. Human creativity is reflected in scientific plans, data, and ideas, and in the arts – poems, music, pictures, sculpture, cartoons, and books. A regional museum has been funded with part of the settlement funds.

This disaster, like other major disruptions both natural and technological, has forced the human species to think new thoughts and to take creative preventive steps. If we can learn, apply, and remember the lessons learned, the increasingly industrialized world of the twenty-first century will be more cognizant of, and responsible for, the shared risks of international economic development. Oil transportation is just one of many aspects of modern industry that links us increasingly across boundaries, including ocean highways.

The *Exxon Valdez* oil spill is a classic example of "self-organized criticality" (Bak and Chen 1991). The accumulated complexities of technology, people, and organizations had reached a critical state. All it took was one small error, embedded in an incredibly complex industry, and the wall came tumbling down. The oil flowed; the plans failed; the storms came; the inadequacies of regulations, surveillance, equipment, and organizations were highlighted. Emotions were heightened; money was applied; and blame was spread from person to person, place to place, organization to organization. Like the single grain of sand in Bak and Chen's experiment that set off the sand avalanche, or the critical threshold of pressure on the earth's crust that initiates an earthquake, or the pile-up of rumours and emotions on Wall Street that sparks a crash, or the single bullet at a critical juncture of history that starts a war, an error on a tanker initiated problems ultimately revealing the intricate network of how one industry is linked to a multitude of others; how one agency overlaps another; how utterly fragmented are the nation, industry, and government at the end of the twentieth century.

If the symptoms of "self-organized criticality" can be recognized in time, protective actions can be taken. But until our knowledge includes a level of refined understanding of the interconnectness of industries, government, and the diversity of local human cultures, including those embedded in corporations and agencies, we remain vulnerable for yet another surprise, zapped again, at unexpected times and in unexpected places.

Obviously, we must increase awareness of technological risks, as well as how they might be compounded by subsequent natural disasters (or vice versa), and we must be alert to more appropriate and sophisticated ways of preventing disasters and minimizing impacts. But it also behooves us to watch for, recognize, and encourage local recovery capabilities.

In this chapter I have indicated how a regional approach with time depth adds a historical dimension for understanding the ability of communities to recover, or not. Three major disasters, each the largest of its kind in the twentieth century in North America, struck the Central North Pacific. Each led to new knowledge and the rearrangement of people. Usually, we think of disasters as destroyers of cultures and civilization; perhaps, in some cases, they provide building blocks. Like small mutations within a genetic structure – slight rearrangements of ACTG codes in DNA – technological and natural disasters may provide organizational "mutations" for society, with concomitant responsibility for us to select new directions, more wholly conscious of the ramifications those choices may have on the long-term survival of an increasingly tightly knit species – our own (Davis 1991).

In the search for indicators of community recovery, many categories might be considered. I suggest that small communities have greater abilities for recovery than are usually recognized. They have kinship, family, history, identity, past experiences, local leadership, all combined and activated by a major event. Resolution of local pre-disaster conflicts may need to occur as part of recovery. External involvement by attorneys, social services, and even inappropriate research, may inhibit recovery processes and prolong or sharpen awareness of the original pain, extending in time the negative impacts.

The Central North Pacific bears many markers of disasters, vestiges of past disruptions – layers of ash from the 1912 Katmai eruption, tangled groves of dead trees in areas that subsided during the 1964 earthquake, and occasional pockets of oil from the 1989 spill. These are remnants of debris in an environment that can – under many circumstances – heal itself and are small markers compared with the larger impact of the original event. Less visible are the remnants of memories in the minds of survivors and communities.

But back to the critical question: have the communities recovered? I cannot answer that directly, for I cannot ask those who were involved, until the court cases are settled and people can talk without fear of jeopardizing their own financial settlements or those of their neighbours. Clearly, social science has not recovered. We may never again enjoy the special kind of independent pursuit of ideas, relationships, and insights that comes from creative research unfettered by the ominous threat of litigation. Constraints on human ideas and discussion may be one of the most enduring negative impacts of the *Exxon Valdez* oil spill in Prince William Sound.

Chronology of the first 10 days

Day 1

Assessment of damage, and gathering of personnel. Concern about ship stabilization, and questions of appropriate methods – burn, boom or use dispersants? After experiencing telephone overload (a technological malfunction), Alyeska reverts to using fax for communication for a while in the morning. A teleconference is held at noon with participation of 13 people and eight agencies. At night, the first boom is deployed.

Day 2

Lightering of oil off the ship is begun. Question of who was in charge is raised. Nighttime burn test; smoke frightens the villagers at nearby Tatitlek, who have not been informed of the test.

Day 3

Conflict between the State, Exxon, and the Coast Guard concerning the use of dispersants.

Day 4

High winds, 73 mph, and the oil moves 40 miles.

Day 5

Committee of three evolves.

Day 6

Continuing discussion about the use of dispersants.

Day 7

First dead bird and two sea otters brought in.

Day 8

M/V *Exxon Valdez* still leaking; boom around it breaks again. Greenpeace incident. Recriminations and blame highlighted. Dispute over dispersants escalates. Gas prices on the West Coast increase 15 cents. Phones into Valdez triple. Warrant for the arrest of Captain Hazelwood, but he cannot be located, having left Valdez four days earlier.

Day 9

Amount of boom positioned: 84,000 feet. Federal presence: 391 Coast Guard, 23 from the Department of Interior, 14 from NOAA, 6 from EPA and 4 from USDA. Third highest day of traffic since the oil spill: 613 flights into or out of Valdez.

Day 10

Number of Exxon employees: 72 Exxon employees on site; 367 contract personnel; 252 contract fishing personnel in Valdez and an estimated 126 contract fishing personnel in Cordova. In total, 189 tons of air cargo arrive; 107 vessels are deployed, as are 111,000 boom feet, 13 skimmers, and 18 aircraft.

Notes

1. This is by no means the largest oceanic oil spill. For example, official estimates released on 13 December 1992 indicate that a Greek tanker spilled 21.5 million gallons of crude oil off the coast of Spain – about twice the volume spilled by the *Exxon Valdez* (see *New York Times*, 14 December 1992).
2. Named by Vancouver in 1794 for Captain Bligh, later famous for the mutiny on the *Bounty*.
3. I gave a paper at that meeting, comparing the earthquake and the oil spill, and I recall being extremely concerned about it. I had resolved by that time that I would maintain my independence and integrity, and assume that neither side would subpoena me. However, the fear still haunts me. I did not pursue funding for the 200 pages of draft material written under a contract with the North Pacific Rim, funded by the Bureau of Indian Affairs. It was clear that any positive findings might be used against the Native persons and their ultimate settlement. I felt, and still feel, restraint on trying to report here that there were *any* benefits to the events related to the oil spill.

References

Alaska Oil Spill Commission. 1990. "Executive summary. Spill. The wreck of the *Exxon Valdez.* Implications for safe marine transportation." State of Alaska. January.

Alyeska Corporate Affairs. 1990. *Prince William Sound Tanker Spill Prevention and Response Plan.* In three volumes (summary in a briefing booklet). Anchorage, Alaska: Alyeska Pipeline Service Company.

Araji, Sharon K. 1990a. "Effects of Exxon-Valdez oil spill on families and communities: A preliminary report." Alaska Anthropological Association, Fairbanks, Alaska, March.

————. 1990b. "Social and psychological effects of oil spill on three communities/ villages: A comparison." Arctic Science Conference, Anchorage, Alaska, October (with Susan LaBelle).

————. 1991. "Hidden effects of the Exxon-Valdez oil spill: A comparison of communities." Pacific Sociological Association, Irvine, Calif., April.

————. 1992a. "The Exxon-Valdez oil spill: Social, economic, and psychological impacts on Homer." Department of Sociology, University of Alaska Anchorage.

————. 1992b. "The Exxon-Valdez oil spill: Social, economic and psychological impacts on Seldovia." Department of Sociology, University of Alaska Anchorage.

————. 1993. "The Exxon-Valdez oil spill: Social, economic and psychological impacts on Port Graham." Department of Sociology, University of Alaska Anchorage.

Bak, Per, and Kan Chen. 1991. "Self-organized criticality." *Scientific American* 264(1): 46–53.

Baker, Jenifer M., Robert B. Clark, and Paul F. Kingston. 1991. *Two Years after the Spill: Environmental Recovery in Prince William Sound and the Gulf of Alaska.* Edinburgh: Institute of Offshore Engineering, Heriot-Watt University.

Betts, Robert C., Christopher B. Wooley, Charles M. Mobley, James C. Haggarty, and Aron Crowell. 1991. "Site protection and oil spill treatment at Sel-188. An archaeological site in Kenai Fjords National Park, Alaska." Report submitted by Exxon Shipping Company and Exxon Company, Houston, Texas.

Browning, Larry D., and Judy C. Shetler. 1993. "Communication in crisis, communication in recovery: A postmodern commentary on the Exxon Valdez disaster." *International Journal of Mass Emergencies and Disasters* 10(2).

Cahalane, Victor H. 1959. *A Biological Survey of Katmai National Monument. Smithsonian Miscellaneous Collections* 138(5). Publication 4376. Washington, DC: Smithsonian Institution.

Clark, Donald. 1984. "Pacific Eskimo: Historical ethnography." In: D. Damas, volume ed. *Handbook of North American Indians. Vol. 5. Arctic.* Washington, DC: Smithsonian Institution, pp. 185–197.

Clarke, Jeanne Nienaber, and Daniel McCool. 1985. *Staking Out the Terrain. Power Differentials among Natural Resource Management Agencies.* SUNY Series in Environmental Public Policy, edited by Lester Milbrath. Albany: State University of New York Press.

Cohen, Maurie J. 1992. "An assessment of the economic impacts of the *Exxon Valdez* oil spill on southcentral Alaska's commercial fishing industry." Paper presented at the 1992 AAAS Arctic Science Conference, Valdez, Alaska.

Cultural Dynamics, Ltd. 1993. *A Description of the Social and Economic Systems of the Kodiak/Shumagin Region.* Technical Report No. 122. Alaska Outer Continental Shelf Region. Social and Economic Studies Program. Anchorage: Minerals Management Service, US Department of the Interior.

Dacy, Douglas C., and Howard Kunreuther. 1969. *The Economics of Natural Disasters: Implications for Federal Policy.* New York: Free Press.

Davis, Nancy Yaw. 1969. "A village view of agencies." Presented at the Alaska Science Conference. AAAS Meetings, Arctic Division. Fairbanks.

———. 1970. "The role of the Russian Orthodox Church in five Pacific Eskimo villages." In: Eugene Hass and Robert W. Kates, eds. *The Great Alaska Earthquake of 1964. Human Ecology. Vol. 4.* Washington, DC: National Research Council, National Academy of Sciences, pp. 125–146.

———. 1971. "The effects of the 1964 Alaska earthquake, tsunami and resettlement on two Koniag villages." Unpublished Ph.D. dissertation in Anthropology, University of Washington. 434 pp.

———. 1977. "An historical overview of the Chugach region." In: *Gwangkumtenek Sungcarluta.* Anchorage: North Pacific Rim Health Department, pp. 1–16.

———. 1984. "Contemporary Pacific Eskimo." In: D. Damas, volume ed. *Handbook of North American Indians. Vol. 5. Arctic.* Washington, DC: Smithsonian Institution, pp. 198–204.

———. 1986. *Sociocultural Description of Small Communities in the Kodiak/Shumagin Region.* Technical Report No. 121. Social and Economic Studies Program. Anchorage: Minerals Management Service, US Department of the Interior. 298 pp.

———. 1987. "Earthquake, tsunami, resettlement and survival in two North Pacific Alaskan Native villages." In: A. Oliver-Smith, guest ed. *Natural Disasters and Cultural Responses.* Studies in Third World Societies. Publication No. 36. Williamsburg, Va.: Department of Anthropology, College of William and Mary, pp. 123–154.

———. 1989a. "Comparisons of the 1964 Alaska earthquake–tsunami and the 1989 Alaska oil spill." 40th Arctic Science Conference, AAAS, Fairbanks, 16 September.

———. 1989b. "Social and economic impacts of the Prince William Sound oil spill on Native residents of the Chugach region." North Pacific Rim Native Corporation. Bureau of Indian Affairs. Draft report in four parts. 210 pp.

———. 1990. "Insights from comparisons: The Great Alaska Earthquake and the Great Alaska Oil Spill." Session on Risk Perception, Response, and Emergency Management in Disasters. A. Oliver-Smith, organizer. Annual Meeting of the Society for Applied Anthropology, York, UK.

———. 1991. "Are disasters to society what mutations are to biology?" Governmental and Institutional Responses to Disaster. A. Oliver-Smith, organizer. Annual Meeting of the Society for Applied Anthropology, Charleston, South Carolina.

Dyer, C.L., D.A. Gill, and J.S. Picou. 1992. "Social disruption and the *Valdez* oil spill: Alaskan Natives in a natural resource community." *Sociological Spectrum* 12(2): 105–126.

Endter-Wada, Joanna, Rachel Mason, Joanne Mulcahy, and Jon Hofmeiser. 1993. "The Kodiak region." In: *Social Indicators Study of Alaskan Coastal Villages. IV.*

Postspill Key Informant Summaries. Schedule C Communities. Part 2. Human Relations Area Files. Alaska OCS Region. Anchorage: Minerals Management Service, US Department of the Interior.

Enge, Marilee. 1993. "Suicide touches nerve left raw by oil spill." *Anchorage Daily News,* 17 May, A1, A8.

Exxon Company. 1992. *Three Years After. Conditions in Prince William Sound and the Gulf of Alaska.* October. Houston: Exxon Company.

Exxon Valdez Oil Spill Trustees. 1992. "*Exxon Valdez* Oil Spill Restoration. 1993 Draft Work Plan." October.

Exxon Valdez Oil Spill Restoration Office. 1993. "Draft *Exxon Valdez* Oil Spill Restoration Plan. Summary of Alternatives for Public Comment." April.

Exxon Valdez Oil Spill Trustee Council. 1993. "Restoration Office. 1993 fact sheet: Restoration actions of the *Exxon Valdez* Oil Spill Trustee Council as of July 1993."

Fall, James A. 1990. "Subsistence after the spill: Uses of fish and wildlife in Alaska Native villages and the *Exxon Valdez* oil spill." Paper presented at the 89th Annual Meeting of the American Anthropological Association.

———. 1991a. "The Division of Subsistence of the Alaska Department of Fish and Game: An overview of its research program and findings: 1980–1990." *Arctic Anthropology* 27(2): 68–92.

———. 1991b. "The *Exxon Valdez* oil spill: Impacts on subsistence uses of fish and wildlife." *Arctic Issues Digest.* October. Cooperative Extension Service, University of Alaska Fairbanks, pp. 12–25.

———. 1993a. "Plenary presentation: Subsistence and the *Exxon Valdez* oil spill." *Exxon Valdez* Oil Spill Symposium. Anchorage, Alaska, 2 February 1993. Division of Subsistence, Alaska Department of Fish and Game.

———. 1993b. "Subsistence uses of fish and wildlife resources in areas affected by the *Exxon Valdez* oil spill." *Exxon Valdez* Oil Spill Symposium. Session IB: Subsistence. Anchorage, Alaska, 4 February 1993. Division of Subsistence, Alaska Department of Fish and Game.

Gramling, Robert, and William R. Freudenburg. 1992. "The *Exxon Valdez* oil spill in the context of US petroleum politics." *Industrial Crisis Quarterly* 6: 175–196.

Griggs, Robert F. 1922. *The Valley of Ten Thousand Smokes.* Washington, DC: National Geographic Society.

Haggarty, James C., Christopher B. Wooley, Jon M. Erlandson, and Aron Crowell. 1991. "The 1990 Exxon Cultural Resource Program: Site protection and maritime cultural ecology in Prince William Sound and the Gulf of Alaska." Report submitted by Exxon Shipping Company and Exxon Company, Houston, Texas.

Harrald, John R., Ruth Cohn, and William A. Wallace. 1992. "We were always re-organizing ...: some crisis management implications of the *Exxon Valdez*." *Industrial Crisis Quarterly* 6: 197–217.

Impact Assessment Incorporated. 1990. "Economic, social and psychological impacts of the *Exxon Valdez* oil spill. The oiled mayors study." In three parts. Alaska Department of Community and Regional Affairs.

Institute of Social and Economic Research. 1993. *Communities' Mitigation Strategies Project. Progress Report: Phase II. Vol. I and II.* Contract No: 4005.003.414 with Regional Citizen's Advisory Council. Prepared in collaboration with Stephen R. Braund and Associates. University of Alaska Anchorage.

269

Jahns, Hans, and Bruce Koons. 1993. "The fate of the oil from the *Exxon Valdez*: A perspective." Speech given to the American Society for Testing and Materials (ASTM) Symposium on Environmental Toxicology and Risk Assessment, 26 April 1993. Exxon Company, Houston, Texas.

Jorgensen, Joseph G. 1993. *Social Indicators Study of Alaskan Coastal Villages. II. Research Methodology: Design, Sampling, Reliability, and Validity.* Technical Report No. 153. Alaska OCS Region. Anchorage: Minerals Management Service, US Department of the Interior.

Keeble, John. 1991. *Out of the Channel. The* Exxon Valdez *Oil Spill in Prince William Sound.* New York: Harper Collins.

———. 1993. "A parable of oil and water. Revisiting Prince William Sound, four years after." *Amicus Journal* (Spring) 35–42.

Kizzia, Tom. 1993a. "Alaskans preach hope to Shetland Islanders." *Anchorage Daily News*, 16 January, pp. A1, A9.

———. 1993b. "Mistake caused oil spill." *Anchorage Daily News*, 26 August, pp. B1, 3.

Martin, George C. 1913. "The recent eruption of Katmai volcano in Alaska." *National Geographic Magazine* 24(2): 132–181.

Mason, Rachel. 1993. "Fishing and drinking in Kodiak, Alaska: The sporadic re-creation of an endangered lifestyle." Unpublished Ph.D. dissertation, Department of Anthropology, University of Virginia.

McNabb, Steven. 1993. "Postspill Key Informant Summaries. Introduction." In: *Social Indicators Study of Alaskan Coastal Villages. IV.* Technical Report No. 155. Schedule C Communities Part 1. Human Relations Area Files. Alaska OCS Region. Anchorage: Minerals Management Service, US Department of the Interior, pp. 5–26.

Mielke, James E. 1990. "Oil in the ocean: The short- and long-term impacts of a spill." Congressional Research Service Report for Congress. The Library of Congress. 24 July.

Mobley, C.M., J.C. Haggarty, C.J. Utermohle, M. Eldridge, R.E. Reanier, A. Crowell, B.A. Ream, D.R. Yesnter, J.M. Erlandson, and P.E. Buck. 1990. "The 1989 Exxon Valdez Cultural Resource Program." Report submitted by Exxon Shipping Company and Exxon Co., Houston, Texas.

Moss, Madonna L., and Jon M. Erlandson (eds.). 1992. "Relationships between maritime cultures of southern Alaska: Rethinking cultural area boundaries." *Arctic Anthropology* 29(2). 5 pp.

National Archives. Record Group 22. Bureau of Fisheries, Department of Commerce and Labor. Entry 91, Box 54, File 351. E.M. Ball 1912 to 1916.

———. Record Group 75. Bureau of Education. Box 48, Entry 86. Departmental-Treasury (Revenue Cutter 1912–1913 Service).

Natural Resource Damage Assessments. 1992. *Document Index List – State of Alaska.* Anchorage, Alaska: Oil Spill Public Information Center Public Release. 49 pp.

Norton, Frank R.B., and J. Eugene Haas. 1970. "The human response in selected communities." In: *The Great Alaska Earthquake of 1964. Human Ecology.* Committee on the Alaska Earthquake of the Division of Earth Sciences. National Research Council. Washington, DC: National Academy of Sciences, pp. 245–399.

Oil Spill Public Information Center. 1992. Bibliography sorted by title. 203 pp.

O'Meara, Jan (ed.). 1989. *Cries from the Heart. Alaskans Respond to the* Exxon Valdez *Oil Spill.* Homer, Alaska: Wizard Works.

Palinkas, Lawrence A., Michael A. Downs, John S. Petterson, and John Russell. 1993. "Social, cultural, and psychological impacts of the *Exxon Valdez* oil spill. *Human Organization* 52(1): 1–13.

Picou, J. Steven, Duane A. Gill, Christopher L. Dyer, and Evans W. Curry. 1992. "Disruption and stress in an Alaskan fishing community: initial and continuing impacts of the *Exxon Valdez* oil spill." *Industrial Crisis Quarterly* 6(3): 235–257.

Reger, Douglas R., J. David McMahan, and Charles E. Holmes. 1992. *Effect of Crude Oil Contamination on Some Archaeological Sites in the Gulf of Alaska, 1991 Investigations.* Office of History and Archaeology Report Number 30. Anchorage: Division of Parks and Outdoor Recreation, Alaska Department of Natural Resources.

Regional Citizens' Advisory Council. Prince William Sound. 1993. *Then and Now. Changes Since the* Exxon Valdez *Oil Spill.* Written and edited by Patty Ginsberg. Anchorage: Northern Printing.

Reynolds, Stephanie. 1993. "Effects of the 1989 *Exxon Valdez* Oil Spill on Cordova, Alaska." In: *Social Indicators Study of Alaskan Coastal Villages.* Technical Report No. 155. HRAF. Alaska OCS Region. Anchorage: Minerals Management Service, US Department of the Interior, pp. 129–422.

Richter, C. Kay. 1990. "T/V Exxon Valdez Oil Spill Chronology. March 23, 1989– May 2, 1989. Day Minus-One through Day Forty." Alaska Oil Spill Commission. Volume IV, Appendix N. State of Alaska. Anchorage, Alaska. (February).

Robbins, Ed. 1993. "Valdez Key Informant Summary." In: *Social Indicators Study of Alaskan Coastal Villages. IV.* Technical Report No. 155. Postspill Key Informant Summaries. Schedule C Communities, Part 1. HRAF. Alaska OCS Region. Anchorage: Minerals Management Service, US Department of the Interior, pp. 31– 126.

Robbins, Lynn A. 1993. "Kenai." In: *Social Indicators Study of Alaskan Coastal Villages. IV.* Technical Report No. 155. Postspill Key Informant Summaries. Schedule C Communities, Part 2. HRAF. Alaska OCS Region. Anchorage: Minerals Management Service, US Department of the Interior, pp. 445–514.

Roberts, Leslie. 1992. "Science in court: A culture clash." *Science* 257: 732–736.

Rodin, Mari, Michael Downs, John Petterson, and John Russell. 1992. "Community impacts resulting from the *Exxon Valdez* oil spill." *Industrial Crisis Quarterly* 6: 219–234.

Rogers, George W. 1970. "Economic effects of the earthquake." in: *The Great Alaska Earthquake of 1964. Human Ecology.* Committee on the Alaska Earthquake of the Division of Earth Sciences. National Research Council. Washington, DC: National Academy of Sciences, pp. 58–76.

Rooks, Curtiss Takada. 1993. "Old Harbor." In: *Social Indicators Study of Alaskan Coastal Villages. IV.* Technical Report No. 155. Postspill Key Informant Summaries. Schedule C Communities, Part 2. Contributions from Joanna Endter. HRAF. Alaska OCS Region. Anchorage: Minerals Management Service, US Department of the Interior, pp. 771–816.

Shaw, David G. 1992. "The *Exxon Valdez* oil-spill: Ecological and social consequences." *Environmental Conservation* 19(3): 253–258.

Sorokin, Pitirim A. 1943. *Man and Society in Calamity. The Effects of War, Revolu-*

tion, Famine, Pestilence upon Human Mind, Behavior, Social Organization and Cultural Life. New York: E.P. Dutton Co.

Stone, Richard. 1993. "Dispute over *Exxon Valdez* cleanup data gets messy." *Science* 260: 749.

Tierney, Kathleen J., and E.L. Quarantelli (eds.). 1992. *Social Aspects of the* Exxon Valdez *Oil Spill. Industrial Crisis Quarterly* 6(3): special issue.

US Department of the Interior. 1992. *Social Indicators Study of Alaskan Coastal Villages.* Technical Report No. 152. Key Informant Summaries. Volume 2: Schedule B Regions (Bristol Bay, Kodiak, Bering Straits). Social and Economic Studies. Alaska Outer Continental Shelf Region. Anchorage: Minerals Management Service, US Department of the Interior.

———. 1993a. *Social Indicators Study of Alaskan Coastal Villages. IV. Postspill Key Informant Summaries.* Technical Report No. 155. Schedule C Communities, Part 1 (Cordova, Tatitlek, Valdez). Alaska OCS Region. Anchorage: Minerals Management Service, US Department of the Interior.

———. 1993b. *Social Indicators Study of Alaskan Coastal Villages. IV. Postspill Key Informant Summaries.* Technical Report No. 155. Schedule C Communities, Part 2 (Kenai, Tyonek, Seldovia, Kodiak City, Karluk, Old Harbor, Chignik). Alaska OCS Region. Anchorage: Minerals Management Service, US Department of the Interior.

United States General Accounting Office. 1989. "Financial Audit." Trans-Alaska Pipeline Liability Fund's 1988 Financial Statements. Report to the Congress. September GAO/AFMD-89-104.

———. 1991a. "Coast Guard. Millions in federal costs may not be recovered from *Exxon Valdez* oil spill." Report to Congressional Requesters. March. GAO/RCED-91-68.

———. 1991b. "Trans-Alaska pipeline." Report to the Chairman, Subcommittee on Water, Power, and Offshore Energy Resources, Committee on Interior and Insular Affairs, House of Representatives. July. GAO/RCED-91-89.

———. 1991c. "Natural resources damage assessment. Information on study of seabirds killed by *Exxon Valdez* oil spill." Report to the Honorable Frank H. Murkowski, US Senate. November. GAO/RCED-92-22.

———. 1993. "Natural resources restoration. Use of *Exxon Valdez* oil spill settlement funds." Briefing Report to the Chairman, Committee on Natural Resources, House of Representatives. August. GAO/RCED-93-206BR.

Vermeij, Geerat J. 1991. "When biotas meet: Understanding biotic interchange." *Science* 253: 1099–1104.

Wheelwright, Jeff. 1991, "Muzzling science." *Newsweek*, 22 April, p. 10.

Wolforth, Charles. 1993. "Hidden damage." *Alaska. A Magazine of Life on the Last Frontier* 59(1): 45–51, 86.

Workman, William B. 1979. "The significance of volcanism in the prehistory of Subarctic Northwest North America. In: P. Sheets and D. Grayson, eds. *Volcanic Activity and Human Ecology.* New York: Academic Press, pp. 339–371.

9

Signposts on the road to recovery

James K. Mitchell

Surprising events and disquieting outcomes

This book has chronicled and analysed a selection of the most widely publicized industrial disasters that occurred during the second half of the twentieth century. All are examples of "surprises" (i.e. unprecedented events). Three are unqualified surprises – Minamata (first-of-a-kind surprise and worst-of-a-kind surprise), Bhopal (worst-of-a-kind surprise), and Chernobyl (worst-of-a-kind surprise). The remaining disasters are less complete surprises, although all contain elements of surprise. For example, long-running underground fires are a staple of coalmining regions but few have led to the extinction of an entire town, as is occurring in Centralia. Many dioxin releases pre-dated the Seveso accident and some of these may have involved greater amounts of that hazardous chemical, but this was the first peacetime release to affect a large civilian population. The *Exxon Valdez* oil spill was certainly not the first tanker accident of its type, nor was it the largest or most destructive spill, but it polluted one of the world's premier fisheries in a flagship wilderness area noted for scenic beauty and scientific importance; it also led to a record-setting court award of punitive damages. Many countries have suffered heavier wartime losses of industrial facilities than Iran, but the Iran–Iraq war was the first significant example of the destruction of a large modern oil industry in a less-developed country.

Industrial disaster surprises like these are public policy problems of increasing global importance. This is not just because they inflict record losses or because they challenge the effectiveness of existing hazards-management programmes: it is also because they signal the need to devise resilient public policies in anticipation of currently unidentified problems that are likely to arise during periods of rapid and far-reaching socio-environmental change. In other words, this problem arena is a test bed for the management of an uncertain, perhaps indeterminate, global future.

As reflected in the case studies analysed here, *the record of human response to industrial surprise is disquieting.* Only in one place (Seveso) is there evidence of more or less successful recovery, although even here the lessons of success are qualified. Elsewhere, the process of recovery has typically been slow, difficult, uneven, and incomplete, although much effort has been expended to bring about a quick and untroubled return to "normal." A disturbingly large number of people are still trying to devise appropriate responses to hidden, chronic, and late-blooming problems. In short, the disasters continue to unfold and societal responses are only partly effective.

Without compelling evidence of successful recovery, *it is difficult to argue that there has been much progress in converting these surprises into routine hazards.* What does apparent failure of the routinization process signify? Several answers are possible. Some kinds of surprise may simply be very resistant to routinization; we may have to allow considerably more time for appropriate coping strategies to emerge. Relatively quick actions – such as the Montreal Convention for control of chlorofluorocarbons (CFCs) – may be the exception rather than the rule. In an era of fast-rising environmental pressures, this is a worrying possibility. Alternatively, not enough effort may have been devoted to unravelling and responding to the surprises reported in these case-studies. Perhaps, because they are mostly local and regional problems, they lack the urgency of threats that are truly global in scope. Or perhaps there are countervailing forces that work against routinization. Contestation and struggle are valuable tools for groups that do not now control many of the circumstances of their lives but seek to do so in the future. Perhaps unroutinized disasters act as lightning-rods in political disputes about issues of equity, justice, or other matters. As long as they are unresolved, there is an opportunity for disaffected groups to gain advantage. Unresolved impacts of surprise may be an indication that political issues are hardier than technical ones. At present it is not possible to determine which answers are correct, but there is clearly a need to seek answers in the context of a broader research agenda.

Today's problems are rooted in specific events that began at various times in an increasingly distant past and are still continuing. The road between initial crisis and successful recovery appears to be a particularly long one. Often, the early impacts remain unresolved and have been joined by new worries and new manifestations of loss. For example, decades after the dumping of mercury in Minamata Bay ended, local fishermen are still coping with a variety of consequences such as embargoes on catches, closures of fishing grounds, attempts to force them into other occupations, and the government's unwillingness to recognize fishermen as a special class of mercury-contamination victims. The situation around Chernobyl is similarly troubling. Nearly a decade after the accident, hundreds of thousands of people in Ukraine, Belarus, and eastern Russia still do not know how much radiation they have absorbed, how long soils will remain contaminated, and what is the prognosis for recovery. In all of the study sites, many of the adults who were present at the time of the original crises are coming to the ends of their lives and whole new generations are reaching maturity in the shadow of lingering disaster. The frustrations of incomplete and slow recovery are too numerous to bear recounting here; let it suffice to say that, in addition to the heavy material, economic, and emotional costs that are borne by immediate victims, the transgenerational effects of continued victimization may also exact a severe toll.

Just as impacts are becoming more protracted or prolonged, *the spatial effects of industrial disaster surprises are also spreading.* Three main processes are involved. Effects spread because disaster agents are often carried far from the scene of initial accidents. The larger the quantity of pollutants introduced into air, water, and soil, the greater the probability that distant locations will be affected. For example, some oil from the *Exxon Valdez* was swept hundreds of miles from Bligh Reef, and Chernobyl's radionuclides were lofted around much of Europe. Sometimes it is the victims who spread out and carry the effects with them. In an increasingly interconnected world, many evacuate or migrate to distant locations in search of medical care, jobs, or assistance. Thus, former residents of Minamata now live, work, and file legal actions about disaster in most of the major cities of Japan. The geographic spread of effects is also transmitted more widely than ever before by new large-scale institutions such as multinational corporations and continental-sized free trade organizations.

275

This was the case in Bhopal, where a US-based corporation was sued for compensation by victims of an accident at an Indian subsidiary. It also occurred throughout the European Community, when member states adopted a sweeping hazards policy directive that grew out of the experience of disaster at Seveso. Indeed, *the entire system of legal responsibilities and jurisdictions over major industrial disasters seems to have been greatly expanded and become more global in light of the events at Seveso, Bhopal, and Chernobyl.*

In summary, compared with other hazardous events, industrial disaster surprises have the capacity to affect more people in more places at more times, thereby greatly complicating the task of hazard management. The implications are striking. Not only are individual problems unprecedented, but involvement of more people raises the demand for protective services; involvement of more places increases the number and variety of environmental factors that must be taken into account; and involvement of longer time horizons exposes the limitations of conventional public decision-making that is typically keyed to short-term returns on investment, short-term plans, and short-term election cycles. Given the complex, pressured setting in which recovery takes place, it is no wonder that the process is impaired and that industrial disaster surprises continue to pose severe policy problems! How can we do better?

Responding effectively to industrial disaster surprises

The resolution of any public policy problem, including industrial disaster surprises, is a function of three main variables – awareness, information, and action. Decision makers, lay as well as expert, must be aware that a problem exists, they must know what to do about it, and they must (be willing and able to) act.

Awareness

The events examined in this book are among the most newsworthy of recent times, so it is probably safe to say that people in the affected areas and public leaders elsewhere were aware of them. Yet, despite the notoriety of these cases, *most of the disasters did not long remain in the forefront of public attention.* A census of mass media reports illustrates this point. Only a handful of stories about the early disasters – Minamata, Centralia and Seveso – have appeared in US newspapers and magazines during the past decade (tables 9.1 and 9.2).

Table 9.1   **Numbers of articles in US newspapers,**[a] **1988–1994**

Event	\multicolumn{6}{c}{Period (month/year)}

Event	1/88–12/88	1/89–12/90	1/91–12/91	1/92–12/92	1/93–2/94	Total
Minamata	0	3	2	2	2	9
Centralia	0	0	0	1	0	1
Seveso	1	0	0	0	1	2
Bhopal	163	99	12	15	4	293
Chernobyl	252	111	86	46	47	542
Iran–Iraq War	2,799	71	43	27	6	2,946
Exxon Valdez	0	540	122	39	39	740

a. *New York Times, Wall Street Journal, Washington Post, Atlanta Constitution and Atlanta Journal, Boston Globe, Los Angeles Times, Chicago Tribune, Christian Science Monitor, USA Today.*

Table 9.2   **Numbers of articles in US magazines,**[a] **1986–1994**

Event	\multicolumn{3}{c}{Period (month/year)}	

Event	1/86–12/89	1/90–12/91	1/92–2/94	Total
Minamata	0	2	1	3
Centralia	1	4	0	5
Seveso	4	0	3	7
Bhopal	59	21	14	94
Chernobyl	294	118	89	501
Iran–Iraq War	283	45	14	342
Exxon Valdez	57	56	58	171

a. Approximately 1,000 general reference periodicals.

Even Bhopal, which was once regarded as a herald of industrial disasters in the third world, no longer attracts much attention from American mass media. The Iran–Iraq war was a hot topic for North American media while hostilities continued but – like most "other people's wars" – it quickly disappeared from public view once peace broke out. Only recent events – Chernobyl and the *Exxon Valdez* – have retained a significant hold on popular consciousness in America: the former is a simmering issue in a volatile stew of Eastern European politics at the end of the Cold War, while the latter is periodically resurrected by high-stakes legal battles in US courts (*New York Times*, 13 June 1994).

Transient public interest is not a promising foundation for the resolution of any policy problem that involves long-term effects. Indeed, the history of successful disaster legislation and other social guides for coping with disaster is that they are usually enacted during the weeks and months immediately following particularly severe disasters, when the heaviest losses are fresh in mind. A high level of public awareness about hazards or disasters has been a *sine qua non* for the emergence of new planning and management systems.

Of course, the fact that journalists no longer write stories about certain industrial disasters does not mean that others – such as victims and stakeholders – have forgotten them. *A vast number of people are intimately associated with the aftermaths of all the disasters examined here*. Apart from a few communities that have been abandoned (e.g. Pripyat) or are disappearing (e.g. Centralia), most affected places still function as active human settlements and are likely to continue to exist, despite the fact that *residents are surrounded by potent reminders of hazard*. Minamata's experience is kept fresh in mind by the presence of the Chisso Corporation's plant, disease museums, and a waterfront landfill. The people of Ukraine, Belarus, and western districts of Russia are aware of contaminated zones that are closed to the public; they also know that several of Chernobyl's reactors are still intact and may yet be brought back into production. Many are also cognizant of the fact that perhaps 16 per cent of the territory of the former Soviet Union can be classified as a disaster area because of chronic environmental despoliation – some of it attributable to Chernobyl (Girardet 1992: 114). Large numbers of oil tankers continue to ply Prince William Sound in full view of fishermen and other coastal residents whose livelihoods depend on the health of surrounding waters. For these people, at least, lack of awareness of hazard is not an important issue.

For the larger public that is not aware of disasters from first-hand experience, a die-off of media interest is more important because it may reduce pressure to keep the disasters on national political agendas. However, a lack of media coverage need not spell the permanent departure of these events from public discourse and an end to prospects for coping with their impacts. There remain at least *four different means for reviving lost awareness of a specific disaster* that can be used by victims and stakeholders who are in pursuit of solutions to lingering problems.

First, *new scientific or technical information* may emerge. Examples include the finding of possible unanticipated cancer clusters around Seveso, decades after the accident; the belated discovery that Chernobyl's meltdown may have been much more serious than first assumed; and the mid-1983 report that confirmed the failure of all previous attempts to stem Centralia's fire. These are representative of scientific findings that effectively refuelled old controversies and sometimes became turning points in subsequent debates. As long as scientists continue to reassess the consequences of past industrial disasters, the verdicts on disaster impacts and management efforts are likely to remain provisional. Eventually, repeated confirmations of hazard or lack thereof will be self-limiting and no new investigations will be mounted. We do not know how long this process of scientific truth-seeking may take but – for industrial surprise disasters – it is likely to be quite lengthy. Twenty years have elapsed since Seveso and closure on the scientific issues that were raised there is not yet complete!

Second, *legal actions* often resurrect an industrial disaster as a public issue. Such mechanisms reminded affected groups about disasters at Minamata, Bhopal, and Prince William Sound (*Exxon Valdez*). It is not simply that lawsuits provide forums in which to re-examine the events of each disaster: they also hold out the possibility of establishing responsibility, fixing blame, and mitigating disaster impacts via compensation awards or punitive damage payments. However, legal suits frequently truncate the range of disaster issues by giving pride of place to those that can be accommodated by the legal system. Moreover, the favoured legal mechanism of financial compensation is often inadequate for qualitative losses such as those that affect personal health, collective security, and community well-being. Finally, unless there is a direct link between blame-fixing by the courts and reform of the industrial disaster-management system, impacts may be compensated but not undone and prospects for future recurrences will remain strong.

Third, *attempts to memorialize past disasters* can revive dormant or otherwise hidden issues and reposition them on the public agenda. For some residents, the creation of disease data centres, museums, prizes, conferences, and commemorative bamboo gardens might signal Minamata's willingness to ring down the curtain on past losses. However, for others, these same facilities serve to perpetuate painful evidence and to "freeze" conflicting interpretations of past events. The capacity of humans to reconstruct their own pasts selectively is well known and the potential for misusing memorialization as a tool for attracting attention to unresolved impacts of past disasters is considerable. None the less, in this context at least, George Santayana's observation remains valid: " Progress, far from consisting in change,

279

depends on retentiveness ... Those who cannot remember the past are condemned to repeat it" (Santayana 1905).

Whereas scientific research, legal proceedings, and memorials are tools that can be used in every era and most societies, the same cannot be said of the fourth mechanism for reviving interest in resolving the lingering impacts of past disasters. *Changes in the general institutional arrangements of society* offer opportunities for reappraising previous decisions and actions. This occurs on a small scale when the previous activities of outgoing governments or departing boards of directors are subject to scrutiny – and sometimes to reversal – by incoming ones. Much greater scope for unearthing past issues arises when regimes and entire systems of governance are overturned. The post-1989 collapse of the Soviet system is a classic example. The full extent of the losses associated with Chernobyl and the blundering attempts to mount an effective response were not clearly revealed until after Ukraine and Belarus came into existence as independent republics separated out of the former Soviet Union. Likewise, the lessons of Seveso could not have been so widely learned and applied throughout Europe if the European Community had not grown beyond its original conception as a customs union and trading bloc to take responsibility for "harmonizing" a wide range of regulations among the 12 member nations.

It should be noted that these *awareness-reviving mechanisms are more available in some places than in others*: third world countries may be at a particular disadvantage. For example, in Iran, industrial hazards of the war with Iraq are not likely to persist for long as a major public issue. Several factors support this conclusion: there has been little scientific inquiry into the effects of such industrial hazards; legal mechanisms for ensuring compensation are overshadowed by bureaucratic ones that are less open to outside inspection; memorialization is largely left to affected localities that have more pressing priorities; and the Islamic Republic has resisted fundamental institutional changes since it came into being after the fall of the Shah. This is not to say that long-term recovery will be impossible in Iran within the lifetimes of the victims. Perhaps there are traditional measures that can substitute for the four processes noted here, although that seems unlikely, given the novelty of the hazards that occurred there. Whether the Iran case is typical of other developing countries is impossible to determine at present but, if it is typical, it implies that *industrial disaster surprises may widen the development gap between rich countries and poor ones.*

All other things being equal, enhancement of public awareness leads to better decision-making about environmental risks. But this should not blind us to the fact that there are also *costs associated with each of the four awareness-reviving processes*. Legal recourse is an obvious example. Litigation is already an important element of public policy for industrial disaster recovery in the United States. Elsewhere, its popularity is growing in response to the global expansion of American-style business practices with their supporting legal regimes and to the accompanying *laissez-faire* philosophies of governments that rely on courts for the resolution of disputes. But there are clear drawbacks to seeking redress through the courts. First, legal action is usually slow; many plaintiffs continue to suffer – and sometimes to die – before their cases come to trial. The definition of victims is subject to political manipulation, and the lure of compensation payments can attract spurious claimants. The fact that deserving victims wait years in the hope of compensation is an index of their desperation and their moral outrage, as well as an indictment of the lack of alternative systems for funding disaster recovery. Second, lawsuits and the threat of lawsuits often deter scientists from investigating certain aspects of industrial disasters or publicizing the results of their work. Such paralysis of scientific inquiry cannot be advantageous to the larger public because it deprives disinterested persons and organizations of information that might help to improve hazard planning and management. Third, resort to legal action encourages the use of blunt decision-making instruments. The resolution of complex, and often fluid, environmental disasters tends to be reduced to a matter of artificial and rigidly constrained legal choices. For these reasons, alternatives to litigation-driven recovery systems need to be preserved and fostered (Gaskins 1989).

In summary, awareness of the industrial disasters surveyed here seems to be high among victims and other directly affected groups, but the declining newsworthiness of such disasters greatly increases the difficulty of mobilizing support from national governments and other non-local institutions for programmes that address lingering or late-blooming problems. The mechanisms for reviving attention to dormant issues offer only uneven and incomplete avenues of redress and mitigation. The search for additional alternatives for raising dormant awareness of "past" industrial disasters may be worth pursuing. However, strengthening linkages between revived awareness and better decision-making is more important. There is considerable *scope for improving coordination and feedback from awareness-*

281

reviving mechanisms to the entire process of industrial investment, facilities planning, and management.

Information

Scientific information is rarely the only basis for public decision-making but it has traditionally been a cornerstone of hazard management. Broadly speaking, information about industrial disasters can be divided into two subsets – analytic information and prescriptive information (i.e. knowing *how* or – sometimes – *why* something happens, and knowing *what* to do about it).

Much analytic information about the case-studies is now available. We know, for example, that impacts are frequently severe, diffuse, delayed, and prolonged; public interest dies off rapidly after the acute stages of disasters; recovery is slow and incomplete; major post-disaster institutional innovations and rearrangements are common; and outcomes are frequently paradoxical (see below). However, the picture is far from complete: much still remains to be discovered.

Key data on the effects and consequences of industrial disasters are often missing. For example, there is no agreement about numbers of people who were affected by Minamata, or Bhopal, or Chernobyl, or who were casualties of the Iran–Iraq War. This is because of different definitions of victims, failure to conduct comprehensive loss assessments, misreporting of known losses, and other factors. Nor can we always be sure about matters like the identity of hazard agents, levels of environmental impact, or the dimensions of affected areas. Thus, the composition of Bhopal's gas cloud and the relative contributions of different oil spills in Prince Edward Sound are still matters of conjecture. Likewise, we know far too little about the interaction of new industrial disaster agents and the physical environment. As the experience of Chernobyl shows, a combination of airborne radiation dispersal plumes, topography, soils, vegetation, hydrology, and farming operations produced complex unforeseen patterns of radiation uptake and contamination that jeopardized the effectiveness of risk-management zones established by hazard managers.

The research community is also hampered by a lack of reliable explanatory models for disaster surprises. As several of the authors in this volume point out, *cyclical models of crisis and response that posit a return to "normal" seem to be of little help* here. Models of disaster recovery provide frameworks for interpreting empirical data and gauging the effectiveness of different measures. Without them, the task of hazards management is slowed and rendered less effective.

A further broad informational issue is that *much of what is known about industrial disaster surprises is highly provisional* and subject to fundamental reinterpretation – sometimes decades after the primary event. For example, earlier explanations of Minamata "disease" have been revised on several occasions after later investigations. Likewise, new and contrary information about the toxicity of dioxin has recently emerged in Seveso. Changes of interpretation occur both because contemporaneous scientific investigations of acute-stage hazards are rarely exhaustive and because latent impacts are slow to emerge. Indeed, "lagging indicators" of industrial disaster surprises are often transgenerational and global in scope. The typical post-disaster reviews and assessments carried out by public agencies and other bodies usually pick up only immediate, clearly detectable, short-term effects and issues.

Important as they are, analytic information gaps may not be the most important ones. *Prescriptive information – knowing what can be done to improve recovery from industrial disaster surprises – is, in many ways, the most difficult challenge for public policy makers.* If the disasters are truly unprecedented, then knowledge useful for guiding action is limited. But there are degrees of surprise: for example, improperly managed, worst-of-a-kind events (level 1 events) are likely to be easier to cope with than unsuspected, one-of-a-kind surprises (level 3 events) because they are nearer to familiar experience (table 9.3).

We know that surprises that were studied here elicited some responses that were familiar to public decision makers, if not always entirely appropriate or successful. (These might be labelled "habitual responses.") For example, the Iranian government did what it is accustomed to do: it began a programme of centralized economic and community planning to guide recovery from war. Likewise, in predictable fashion, legal actions were begun against those allegedly responsible for Minamata, Bhopal, and the *Exxon Valdez*. Other responses were clearly of an ad hoc, trial-and-error nature ("experimental responses"). Examples of these include attempts to tunnel under and shore up the Chernobyl reactor after it threatened to collapse into the ground water-table when a concrete sarcophagus was being constructed above ground. Efforts to clean the shores of Prince William Sound with various media such as steam, chemicals, and

Table 9.3 **Levels of difficulty in recovering from surprises**

Remoteness from experience	Potential degree of control		
	Unsuspected	Improperly managed	Instrumental
One of a kind			Iran–Iraq war
	– – – – – – – Level 3 – – – – – – –		
First of a kind	Minamata[a]		
	– – – – – – – – – – – Level 2 – – – – – – – – – –		
Worst of a kind	Minamata	Bhopal	
		Chernobyl	
		Centralia	
		Seveso	
		Exxon Valdez	
	– – – – – – – – – – – Level 1 – – – – – – – – – –		

a. Minamata appears twice because it was originally the first significant event of its kind (level 2) but later became only one of at least thirty known sites of methyl mercury contamination worldwide (level 1).

paper towels also belong to a class of experimental responses. A third set of responses included novel but well-thought-out measures that were designed in light of the disaster experience and put into practice after much consultation among governments and other parties. The Seveso Directive is a prime example of what might be called "innovative responses."

Unfortunately, beyond these anecdotal examples, *information about decision makers' knowledge of adjustments to surprise is highly incomplete*. We do not know much about how the mix of habitual, experimental, and innovative responses varied among the different cases. It would be valuable to know whether hazard managers, victims, and other stakeholders knew and canvassed the full range of existing possibilities for speeding recovery and avoiding a repetition of disaster. Presumably, a population that knows what might be done is in a better position to cope with disasters than one which lacks that information. But such a statement implies that a reliable body of knowledge about appropriate coping behaviour exists, at a time when there is reason to doubt that it does – at least for unprecedented industrial surprises. However, it might be possible to answer less exacting but none the less illuminating questions: are managers, victims, and stakeholders aware of the experience of other communities that have been affected by similar industrial disasters? What do the leaders and citizens of southern Iran know of recovery in Viet Nam or other war-ravaged societies? What do the residents of Prince William Sound know about recovery from oil pollution in places that experienced similar disasters (e.g. the shores of Brittany affected by the *Amoco Cadiz* oil spill)? Are they also aware of the accumulated expertise about recovery from other (non-industrial) types of disasters (e.g. earthquakes, cyclones)? Have they made use of such borrowed experience? Since none of the case-studies (and few other accounts) have explicitly addressed these questions, it is not possible to provide clear answers. The investigation of awareness about alternative adjustments to major industrial hazards is a much-neglected field in the professional literature.

A fast-breaking emergency may not be the most appropriate time for public decision makers to canvass the experience of others. However, that does not excuse the failure to undertake post hoc assessments of the long-term recovery process. The principle of interrogating the performance of human and engineered systems in response to extreme natural events is well established in the United States. So-called "quick-response" investigation teams are routinely sent to the scenes of hurricanes, floods, earthquakes, and similar events by many agencies of the US government. The National Transportation Safety Board performs in a similar role for transportation accidents. Most of the impacts of natural disasters and transportation accidents show up within hours to months of the events, whereas many of the impacts that have been discussed in this book involve much longer periods. In light of these differences, perhaps it is time to extend the general principle of post hoc disaster assessments to include longer-term evaluations of recovery from industrial disaster surprises.

Action

Lack of willingness to act does not rank high among the problems that have frustrated coping with industrial surprises. In every case-study it is evident that a wide range of responses to these problems were tried – with varying degrees of success. Rarely are there examples of actions that were proposed but not attempted. It is not appropriate to repeat all the examples of actions taken that are reported in the case-studies. Instead, let us focus on one particularly significant category of responses – institutional changes.

Usually, institutional changes are believed to occur slowly. Changes in public policy are a good example. The development of public policy in modern bureaucratic states has been characterized as a process of disjointed incrementalism, whereby change occurs in irregular spurts and new policies are only marginally different from old ones. Policies also become integrated: separate policies with limited goals are gradually knitted together in pursuit of broader objectives. A typical sequence of policy development might begin with single-purpose/single-means policies and end with multiple-purpose/multiple-means policies (White 1969). Nuclear power station policies are a good example. In more-developed countries, nuclear power stations were once designed as stand-alone fail-safe technologies largely under the control of plant operators. These measures are now routinely backed up by broad programmes of siting controls, emergency planning, and response that involve a great many governmental authorities and public organizations. Furthermore, the entire nuclear fuel cycle is becoming a basis for planning and management, rather than just the power station portion of the cycle. The mining and processing of reactor fuels, the diversion of spent fuels for use in nuclear weapons, and the storage of nuclear wastes are also parts of the management nexus. Similar trends toward broader, more integrated, policies are thought to be occurring in other fields of hazardous technology.

Virtually all the case-studies show that important institutional changes occurred, or were attempted, in the wake of the disasters. Some changes were formal and official; others were informal and unofficial. Among the former are post-*Exxon Valdez* initiatives such as the Ceres Principles (a set of environmental guidelines for business); a pathbreaking piece of pollution-control legislation (the Oil Pollution Act of 1990) that led in turn to other innovations, such as a new national oil-spill clean-up organization established by the US petroleum industry; and record monetary awards made to plaintiffs in legal actions against the Exxon oil company. Other formal institutional changes include the European Community's Seveso Directive, precedent-setting legal decisions about the jurisdiction of courts in one country (the United States) over industrial accidents that occur in another (India), and the creation of a national disaster-management institute at Bhopal. Chernobyl's disaster enhanced the role of the International Atomic Energy Agency as a monitor of reactor safety and nuclear security. It spurred the creation of a plethora of governmental and non-governmental organizations in Russia, Ukraine, and Belarus. It also highlighted the issue of secrecy and openness of nuclear facilities to international inspections – an issue that subsequently assumed great prominence in diplomatic relations between the United States and the governments of Iraq and North Korea (e.g. 1992 Gulf War; 1994 crisis over North Korean nuclear weapons).

Informal institutional changes were also significant. The Minamata disaster provoked a breakdown in long-established traditions of mutual aid among neighbours and gave an unprecedented stimulus to grass-roots environmental activism in Japan, which ushered in a period of national soul-searching about the costs of unrestrained economic development. As in Minamata, citizen protest movements emerged in Centralia, although their efforts were less successful there. Information about institutional changes in Iraq is sparse, but the fact that housing reconstruction was largely exempted from central government control indicates that wartime disaster forced some modification of a highly centralized state policy-making and administration apparatus.

Despite these reforms, the growing catalogue of industrial disaster surprises shows that the limits of emerging broader policies are clearly being tested and found wanting. Moreover, the types of issues that are being raised by surprises are difficult to address within the context of existing policies and programmes. This may be the very reason why institutional reforms and innovations continue to blossom in the wake of the case-study disasters! The fact that existing industrial disaster policies are not sufficiently broad to take account of vital issues is illustrated in all the case-studies.

In every case, actions to cope with surprise have become caught up in paradoxes that signal the limitations of existing public policies and imply a need to find alternatives that address broader contexts of decision-making. In Minamata, a bedrock community myth of "shared destiny" between the city's main corporate employer and the residents blocked many efforts to improve the recovery process. In Centralia, existing disaster policies have resolved the hazard by extinguishing the community; the operation was successful but the patient died! A more enlightened policy would try to avoid such Draconian alternatives. In Seveso it is clear that the very policy that produced a more or less successful response carries within it the seeds of future failures. The conditions that made for successful recovery from one airborne release of dioxin possibly cannot be replicated in the "improved" regulatory system that was developed after the disaster. In the Bhopal case, a dominant institution (e.g. a multinational corporation) has been shown to be vulnerable to the disaster that it inflicted on a local public. Taken together, Chernobyl and the Iran–

Iraq war raise questions at opposite poles in a debate about the appropriate scale for formulating public policy. Chernobyl underscores the limitations of national and multinational political–economic restructuring as a panacea for local socio-environmental ills. Here, the kind of decentralized decision-making about risky technologies that might reduce the likelihood of future disasters may also hinder the management of any large-scale disasters that slip through the safety net. Yet Iran's record of recovery from war with Iraq suggests that the same lesson can operate in reverse – central governments may be the only institutions capable of articulating and carrying through policies for devastated local communities. Finally, the *Exxon Valdez* experience suggests that the procedures of a legal system that is dedicated to administering justice may require that scientists make no public statements about their research in the wake of disaster.

Most, perhaps all, existing disaster-management policies do not directly or indirectly address the kinds of problems just mentioned. What might be done differently? How might such policies be better framed?

Recommendations

Some general recommendations can be offered at this point. They are not meant to constitute an exhaustive list or to be finely calibrated to different cultures, different organizations, or different management systems. Rather, they provide indications of the directions in which research and public policy might move if society is to do a better job of coping with industrial disaster surprises. Because the seriousness of these problems warrants broad mobilization of intellectual and material resources, a mixture of pragmatic recommendations and idealistic suggestions is included.

First, there is a need for more empirical research on recovery from industrial disaster surprises. This includes better assessment of impacts (especially long-term impacts) so that affected communities are adequately informed about the problems that face them. Better evaluation of available responses is also necessary – including identification of alternatives when existing means are inadequate. The capability of existing institutions to handle global and semi-global impacts needs to be clarified, as well as legal jurisdictions over transboundary hazards that involve multinational corporations. It is also important to understand how some surprises become routine disasters. Which factors aid this transition and which retard it? What are the best ways of encouraging the process? Finally, existing models of disasters and disaster recovery provide inadequate explanations of surprises and long-lasting disasters. New ones are needed.

Second, a system of long-term post-disaster assessments should be institutionalized, wherever possible. Disaster reassessment reports might be prepared under independent direction at regular intervals for several decades after the initial disaster event. The system's goal would be to inform public policy-making about the need for timely corrections of hazard-management actions to take account of lingering impacts that have resisted resolution, as well as unanticipated late-blooming impacts.

Third, it will be important to encourage wider and more carefully targeted exchange of experience with industrial disaster surprises among affected individuals, communities, and institutions. People who face highly unusual or unprecedented problems need to know how others elsewhere have attempted to cope with related problems. The establishment of global or regional clearing-houses for information could assist this process; so, too, could reciprocal community-level initiatives that do not depend on customarily slow channels for the diffusion of scientific and managerial information (Perlman 1993).

Fourth, the policy-making and planning process for hazards management should be modified to seek inputs from groups that are suffering from lingering and late-blooming effects of disasters that have otherwise disappeared from public view. This will require improving feedback from various mechanisms for reviving awareness of past disasters and changes in the predominantly short-term planning horizons of policy-making bodies and hazard-management agencies.

Fifth, industrial disaster surprises need to be addressed in much broader contexts than heretofore. This is perhaps the most important task that faces researchers, managers, and public policy-makers. Ironically, single-minded attention to hazards and the mitigation of hazards *per se* may not identify the most promising choices for recovery. Communities typically suffer from a variety of problems that intersect with hazards and must also be addressed jointly if hazards are to be successfully coped with. Economic investment problems are one obvious candidate. For example, it is clear that the process of deindustrialization is closely connected with the opening up of possibilities for speeding recovery from Minamata's disaster. Facing the decline of Chisso Corporation's local plant, the community is being forced to look for alternative economic investments. A heretofore odious reputation as a toxic monument is being turned to advantage as Minamata seeks to become a focus for tourists interested in environmental regeneration. In the process, the adversarial stance of victims and plant personnel is no longer such an impediment to recovery. Elsewhere, changes in political culture and disaster recovery are tightly interwoven. This is so in Eastern European communities affected by Chernobyl. There, prospects for recovery are as much bound up with changes in ideologies, governmental structures, and the role of science in public decision-making as they are with technical issues such as victim compensation, improved monitoring of radiation, and decontamination of soils and water (Mitchell 1993). There is already growing recognition that environmental problems and economic problems are often interrelated and may require joint action. This has given rise to the concept of sustainable development, which also provides one of the more promising contextual frameworks for addressing disaster surprises.

Contextualization of hazards research and hazards management will undoubtedly improve prospects for recovering from, and mitigating, industrial surprises. But explicitly taking account of overlapping issues and problems does not alone guarantee success. Such issues and problems are subject to substantial change at the time-scales that affect recovery. Since recovery times are typically measured in decades, the process of recovery is hostage to a wide variety of more or less unpredictable scientific, technical, and societal changes. In other words, environment, society, and hazards-management systems may not be stable throughout the recovery period, and assumptions about appropriate choices of responses may become outdated and faulty.

This poses difficult problems for policy makers and the public as a whole. Decadal-scale predictions of societal and technological change have previously not proved to be very reliable and there is not much indication that they will improve significantly in the near future; it is, therefore, not likely that such predictions will be particularly helpful to those who must cope with, and recover from, industrial surprises. In the absence of accurate predictions, one alternative is to take a proactive stance towards change – that is, to shape its outcomes rather than adjust to its constraints. It would be both premature and presumptive to specify the form that such interventions will take; however, they will probably require redirection of deep-seated parts of the social system that structure our values and behaviour. These include – among others – education, cultural myths, and ethical guidelines. For most of human history, education, myths, and ethics have worked slowly and unevenly – but often comprehensively – to bring about changes in human behaviour. We are now faced by the possibility that industrial disaster surprises will pose new challenges that require society to speed up the operation of these mechanisms to cope with a set of hazards that is both emerging more quickly and lasting longer than heretofore.

The desire to rid the world of environmental hazards and disasters appears to be deeply embedded in Western culture. Only within the last few decades have researchers and scholars come to accept a different view – namely, that it may be better to learn to live with (and adjust to) many types of threats. This book suggests that industrial disaster surprises are putting our capacity for adjustment to a rigorous test.

References

Gaskins, Richard H. 1989. *Environmental Accidents: Personal Injury and Public Responsibility*. Philadelphia: Temple University Press.

Girardet, Herbert. 1992. *The Gaia Atlas of Cities: New Directions for Sustainable Urban Living*. London: Gaia Books.

Mitchell, James K. 1993. "The future of Russian science is of concern to all nations." *Scientist* 7(19): 11–15.

Perlman, Janice. 1993. "Mega-cities and the innovative technology: An assessment of experience." Hubert H. Humphrey Lecture on International Comparative Planning, Edward J. Bloustein School of Planning and Public Policy, Rutgers University, New Brunswick, NJ, October.

Santayana, George. 1905. *The Life of Reason*. London: Constable.

White, Gilbert F. 1969. *Strategies of American Water Management*. Ann Arbor: University of Michigan Press.

Contributors

Hooshang Amirahmadi, Department of Urban Planning and Policy Development, Edward J. Bloustein School of Planning and Public Policy, Rutgers University, New Brunswick, New Jersey 08903, USA.

Stephen R. Couch, Department of Sociology, Pennsylvania State University – Schuylkill Campus, 200 University Drive, Schuylkill Haven, Pennsylvania 17972, USA.

Nancy Yaw Davis, Cultural Dynamics, 719 N Street, Suite 3, Anchorage, Alaska 99501, USA.

Silvio O. Funtowicz, Joint Research Centre, Institute for Systems Engineering and Informatics, Industry Environment Unit, T.P. 321, 21020 Ispra, Italy.

Bruna De Marchi, Institute of International Sociology, Via Mazzini 13, 34170 Gorizia, Italy.

David R. Marples, Department of History, University of Alberta, Edmonton, Alberta T6G 2H4, Canada.

Sadami Maruyama, Department of Literature, Kumamoto University, 2-40-1 Kurokami, Kumamoto-shi, Kumamoto-ken 860, Japan.

James K. Mitchell, Department of Geography, Rutgers University, New Brunswick, New Jersey 08903, USA.

Jerome R. Ravetz, Joint Research Centre, Institute for Systems Engineering and Informatics, Industry Environment Unit, T.P. 321, 21020 Ispra, Italy.

Paul Shrivastava, Department of Management, Bucknell University, Lewisburg, Pennsylvania 17837, USA.

Index

Abadan [Iran]   *151*, 160
accident response facilities   220, 259–
    260
accidents
    definitions   35n(9), 108
    trends
        global   *20*
        USA   *21*
    types   19–20
acid precipitation   22, 108
adaptation   29–30, 255
Afognak [Alaska]   241, 242
Agano river basin [Japan], mercury
    pollution   49, 58n(1)
Akhiok [Alaska]   242, 247
Alaska
    earthquake [1964]   241–243
    Exxon Valdez oil spill   231–232, 235–
        236
        chronology of events   265–266
        community impact   243–251
        recovery   246, 251–265
    geology   238
    human settlements   239
    oil industry   233–234
    volcanic eruption [1912]   240–241

see also Exxon Valdez oil spill
Alaska Department of Fish and Game
    Habitat and Restoration Division
        259
    Subsistence Division, studies   243,
        246, 252, 261
Alaska State, Department of Natural
    Resources, archaeological impact
    studies   246–247
Alaska Tsunami Warning Center
    (ATWC)   242
Alutiiq Native population [Alaska]   239
    elders' conferences   262
    oil spill studies   247–249
    recovery capability   255
    religious affiliation   249
Alyeska Pipeline Service Company
    234, 252, 259
Alyeska Ship Escort and Response
    Vessel System   260
Amoco Cadiz oil tanker disaster   285
archaeological impact studies, Alaska
    246–247
Arctic ecosystems, effect of Trans-
    Alaskan Pipeline   234
Atom [UKAEA magazine]   215, 216

Belarus
  birth/mortality rates   203
  charitable Chernobyl-centred funds/
    societies   209–210
  costs due to Chernobyl disaster
    225n(22)
  emergency actions after Chernobyl
    disaster   203–204
  evacuation after Chernobyl disaster
    190, 203
  governmental actions   203–204
  lack of funds for disaster relief   204
  map   *185*
  political climate   200, 226n(35)
  Popular Front (BPF)   206–207
  radioactive-fallout patterns   198
  victim action groups   206–208
Belarusian Charitable Fund for the
    Children of Chernobyl   207, 208
Bhopal city [India]
  Hindu–Muslim riots   133
  history   *124*, 125–126
  infrastructure lacking   126
  population growth   126
Bhopal Gas Leak Disaster Ordinance
    131, 144
Bhopal [India] crisis   6, 121–145
  background history
    inside company/plant   123, *124*, 125
    outside plant   *124*, 125–126
  chemical plant accident as cause   122,
    125, 136
  company view   127
  compared with Seveso crisis   103, 109
  compensation paid   129–130, 132,
    133
  death toll   122, 132
  economic losses   129
  factors affecting impact
    inside plant   122, *124*, 125, 126, 136
    outside plant   *124*, 126
  financial survival of Union Carbide
    threatened by   6, 133, 135
  government view   127
  mass exodus after accident   123
  medical information lacking   128
  multiple-perspectives analysis   126–
    127

  number of people affected   122, 129,
    132
  policy implications   143–145
  political management   132, 137–139
  sabotage claim   136
  type of disaster   22
  victims   122, 132–133, 139, 142
Black Triangle [Central Europe]   1, 3,
    8n(1)
blame attribution   32
  Bhopal crisis   136
  Chernobyl disaster   195, 211–212,
    219, 223
  link with reform of disaster-
    management system   279
  Minamata disease   45, 49, 58
  Seveso disaster   104
Blix, Hans   192
boiler explosions   17, 34n(7)
Braer oil tanker   231

caesium-137   197, 198
Canada
  nuclear reactor accident   226n(40)
  transportation accident   22
cancers
  dioxin-associated   116n(7), 278
  radiation-caused   201–202
Centralia [USA]
intracommunity conflict   60, 65–66, 67,
    73
  location   *61*
  population
    attitudes   63, 67
    evacuation/relocation   64, 66–67,
      73, 81
    numbers   61, 63
    remaining citizens   67
  socio-economic history   61–63
  underground coalmine fire   5, 60,
    63–67
    attempts to extinguish   63, 76
    diverse community reactions   64–
      65
    extent   63, *64*, 66
    origin   63, *64*
Ceres Principles   286
Challenger space shuttle disaster   13, 22

chemical plant accidents 23, 86, 121, 125
  see also Bhopal crisis; Seveso disaster
chemical weapons 150–151
Chenega [Alaska] 241, 242, 247–248
Chernobyl [Ukraine] nuclear power
    station 186
  accident 183
    cause 217
    compared with Seveso disaster
      103, 109
    costs 225n(22)
    death toll and casualties 183, 193,
      200–201, 225n(25), 227n(44)
    effects on community 32, 196–202
    fire-fighters 188, 189
    governmental reactions 189–194,
      203–204
    and IAEA 192, 195
    institutional changes resulting 6–7,
      207, 208–210, 222, 286
    international nuclear energy
      industry's response 215–217,
      219
    number of people affected 24, 196,
      200, 225n(23)
    off-site effects 24–25, 26, 183, 198
    political aspects 189–190, 211, 212
    pretence of normality afterwards
      191–193, 218–219
    radiation levels 191, 192, 224n(13)
    radioactive-fallout maps/patterns
      198, 210, 223, 225n(20)
    recovery 202–210
    type of disaster 22, 23, 25, *27*
  faults/problems in manufacture 186–
    187
  location 184, *185*
  reactor design 186, 195, 216, 217
  sarcophagus over fourth reactor 197,
    223
  Station Director 188, 189, 223
Chignik Bay [Alaska] 247, 248
China, workplace fatalities 34n(5)
Chisso Company/Corporation
  disinformation from 48, 50
  effluent treatment facilities 50
  influence in local community 45–46,
    54

litigation 44, 52, 58
pollution 41, 46–47
reclamation projects 56
reparations 52–53
  see also Minamata disease
chloracne, dioxin-caused 113
Chugachmiut 260, 262
  see also North Pacific Rim
Cimmino Commission 112, 113
clean-up techniques
  oil pollution 237, 265
  radioactive contamination 204
clean-up workers
  Chernobyl disaster 183, 196,
    225n(24, 25)
  Iran–Iraq war 175
coal-burning power stations 8n(1), 187
  environmental impact 1, 219
coalmine disasters
  community conflict resulting 60–83
  factors affecting death rates 18
  USSR data 219
coalmining communities
  collective actions 62
  influence of mining companies 62
Comet airliner crashes 22–23, *27*
Community Documentation Centre on
    Industrial Risk (CDCIR) 95
community responses, evolution 17–19
company towns 45, 61
  see also Centralia; Minamata
compensation *see* reparations
conflictual community 60
  see also intracommunity conflict
confusion
  caused by authorities in Chernobyl
    disaster 190, 220, 221
  as community reaction to
    disasters 122, 189, 218
contamination disasters
  outcomes
    relocation 75, 76
    technological solution 75–76
  recommendations on national
    policy 80–83
  socio-economic classification of
    victims 44, 78
  stage model 69–74

contamination disasters *(cont.)*
  definitional stages *70*
  political stages 70–74
  see also Bhopal crisis; Centralia;
    Chernobyl nuclear power station;
    Exxon Valdez oil spill; Minamata;
    Seveso disaster
Cook Inlet [Alaska]
  map *237*
  Regional Citizens' Advisory Council
    257
Cordova [Alaska] 239, 250
criminal prosecution [of directors/
  executives] 114, 139, 223
crisis, meaning of term 145n(1)
crisis management
  Alaskan Native communities 249,
    255
  legal aspects 130–132, 211–212
  limitations of existing public policies
    287–288
  mass-media involvement 65, 111,
    212–213, 214
  medico-legal documentation required
    128, 144, 221
  political aspects 137–139, 189–190,
    211, 212
  role of victims 66, 111, 115, 144–145,
    166, 212
crisis morphology 141–142
culpability
  Chernobyl disaster 219
  see also blame attribution
cultural differences [between local
  community and external agencies]
  Alaska 248–249, 253–254
  Centralia [USA] 80
  Iran's attempts to minimize effects
    166, 167, 175
cyanide poisoning 129
cycle/stage model [for disasters] *30*, 31
  non-applicability 31, 282
  see also stage model

death toll
  Alaskan earthquake 241–242
  Bhopal crisis 122

Chernobyl disaster 183, 193, 200–
  201, 225n(25), 227n(44)
developing countries
  recovery from disasters 31, 280
  risk-reduction measures required
    145
  technology transfer 18
  see also India; Iran
dioxin
  characteristics 89, 90
  contamination by 24, 86–90, 273
  dread associated 89, 106
  scientific uncertainty about effects
    106, 109–110, 117n(7)
  see also Seveso disaster; Times Beach
    landfill site
direct action, effect on communality
  54, 66
disaster
  cycle/stage model *30*, 31
    non-applicability 31
  definitions 8n(2), 108, 145n(1)
disaster management *see* crisis
  management
disaster reassessment reports 289
disaster subculture 64–65, 79
disempowerment [of victims] 131, 144
Dnieper River [Ukraine] 185, *185*, 186

early warnings [of disasters] *124*, 144
earthquake, Alaskan 241–243
East Ural Radioactive Trace 16
economic losses
  Alaskan earthquake 241
  Bhopal [India] crisis 129
  Chernobyl disaster 225n(22)
  Iran–Iraq war 155, 156–160, *161*
education policy
  effect of Iran–Iraq war 152
  role in reconstruction process 172
emergency stage [in disaster planning]
  30, 31, 176
  actions in Chernobyl disaster 203–
    204
English Bay [Alaska] 247, 256
environmental impact
  industrial processes 25, 108

oil spills   154–155, 236
wars   148, 153–155
waste material dumping   44, 55
Environmental Protection Act [India]
   139–140
Environmental Protection Agency
   [USA]   81, 117n(7)
epidemiological monitoring programmes
   221
   Bhopal [India]   128–129
   Chernobyl area   202, 204
   Seveso [Italy]   105–106, 113, 116n(7)
European Commission [Commission of
   the European Communities]   *92*,
   116n(4)
   accidents to be reported   94
European Community/Union (EC/EU)
   Directives   91
      procedures for adopting   91–92
      Seveso Directive   90, 91, 92–95,
         280
   legislative structure   *92*
   members   116n(4)
   treaties as basis   116n(4)
European Council of Ministers   *92*,
   116n(4)
European Court of Justice   *92*, 116n(4)
European Parliament   *92*, 116n(4)
evacuation [of affected people]
   Alaska   240
   Bhopal   123
   Centralia [USA]   64, 66–67, 75
   Chernobyl area   190, 203, 220,
      227n(45)
   factors affecting decision   220,
      227n(45)
   in Iran–Iraq war   152
   Seveso area   103, 112
   see also relocation
experimental responses   283–284
exporting/externalizing of hazards   78,
   88–89, 115
external support   54, 65, 79
Exxon [oil company]
   service organization   248
   in Trans-Alaskan Pipeline consortium
      234

unfamiliarity of staff with Alaskan
      Native culture   234, 253
Exxon Valdez oil spill   7–8, 231–266
   accident details   235–236
   amount of oil spilled   232
   archaeological impact studies   246–
      247
   chronology of events   265–266
   community impacts
      towns   249–251
      villages   247–249
   creative activities resulting   261, 263
   cultural/psychological/social impacts
      243–247
   litigation   238, 252–253
      effect on scientific research   7–8,
         252, 253, 265
   location   231–232
   organizational responses   257–260
   recovery   246, 251–262
   seabird casualties resulting   236
   ship's description   235
   shoreline pollution caused   236, *237*
   type of disaster   22
   uniqueness   273
Exxon Valdez Oil Spill Trustees
      Council   258
   projects funded   247, 258–259

farmland, effect of Iran–Iraq war   153–
   154
Federal Emergency Management
      Agency   81
fish contamination   44–45
   effect on fishermen   44, 47, 250
   measures to lessen impact   47–48, 49
   see also Minamata disease
Flixborough [UK] chemical plant
      explosion   90, 116n(3)
foetal damage
   dioxin contamination   117n(7)
   mercury toxicosis   43
forest death [*Waldsterben*]   22
   meaning of term   35n(10)
forests, effect of Iran–Iraq war   153
frequency/severity graphs   21
   uses   21–22

GAF Corporation, take-over bid for
  Union Carbide   133–134
Gale, Robert   196, 227n(44)
Giovanardi Commission   112
Gittus, J.H.   215–216
Givaudan [Roche subsidiary]
  admission that dioxin released at
    Seveso   111
  civil damage cases   114–115
  as owner of ICMESA Meda plant
    116n(1)
  Technical Director   110
    criminal conviction   114
  see also Hoffman La Roche; ICMESA
    chemical plant
glasnost, failure over Chernobyl disaster
  218
global warming
  causes   25, 29
  effects   25
Gorbachev, Mikhail   194, 195, 196, 222
governmental reactions
  Bhopal crisis   129, 130, 131, 137–139
  Centralia coalmine fire   66
  Chernobyl disaster   189–194, 203–
    204, 218
  Exxon Valdez oil spill   257–260
  Iran–Iraq war   162, 163–165, 166
  Minamata disease   45, 52, 53
  recommendations on policy   81–82
  Seveso disaster   99, 111–114
greenhouse gas build-up   22, 25
  mitigation of effects   29
Greenpeace International   208, 222
Green World ecological association
  [Ukraine]   205, 206, 212

habitual responses   283
Hammer, Armand   196
hazardous industry regulation
  harmonization throughout EC/EU
    93, 280
  Indian   139–141
  UK   18, 89
hazards
  assessment   175
  classification   23
  definition   8n(2)

  see also industrial hazards
health effects
  Bhopal crisis   128
  Centralia coalmine fire   64
  Chernobyl disaster   189, 201–202
  Exxon Valdez oil spill   244
  influence of pre-existing health status
    129, 202, 210
  Iran–Iraq war   154
  Minamata disease   43, 45
  Seveso disaster   88, 110, 111
Hiroshima [Japan], atomic bomb effects
  27, 28, 117n(8)
Hoffman La Roche   116n(1)
  Director of Clinical Research   111
  see also Givaudan; ICMESA chemical
    plant
housing
  decontamination/demolition at Seveso
    113, 114
  reconstruction policy   171–172
    after Iran–Iraq war   164, 168
Human Relations Area Files, Inc.,
  Alaskan study   245
Hunter and Russell's syndrome   52,
  59n(6)
hurricane Andrew, effects on offshore
  gas/oil platforms   17

ICMESA chemical plant [Italy]
  demolition   104, 109, 114
  dioxin released   86–89, 110
  directors arrested   99, 111
  first established   115
  out-of-court settlements   114
  ownership   116n(1)
  Production Director
    arrest   99, 111
    assasination   99, 114
  products   115n(1)
  Technical Director   110, 111
    arrest and conviction   99, 111,
      114
  see also Seveso disaster
Impact Assessment, Inc., Alaskan study
  244
India
  chemical accident   121–125

hazardous industry regulation 139–141
see also Bhopal crisis
Indian government
  political changes 137, *138*, 139
  reactions to Bhopal crisis 127, 129, 130, 131, 137–139
industrial disasters
  global losses 15
  information required 282–285
  lessons to be learnt 10–11, 145
  nature 11–15
  suggestions for recovery model 220–222, 288–291
  terminology used 8n(2)
  see also routine disasters; surprises
industrial hazards
  causes 11–12
  changes 17
  climatic effects 25
  components *12*
  explanations 13–14
  ignored in reconstruction process 179
  management, social learning model 18–19
infrastructure
  Belarusian 204
  Bhopal [India] *124*, 126
  supplementation in developing countries 145
  war damage 152, 154, *158*, 159
  reconstruction strategy 172
innovative responses 284
institutional changes [after disasters]
  Bhopal crisis 139–141, 286
  Chernobyl disaster 207, 208–210, 222, 286
  Exxon Valdez oil spill 257–260, 286
  Seveso disaster 92–95, 286
institutional uncertainty *97*, 98
  not dealt with in EC/EU regulations 101
international assistance
  Chernobyl disaster 191, 194–196, 208–210, 225n(22)
    aid-group diversity 208–210
    information problems 210
    organizational constraints 208
  in emergency stage [of disaster] 176
  Iranian war damage repair 165, 178
  permanent system suggested 221–222
International Atomic Energy Agency (IAEA)
  and Chernobyl disaster 192, 195, 212, 217
  dual role 212, 222
International Decade for Natural Disaster Reduction 35n(8)
International Monetary Fund (IMF)
  aid for Iran 180n(5)
  recommendations for Iran 162, 163
intracommunity conflict
  Alaska 248, 249, 250, 261
  Centralia [USA] 60, 65–66, 67, 73
  Chernobyl 197–198
  Minamata [Japan] 43–44, 52, 53–55
  recommendations on mediators 82
iodine-131 198
  health consequences 201
Iran
  coastal region 154
  economic policy [post-war] 162
  governmental borrowings 162
  imports 160
  industries
    losses in 1980–1988 war *157–158*, 159–160, *159*, *161*
    reconstruction after war 168–169
  national reconstruction plans 163–165
  oil industry 156
    losses due to war 156, *158*, *159*
  population
    demographic profile 150, 152
    growth 152, 153, 162
Iran–Iraq war [1980–1988] 148–179
  homeless due to war 152
  impacts
    economic losses 155, 156–160, *161*
    educational system 152
    environmental damage 153–155
    human losses 152–153
    human-settlement losses 155
    military/strategic context 150–151
    recovery after war 7, 160, 162–169

Iran–Iraq war [1980–1988] *(cont.)*
  housing reconstruction   164, 168
  industrial reconstruction   163, 168–
    169
  international support   165
  local-community support   165–167
  national reconstruction plans   163–
    165, 166
  rural reconstruction   163
  urban reconstruction   167–168
Italy
  chemical accident   86–117
  see also Seveso disaster

Japan
  environmental activist movement   28
  mercury toxicosis   41–57
  radioactive waste leakage   215
  see also Minamata disease
Jorgensen, Joseph G.   245
Jovanovich, Prof. Jovan   216, 217,
  224n(17)

Kaguyak [Alaska]   241, 242
Karin B incident   101
  uncertainty management model
    applied   101
Karun River [Iran]   *151*, 154
Katmai [Alaska], volcanic eruption
  [1912]   240–241
Kharg Island [Iran]   *151*, 156
Khorramshahr [Iran]   *151*, 155, 167
Kodiak City [Alaska]   239
  earthquake effects   241, 242
  funding of museum   247, 259
  oil-spill impact   251
  volcanic-eruption effects   240
Kumamoto University [Japan], research
  on Minamata disease   48, 49
Kuwaiti oil well fires, type of disaster
  22, 27
Kyshtym [Russia], nuclear waste storage
  disaster   16, 22, 27

lawsuits *see* litigation
legal/moral uncertainty   97
  examples   99

legislation
  hazardous industry regulation
    EC/EU   90, 91, 92–95
    India   139–141
  nuclear plant design [Russia]   222
  oil spill prevention [USA]   257–258
litigation
  Chisso Company/Corporation
    [Minamata, Japan]   44, 52, 58
  Exxon Corporation [Alaskan oil spill]
    238, 252–253
  ICMESA/Givaudan [Seveso, Italy]
    114–115
  inadequacies of system   279, 281
  increasingly global extent   275–276
  research affected by   7–8, 252, 253,
    265, 281
  Union Carbide Corporation [Bhopal,
    India]   130–132, 135–136
Love Canal [USA] landfill site   22, 76,
  78
low-income groups
  effects of contamination/pollution
    44, 78, 129, 245
  and post-war reconstruction   173

Maastricht Treaty [on European Union]
  116n(5)
Major Accident Reporting System
  (MARS)   95
management failure, as cause of
  disasters   23, 86, 223
man-made disasters   19, 107
Marine Spill Response Corporation
  (MSRC)   258, 286
mass media
  reactions to disasters   212–213, 218,
    276, *277*
  see also publicity
Meda [Italy]
  chemical plant
    accidental release of dioxin   86–89,
    110
    demolition   104, 109, 114
  out-of-court settlement by
    ICMESA   114
  see also Seveso disaster

medical information, absence 48, 128,
    210
medical recovery/relief
    Bhopal victims 128–129
    Minamata disease victims 51
medico-legal documentation 128, 144,
    221
    Belarusian 204
Medvedev, Zhores 187, 224n(6),
    227n(42)
memorialization [of past disasters] 56,
    279
mercury toxicosis/poisoning 41
    see also Minamata disease
methyl isocyanate (MIC)
    escape at Bhopal [India] 122, 125
    in pesticide manufacture 123
    physiological effects 128
    reaction with water 125
methyl mercury
    dumping in sea 41
    physiological effects 43
    see also Minamata disease
Metropolitan Edison company [USA]
    213, 214, 215, 218
military personnel, clean-up and
    reconstruction using 175, 196
military technologies
    advances 149
    hazards 23–24
mimaikin [consolation payment] 46, 52,
    57, 59n(5)
Minamata Bay [Japan]
    contaminated sludge dumping 41
        effect on fish and seafoods 44–45,
        50
        movement/removal of sludge 58,
        59n(4)
    location 41, *42*
Minamata disease 4–5, 41–59
    actions to lessen impact
        ban on fishing 47–48
        halting dumping of waste 49–50
    cause 15, 41
    certification procedure 52
    community reactions 15–16, 43, 53–
        55

first signs 44–45
    lack of medication 43
    lessons to be learnt 55
    medical research 48–49
    official/public recognition 45, 49, 57
    second occurrence 49, 52, 58, 58n(1)
    symptoms 43
    victims 42–44
        discord expressed 56
        financial losses 43
        litigation 44, 52, 58
        numbers 43
        ostracization by community 43,
        53–55
        relief for 51
        reparations 51–53
        as scapegoats 55
Minamata Disease Data Hall 56
Minamata [Japan]
    influence of Chisso company 45–46,
        54–55
    need to reduce community
        dependence 55, 289–290
    international conference 2, 56
    location 41, *42*
    measures to aid fisheries 53
    toxic waste disposal by Chisso
        company 41, 46–47
        actions to reduce levels 46, 49–50
        change in discharge point 50, 57
        effect on fisheries 44, 47–48
        environmental impact 44
        protest by fishermen 48, 49–50
    type of disaster 22, 23, *27*
Minamata River [Japan] *42*, 50
Mississauga [Canada] train
    derailment 22
mitigation 28–29
mobilization of resources, post-war
    reconstruction 175
moral hazard [insurance] 105
moral uncertainty *see* legal/moral
    uncertainty

Nagasaki [Japan], atomic bomb *27*,
    28
Nanwalek [Alaska] 247, 256

natural disasters
  compared with industrial
    accidents   108
  global awareness   32
  recovery processes   30–31
natural hazards
  classification   35n(8)
  effect on industrial disasters   24
  factors affecting   25
"need-to-know" principle   91
no-fault principle [insurance]   105
normal accidents   19–20, 107–108
North Pacific Rim [Alaskan Native
    service organization]   252
  name change   262
  personnel levels   260, 262
nuclear energy industry
  integrated policies   222, 286
  US   12–13, 213–215
  USSR   188
    reactor types   186, 195, 216
  see also International Atomic Energy
    Agency (IAEA); United Kingdom
    Atomic Energy Authority
    (UKAEA)
nuclear power station accidents   22, 23,
  183–227
Nuclear Regulatory Commission (NRC)
  214, 215
nuclear waste, disasters associated   16,
  22

offshore gas/oil platforms, effect of
    hurricane Andrew   17
off-site effects
  chemicals pollution/contamination
    41, 49–50, 87, 122, 275
  nuclear power station accidents   13,
    24–25, 26, 183, 198, 275
oil and gas industry
  industrial disasters   3, 154–155, 231–
    266
  Iranian   156
  losses due to war   156, *158*, *159*
Oil Pollution Act (OPA 90)   257–258,
  286
Oil Spill Public Information Center
  (OSPIC)   259

oil tanker accidents
  first major disaster   23
  North American   22, 231–266
  in Persian Gulf   154
  see also Amoco Cadiz oil tanker
    disaster; *Braer* oil tanker; *Exxon
    Valdez* oil spill; *Torrey Canyon* oil
    tanker disaster
Old Harbor [Alaska]   241, 242, 246, 247
Ore Mountains [Central Europe]   2,
  8n(1)
Organisation for Economic Co-operation
  and Development (OECD), recommendations   96
out-of-court settlements   114, *131*, 132
Ouzinkie [Alaska]   241, 247, 248
ozone depletion   22, 27

peace strategies   174–175
Perryville [Alaska]   240, 247
Persian Gulf, effects of pollution   154–
  155, 180n(3)
Persian Gulf War [1990–1991]   148
  environmental effects   3, 155
political aspects
  Bhopal crisis   132, 137–139
  Centralia coalmine fire   65, 66
  Chernobyl disaster   189–190, 211,
    212
  Minamata disease   46, 54
  post-war reconstruction   172–173
  in stage model   70–74
pollution, effects   55
pollution-control legislation   257–258,
  286
Port Graham [Alaska]   247, 256
Port Lions [Alaska]   242, 247
post-war reconstruction, conceptual
  framework   169–177
Prague exhibition [on Black Triangle]
  1, 8n(1)
pre-disaster community attitudes, effect
  on response   47, 62, 64–65, 70, 166
prescriptive information   283
Prince William Sound [Alaska]
  oil spill   231–232, 235–236
  Regional Citizens' Advisory Council
    (RCAC)   246, 257, 258

Pripyat Industrial and Research
    Association   197, 226n(30)
Pripyat [Ukraine]   184–185, *185*
    population   185, 186
        evacuation   197, 223
    see also Chernobyl nuclear power
        station
proprietary uncertainty   *97*, 98
    examples   100
psychological impacts/symptoms   128,
    202, 244
public awareness [of industrial disasters]
    transient nature   276–277
    ways of reviving   278–280
publicity
    Centralia coalmine fire   65
    Chernobyl disaster   207, 213, 218,
        223, 226n(39)
    clean-up/reconstruction results   177
public responses
    Chernobyl disaster   189, 191, 192,
        193–194, 213
    energy-industry accidents   219–220
    Three Mile Island accident   214–215,
        218

rad, definition of term   224n(11)
radioactivity
    data on effects   26, 28, 210
    levels at Chernobyl   191, 192, 198,
        224n(13)
Rafsanjani, A.A.H. [President of
    Iran]   162
railroad accidents
    Canadian [Mississauga] derailment
        22
    first US death   34n(7)
reconstruction   *30*
    post-war
        framework   *170*
        importance of community
            involvement   164, 165–167
        importance of timing   175
        Iran–Iraq war   160, 162–169
        issues to be decided   160
        process of reconstruction   173–
            177
        strategy   169–173

risk-reduction strategies incorporated
    174–175
    symbolic   30, 56, 106
    as therapy   174
recovery [from surprises]   30–33
    Bhopal crisis   127–133
        economic recovery   129–130
        medical recovery   128–129
    broad-context integrated approaches
        289–290
    Chernobyl disaster   202–210, 220–
        223
    in contamination disasters   56–57,
        76–77, 103–104, 127–133, 202–
        210, 251–262
        factors affecting   104–105, 108–
            109
        moral aspects   105, 109
        social aspects   77–78
    definitions   127, 262
    exchange of experience/information
        284–285, 289
    Exxon Valdez oil spill   246, 251–262
        community responses   254–257
        litigation initiatives   252–254
        new risks resulting   260–261
        organizational responses   257–260
        other activities   261–262
    improvement of process   29–30, 34,
        178, 220–222, 288–291
    Iran–Iraq war   160, 162–169
    research required   288–289
    Seveso disaster   88, 103–104, 106
    stages   *30*, 31, 56
    time required   33
Red Cross, International   208, 222
relief
    Bhopal victims   128
    Minamata victims   51
relocation [of affected people]   33, 75,
    76
    Alaskan Natives   240, 242
    Centralia [USA]   64, 66–67, 75
    effect of policy   80
    Iran's policy   164
    Minamata [Japan]   44
    see also evacuation
rem, definition of term   224n(11)

reparations
  Bhopal crisis   130, 133, 137–138
  effect of safety regulation   104–105
  Exxon Valdez oil spill   252, 258
  fishermen affected by Minamata
    pollution   53
  Iran–Iraq war   180n(5)
  Minamata disease victims   51–53
  Seveso disaster   104, 105, 114
research
  on effect of surprises   28
  litigation affecting   7–8, 252, 253, 265,
    281
  Minamata disease   48, 49
  on recovery   288–289
Resources for the Future [think-tank]
  definition of industrial accidents
    35n(9)
  disaster data   15, 20
"right-to-know" principle   91, 94
risk analysis   2–3
risk reduction
  factors affecting   14–15, 145
  strategies incorporated into
    reconstruction process   174–175
risks, definition   14
risk society   14
risk transition   17
rivers/waterways, pollution   50, 154, 155
Roche *see* Hoffman La Roche
routine disasters   19–20
  definitions   11, 19–20, 107–108
  global trends   20
Rukh (Popular Movement for
  Perestroika)   205, 206
Russia
  nuclear power programme   186, 222
  nuclear waste storage disaster   16, 22
  radioactive fallout from Chernobyl
    198, 210
  see also USSR
Russian Orthodox Church, influence in
  Alaska   249

sacrificial zones   80
safety
  failure of devices at Bhopal   125, 136

meanings of term   102
and Seveso Directive [EC/EU]   103
Seveso disaster as benchmark   107
safety regulation, community recovery
  affected by   105
Sakharov, Andrei, quoted   192–193
scientific uncertainty   97, 98
  examples   99, 106, 109–110, 283
seafoods, effects of pollution   44–45, 50,
  155
self-organized criticality   263
  examples of effects   263–264
Seveso Directive [EC/EU]   6, 90, 91,
  92–95, 286
  amendments   94–95
  implementation in UK   116n(3)
  information to be provided to
    public   93–94, 116n(6)
  institutional effects   95–96
  revision/updating procedures   94
  and safety   103
  similar directives   95–96
  uncertainty management model
    applied   100–101
Seveso [Italy] disaster   5–6, 86–89, 110
  abortion allowed as result   112
  amount of dioxin released   115
  area affected   87, 111, 112, 113
  background history   90–91
  children affected   110, 111
  chronology   110–115
  compared with Bhopal and Chernobyl
    disasters   103, 109
  compensation payments   104, 105,
    113
  decontamination work   113, 114
    fate of contaminated material   114,
      115
  epidemiological monitoring
    programmes   105–106, 113,
    116n(7)
  evacuation of people from affected
    area   103, 112
  health effects   88, 110, 111
  hypothetical effects of Seveso
    Directive   103
  lessons to be learnt   96–109

location 87, *88*, 111
moral paradox 105, 109
operational action programmes 113
as safety benchmark 107
scientific paradox 105–107, 109–110
successful recovery/response 103–
   104, 106
   factors affecting 104, 108–109
type of disaster 22
uncertainty management model
   applied 99–100
see also ICMESA chemical plant
Seward [Alaska] 239, 242, 251
Shatt-al-Arab waterway [Iran/Iraq]
   155, 179n(2)
Shcherbak, Yurii 205, 206, 225n(23)
Shcherbytsky, Volodymyr 188, 205–
   206
sheep farming, effect of Chernobyl
   disaster 26
Showa Denko K.K., mercury pollution
   by 49, 58n(1)
Silver, L. Ray 226n(41)
situational uncertainty 96–97
   examples 99
   not dealt with in EC/EU regulations
   101
Slavutich [Ukraine] 197, 225n(18)
small communities, recovery capability
   255, 264–265
social learning model [of industrial
   hazard management] 18–19
societal uncertainty 97–98
   examples 99
   not dealt with in EC/EU regulations
   100
socio-economic classification [of victims],
   recovery affected by 44, 78, 142–
   143
Soviet Union *see* USSR
stage model [for disasters] *30, 31, 69*
   applications
      Centralia coalmine fire 5, 68–73
      Iran–Iraq war 176–177
   contamination disasters 69–74, 143
      definitional stages 70
      political stages 70–74

signal events 71, 72
   warning/threat/impact stages *69*,
      74
emergency stage *30*, 31, 176
natural disasters 68–69
non-applicability 31
pre-disaster stage to be added 70,
   143
reconstruction/replacement stage *30*,
   31, 177
restoration/recovery stage *30*, 31,
   176–177
strict-and-absolute liability principle
   140
surprises [industrial disasters] 4, 20–25
   characteristics 27
   classification 4, 22–23, 25–27, *284*
   effective responses 11, 276–288
      actions 285–288
      awareness of problem 276–282
      informational issues 282–285
   examples 4, 11, 22, 273
   failure to convert to routine hazards
      274–275
   first-of-a-kind 22–23, 27, 273
   meaning of term 22
   one-of-a-kind 22, 27
   recovery 30–33
      broad-context integrated
         approaches 289–290
      cycle/stage models *30*, 31, 282–283
      exchange of experience/information
         284–285, 289
      levels of difficulty *284*
      long timescales 275, 290
      recommendations for improvement
         288–291
   reduction of impact 27–30
      by adaptation 29–30
      by mitigation 28–29
      by research 28
   routine hazards principles not
      applicable 26
   sources 21
   spatial effects 275
   worst-of-a-kind 23, *27*, 273
sustainable development 290

Swiss Reinsurance Company, disaster
data   15, 19
symbolic reconstruction   30, 56, 106

Tatitlek [Alaska]   242, 247
technological solutions [for
contamination]   75–76
failure at Centralia coalmine fire   63,
76
territorial basis [of community]   79–80
2,3,7,8-tetrachlorodibenzo-*p*-dioxin
(TCDD)
accidental release 86–89
see also dioxin; Seveso disaster; Times
Beach landfill site
threats, definition 14
Three Mile Island (TMI) nuclear plant
accident
causes   12–13, 213–214
mass-media reactions   214–215
off-site effects   13, 214
thyroid cancers   201–202
Times Beach [USA] landfill site   23, 24,
32
Torrey Canyon oil tanker disaster   23
toxicology, effect of industrial disasters
106–107
Trans-Alaskan Pipeline   233
ecological effects   234
transnational effects [of industrial
disasters]   210–211
action required   221, 222
transportation disasters   22–23, 231–
266
investigation teams   285
transportation industry, damage in Iran–
Iraq war   158, 159, 160
Treaty of Algiers [1975]   150, 179n(2)
Treaty of Paris [1951]   116n(4)
Treaty of Rome [1957]   116n(4)
see also European Community/Union
2,4,5-trichlorophenol (TCP)
production, accidents involving   86,
89
safety precautions   89–90
see also dioxin
tsunami
damage caused   241–242

warning centres   242
Tsuruga [Japan], radioactive waste
leakage   215

Ukraine
birth/mortality rates   203
costs due to Chernobyl disaster
225n(22)
distrust of central government   199
evacuation after Chernobyl disaster
190
governmental actions   203
government chief   188, 205–206
lack of funds for disaster relief   204
map   185
nuclear power stations   186
political events   200, 205–206
radioactive-fallout maps/patterns
198, 225n(20)
victim action groups   205–206
see also Chernobyl nuclear power
station
uncertainty management model   96–99
applications
Karin B incident   101
Seveso Directive   100–101
Seveso disaster   99–100
strategies for communication   97, 98–
99, 100
types of uncertainty   96–98, 97
Union Carbide Corporation
accident at Bhopal [India] pesticide
plant   121
effect on financial structure   6,
133–135
official company view   127
sabotage claim by company   136
directors/executives   134
arrest and prosecution   137, 139
Indian subsidiary company   123, 135
litigation   130–132, 135–136
chronology   131
profits compared with other
companies   135
take-over bid by GAF   133–134
see also Bhopal crisis
United Kingdom Atomic Energy
Authority (UKAEA)   215

United Kingdom (UK)
  hazardous industry regulation   18, 89,
    116n(3)
  nuclear power industry
    accidents   23, 211, 218
    Soviet article   194
United Mine Workers' Union   63
United Nations administration,
    international aid programmes   165,
    221–222
United States of America (USA)
  accident data   *21*
  attitude to Iran   162, 180n(5)
  coalmine disasters   18, 60–83
  nuclear power industry
    accidents   12–13, 211, 213–215
    Soviet article   194
  quick-response investigation teams
    285
  recommendations on industrial
    disaster policy   81–82
  transportation accidents   34n(7)
  workplace fatalities   *21*, 34n(5)
US Council for Energy Awareness
    216
US Department of the Interior (DOI),
    Minerals Management Service
    (MMS) research   243
USSR [Soviet Union]
  collapse of Union   199
  energy policy   186, 219, 222
  government reactions to Chernobyl
    disaster   189–194
  international cooperation after
    Chernobyl disaster   194–196
  migration to towns   203
  nuclear power industry   188, 222
    accidents   22, 23, 183–227
    reactor types   186, 195, 216
  propaganda strategy   191, 192, 193–
    194
  see also Belarus; Russia; Ukraine

Valdez [Alaska]   239
  earthquake effects   241, 242
  oil-spill effects   250–251
VECO Inc., hiring policies in Alaska
    248
victim action groups
  Centralia [USA]   65, 66, 73
  Chernobyl disaster   205–208, 212
  as foci for quasi-opposition movements
    207
  Minamata [Japan]   54
  Seveso [Italy]   115
victims
  Bhopal crisis   122, 132–133, 139, 142
  Chernobyl disaster   24, 32, 196–202,
    275
  Minamata disease   42–44, 53–55, 275
  Seveso disaster   110, 111
volcanic eruptions, Alaskan   240–241

war, characteristics   149, 179
war-related industrial disasters   148–
    179
waste material dumping   41, 55
Windscale [UK] nuclear power station
    accident   23, 211, 218
workplace fatalities
  in China   34n(5)
  global trends   *20*
  in USA   *21*, 34n(5)
workplace safety, public policy   13
World Bank
  aid for Iran   180n(5)
  recommendations for Iran   7, 162,
    163